CHILD DEVELOPMENT:

Parenting & Teaching

CONTENT REVIEWERS

Johanna Huggans, Ph.D.
Director
Child and Family Laboratories
University of Texas—Austin

Garrett Lange, Ph.D.
Professor and Chair
Department of Child Development and Family Relations
University of North Carolina—Greensboro

William H. Hooks
Director
Bank Street College Publications
Bank Street College
New York City

CHILD DEVELOPMENT:

Parenting & Teaching

V. Thomas Mawhinney, Ph.D.
The Psychology Department
Indiana University at South Bend

Corlice J. Petersen, Ph.D.
Child Development Department
College of Home Economics
Iowa State University

Published by
SOUTH-WESTERN PUBLISHING CO.

CINCINNATI   WEST CHICAGO, IL   DALLAS   PELHAM MANOR, NY   LIVERMORE, CA

To our mothers and fathers with love and appreciation.

ISBN: 0-538-32200-4

Library of Congress Catalog Card Number: 84-52588

1 2 3 4 5 6 7 8 D 2 1 0 9 8 7 6

Printed in the United States of America

CONTENTS

ACKNOWLEDGMENTS

For permission to reproduce the photographs on the pages indicated, acknowledgment is made to the following.

page 2: Photo Courtesy of Kinder-Care Learning Centers, Inc.

page 14: French Government Tourist Office

page 36: © L. S. Williams/H. Armstrong Roberts

page 50: © Ron Meyer/White Eyes Design

page 62: New England Memorial Hospital

page 74: © Betty McKenney

page 90: © Ron Meyer/White Eyes Design

page 140: National Easter Seal Society

page 156: © Joan Menschenfreund/Taurus Photos

page 176: © Frank Siteman MCMLXXXIII/Taurus Photos

page 192: © Shirley Zeiberg/Taurus Photos

page 218: World Bank Photo by Kay Chernush

page 244: © Ron Meyer/White Eyes Design

page 262: Courtesy of Six Flags Over Georgia

page 278: HUD Photo

page 294: © Ron Meyer/White Eyes Design

page 310: National Easter Seal Society

page 324: © Ron Meyer/White Eyes Design

page 340: State of New Mexico Economic Development & Tourism Department

page 350: USDA Photo by Larry Rana

page 368: UNRWA

page 382: © Ron Meyer/White Eyes Design

page 394: Texas Department of Highways

page 410: © Ron Meyer/White Eyes Design

page 424: H. Armstrong Roberts.

PREFACE

In earlier generations, child-care responsibilities and parenting skills were taught within the extended family. In today's mobile society, the extended family and the parenting models it provided are now rare. Nuclear families are still abundant, but are smaller and dramatically changed due to contemporary philosophical, social, and economic factors. Family patterns are changing. Single-parent families and stepparent families are increasing in number. To cope successfully with these complex and relatively recent changes in our society, high school students are in need of formalized study of child development and parenting. *Child Development: Parenting and Teaching* will help prepare high school students for their responsibilities in the lives of the children around them now and in the future.

The authors view child development as an intriguing and miraculous journey. We have all experienced this journey through our own development and that of the children in our lives, but many people are still unaware of the "hows" and "whys" of child development and child care. This text helps readers to learn the answers to the hows and whys by exploring human conception, pregnancy, and child development. In its personalized approach, *Child Development: Parenting and Teaching* explains well-researched and important concepts of child development through concrete examples, which allow the reader to empathize with the thoughts, feelings, and needs of both children and parents, and other care givers.

The text addresses three broad but integrated areas: child development, parenting, and teaching. *Child development* concerns a review of important, orderly changes in an individual as he or she grows. These changes result from both maturation and experience. The topic of *parenting* relates to the joys and responsibilities involved in fostering warm and loving human relationships between parents and children, and ensuring that children's developmental needs are fulfilled and their rights are protected. *Teaching* involves identifying and strengthening specific skills and abilities in children which are necessary and beneficial to their overall development. Information regarding these three subject areas is first discussed individually and then, as in real life, is intertwined throughout the text.

The text covers not only the more traditional topics of child development, such as physical and cognitive development, but also increasingly important topics, such as teen pregnancy, day care, and parental goals and objectives, which are closely related to today's social and economic environment. The authors discuss basic principles of teaching and learning, such as respondent learning and operant learning, and explore matters of child discipline. Here the authors label the dangers of harsh discipline, discuss the widespread problem of child abuse, and familiarize the reader with generally mild, effective, and constructive discipline techniques. Parenting and teaching methods and philosophies are described in practical, realistic situations.

Child Development: Parenting and Teaching brings the study of child development to a practical and true-to-life level through its many learning aids:

- Part openers identify the major goals of each of the five parts of the text.
- Many illustrations reinforce the material.
- Italicized terms, fully defined.
- Personalized case studies.
- Lists and tables of useful tips and developmental information.
- Study questions at the end of each chapter, presented in the same order in which they are discussed within the chapter.
- A complete Glossary of terms and concepts.
- A comprehensive Index.

A Student Activity Guide provides the student with a variety of thought-provoking and challenging activities. The accompanying Teacher's Manual includes a ready list of references to further readings and audio/visual supplements. Also included are suggestions for class discussion, field trips, class projects, and further clarification of difficult text concepts.

Through the study of *Child Development: Parenting and Teaching*, readers will gain a greater appreciation and understanding of themselves as well as of the children in their lives.

We are indebted to several individuals who have contributed to the successful completion of this textbook. We are particularly grateful to Lisa Clyde Cassidy, whose excellent editorial work has improved our efforts immeasurably. We also thank Maureen A. Skurski, Jean H. Badry, and Lisa K. Sexton for their encouragement and assistance.

A PERSONAL LETTER TO OUR READERS

V. Thomas Mawhinney

Corlice J. Petersen

Dear Reader:

We hope you will enjoy reading *Child Development: Parenting and Teaching*. We have designed the book to be an enjoyable and helpful learning experience that will be important to you both now and in the future.

We have written this book for many reasons. Most of all, we want to share what we and others have learned about children. We believe that this knowledge will be valuable to you and will add to the richness of your life. Another reason is that as parents, teachers, and therapists, we have seen the positive results that occur when children receive skillful and loving care. Learning about child development has been among the most valuable experiences in our lives. We hope to communicate the joys and benefits of these experiences to you and, through you, to others.

The focus of *Child Development: Parenting and Teaching* is upon successful child development and the positive things that parents and others can do. However, we are not blind to the problems that some children grow to experience. Often, adults who are involved in violent crime, drug or alcohol abuse, child abuse or neglect, suicide, or mental illness were in need of help as children. We would be gratified if our efforts contribute in any way to the prevention of such tragic child-development outcomes.

As you read our book, remember that the developments we describe were once accomplished by you, your parents, and your brothers and sisters. These developments will surely be descriptive of all the children in your present and future. If we help the children in our lives, they will grow to benefit us all.

Tom Mawhinney

Corlice J. Petersen

PART

A

INTRODUCTION TO CHILD DEVELOPMENT AND PARENTING

In Part A we address some general but important ideas and concerns about child development and parenting: Why is it necessary and valuable to learn about children? What are the methods commonly used to learn about children? How does learning about children enrich our lives?

We attempt to strengthen an understanding of the enormous responsibility that becoming a parent represents: What are the requirements for competent parenting in our society? What are the rights of children? What are the special problems of teenage pregnancy and parenting? Why do so many people choose to become parents?

CHAPTER

1

Why Learn About Children?

"Every child belongs to mankind's family
Children are the fruit of all Humanity
Let them feel the love of all the human race
Touch them with the warmth, the strength of that
    embrace"

> —*Words from* Children of Sanchez *by
> Chuck Mangione. Copyright © 1978
> Gates Music, Inc. All rights reserved.
> Used with permission.*

Probably no subject is more important than learning about children. The subject of child development is about everyone's past, present, and future.

When we read about a baby's development in the mother's womb, we are learning about something that has happened to everyone. When we read about infants who learn to recognize their parents, sit up, crawl, stand, or say "da da," we are reading about our own accomplishments and those of every person in our lives.

It is astonishing that children learn so much and develop in so many ways. Yet it is hard to be fascinated or amazed by things that are as common and natural as a child's development. The sun, as another example, rises and sets each day, and most people think little of it. But when we take the time to sit quietly and watch a sunrise, we agree that it is truly a grand event. How much would we pay to see a sunset if we had never seen one before? How much would we pay to see a child grow and develop if we had never experienced this before?

Millions of children are born, grow, and develop each year. This happens so often that it is easy to start believing that the birth and development of a child are nothing special, that they are really sort of boring. Nothing could be further from the truth.

People study child development for many different, specific reasons, such as to learn about the development of memory, sight, and emotions. A shared or common reason for study, though, is that child development is important to our future and the future of our loved ones. In this chapter, we discuss why child development is such a popular field of study. We also explore what areas of child development scientists study, the methods they use, and why the study of child development is valuable for you.

WHY SCIENTISTS STUDY CHILDREN

Scientists who study children are interested in finding out one thing, above all others. They want to learn the facts—the truth about how children develop. This is hard to do when studying children. Sometimes, what is thought to be factual or true at the time of study is found to be less true, or even a mistake, in the future. That is why scientists find the study of children to be especially interesting and challenging.

© Craig Aurness/West Light

© Betty McKenney

Figure 1-1. Because so many children are born and develop each year, we sometimes fail to appreciate that childhood is actually a wondrous time of discovery and exploration.

© Ron Meyer/White Eyes Design

People once thought that the world was flat, and that the sun revolved around the earth. At one time, people with high temperatures were thought to have too much hot blood. It was believed that *bleeding*, or draining blood from people, could help to reduce body temperature. We now know that these beliefs were mistaken.

Other mistakes of the past related directly to children, and undoubtedly made life difficult for them. Dorothy Rogers, in her book *Child Psychology*, reports on some advice given in the eighteenth century for the care of sick children. The advice included bleeding several ounces of blood every third day, giving three pills daily of turpentine and deer's dung, and constant horseback riding.

In 1750, milk was thought to be white blood. It was believed that children came to look like their parents by drinking mother's milk. Later, doctors warned mothers not to nurse their babies when they were angry, because it might kill their babies.

A well-known scientist named J. B. Watson recommended in 1928 that parents treat children as though they were young adults. He advised parents to be objective and firm, and to avoid showing warm affection. This advice was relatively popular, and thousands of copies of Watson's book were sold.

Today, scientists believe that ideas about child development and teaching should be tested and carefully examined many times before giving advice about child rearing. After reading the previous descriptions of child-rearing advice, it easy to understand why scientists now believe in careful testing of ideas. Can you think of any old and possibly false beliefs about children that should be tested more carefully before they are accepted as truth?

Scientists are aware of how easy it is to make mistakes. They work hard to find ways to study child development—ways that are less likely to lead to mistaken conclusions. This open-to-change attitude of scientists, based upon new evidence or information, is a healthy sign for the future. Science has done a reasonably good job in the study of children. However, much remains to be learned about children and their development.

WHAT SCIENTISTS STUDY

In many colleges, universities and research centers throughout the world, thousands of people are studying child development. Study can begin once researchers and special human-rights committees are sure that the research projects will be harmless to children.

What is studied? Researchers study anything and everything which they feel is important and is of interest to them and others. Some of the things researchers have studied about children are listed below. As you read the list, think of some other topics about infants and children that might interest you.

- Aggression
- Anxiety
- Taste perception
- Visual perception
- Creativity
- Depth perception
- Emotional attachment
- Imitation
- Laughing
- Moral development
- Breathing
- Separation anxiety

- Smiling
- Vocabulary
- Frustration
- Heart rate
- Bed wetting
- Thinking
- Crying
- Early stimulation
- Eye blinks
- Intelligence
- Love
- Smell perception
- The effects of rocking
- Sex differences
- Underachievement
- Speech
- Salivation
- Hearing
- Body build
- Reflexes
- Cuddling
- Emotion
- Hunger
- Kicking by infants
- Memory
- Play behavior
- Retardation
- Sex-role identification
- Values
- Vocalization

Research findings that are interesting, useful, or simply new are often published in professional journals. This huge amount of information is read by researchers, educators, physicians, psychologists, teachers, parents, and many others. (A *physician* is a medical doctor. A *psychologist* is a person who studies human behavior, learning, feelings, and other mental processes.)

Some of the many professional journals that contain articles and research findings about children are listed below. Individuals can buy these journals or find many of them in libraries.

- *Journal of Child Psychology and Psychiatry*
- *Journal of Genetic Psychology*
- *Child Development*
- *Journal of Psychology*
- *Journal of Experimental Analysis of Behavior*
- *Journal of Applied Behavior Analysis*
- *Journal of Educational Psychology*
- *American Psychologist*
- *Journal of Experimental Child Psychology*
- *Young Children*
- *Journal of Comparative and Physiological Psychology*
- *Education and Treatment of Children*
- *Behavior Research and Therapy*
- *Behavior Modification*

People who study child development search for new information in their own areas of interest. Sometimes they may find new ideas that help them to better understand, for example, language development or emotional development. These professionals, in turn, may write articles that summarize new findings from a number of different journals. Or based upon the research findings of others, an author-researcher may publish a new *theory*, or possible explanation, about how children develop. The new theory may stimulate other researchers to do different studies of children which may either support or fail to support the new theory.

Researching and learning about children is an exciting and ever-changing field. Our understanding of child development is growing steadily. As we learn, we move closer to finding answers to yet more questions about child development. The following is a list of some important general questions about child development.

• What are normally developing children like at different ages?
• How do children in different parts of the world develop? What are the similarities, and what are the differences?
• What personal experiences may help or hurt a child's development?
• What are the signs that a child may be *handicapped* (at a physical, mental, or emotional disadvantage) and in need of special professional help?

Brazilian Tourist Authority

• How do young children learn best?
• How can children best be helped to enjoy healthful and successful development?

Can you think of other important general questions that you would like to study?

RESEARCH METHODS

Scientists and others have used many methods to research or learn about child development. Some of these methods are described in this section.

Controlled Naturalistic Studies

In *controlled naturalistic studies* children are carefully observed to see how they learn and

Figure 1-2. Children around the world have many cultural differences in their languages, foods, and daily lives. But they still develop in similar ways.

Free China News and Information Bureau

develop. Observers are careful to accurately describe the child's surroundings in great detail. The child's behavior is also described using very clear terms. For example, instead of reporting that a child "showed anger," the observer will use carefully chosen *labels*, or names, for the precise behavior. Some such labels may be "yelled," "hit," or "pushed." The observer also describes what happened just before the child showed the behavior ("parents said no"), and immediately after

the behavior occurred ("parents gave the child a toy").

The controlled approach to studying children is useful because it helps researchers to see exactly what a child does. Its weakness is that it does not answer *why* the child behaves in a certain way.

Surveys and Interviews

If researchers want to know something about how children *behave* (act) at the age of two

Figure 1-3. We can learn many valuable things about children by observing them during their daily activities. (Binney & Smith Inc.)

years, they may write a list of questions about what the children do. For example, they may ask what the children play with, what they say, how often they cry, and so on. Then the researchers can have the parents answer the questions. This method of *surveys* and *interviews*—asking questions and recording the answers—can provide interesting and valuable information.

A weakness of surveys and interviews is that parents do not always accurately describe their children's development. This is probably not due to lying, but more to forgetting or not observing accurately. Sometimes emotional closeness to children interferes with clear analysis. A parent might say, ''He *is always* such a sweet child. We just love him to pieces.'' Here the parent has overlooked the fact that all children have their emotional ups and downs.

Longitudinal Studies

Sometimes researchers want to know how children develop over a long time period. To learn this, researchers do *longitudinal studies*. Researchers following this approach may use controlled naturalistic observations, interviews, surveys, intelligence tests, or direct measurements, to name a few of the available methods. But the important or common point is that the same children are studied over time as they grow and develop.

For example, one way to find out how tall children are at various stages is to measure the heights of a certain group of children every six months until they finish high school. This is a longitudinal method. In this way, the average height of this group of children for each six-month period can be obtained. Researchers can also examine the information to learn when *growth spurts* (periods of unusually fast physical development) occur.

The main problems with the longitudinal approach are that it is sometimes very expensive, and it can take a very long time to do. Also, information collected early can become ineffective. This is because during the years required to complete measurements, the researchers may lose track of the children because of moves in residence. Or the research may end due to other factors, such as lack of research money or the death of a main researcher.

Cross-Sectional Studies

The method of *cross-sectional studies* can produce the same sort of information as the longitudinal approach. But the same group of children is not measured over time. Instead, researchers using the cross-sectional method may measure different groups of children at different ages. In this way, measurements can be taken quickly. However, one disadvantage is that researchers cannot watch how an individual changes over time.

Experiments

Experiments are designed to do a very special and difficult job: to identify cause-and-effect relationships. In the research methods discussed earlier, all that can be learned is what is happening in development. In comparison, experiments are used to discover both what is happening and why it is happening.

Experiments require that a specific activity be measured. The specific activity (child behavior) is called the *dependent variable*. This variable, or behavior, is expected to change in some way dependent upon a specific treatment to be tested. The specific treatment is called the *independent variable*. This variable, or treatment, is the one that will be changed in some way.

Interfering variables are other factors that might influence the dependent variable. Interfering variables are controlled (kept out of the results). For example, a researcher named Yvonne Brackbill did an experiment with infants in 1958. She chose a quiet room, placed the infants in cribs, and made sure that no one else touched or talked to the infants. In this way, Brackbill controlled interfering variables that could influence the infants' behavior. Brackbill counted the number of times the infants smiled during a specific length of time. Smiling was the dependent variable.

After learning how much the infants smiled under these controlled conditions, Brackbill applied the independent variable. Every time an infant smiled, she "rewarded" the child: she smiled back, spoke softly, and picked up the infant. Later, she stopped the reward treatment and simply counted the smiles as before.

Brackbill theorized that babies can learn to smile more frequently if they are rewarded for smiling by a loving person. When the infants' smiles were not rewarded during the experiment, the smiles happened much less often. This experiment suggested that parents who respond to their infants' smiles may help the infants to smile more often in the future.

WHY SHOULD YOU STUDY CHILD DEVELOPMENT?

Whether or not you choose to become a parent, there are many good reasons for you to study child development. Earlier in this chapter, we discussed why and how scientists study children. In this section, we explore some of the reasons why it is valuable for you to learn about children.

Reasons for You to Study Child Development

The study of child development has immediate uses, and can be of benefit throughout your life. The following are among the uses and benefits.

To Learn about Yourself. As you study the developing child, you will re-visit many developments which you have already accomplished. This process is like renewing an old friendship. You have changed over the years, and it is sometimes hard to remember who you were and what life was like at different times in your development.

To Learn What You Can Expect from Normally Developing Children. As a parent, teacher, or friend of children, you will want to help them grow and develop well. By understanding normal development, you will find it much easier to know when and how to help children with new achievements.

To Learn How to Help Children Develop Normally. Researchers and others have learned a great deal about ways to help children develop normally. By learning about child development, you will be able to help children to deal with fears, strengthen language development, encourage independent thinking, and much more.

To Learn How to Help Children Learn. As we discuss in later chapters, children are capable of learning a great deal on their own. However, adults can assist children to learn. Adults can help by such actions as arranging children's environment in helpful ways, setting good examples, encouraging, and praising. (The *environment* is all of the surrounding things, conditions, and influences which affect children's development.)

To Learn to Avoid Mistakes that May Limit Development. There are many good ways to strengthen a child's development. There are also a variety of errors that parents and other care givers can make that are not beneficial. By learning about children, you can not only identify positive things to do with children, but can be aware of some common mistakes to avoid.

To Help You Consider if You Would Like to Enter a Profession that Relates to Children. It may be too early for you to know what you would like to do with your life. Many people have chosen careers that involve helping children to grow and develop. By learning about children, you can think about this possibility more carefully.

To Help You Understand, Appreciate, and Help Children Who Are in Your Life Now. When people learn about nature, they often acquire a deeper appreciation and enjoyment

Figure 1-4. How do the children you know add to the quality of your life? (USDA Photo by Warren Utzel)

of their world. Human growth and development are a part of nature.

To Understand the Knowledge, Maturity, and Sacrifice Needed to Rear Children Responsibly. You can learn what the demands of parenting are. You can begin to consider when, or if, you will be willing to meet those demands.

To Understand How, by Helping Children, You Can Make the World a Better Place. Perhaps you remember someone who was kind to you when you were young, or how you helped a child. If you help children in kind and good ways, they are likely to use what you have given them and also pass it on to others. This chain can continue for generations into the future. This is a way that you can help make the world a better place to live.

To Marvel at the Development of a Child. By studying child development, you will learn to appreciate its beauty, complexity, and enormous promise for everyone's future.

SUMMARY

Most of us enjoy looking at old photographs of ourselves, our family, and our friends. We also enjoy hearing stories about our past. Studying child development can serve to satisfy our curiosity about our own beginnings, and how we have become what we are now. This process of learning about ourselves will expand naturally into a healthy curiosity about other people.

If you choose to become a parent, you will be much more prepared and responsible as a result of learning about child development. Being a responsible parent requires education in general ideas and skills in child development. Each person is complex, and our society is complex. Parenting, then, cannot be left only to common sense. Parenting—being a parent—is an important job, and people should prepare for it. There are several areas of achievement which are very important for parents. These achievements involve biological readiness, social and emotional readiness, and financial readiness.

If you should choose to work in a field related to child development, the advantage will be yours when it comes to knowledge about children. Your knowledge will help you to get a job, enjoy it, and make a worthwhile contribution to it. Jobs for teenagers in this area include babysitting, lifeguarding, becoming a camp counselor, and helping to coach children in sports. Other jobs are working in day-care centers or as an aide in hospital *pediatric* (children's) wards. Many people are needed to work with handicapped children and others with special needs.

If jobs in these areas are not available when you first apply, *volunteer work* (work without pay) will provide experience. It will also help you when competing with others for future employment. Volunteers are appreciated in nearly all of the same places where you might seek employment related to children.

We have discussed some of the reasons for studying child development. Perhaps the reasons can best be summarized in this way: Learning about children is one way to show that we care about them. Caring about children is one way of showing that we care about ourselves, our fellow humans, and our future together.

QUESTIONS FOR GROWTH

1. Describe two ''mistakes of the past'' that people made related to children that sound ridiculous by today's standards.
2. List several reasons why scientists study child development.
3. List five topics of study about children that interest you, and explain why they interest you.

4. Name and explain five different methods that scientists use to study children.

5. Describe what you consider to be the three most important reasons to study children.

6. Why are you interested in studying children?

7. Describe several jobs for which teenagers skilled in child development are qualified.

8. If paid work in child care is currently unavailable in your area, explain how you can still gain some useful experience.

CHAPTER

2

Parenting: Do You Have What It Takes?

Have you ever wondered what it would be like to be a parent? Whether or not you wish to be a parent someday, now is not too soon to begin thinking about a big question: What does it take to be a good parent?

No one has designed and tested the ''perfect parent.'' There is probably no such thing as a perfect parent, because people—both parents and children—differ so much and have different needs. It is probably more useful to explore what it takes to be a *competent*, or able, parent. Researchers and others have learned some of the qualities of competent parents. They have also helped people to realize many of the demands that are faced in parenting. Yet what it takes to be a good parent remains a topic of discussion, because no one has all of the answers.

In this chapter, we discuss the role of parenting. We discuss the rights of children,

the responsibilities of parents, and the signs of readiness for parenthood.

UNDERSTANDING A CHILD'S RIGHTS

It is not easy for anyone to really know when he or she is ready to be a parent. This is especially true if the person wishes to make a careful and responsible decision about his or her readiness for parenting. Parenting is a big and important job (see Box 2.1).

A good way to think about what it takes to be a parent is to consider a child's rights. This may sound unusual, because people often think more about the rights of teenagers and adults than about the rights of children. But children do have rights, and parents have the main responsibility to insure

BOX 2.1

Parenting: Do You Want This Job?

Hours: Whenever and wherever you are needed, day or night, 7 days a week, 365 days a year, all the years of your life.

Salary: You pay approximately $8,900 per year until your child finishes school. Somewhat reduced expenditures likely during the remaining years of your life.

Retirement Benefits: Absolutely none guaranteed. In fact, retirement is forbidden.

Other Fringe Benefits: For those with skill and good luck, quiet pride in a job well done and feelings of warmth for as long as you live. Expectations of other benefits are not guaranteed.

their children's rights. If you can identify what you believe are the rights of children, you may also clarify your own views of the responsibilities of parents.

Figure 2-1. *Providing children with consistent love and security is an important part of parenting. (USDA Photo)*

Box 2.2 is a partial list of the "bill of rights" that many people believe should be guaranteed to children. After thinking about this bill of rights, it should be clear that the decision to have children is a serious and important one. (A *decision* is the act of choosing among *alternatives*, or choices.) Such a decision requires careful thought and preparation. Through the study of child development and parenting, much of the unnecessary pain and trouble that some children and parents experience can be reduced.

WHAT PARENTS MUST LEARN

More is known about child development and parenting today than was known 50 years ago. However, child rearing is much more

BOX 2.2

A Child's Bill of Rights

1. *The Right to Secure and Loving Human Relationships.* It is important that infants and young children experience a close, loving relationship with parents or, if need be, a good parent substitute. Someone must be present to attend to the infant's needs in a gentle, reliable way: to hold, cuddle, stimulate through speech and play, and to protect from physical harm. Research shows that when these forms of early love and security are missing, infants cry more, smile less, vocalize less, are less attentive, and, in some, cases, even come to reject physical closeness with human beings. It is from close relationships that parents gain their great power to teach and children gain their equally powerful desire to learn.

2. *The Right to Proper Nutrition, Healthful and Safe Living Conditions, Preventive and Curative Medical or Psychological Care.*

3. *The Right to Be Taught Essential Skills in an Effective and Humane Way.* Infants and young children are in no position to predict the kinds of skills that will be needed for future success and happiness in life. Effective parents must recognize what these skills are and then help their children to learn them. Identifying and strengthening these skills are essential for proper development.

4. *The Right to Humane and Nonabusive Discipline.* Parents are responsible for teaching their children to follow many rules for self-conduct, while not unnecessarily restricting their personal freedom. Teaching rules need not involve punishment. While some forms of punishment may be needed occasionally, they should not be too harsh or overused.

5. *The Right to Learn Sound Values and Moral Behavior.* Parents and teachers must give careful attention to identifying, demonstrating, and strengthening the basic values and morals which are likely to lead children to sensitive, respectful, and law-abiding behavior toward people, other living things, the environment, and the property of others.

6. *The Right to Develop as an Independent and Unique Individual.* One of the greatest challenges of parenting is to teach a multitude of basic skills while still allowing children the freedom to develop as individuals. Each infant born into this world is unique. Parents must preserve and strengthen the positive aspects of this individuality as they teach.

7. *The Right to Be Protected from People, Parents Included, Who May Physically or Mentally Harm Them because of Uncaring or Painful Treatment.* It is everyone's responsibility to
Continued on next page

A Child's Bill of Rights (Continued)

provide such protection for children. Many states have laws to protect concerned citizens who report what they truly believe to be instances of child abuse to social-welfare agencies. Child abuse may include sexual, emotional, or physical mistreatment as well as neglecting children's basic needs.

8. *The Right to Develop Individual Talents.* Each child is an individual with individual strengths and talents. Children have a right to be cared for by adults who will recognize special talents and who will help children to become all that their unique capabilities will allow.

difficult than it used to be. In some ways it is now harder to learn how to be a parent. Today's families tend to move more often from one community to another, and

Figure 2-2. Today's complex world places increased demands on parents and teachers to prepare children for adulthood. (Courtesy Digital Equipment Corporation)

parents are often more isolated or apart from others who have reared children. Because people in our society move around so frequently, it is often harder to turn to relatives for help. Professional assistance from physicians or psychologists can be expensive, and friends are less likely to be experienced with children than in times past. Also, our culture is rapidly becoming more complex in its technology and knowledge. This requires that children be helped to learn more now than ever before in order to deal with life well.

Parenting today requires more skill under more changing circumstances, but there is a bright side to this picture. We can now easily identify basic information about child development that everyone, who is in any way responsible for children, should know. For example, we now know much more about the steps in normal child development and how children learn about their world.

Also, many communities now provide support groups and services for families who have become isolated from the aid and support of friends and relatives.

Parents and other concerned people need to know what they are doing with children. When it comes to teaching and rearing children, it is important to avoid common errors and problems. The old saying, ''An ounce of prevention is worth a pound of cure,'' is good advice. Once made, even easily avoided mistakes in child rearing can be difficult to undo.

DETERMINING READINESS FOR PARENTHOOD

It was once thought that knowing how to help children develop came naturally. Today, it is clear that potential parents have much to learn. In addition to learning about child development, parents should have achieved important personal developments. These developments are biological readiness, social and emotional readiness, and financial readiness. True readiness is necessary for successful parenthood.

Biological Readiness

Puberty is the physical beginning of manhood or womanhood which results in being able to produce *offspring* (children). Puberty in both sexes has occurred at younger ages in the past few generations. The trend of earlier physical maturity is thought to be largely a result of improved nutrition.

Today, about one-third of girls in the United States reach puberty by the age of 12 years. American boys reach puberty at approximately 13 or 14 years of age. At about 12 or 13 years, most females are *fertile*, or capable of producing offspring. The start of menstruation is the clearest sign that a female is biologically capable of becoming pregnant. Many males are fertile at about 14 years of age.

Women between the ages of 21 and 35 are most likely to have successful pregnancies and give birth to normal children. Pregnancies that occur much before or after these ages increase the risks to the developing infant.

The pregnant teenager faces some special *risks*, possible dangers. Her own body has not yet finished developing. Therefore, the baby within her must compete for nutrients needed by both mother and baby for proper growth. This natural competition places both the mother and baby at higher than normal risk for many diseases.

Teenager mothers tend to have babies with low birth weight. According to the National Foundation of the March of Dimes, the greatest single factor associated with birth defects is low birth weight. Babies born to teenagers are two to three times more likely to die in their first year of life. Babies born to mothers who are less than 18 years of age are more likely to show behavioral problems and lower intelligence quotients (I.Q.s). Mental *retardation*, in which a child's development is much slower than others of the same age, occurs more often in children born to mothers who are under the age of 20.

These unfortunate outcomes may be caused by teenage mothers not reaching full biological maturity, poor nutrition, or poor medical care. Another possible cause may be psychological *stress* (pressures or tension) during pregnancy. While we do not fully understand the reasons for the increased risks in teenage pregnancy, the risks are very clear.

If a teenager thinks she might be pregnant, the most important thing to do is face the facts. The female who has been sexually active and who is 40 days past her menstrual period (normally every 28 days) must have a pregnancy test. To deny the possibility of a pregnancy under these conditions greatly increases the risk to the infant who may be growing inside the mother. A pregnancy test can be given by a physician, or a test kit can be purchased from a drug store and given at home.

If the teenager is pregnant, it is essential to obtain immediate medical care. Counseling about the pregnancy is also valuable. Many communities have planned-parenthood organizations where the teenager can obtain help in considering the options of abortion, putting the baby up for adoption, or keeping the baby. Should the decision be made to have the baby, it is important to attend parental education classes and to attend support groups for pregnant teens. The pregnant teenager should also learn as much as possible about how to protect the health of the developing baby. Proper nutrition and avoidance of alcohol and nonprescribed drugs are required to protect the developing baby from harm. Good health care is essential during pregnancy. These topics are described in detail in Chapter 3.

Facts and Problems Associated with School-Age Motherhood

The following material is based upon *School-Age Parenthood: Consequences for Babies, Mothers, Fathers, Grandparents, and Others* by Ivan Nye.

1. Teenage pregnancy rates in the United States are among the highest in the world. Each year, approximately ten percent, or one million, of American teenagers become pregnant. About 30,000 of these girls are under 15 years of age. Although the nation's overall birth rate is declining, the birth rate among teenagers is increasing.

2. Babies of teenage mothers are two to three times more likely to die before their first birthday than are infants of physically mature mothers.

3. The infants of teenage mothers are more likely to be born with birth defects.

4. Mental retardation occurs more often among children born to mothers under the age of 20 years.

5. Babies born to mothers under 18 years of age are more likely to be classified as having behavioral problems and lower I.Q.s.

6. Unless pregnancy occurs within the last year of high school, progress toward graduation is usually interrupted.

7. After birth, the baby's need for constant care separates the teenager from her friends.

8. It is estimated that 80 percent of marriages of brides under the age of 16 years will fail. Another study estimated that about 67 percent of marriages of school-age girls end in divorce within the first five years. Another study estimated that about 50 percent of marriages of pregnant high-school girls ended within four years.

9. Teenage pregnancy normally does not provide more freedom to the girl; it provides less freedom.

10. Teenage mothers appear to be less happy than their peers. They are seven times more likely to attempt suicide than teenage girls who do not have children.

Facts and Problems Associated with School-Age Fatherhood

The following material is based upon *School-Age Parenthood: Consequences for Babies, Mothers, Fathers, Grandparents, and Others* by Ivan Nye.

1. Teenage fathers have equal responsibility for their children.

2. Teenage fathers who marry frequently interrupt their schooling or training that could prepare them for better jobs.

3. Teenage fathers often marry girls they may not choose otherwise. They face a higher likelihood of divorce and of having a child with birth defects.

4. Many teenage fathers feel guilty and unhappy about sharing responsibility for a pregnancy. The pregnancy may be terminated, or the child may be offered for adoption or kept by the mother. However, the decision is usually made only by the mother.

5. The father is legally responsible to support his child until the child is 18 years old. Fathers as young as 14 years have been sued for financial support of their children.

6. The federal government is now responsible for locating and collecting child support from parents who are not contributing to the support of their children.

Social and Emotional Readiness

Development continues throughout life. However, successful social and emotional growth during the teenage years is perhaps the most challenging developmental task of all. Teenagers often have the most rapid physical and mental changes, and the greatest needs for personal adjustment.

Physical changes alone require a great deal of adjustment. Boys tend to experience a period of very rapid growth between 13 and 14 years of age. Girls tend to experience such growth spurts between 11 and 12 years. No one can predict exactly when a certain person will experience these spurts. Some girls begin as early as 7½ years of age, and some boys start at about 10½ years. One of the tasks of maturing is becoming comfortable with the rapid physical changes. Most teenagers need time to adjust to their changing bodies. Some are frustrated because their development occurs earlier or later than that of their peers. The same is true of sexual *maturation* (growth), which occurs at about the same time of the growth spurt. Physical changes related to sexual maturity require still more personal adjustments by teenagers.

Personal adjustments to physical growth and sexual maturity are major developmental tasks during adolescence. *Adolescent* is a term often given to a teenager. An adolescent is

CASE STUDY

Sahra and Freddy

Adolescent pregnancy may be the beginning of a difficult time. Adolescent parents are frequently not prepared to care for a baby. The adolescent father often deserts the mother and infant.

When the psychologist entered the hospital room, he saw Sahra and her two-year-old child, Freddy. Sahra had given birth to Freddy when she was 16 years old. Sahra was tired, fearful, and alone. As she wept, she looked much older than her 18 years.

Freddy was in the hospital because he was extremely active. As an infant, he did not sleep well and he cried constantly. He resisted cuddling. Now Freddy constantly screamed, ran, and climbed on furniture and window sills. Freddy was very clumsy and had many bruises and scars from frequent and dangerous falls. He seldom slept more than an hour or two before he would awaken and become uncontrollable.

Sahra's early home life had been marked by violence and stress. Her father was an alcoholic, and he often beat Sahra's mother.

Sahra talked to the psychologist about the pain of failing in school. She talked about meeting her first boyfriend and feeling loved and wanted for the first time. Sahra became pregnant and left school when she was 16. She and her boyfriend lived together until Freddy was born. Sahra's boyfriend lied to her, dated other girls, and occasionally beat her. Finally Sahra went to a women's shelter, a temporary home for abused women.

Later Sahra met another man who gave her attention. He suggested that they go to another state to find work. They went, but their relationship lasted only a short while. They began arguing, and Sahra was beaten again. She moved in with another man because she "had no other place to go." This relationship soon ended. Eventually Sahra returned to her hometown.

Continued on next page

CASE STUDY (Continued)

Now, in the hospital room, Sahra cried. She was living in a public housing project and had no friends or work. She was alone with Freddy and she felt defeated and hopeless. She was also six months pregnant.

Do you think that Sahra's situation could have been prevented? How? How could her problems be solved? Could this situation happen to anyone you know?

---

a person growing up from childhood to adulthood, especially from the ages of about 12 to about 20. Adolescents not only must adjust to physical changes, but also must develop socially and emotionally. For now, we will focus upon this psychological development and how this process relates to readiness for parenthood.

Psychologically, it is clearly best for the adolescent to delay parenthood. The main task of teenagers is to discover who they are and what they can become. Teenagers need much time and many social experiences to experiment with different roles, such as student, athlete, and friend. This is their time to find the personal identities that fit them comfortably.

Teenagers are in the process of self-discovery. They are trying to establish their own sense of identity. This period of life can be a difficult time. Because they themselves are growing, it is very difficult for teenagers to have the patience and psychological maturity required to parent a child successfully.

Some of the main questions for the teenager appear to be "Who am I?", "Where am I going?", and "How will I get there?". Answering these questions requires the answers to many other questions. Adolescence is normally marked by an increase in

Figure 2-3. Babysitting can help a teenager understand the developing child.

Figure 2-4. *Adolescence is a time for personal growth and self-discovery.*

cognitive ability—the ability to think. Earlier in development, judgments of wrong and right have much to do with what others in authority judge is wrong or right. In adolescence, individuals are more likely to become concerned with what they themselves believe is right. Their thoughts and questions are likely to extend to many areas of human activity, such as sexual conduct, drug and alcohol use, religion, politics, and justice. This process is important preparation for yet another adolescent task: gaining greater independence from the guidance of family, teachers, and, eventually, friends.

In adolescence, friends become very important. Increased social involvement holds the potential for increased social skills and maturity. The enjoyments of parties, dances, and dating contain valuable lessons for adult life. Learning to meet and get along with many different people is an important skill to develop and practice.

During social and emotional development, pieces to the puzzle of "Who am I?" become available. The adolescent's questions are nearly endless. This kind of serious and far-reaching questioning occurs throughout life. But in adolescence, self-questioning begins with a rush.

Adolescence is a time for both work and play. Valuable lessons are learned from both. It is a time for rapid personal growth that requires increased freedom.

Being a parent requires social, moral, and emotional maturity. Such maturity is more likely to be achieved after full involvement in, and mastery of, the tasks of adolescent development. Having a child before these tasks are completed can interfere with a parent's personal growth and development, and can also interfere with the successful development of a child.

Financial Readiness

Anyone thinking about making an investment for the future will want to know how much the investment will cost. This is normally the first question when considering a business investment or the purchase of a home or car.

Few people, however, consider what it will cost to have and raise a child. Thinking about the costs of having a child may seem out of place or selfish. But it is not selfish to consider the rights of a child and what it will cost to provide the child with shelter, clothing, food, health care, recreation, education, and so on. Individuals who consider the costs show a mature, responsible, and unselfish concern for a child's future.

No one can say exactly how much money is needed to raise a happy and healthy child to young adulthood. Wealthy families can fail and poor families can succeed in raising a happy and healthy child. This fact shows that factors other than money are of great importance. Yet without enough money, sucessful child rearing can be very difficult.

A recent estimate, Box 2.3, puts the total cost of raising one child for 18 years at about $160,000. According to this estimate, the total expenses for one child could average about $740 per month, or approximately $8,900 per year. The costs of raising a child include housing, food, clothing, medical care, education, transportation, and recreation.

BOX 2.3

The Costs of Bringing Up Baby

This article is by Christine Denzin Dippold and appeared in the *Des Moines Register*, November 15, 1981. Used with permission.

Costs for Raising a Child from Birth to Age 18*

Housing	$ 52,177
Food at home	37,899
Transportation	26,560
Clothing	13,578
Medical care	8,052
Food away from home	4,429
Education	2,740
All other	18,030
Total	**$163,465**

*Assumes 8 percent yearly inflation rate. Figures are averages for moderate-cost child growing up in an urban, North Central region family.

The average direct cost of raising a child born in Iowa this year to age 18 could exceed $160,000, estimates Christine Denzin, extension family economist at Iowa State University in Ames. That estimate assumes just an 8 percent annual inflation rate.

To arrive at this price tag, Denzin started with a cost of $75,239, the average total cost of raising a "moderate-cost" child from birth to age 18 in an urban area of the North Central region (which includes Iowa). This figure is based on May 1981 costs for goods and services.

According to the Family Economics Research Group of the U.S. Department of Agriculture, which publishes child-raising cost estimates, costs are often slightly less for rural families. Not included in the figure are the actual cost of a birth and savings for education after high school.

If inflation keeps up at an annual pace of 8 percent, the same child referred to in the example above turns into a $163,465 bundle by the time he or she reaches age 18, according to Denzin's calculations. Accounting for almost one-third of the total is housing at $52,177 over the 17-year period. In addition to shelter, this figure includes the child's share of utilities, household operations, furnishings and equipment.

Other major costs are food, which includes home-produced food and school lunches ($37,899), and transportation ($26,560). (These figures also take into account the 8 percent annual inflation rate.) "Housing, food and transportation are the major expenses in most family budgets, whether there are children present or not," the family economist says.

Even though inflation may average 8 percent annually over the next 17 years, the cost of raising a child born in 1981 may not reach the $160,000-plus price tag.

Continued on next page

The Costs of Bringing Up Baby (Continued)

''These are average prices. Every family's buying practices are different,'' Denzin says.

But even for frugal parents whose child-rearing costs fall well below this average, Denzin gives the reminder that these are only out-of-pocket expenses. Not included are services economists call ''in-kind'' (when a family member cares for a child, for an example); public services the child will use, such as schools and libraries; and lost earnings if one parent elects to stay out of the labor force to care for the child.

The decision about having a child isn't just an economic one, Denzin notes. But she says the cost estimates of raising a child can be helpful in making decisions about the spacing and number of children.

If the total cost is discouraging, Denzin says to remember that the costs are spread over a considerable length of time.

Whether or not a person eventually becomes a parent, a major task of adolescence is to prepare for future employment and financial independence. To do this, the individual must identify his or her special interests and talents. It is also important to make a thoughtful study of the employment opportunities that will be available in the future. It is wise to consider work satisfaction and lifestyle as well as financial earning capabilities.

Choosing to have and rear children should be an informed decision. Planning how to handle the costs involved is part of responsible decision making.

WHY PEOPLE CHOOSE PARENTHOOD

Under the best circumstances, children are born because mature and loving parents are ready to spend much of their lives to help them grow into happy and successful adults. These parents understand the personal commitment they have made, and they are physically, emotionally, and financially prepared.

We will explore some of the reasons people give for having children. We first explore some of the poor reasons given for having children.

Poor Reasons for Having Children

Sometimes people have children for the wrong reasons. As you read and think about the following, perhaps you can identify other reasons for having children that you feel are wrong.

• **Do not have a baby because of social pressure.** Pressure for everyone to have children is not appropriate. People often bend to the wishes and expectations of friends and relatives to have babies. However, many people are not prepared. Some simply do not want to have and rear children. They may feel they do not have the necessary patience, interest, or commitment. Perhaps they wish to contribute to society in other valuable ways.

• **Do not have a baby because some people consider it a "status symbol."** About one million teenagers become pregnant each year. The number of pregnant teenagers has been rising since 1960. One possible reason for this trend is that some teenagers think that having a baby proves their maturity and earns respect among their friends. In other words, they think having a baby is a status symbol. This implies that the baby is a possession or a reflection of the parent rather than a person with individual rights.

• **Do not have a baby because "it will love me."** Sometimes people have children because they feel lonely and unloved. They expect a baby to make them feel needed and loved. But babies are naturally very *self-centered*; they are concerned only with their own needs. When they are hungry, cold, wet, tired, or bored, they may cry and scream. Even after parents have done everything possible, sometimes babies still cry, scream, and show no gratitude. The person who has a baby to be loved and appreciated by another is in for a serious disappointment. Immature mothers and fathers have become angry. Some have even physically injured their babies because they mistakenly felt the babies did not love them and were rejecting them.

• **Do not have a baby to save a marriage.** Troubled couples sometimes admit that they had a child to save their marriage. They hoped that the love for their baby would draw them closer together. This often fails, because child rearing demands increased patience and cooperation from both parents. Often, the result is that existing marital problems become worse.

Good Reasons for Having Children

One of the best reasons to have a baby is because the parents have thought long and hard about the possibility and have decided that they are ready. This is called the *rational approach*. The rational approach to having children will not guarantee a good decision, but it makes a good decision more likely.

When a couple considers having children (biologically or through adoption), they should not do so because of outside pressure. Rather they should have children because of their own sincere desire to do so. Such people may wish to have children to enrich and strengthen an already strong and rewarding marriage. They are ready to make a commitment and to share themselves unselfishly with a child. They also have the time, energy, and maturity to do so. The parents have learned about the demands of parenthood and the rights and needs of children, and are ready to meet the challenge.

COMPETENT PARENTS

While each parent is unique, competent parents often share some general *characteristics*,

Figure 2-5. *Couples who have prepared themselves and who fully understand the demands and responsibilities of parenting are more likely to be happy and successful as parents.*

or special qualities or features. Today, parents who are competent are likely to have planned and prepared to become parents. They have learned something about children and child rearing through experience (volunteer work, babysitting, or caring for siblings) and through reading (either independently or in school). They generally have a good, realistic idea of what can be expected in child rearing.

Competent parents look forward to the tender and loving times they will have with their children. But they are also aware and ready to willingly make the sacrifices required in parenting.

Figure 2-6. *New parents often say that successful parenting takes more time, money, love, and patience than they had ever imagined.*

Many of the satisfactions from having and raising children are unique and personal. So, too, are the *sacrifices*, or things which must be given up. A handicapped child is rarely expected, yet children with mental or physical handicaps are born. Their care may require many sacrifices. Normally healthy children may become ill, be injured in an accident, or suffer emotional turmoil. Many parents have had to cancel plans in order to nurse their children back to health. Babysitters will be needed—but babysitters have been known to cancel, often at the last minute. Prized possessions may be broken by exploring children, and the parents' time together will be limited and interrupted. It takes a lot of time to rear children, and time for oneself may become rare.

Competent parents give love freely and willingly, but also discipline themselves to humanely discipline their children. They enjoy their children's dependence upon them, yet they encourage growth and development to independence. Competent parents care enough to be dependable. They work on their own habits so that they show the kind of behaviors they wish their children to see and imitate. Competent parents care enough to learn and to do what is necessary to help their children grow successfully to adulthood.

Not everyone can or should be a parent. Being a competent parent requires special skills and capacities that not everyone has or wants. Having children requires a long-term commitment from both the mother and the father. In the song lyrics to *Cat's In the Cradle*, shown in Box 2.4, Harry Chapin gives potential parents some food for thought.

BOX 2.4

Cat's In the Cradle

This song was written by Harry and Sandy Chapin. Copyright © *1974 Story Songs, Ltd. (ASCAP). All rights reserved. Used with permission.*

> *My child arrived just the other day.*
> *He came into the world in the usual way.*
> *But there were planes to catch and bills to pay.*
> *He learned to walk while I was away.*
> *And he was talkin' 'fore I knew it, and as he grew*
> *He'd say "I'm gonna be like you, dad,*
> *You know I'm gonna be like you."*
>
> *And the cat's in the cradle and the silver spoon*
> *Little boy blue and the man on the moon.*
> *"When you comin' home dad?"*
> *"I don't know when, but we'll get together then.*
> *You know we'll have a good time then."*
>
> *My son turned ten just the other day.*
> *He said "Thanks for the ball, dad, come on let's play.*
> *Can you teach me to throw?" I said "Not today*
> *I got a lot to do." He said "That's O.K."*
> *And he walked away, but his smile never dimmed,*
> *And said "I'm gonna be like him, yeah,*
> *You know I'm gonna be like him."*
>
> *And the cat's in the cradle and the silver spoon*
> *Little boy blue and the man on the moon.*
> *"When you comin' home dad?"*
> *"I don't know when, but we'll get together then.*
> *You know we'll have a good time then."*

Continued on next page

Cat's In the Cradle (Continued)

Well he came from college just the other day
So much like a man I just had to say
"Son, I'm proud of you can you sit for awhile?"
He shook his head and said with a smile
"What I'd really like dad is to borrow the car keys.
See you later. Can I have them please?"

And the cat's in the cradle and the silver spoon
Little boy blue and the man on the moon.
"When you comin' home son?"
"I don't know when, but we'll get together then.
You know we'll have a good time then."

I've long since retired. My son's moved away.
I called him up just the other day.
I said "I'd like to see you if you don't mind."
He said "I'd love to dad if I can find the time.
You see my new job's a hassle and the kids have the flu
But it's sure nice talking to you, dad,
It's been sure nice talking to you."

And as I hung up the phone it occurred to me—
He'd grown up just like me.
My boy was just like me.

And the cat's in the cradle and the silver spoon
Little boy blue and the man on the moon.
"When you comin' home son?"
"I don't know when, but we'll get together then.
You know we'll have a good time then."

QUESTIONS FOR GROWTH

1. Why is it difficult to describe the perfect parent?

2. What is a good way to identify some of the things required of a competent parent?

3. What did you learn from the job description of parenting in Box 2.1?

4. List the major points included in the child's bill of rights in Box 2.2. Add some ideas of your own.

5. How was parenting 50 years ago likely to differ from parenting in the 1980s?

6. In what ways are teenage girls less ready for motherhood than females of older ages?

7. What are the excessive risks to mother and child in teen pregnancies?

8. What are some of the social and emotional growth tasks during adolescence?

9. What are some of the costs associated with raising a child?

10. What is the moral to be found in the lyrics of the song *Cat's In the Cradle*?

11. Summarize your ideas about what competent parents are like.

PART

B

PRINCIPLES OF DEVELOPMENT

Part B provides an overview of basic child development. This introduction will help you to obtain a clearer image and understanding of the developing child as a whole person. A general understanding of child development is valuable in itself. But it also forms the basis for a better appreciation of the many examples of parenting and teaching which are presented throughout the text.

Part B will help you to understand human conception, growth, birth, and how infants inherit their individual features. Included is an emphasis upon cognitive development as well as the basic needs of infants and children for healthful social and emotional development.

CHAPTER

3

Conception, Genetics, and Prenatal Development

Do you know how your life began and how you became who you are? Many people never seek the answers to these questions. They never learn about how they began life as a human being, and why they are special.

Every human being is unique. No two people have ever been exactly alike. This uniqueness is first established by the combination of the parents' genes. The study of how human life begins is fascinating.

THE UNIVERSE WITHIN

Carl Sagan, a noted scientist, stated that "within each of us is a universe." Within each human body are billions of microscopic cells. In the nucleus (center) of each cell are chromosomes, tiny strands of DNA (deoxyribonucleic acid) protein matter. The chromosomes normally come in pairs. There are 23 pairs of chromosomes within most of the cells in the human body. This equals a total of 46 chromosomes per cell.

Chromosomes carry genes, which are special biochemical "messages." Genes are the key to each person's uniqueness. These genes strongly influence the physical and mental characteristics of every person, because each person receives different combinations of genes from both parents. The combinations of these genes can vary enormously. Your physical appearance depends largely upon which genes were combined when your mother became pregnant with you. This is a major reason why brothers and sisters may look so different.

CONCEPTION

The human body contains a certain type of cell called the *sex cell* which is very different from other types of cells. The function of the sex cell is to produce new life. At first, a sex cell contains 46 chromosomes like other cells in the human body. However, through a process called *meiosis*, each sex cell divides itself in half, producing two new cells which contain only 23 chromosomes each. The sex cells then divide a second time, making exact copies of themselves.

In the male, the sex cells are called *spermatozoa*, or *sperm*. Each sperm has a tail and moves using a swimming motion. The sex cells of the female are eggs, called *ova* (plural of *ovum*). The ovum is much larger than a sperm. See Illustration 3.1. When male and

Figure 3-1. Depending upon the combinations of genes, children of the same parents may look similar to or different from one another. (Gerber Products Company)

female sex cells meet and combine, *conception* has occurred. Conception is the moment when the female becomes pregnant.

When a female reaches puberty at around 12 years of age, she begins a biological cycle in which, usually, one ovum is released from either of two *ovaries*, the storage structures for the ova. Once an ovum is released, it is moved downward by tiny waving hairs in the wall of a pipeway called a *fallopian tube*.

If sperm are deposited in the vagina when an ovum has been released from the ovaries, about 400 million of them stream toward the ovum. The *vagina* is a passage leading from the external genital organs to the *uterus*, a soft, spongy place. The sperm swim up the vaginal canal into the uterus, and then into the fallopian tube. When the sperm meet the ovum, only one sperm may penetrate the ovum. This is the moment of conception. Some of the organs and processes involved in conception are shown in Illustration 3.2.

If conception occurs, the ovum then rejects all other sperm and they soon die. Then the fertilized ovum, now called a *zygote*, moves out of the fallopian tube and attaches itself to the wall of the uterus. In the uterus, the zygote will grow and receive nourishment.

If conception does not occur, the uterus sheds its inner layer and *menstruation* begins. The normal bleeding which occurs during menstruation usually lasts for four to seven days, and is caused by the shedding of the uterus lining. Each female has her own menstrual cycle, usually every 28 days. An ovum is released from one of the ovaries near the middle of each cycle. Pregnancy is most likely to occur within the first 12 hours after an ovum is released. However, sperm deposited

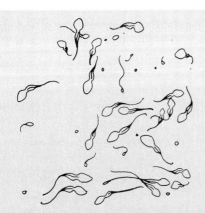

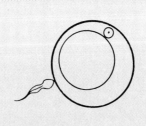

(a) Living human spermatoza, shown as they appear when magnified. The waving tail moves the sperm toward the ovum. The head contains the nucleus of the cell, which carries the chromosomes.

(b) A living human ovum, shown as it appears when magnified.

Illustration 3.1. *The human sex cells*

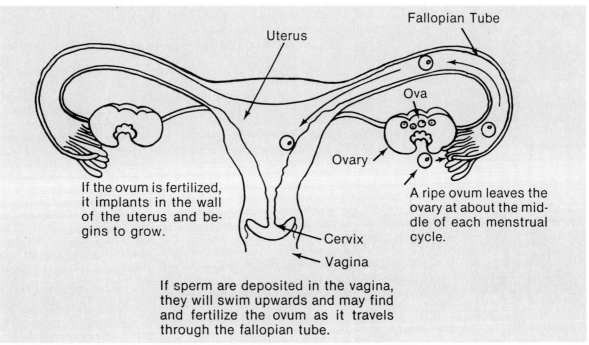

If the ovum is fertilized, it implants in the wall of the uterus and begins to grow.

A ripe ovum leaves the ovary at about the middle of each menstrual cycle.

If sperm are deposited in the vagina, they will swim upwards and may find and fertilize the ovum as it travels through the fallopian tube.

Illustration 3.2. *Some of the organs and processes involved in conception*

in the vagina can live for about 48 hours until an ovum is released. Therefore, sexual intercourse near the middle of the menstrual cycle can produce pregnancy. The female fertility cycle repeats itself continually for 30 years or more.

GENETICS

Genetics is the study of how genes function to influence development. After conception, the ovum contains the 46 chromosomes needed for life to develop. Twenty-three chromosomes from the father's sperm have joined with 23 chromosomes from the mother's ovum. Genes are carried upon each of the 46 chromosomes in the fertilized ovum. See Illustration 3.3.

The special features or capacities which are inherited from the parents and grandparents are determined by the genes at the moment of conception. These genes are carried on every chromosome in every cell of the body for the rest of the person's life. Should the person become a biological parent, some combination of his or her genes will be passed on to the child.

At conception, genetic inheritance influences human development in major ways.

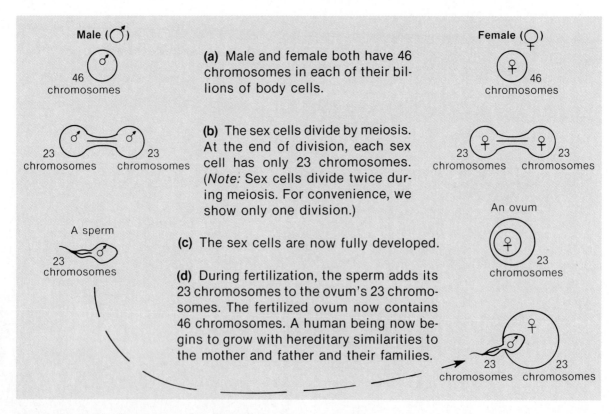

Illustration 3.3. How parents contribute their genes at conception

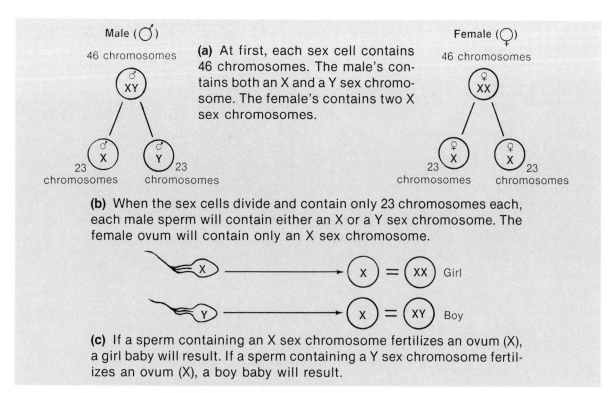

Male (♂)

46 chromosomes

(a) At first, each sex cell contains 46 chromosomes. The male's contains both an X and a Y sex chromosome. The female's contains two X sex chromosomes.

Female (♀)

46 chromosomes

23 chromosomes   23 chromosomes

23 chromosomes   23 chromosomes

(b) When the sex cells divide and contain only 23 chromosomes each, each male sperm will contain either an X or a Y sex chromosome. The female ovum will contain only an X sex chromosome.

X ⟶ X = XX Girl

Y ⟶ X = XY Boy

(c) If a sperm containing an X sex chromosome fertilizes an ovum (X), a girl baby will result. If a sperm containing a Y sex chromosome fertilizes an ovum (X), a boy baby will result.

Illustration 3.4. *How a child's sex (gender) is determined*

Genetic inheritance means the characteristics that a child receives through the genes of both parents. Genetic inheritance is also called *heredity.* One's sex, eye color, hair color and texture, and skin color are among the characteristics influenced by heredity. Size and build, blood type, metabolism, resistance to disease, intelligence, and personality are some other characteristics that are also influenced. How sex is determined is shown in Illustration 3.4. Genes exert their influence throughout an individual's life, turning growth off and on, affecting the sequence of physical development and even how the person ages in later life.

This discussion of genetics is very simplified. Actual genetic influences are amazingly

Figure 3-2. Even twins show differences from each other as a result of genetic inheritance. (USDA Photo)

complex. To illustrate this point, think about the following facts:

• Each chromosome contains about twenty thousand genes.
• Forty-six chromosomes in each cell produce about one million sources of information for each of billions of cells.

Scientists can now explain why people are born with certain characteristics, such as eye and hair color. However, there is still much to be learned about genetics. For example, *geneticists* (scientists who study genetics) still do not know exactly how two cells with 23 identical pairs of chromosomes and genes become different body parts. One cell may become part of the brain tissue. The other may become part of the kidneys or muscle tissue.

Genetic and Environmental Influences

While genetics are a powerful influence in human development, environmental factors are also important. The *environment* is all the nongenetic things and conditions affecting the development of a person. The home, people, natural objects, food, exercise, and emotional atmosphere are part of a person's environment. For example, while your genes carry chemical instructions for your height, the food you eat also plays a part in determining your height. Genes influence your intelligence, but early learning experiences also affect how well you learn. Genes also influence your personality. But how you are treated by others also influences your personality.

Figure 3-3. A grandmother can influence a child genetically and environmentally. (USDA Photo)

Many people argue about which is the bigger influence on development—genetics or environment. Both are very important. It could be said that genetics "deals the cards" and environment "plays the hand." From the moment of conception, genetic inheritance is fixed. Following conception, environmental influences begin to affect development.

PRENATAL DEVELOPMENT

Prenatal development is the growth of the new life in the mother's body from the time of conception until birth. (*Prenatal* means "before birth.") The growth and development during the prenatal period is more rapid and dramatic than anything the individual will ever experience again. The timing and specific developments that occur during the prenatal period are about the same for all developing humans. Yet, miraculously, we are each born an individual unlike any other person who has ever lived.

In only nine months, we each grew from a single cell smaller than the size of a period on this page and weighing only $\frac{1}{20}$-millionth of an ounce to a newborn infant. At birth, the human body contains about 200 billion highly specialized cells and usually weighs about 7½ pounds. The entire prenatal process is separated into three distinct periods of development: the period of the zygote, the period of the embryo, and the period of the fetus.

The Period of the Zygote

The *period of the zygote* lasts from fertilization (conception) until the zygote is implanted in the wall of the mother's uterus. This period lasts for about 10 to 14 days. The zygote grows to about the size of a pin head. Roots then grow from the zygote into the wall of the uterus, which captures a supply of nutrients from the mother's blood. At this point, the period of the zygote is over, and the period of the embryo begins.

The Period of the Embryo

As the zygote enters the *period of the embryo*, it no longer moves freely. The zygote is now firmly attached to the mother and is totally dependent upon her for continued life. At this point, the zygote is now called an *embryo*. Development during this period of the embryo is very rapid. This period lasts from about two weeks to eight weeks after conception.

During the period of the embryo, all of the organs that will be present at birth are formed. Throughout this period, the embryo is surrounded by the *amniotic sac*, a sack filled with liquid. The amniotic sac allows the embryo to float in a watery substance called *amniotic fluid*. The fluid protects the embryo from bumps, bruises, and temperature changes.

The navel (belly button) is a tangible reminder of the embryonic period, because during this period the umbilical cord is formed. The *umbilical cord* is the lifeline that reaches from the embryo's stomach into the wall of the mother's uterus. The umbilical cord contains two arteries. One artery carries waste products away from the embryo to be purified by the mother's blood system. The other artery carries fresh oxygenated and nutrient-rich blood back to keep the embryo alive. The embryo's blood supply and that of the mother do not mix directly, but they exchange products by a process called *osmosis*. Through osmosis, chemicals necessary to maintain life seep back and forth through tissues between the two blood supplies.

The Period of the Fetus

The *period of the fetus* (also called the fetal period) extends from the end of the second month of pregnancy until birth. The embryo is now called a *fetus*. During this time, the various body parts and systems formed in the period of the embryo become much more developed and start to function. It is exciting to learn about the development during the fetal period because the fetus begins to look like a human being. The human features increase in clarity with each passing week. A summary of prenatal development is contained in Table 3.1.

Table 3.1

Summary of Prenatal Development

Age	Activity
Conception and First Month	Descent of the fertilized ovum from the fallopian tube to the uterus. Early cell division and formation of the embryonic mass. A special protective layer forms in the uterus which becomes the *placenta*. Another layer of cells forms the amniotic sac around the embryo. The heart tube forms and begins to pulse; blood circulates about the zygote. The nervous system begins to develop; the early neural tube forms. The intestinal track, lungs, liver, and kidneys begin to develop.
2 Months	The embryo increases from ¼ inch to about 1½ inches in length. Bones and muscles begin to form. The face and neck begin to take on human form. The brain develops very rapidly. Limb buds form and grow, and the sex organs begin to appear.
3 Months	The fetus continues sexual development. Buds of the temporary teeth are formed. The digestive system becomes active and the stomach secretes fluids. The liver and kidneys begin to function. Spontaneous movement of arms, legs, and fingers occurs.
4 Months	Lower parts of the body show accelerated growth. Hands and feet become well formed; the skin appears dark red. Finger closure is possible. Reflexes become more active. The fetus begins to stir and move the arms and legs.
5 Months	Skin structures begin to reach their final form. Sweat glands are formed and begin to function. Fingernails and toenails begin to appear. The fetus is now about one foot long and weighs about 1 pound. If born, the fetus will breathe for a short time and then die; the maturity of the nervous system is inadequate for prolonged life.
6 Months	Eyelids, which have been fused shut, now open. The eyes are completely formed. Taste buds appear on the tongue and in the mouth.
7 Months	The fetus is now capable of life outside the uterus. Cerebral hemispheres cover almost the entire brain. The fetus can make a variety of reflex responses—startle, grasp, and swim movements. The fetus is generally about 16 inches long and weighs about 3 pounds. If born, the fetus can breathe, cry, swallow, and live, but is very prone to infections.
8 and 9 Months	Final preparations for birth and life are made during these months. Fat is deposited for later use. Activity is greater; the fetus can change position and is usually head down. The periods of activity alternate with periods of quiet. The organs increase their activity. Fetal heart rate increases to become quite rapid. The digestive system continues to work. Finally, uterine contractions begin and birth occurs.

Figure 3-4. *A human fetus at about four-and-one-half months of development. (Petit Format/Nestle/Science Source/Photo Researchers, Inc.)*

ENVIRONMENTAL INFLUENCES ON FETAL DEVELOPMENT

If people are asked when the environment starts to influence a developing baby, many suggest some time following birth. However, even a newly fertilized egg is already in touch with the environment. As the zygote rests in the womb, it is influenced by many factors that relate to the outside world, which is, of course, only inches away.

As the pregnant woman interacts with her external environment, she repeatedly changes her own, and her developing child's, internal environment. To aid proper development, the pregnant woman must protect her own health and that of the internal environment in which the fetus develops.

The Womb Is an Environment

Development from conception onward is not purely genetic. From the beginning, the mother's health, emotions, what she eats, drinks, or smokes, and the various drugs she may take all affect the fetus. It is thus very important for a woman who thinks that she is pregnant to visit her physician right away. The physician can provide advice and medical care for the woman and the developing fetus.

FACTORS HARMFUL TO DEVELOPMENT

Researchers have been able to identify some of the specific harmful effects of the environment on human development. It is very clear that unborn infants should not be exposed to drugs by way of the mother. Many chemicals can harm or even kill them. Some chemicals that are thought to be safe for adults may have very damaging effects on the fetus.

Many of the mother's bodily chemicals filter through to the fetus's blood. Researchers are trying to determine which drugs get through to the fetus and which ones cause harm. There is now evidence that many influences may have negative effects on the growing fetus, as discussed in this section.

Tranquilizers and Hypnotics

Tranquilizers and *hypnotics* are drugs which rapidly enter the body of the fetus. They are stored in the brain and liver. The concentration of these drugs is high in the fetus because the underdeveloped kidneys work poorly. Babies of mothers who are addicted to these drugs are often born with *tremors* (shaking), are overactive, and scream fitfully.

LSD

LSD, a hallucinogenic drug, is absorbed into the fetus's brain. Animals given LSD during pregnancy show a greater risk of having dead babies. The babies also tend to have malformations, incomplete growth, and chromosome damage. Human mothers who took LSD during pregnancy have borne infants with spine and bone abnormalities. Similar or related drugs such as *mescaline, psilocybin,* and *peyote* may also have damaging effects.

Marijuana

Little is known about the effects of the drug *marijuana* upon developing human fetuses. However, it appears that marijuana has harmed fetal development in some animals. It is therefore wise not to expose human fetuses to marijuana.

Anesthetics

Anesthetics are pain killers. Pregnant women's use of anesthetics has been associated with high risks of *spontaneous abortion* or *miscarriage*. These terms refer to birth which occurs before life is possible outside of the mother's body. Anesthetics have also been associated with birth defects.

Narcotics

Narcotics such as heroin and morphine are bad for the fetus. Heroin is associated with abnormal prenatal growth and complications during labor and birth. Seventy percent of babies born to heroin addicts have drug-withdrawal symptoms. If the resulting symptoms of diarrhea, anxiousness, and fits of screaming are not effectively treated by the physician, a baby may have convulsions, enter a coma, and die.

Alcohol

Alcohol can damage unborn babies severely. An average of six drinks per day can have devastating effects on the developing infant. Some pregnant mothers can injure their infants by drinking much less because alcohol influences people in different ways. Occasional ''binge'' drinking is also very dangerous to the fetus. Alcohol enters the fetus's blood rapidly, and its underdeveloped liver cannot process it. The result can be *fetal alcohol syndrome*. The effects of fetal alcohol syndrome are:

1. Growth deficiencies before birth.
2. Facial irregularities, small heads, and heart, joint, and limb defects.
3. Mental retardation.

Clearly, women should avoid alcohol when pregnant.

Tobacco

When a pregnant woman smokes *tobacco*, nicotine and carbon monoxide (a poison) enter her bloodstream. These chemicals then enter the fetus's bloodstream. The fetus's heart rate speeds up shortly after the mother smokes.

It is possible that products which enter the fetus's bloodstream after the mother smokes can damage the fetus's heart, circulatory system, and other organs. Premature (early) births among smoking mothers are almost twice that for nonsmoking mothers. It is likely that nicotine constricts the blood vessels that supply nutrition and oxygen to the fetus, thereby limiting the nutrition and oxygen that the child receives.

Maternal (Mother) Age

The best time for a woman to have babies is between 21 and 35 years of age. The chances of maternal death, miscarriage, *stillbirth* (infant born dead), and other developmental complications are increased for pregnancies that occur at ages outside of this range.

Maternal Diseases

Many maternal diseases that may occur during pregnancy can damage the unborn child. Such diseases are rubella (German measles), syphilis, smallpox, Asian flu, typhoid, herpes, and acquired immune deficiency syndrome (AIDS). It is important for a pregnant woman to remain under the continual care of a physician and to care for her health during pregnancy.

Maternal Nutrition

The pregnant mother feeds the fetus within her by feeding herself. It is very important that both she and the developing fetus have healthful, nutritious diets. Ideally, the mother should be well nourished before the pregnancy. During pregnancy, the mother will need about 1,800 to 2,200 calories per day to sustain herself and the fetus. These calories should not be of the empty variety (such as from sweets, soda pop, and french fries). Rather, they should be rich with the vitamins and minerals essential for health and growth. It is important to eat foods from all of the food groups (milk/dairy, vegetable/fruit, meat, and cereals).

Figure 3-5. *Good nutrition during pregnancy is essential for both the mother and the fetus.*

Poor nutrition for the mother results in poor nutrition for the fetus. Protein and vitamin deficiencies may cause miscarriage, stillbirth, physical weakness, rickets, scurvy, stunted growth, poor general health, and mental retardation. The mother who eats well-balanced and nutritious meals has taken a large step to insure the healthy development of the fetus.

Maternal Emotions

Research suggests that the emotional states of the mother can influence the emotions of the unborn child. It is likely that the fetus's chemistry changes with the mother's blood chemistry as she experiences anxiety or emotional upset. Researchers have found that mothers who are anxious during much of their pregnancy often have babies who are unusually irritable and overactive and who have more feeding problems.

With this possibility in mind, it is wise for pregnant women to try to avoid anxiety-producing experiences whenever possible. Pregnant women might also benefit from counseling or from reading books and articles about how to relax and control stress and anxiety.

Parental Blood Types

Blood is either *type Rh positive* (Rh +) or *type Rh negative* (Rh −). When an Rh − female and an Rh + male produce an Rh + child, the possibility exists for blood complications in their future children. This can happen when the mother's and infant's blood mix during the birth process. The result can be a change in the mother's blood chemistry which is dangerous to her next pregnancy. A physician can easily avoid this problem by introducing a special substance into the mother's blood.

OTHER DEVELOPMENTAL CONCERNS

Our understanding of human genetics has advanced so far that specialists are now able to provide *genetic counseling*. Genetic counseling is done by examining medical reports about the potential parents and their relatives. By identifying the prescence or absence of certain genetically based diseases in the couple's families, an estimate can be made of the likelihood of such problems in the couple's children.

Babies can inherit a variety of abnormalities through their parents' genes. If either parent's family is known to have a history of retardation, hemophilia, sickle-cell anemia, congenital deafness, PKU (phenylketonuria), muscular dystrophy, or other inherited diseases, the parents-to-be should seek genetic counseling. A medical association or physician can guide potential parents to the proper specialists who can help them learn what the genetic risks are if they have a baby.

Genetic counseling can also be helpful when a couple has already given birth to a child who has genetically related problems. The parents often wish to know if there is a likelihood of their next child being impaired in the same way.

Genetic counselors often can help parents to estimate the possibilities of genetic diseases in their children. But it is the parents who must decide whether or not they wish to have children biologically. In some cases, couples have chosen to not have children rather than risk having an abnormal child. Many have preferred to adopt one or more of the many children who need loving parents.

Women who are already pregnant and who are concerned about the health of the unborn baby can undergo *amniocentesis*. This medical test involves using a special needle to obtain a sample of the amniotic fluid located within the pregnant woman's uterus. The fluid is analyzed for signs of a variety of fetal abnormalities. If an abnormality is found in the fetus, the parents can decide whether to continue the pregnancy or to have an abortion.

Pregnancy and prenatal development is a complex and amazing process. The pregnant woman who seeks continual medical care and who protects her health in the ways discussed in this chapter has done much to help insure the birth of a healthy infant.

QUESTIONS FOR GROWTH

1. Explain what chromosomes are and why they are important in genetics.

2. How many chromosomes are there in most body cells?

3. What are the sex cells of human males and females called? How do the sex cells differ from other body cells?

4. Briefly describe what happens during the female fertility cycle. About how long does the cycle take?

5. Explain how genetic inheritance is fixed at the moment of conception.

6. Tell what genes are and where they are located.

7. List some personal features which are influenced by genetic inheritance.

8. How do the environment and genetic inheritance work together to influence an individual's characteristics?

9. What is the broad meaning of the term *prenatal development*?

10. Describe the main developments that occur during the period of the zygote. How long does this period last?

11. Describe the main developments that occur during the period of the embryo. How long does this period last?

12. Describe the main developments that occur during the period of the fetus. How long does this period last?

13. Explain how the mother's environment (what she eats and drinks, her emotions, etc.) can influence the fetus.

14. List five drugs which, when taken by a pregnant woman, might harm the fetus. Explain the specific effects of these drugs upon the fetus.

15. Explain genetic counseling and tell when it may be necessary.

CHAPTER

4

Birth and The Newborn

The last month in the mother's uterus is a busy time for the fetus. Much remains to be finished before the day of birth. During the last several weeks in the uterus, the fetus gains about one-half pound of fat per week. The fat accumulates under the skin until birth, helping the fetus to stay warm. The fat also provides the fetus with nutrition in the days following birth, when the digestive system functions poorly.

In the ninth month of pregnancy, the fetus receives antibodies from the mother's blood for protection from various diseases. The mother had been able to feel the fetus's movements during the previous five months. In the ninth and final month of prenatal life, the fetus becomes less active, but the movements are stronger. Sometimes these strong movements even move the surface of the mother's stomach. This is an exciting time for the parents, who are looking forward to their new arrival.

As the time for birth nears, the baby's growth has filled the uterus. The baby is tightly packed, with little room for movement. If the pregnancy is normal at this stage, the baby is positioned upside down and has slipped further down with the head resting in the lower part of the uterus.

BIRTH

Active labor is the birth process or period of contractions preceding the delivery of a child. Labor begins when the cervix begins to dilate, or open. The *cervix* is the opening in the uterus that leads to the vagina, or birth canal. Although other things are occurring within her body, the mother is likely to notice a sudden rush of liquid from her vagina. This liquid is amniotic fluid from the amniotic sac which, after protecting the growing baby for nine months, breaks. This is a normal occurrence which often signals the beginning of the birth process.

Active labor pains are involuntary contractions of uterine muscles. These contractions help to move the fetus into the birth canal. As labor progresses, these contractions occur at shorter intervals and become longer and more forceful. In the beginning, the contractions occur about 15 or 20 minutes apart. They become almost continuous just before birth. The average time for labor for a woman's first baby is about 15 hours. The birth process is painful; that is why it is called labor.

If the birth is normal, the uterine contractions produce pressure to push the baby headfirst into the birth canal, and then out into the world. The newborn has arrived.

The baby's umbilical cord is clamped and cut. This is not painful, because there are no nerves in the umbilical cord. Special openings in the baby's heart close, and for the first time blood flows to the baby's lungs. From the lungs, the baby obtains life-sustaining oxygen which is delivered to the rest of the body through the blood system. In about 15 minutes, the *afterbirth* (the placenta and other membranes) leaves the mother's body through the vagina. The *placenta* is the protective sack which held the fetus and amniotic fluid. The birth is now complete. See Illustration 4.1.

Immediately following birth, the attending physician and staff clean the baby's throat and nose of mucus. Medicine is placed in the baby's eyes to protect them against infection. The baby is then bathed and laid with the head tilted down. In this way, the lungs and airways can continue to drain of remaining amniotic fluid which could interfere with breathing.

The physician also conducts a physical examination of the baby. Health is probably assessed according to the APGAR scoring system or a similar system. The *APGAR* system evaluates or examines five vital signs: heart rate, respiration effort, reflex irritability, muscle tone, and body color. See Table 4.1. Further medical care is then provided as indicated.

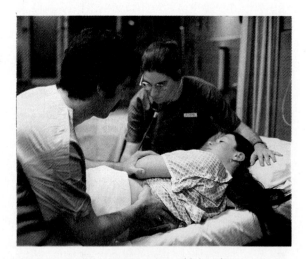

Figure 4-1. *The average time of labor for a woman's first baby is fifteen hours. (© Jeffrey Reed/Medichrome div./The Stock Shop)*

Emotional Bonding

It is now believed that there is an important period of time, soon after birth, during which close physical contact between infant and parents creates a greater emotional *bond*, or tie, between them. Marshall Klaus has observed that infants are particularly alert in the first hour after birth. During this period, infants may stare intently at their parent's faces and may even imitate their facial expressions. As a result of these findings, many hospitals are allowing parents to spend time with their infant immediately after birth, and as often as possible before the family returns home.

Many communities offer classes for expectant couples. In a popular technique, breathing exercises designed by Fernand LaMaze and relaxation methods are taught to the mother. The father is trained to coach the mother and help her through a successful delivery. Involving the father in such a way

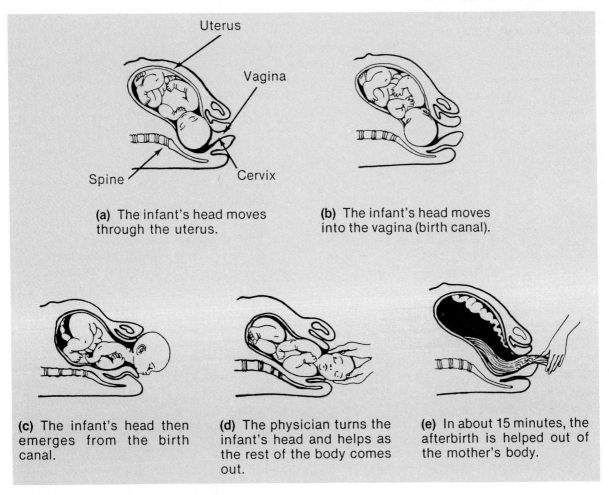

(a) The infant's head moves through the uterus.

(b) The infant's head moves into the vagina (birth canal).

(c) The infant's head then emerges from the birth canal.

(d) The physician turns the infant's head and helps as the rest of the body comes out.

(e) In about 15 minutes, the afterbirth is helped out of the mother's body.

Illustration 4.1. The birth of an infant

Table 4.1

The APGAR Evaluation Method

Score	Heart Rate	Respiratory Effort	Reflex Irritability	Muscle Tone	Body Color
2	100-140	good respiration accompanied by normal crying	normal	good flexion	pink all over
1	< 100	irregular and shallow	moderately depressed	fair flexion	pink body with blue extremities
0	no beat obtained	no breathing for more than 30 seconds	absent	flaccid and limp	blue or pale body and extremities

Total scores: 8-10 good; 3-7 fair; 0-2 poor.

Source: International Anesthesia Research Society. Used with permission.

is viewed as being very helpful to both parents. It also aids in strengthening the father's emotional relationship with the mother and the new baby.

Physicians and hospitals are willing to adapt their methods to help the parents to be comfortable with the birth process. Expectant parents should discuss what choices are available with their obstetrician. An *obstetrician* is a physician who specializes in caring for pregnant women and delivering babies.

Prematurity

A *premature infant* (*premie*) is one born at less than 37 weeks of development, with a body weight of less than 5½ pounds. (Some infants may develop within their mothers for more than 38 weeks but still weigh less than 5½ pounds. These infants are called *small-for-date infants*.)

The survival of an infant who weighs less than 2 pounds at birth is at risk. Generally, the more a premie weighs, the greater the chances for survival, as shown in Table 4.2. A premie who weighs more than 4 pounds has more than a 96-percent chance to live.

Premature babies need special assistance to breathe and stay warm, among other things. Modern medicine is now able to help premies with special incubators and other equipment. However, prematurity remains closely associated with lowered intelligence,

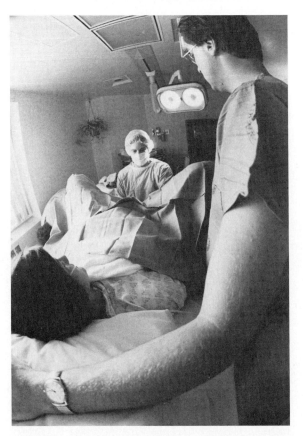

Figure 4-2. Today, fathers are encouraged to help in the birth process. (Photo by Bob Ohr for The Christ Hospital, Cincinnati, Ohio)

retardation, and other physical and developmental problems. Mothers most prone to premature delivery are malnourished teenagers with little or no prenatal care.

THE NEWBORN

The chubby, smooth-skinned, smiling babies that we often see presented as newborns in movies or advertisements are not really newborns. In real life, newborn babies look quite different. They are certainly lovable and cute, but they do not look like what we see on baby food and diaper packages.

The newborn is often called a *neonate*, because ''neo'' means new and ''natal'' means birth. The neonatal period extends for the first two weeks of life. The neonate looks almost like a tiny, very old adult. The skin is wrinkled and blotchy. The head is big and distorted by the pressures of the birth process. The head is about as big around as the chest, and it equals about one-fourth of the total body length. The neonate's neck is very short, and the face and nose are flattened and puffy. The eyes look much too large in *proportion* (size relation) to the little, pudgy face.

Another notable feature is the neonate's belly. It is large and looks bloated. The

	Table 4.2	
	Birthweight and Infant Mortality (Death) Rate	
Birthweight (pounds)		Mortality Rate (per 1,000 live births)
2 lb, 3 oz or less		919
2 lb, 4 oz-3 lb, 4 oz		548
3 lb, 5 oz-4 lb, 6 oz		207
4 lb, 7 oz-5 lb, 8 oz		58
5 lb, 9 oz-6 lb, 9 oz		19
6 lb, 10 oz-9 lb, 14 oz		9
9 lb, 15 oz or more		13

Source: U.S. Department of Health, Education, and Welfare, Health Services and Mental Health Administration, National Center for Health Statistics.

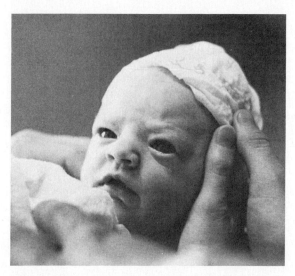

Figure 4-3. Newborns can be surprisingly alert and may already show their own unique personalities. (Photo by Bob Ohr for The Christ Hospital, Cincinnati, Ohio)

shoulders and hips are small in contrast. The legs are short and bowed, tending to fold up against the stomach.

NEONATES ARE INDIVIDUALS

Neonates are not all the same. Each neonate has his or her own personality and characteristics. Some babies are relatively contented, easygoing, and cuddly. Others may be tense, active, cry often, and appear to dislike being held. Researchers have found that neonates differ in activity level, sleep patterns, alertness, and irritability.

The neonate contributes that unique individuality to the family. Both influence each other in ways which stimulate further development. No two children are ever born into

the exact same situation. Each child has unique, biologically based behavioral differences, and the family responds differently to each individual.

SIMILARITIES AMONG NEONATES

We have discussed some of the ways in which newborn babies differ from one another. Although neonates are individuals, they also share many similarities. Some of the similarities are described in this section.

Size and Weight

The average neonate is 20 inches long, but may range from 18 to 21 inches. Newborns normally weigh about 7½ pounds and may range from 6 to 10½ pounds. Boys are usually a little heavier and larger than are girls.

Both sexes grow in a *cephalo-caudal* (head-to-tail) fashion. At birth, the head is the baby's largest feature. Subsequent growth and development will tend to continue the progression from the head down to the toes.

Sleep, Feeding, and Elimination

The neonate's sleeping and waking times are powerfully influenced by the need for food. During the first few days after birth, the neonate probably sleeps about 70 percent of the time. Newborns generally sleep between two to four hours before awakening for a feeding. With each awakening, the parent or other care giver normally changes the neonate's diapers. The newborn is then fed and probably held or rocked for a short time before dozing off again. This routine continues around the clock and is very challenging for the parents.

Most newborns need food about every three hours. By the age of ten months, babies normally reduce these requirements to three meals per day.

Of course, the infant who eats frequently will need to eliminate waste frequently. A neonate may urinate up to about 18 times and have between 4 and 7 bowel movements in a 24-hour period. By the age of about two months, the bowel movements decrease to about twice per day, and the frequency of urination is also reduced. Infants keep their parents busy!

Sensory Abilities

It is very common for people to underestimate the sensory abilities of the newborn. One mother remarked that her baby was really enjoyable to care for when her daughter "became aware of her world at about three months" of age. This mother had seriously underestimated her child's abilities. As a result, she may not have taken the time and effort to help her newborn to sense the many aspects of the world around her. Newborn humans are remarkably sensitive to the new world.

Vision

Unlike many other animals, humans are born with their eyes open, although the eyes are only able to focus (see clearly) upon objects that are about seven inches away. The neonate can also see large objects that are farther away, can detect light and dark patterns, and can see movement. By around six weeks of age, the baby is able to focus upon things at various distances, and by four months the baby can focus about as well as an adult.

At first, the baby's vision is probably in black and white. As the color-sensitive cells in the eyes develop, the infant begins to see more colors. By around two months, the baby can see the differences among colors, and by around four months of age, color vision is as good as that of an adult.

Hearing

Newborns can hear. By two months before birth, in fact, the fetus can hear. By one month before birth, the fetus is able to direct attention toward a sound. The first sounds the baby hears after birth are probably muffled because of amniotic fluid which is trapped in the neonate's middle ear. Yet the neonate still can hear faint sounds.

Taste and Smell

The newborn probably prefers the taste of milk or sweet liquids to the taste of salty ones. The infant's taste sensitivities become more developed within several days, and the baby can also tell the difference among other tastes.

The sense of smell is keen. At birth, the neonate will react to strong odors and will turn away from the smell of ammonia or vinegar. Within several days after birth, an infant may even show a memory for certain odors. It has been observed that newborn infants often turn their heads toward their nursing mother's breasts before they have a chance to see or feel them. It is believed that this action is due to the sense of smell.

Furthermore, evidence has been found that infants of about six to ten days of age can smell the difference between their mother's milk and that of other mothers.

Other Sensory Abilities

The remarkable ability to sense the world at birth includes more than seeing, hearing, tasting, and smelling. The newborn's skin is sensitive to pressure, pain, cold, and heat. These senses are not perfect at birth, but they do operate. For example, the neonate is more able to perceive touches to the lips and cheeks than to the arms and legs. This is one example of the cephalo-caudal (head-to-toe) direction of development described previously. Also, although sensitive to pain and pressure at birth, the neonate becomes even more sensitive during the first few days of development. Evidence also suggests that the sense receptors stimulated by the movement of limbs, and also balance receptors, are operating at birth.

Reflexes in the Infant

Much of human behavior is reflexive. A *reflex* is a biological reaction to a specific stimulus. For example, the mouth waters for food, and the body jerks in response to a loud noise or moves away from a hot surface. These are some of the biological reflexes designed into the human body. A reflex is automatic.

The newborn is equipped with a variety of reflexes. These reflexes are *unlearned*; that is, the infant is born with these responses. Many of the reflexes that are shown at birth disappear as the infant matures.

The reflexes of the infant are very interesting. Some reflexes obviously help the infant to stay alive, such as the sucking reflex or the sneeze (which clears respiratory passages to improve breathing). Other reflexes, though, appear to be strangely useless in today's world, such as the Babinsky reflex (the toes fan out when the sole of the foot is stroked). Perhaps this variety of reflex once, millions of years ago, helped to protect newborns. On the other hand, such reflexes may only be interesting evidence of immature neurological (related to the nervous system) development.

Physicians observe the strength, appearance, and disappearance of reflexes to judge the health and development of infants. The following list describes some of the more interesting reflexes displayed by infants.

• **The rooting reflex.** If you stroke the corner of an infant's mouth with your finger, the infant is likely to move the tongue, mouth, or head toward the source of stimulation. The rooting reflex helps the infant to find food.

• **The sucking reflex.** If a nipple-sized object is placed on the infant's lips, the baby will suck. This reflex allows the infant to ingest food.

• **The blink reflex.** An infant's eyes will open and close in response to a touch on the face, a bright light, a loud sound, a strong odor, or a bitter taste. This reflex serves to help protect the eyes.

• **The pupilary reflex.** An infant's pupils open automatically in response to weak light and contract in response to bright light. This reflex not only allows for better vision, but it also protects the eyes.

- **The grasp reflex.** If the fingers or the palm of a baby are touched, the baby's fingers will close with a grip tight enough to support the child's own weight.
- **The walking reflex.** If the infant is held erect with the feet placed in contact with a surface, the infant will make steplike movements. It is interesting that this reflex occurs even if the baby is held upside down and the feet are placed against a surface overhead.
- **The Flexion reflex.** The infant will bend the leg if the foot or leg receives painful stimulation. This reflex could protect the infant from harm.
- **The Babinski reflex.** A baby will fan (extend) the toes when the soles of the feet are stroked. This reflex disappears at about the age of six months, and then the infant curls the toes downward in response to this stimulation.
- **The startle reflex.** The startle reflex can be produced by a sudden loud noise. In this case, the infant's arms are quickly drawn in near the chest, and crying normally results.

WHAT ALL INFANTS NEED

Newborns are completely dependent upon others to maintain life and healthy development. However, newborns are capable of far more than many people expect or can imagine. By understanding the real abilities of young infants, parents are better able to appreciate their extraordinary children. They are also better able to provide the care and stimulation needed for continual growth and development.

Abraham Maslow was a psychologist who was concerned about the development of healthy personalities. Maslow considered the person with a "healthy personality" as being one who showed no signs of mental illness. He also considered such individuals to be happily involved in developing and using their own unique talents and capabilities. Such individuals were said to be *self-actualizing*.

By studying the lives of many successful and mentally healthy adults, Maslow began to formulate a theory of basic and advanced human needs which he felt must be met before a healthy, self-actualizing individual could develop. Maslow designed a *pyramid of needs*, Illustration 4.2. Self-actualization, the top of the pyramid, can only be achieved when the needs that are lower on the pyramid have been met.

Maslow's theory relates to children because all children must have certain needs met in order to fulfill their tremendous potential. According to Maslow and many other specialists, infants need the following.

1. Infants need to have their *physiological needs* met. The physiological (physical) needs are best met when infants are kept clean, warm, and dry. Infants also need sleep, and must have food and water whenever they are hungry or thirsty.

2. Infants' *safety needs* must be met. Infants should be raised in environments free from physical or psychological threats, fears, and terror. The home environment should be predictable and responsive to the infant.

3. *Belongingness* and *love needs* must be met. These needs are met when a family provides an infant with unqualified love and affection. Love, affection, and acceptance are shown

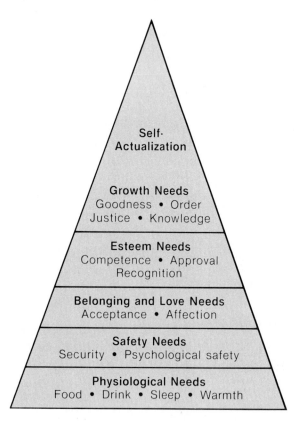

Illustration 4.2. Maslow's pyramid of needs

5. The highest needs in Maslow's pyramid are called *growth needs*. These needs relate to children's becoming unique individuals who pursue knowledge and understanding. Children whose growth needs are met seek their own definitions of goodness and justice and come to appreciate beauty. All of these things, and more, represent the ongoing process of self-actualization.

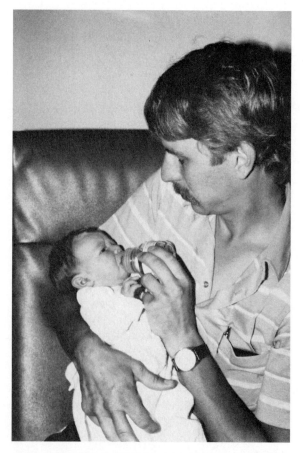

Figure 4-4. Think of Maslow's theory of needs. Which needs are being met by this father? (© Jim P. Garrison 1985)

consistently through social expressions, words, tones of voice, and physical caresses.
4. Infants and children must have their *esteem needs* met. In other words, they must learn to think of themselves as valuable and competent human beings. (This positive view of oneself is known as *self-esteem*.) Attitudes about self-competence and self-esteem are strengthened as children experience success in learning the many developmental tasks and challenges that lay before them. Self-esteem is further strengthened when loved ones and others provide approval and recognition for these accomplishments.

Erik Erikson is another person whose views about the needs of humans for healthy development have gained wide acceptance. Erikson described eight stages of psychological and social development, which include adulthood. His theory about the first stage of this "psychosocial" development is called *Trust vs. Mistrust*.

Erikson thought that the most basic part of a healthy personality is the development of trust. An infant who is not consistently cared for—is left crying for unreasonable periods of time or is not fed regularly—will not develop a sense of trust. However, an infant who has learned to trust the environment is capable of feeling secure and comfortable.

Both Maslow and Erikson expressed similar theories about the needs of infants. Each assumed that infants require consistent and loving care which is responsive to basic physical and emotional needs. Maslow and Erikson also maintained that when infants consistently experience these conditions, the basis for future healthy development is strengthened.

QUESTIONS FOR GROWTH

1. During the last few weeks before birth, what are the main changes in the unborn baby's body?

2. Explain some of the experiences that a woman probably has during the birth process. Use the following terms in your explanation: active labor; amniotic fluid; vagina; uterine contractions; and afterbirth.

3. Explain how the baby exits the birth canal and what the physician does after birth. Use the following terms in your explanation: umbilical cord; heart, lungs, oxygen; eye medication; bath; airway drainage; and APGAR.

4. What are many hospitals doing to help infants and parents in the bonding process?

5. What is the APGAR test, and what are the five things it evaluates?

6. How is prematurity defined, and what is its effect on infant health?

7. Tell how a newborn differs from the babies normally used in advertisements.

8. What is a neonate?

9. Describe some of the ways that newborns may differ from one another.

10. Tell the average length and weight of a newborn.

11. Explain what is meant by cephalo-caudal growth.

12. Describe the newborn's typical eating and sleeping patterns.

13. Explain the following sensory abilities in the neonate: **(a)** vision, **(b)** hearing, **(c)** taste, and **(d)** smell.

14. Explain how infants show the following reflexes. Also tell what stimulation causes the reflex: **(a)** rooting reflex, **(b)** sucking reflex, **(c)** pupilary reflex, **(d)** blink reflex, and **(e)** grasp reflex.

15. Describe the main needs of infants according to Abraham Maslow and Erik Erikson.

CHAPTER

5

Physical Development

The physical development of a human being from two weeks following birth to the seventh year is a complex process. The casual observer notices only an overall impression of gradual development. When studied carefully, though, physical development can be seen as a complex, yet logical, progression. Development occurs in a continuous and predictable way. But each child moves through the steps of development at his or her own speed.

When standing very close to a beautiful tapestry, you can see its close detail, where the countless threads of many colors begin, end, meet, and blend. To view the tapestry from close up is to see and appreciate an unimagined complexity. When viewing the tapestry from a greater distance, you gain another kind of appreciation and understanding. The many changes in pattern which once seemed unrelated now seem to create a whole. Now there is another level of beauty.

In the same way, in child development it is important to appreciate how the many small changes in actions and patterns become related and whole. To study the developing child is to learn what is meant by the saying, ''The whole is greater than the sum of its parts.''

The close-up view of individual changes in the developing child is very different from what we see as we stand back to watch the five- or six-year-old playing. The parts—reaching, grasping, crawling, standing, thinking, speaking, laughing, and so on—sometimes seem less interesting than the whole: the playing child. However, the parts represent important and fascinating achievements. In this chapter, we discuss the ways in which the parts and patterns of physical development and *coordination* (skillful movement) work together to create an impressive whole: a happy and normally developing child.

PHYSICAL GROWTH

Physical growth occurs as a result of billions of specialized cells multiplying in number by dividing themselves. Physical growth does much more than make people larger. It also changes what children can do and experience in thousands of other ways.

As the brain grows, children gain the ability to coordinate their movements, to think, and to learn language. When bones harden and thicken, they become capable of supporting the weight of a crawling or standing baby. Muscles that grow provide the strength to move about, to lift, to roll things, and so

Figure 5-1. Some parents believe that helping their young children learn to swim improves their physical development. (© Jim P. Garrison 1985)

on. Height and weight increase as growth continues. When sitting and standing, children can see, *manipulate* (handle and move or change), and learn from things that were unavailable when they were smaller and could only lie down and wiggle around.

Changes in size, weight, and strength influence the ways that parents and other adults view and treat children. Parents may be tempted to overprotect the child who is small and weak. In comparison, the large and strong child may be encouraged to be more independent, or may be expected to be more skilled. Because of this expectation and encouragement, a child may actually become more independent and skilled. However, if expectations are too high, they can be a source of frustration and failure for children. Expectations that are too low can also lead to frustration and failure.

In these and other ways, physical growth can influence the growth of a child's personality. Physical growth, or the lack of it, may affect what young children can do and what others think they can do. What others think a child can do influences what they allow the child to do. This, in turn, influences what the child may come to learn.

The young child's physical growth is influenced by the same main factors as in adolescence. These factors include the genetic inheritance from the parents and their families, the quality of food eaten, rest, exercise, and general health. If we were to measure six years of growth of one hundred infants born on the same day, there would be many growth differences that would be considered normal. **NOTE:** The growth patterns described in this book are averages. Remember that a child's growth can differ considerably from these averages and still be considered normal.

Two Laws of Developmental Direction

The body does not grow in all directions all at once. Children's growth is guided by two *laws of developmental direction*:

1. The cephalo-caudal principle. Bodily growth begins at the head and then spreads down the body to the legs and feet. This is the same principle that applies to prenatal development. An example of cephalo-caudal development is that infants learn to lift and control their heads and shoulders before they are able to use the lower body to crawl. How the cephalo-caudal principle affects the proportions of the human body is shown in Illustration 5.1.

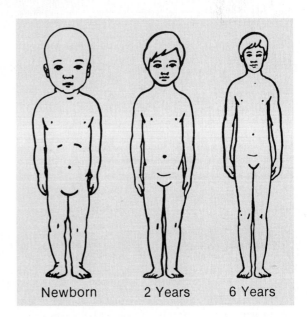

Illustration 5.1. How the proportions of the human body change during the first six years of life

Table 5.1

*Average Height and Weight of
American Children at Different Ages*

	Height (in)		Weight (lb)	
Age	Girl	Boy	Girl	Boy
Birth	19¾	20	7½	7½
6 months	25¾	26	15¾	16¾
12 months	29¼	29½	21	22¼
18 months	31¾	32¼	24¼	25¼
2 years	34	34½	27	27¾
2½ years	36	36¼	29½	30
3 years	37¾	38	31¾	32¼
3½ years	39¼	39¼	34	34¼
4 years	40½	40¾	36¼	36½
4½ years	42	42	38½	38½
5 years	43	43¼	41	41½
5½ years	44½	45	44	45½
6 years	45½	46¼	46½	48¼

Source: Adapted by the Health Department, Milwaukee, Wisconsin; based on data by H. C. Stuart and H. V. Meredith. Used with permission of the Milwaukee Health Department.

2. Proximal distal development. This is another law of developmental direction. It occurs first with growth in the central regions of the body, and then extends outward to the arms, hands, and fingers. An example of this trend of development is the way in which infants learn to control the large muscle movements of their arms before learning to manage their fingers.

Growth rates and proportions of the head, face, shoulders, arms, and legs differ during development. Growth rate comes in waves—at first fast, and then slower. This is fortu-

nate. If you weighed 7 pounds at birth and the growth rate of your first year continued unchanged until your eleventh birthday, you would weigh about 1,240,029 pounds!

Physical development continues throughout life. But development occurs at a faster rate in young children. Near the end of the first year, growth begins to slow. The growth rate then continues to decline until the next major increase in rate, at puberty. See Table 5.1.

PHYSICAL COORDINATION

One of the first great challenges for a baby is to learn how to control the body. During the first weeks of life, the sensory abilities—sight, smell, touch, hearing, and tasting—improve. Yet the baby cannot move much and is completely helpless. The child's ability to coordinate movements of the head, eyes, shoulders, arms, hands, and legs appears much later than the sensory abilities.

During this period of helplessness, the parents or other care givers must care for the infant's every need. As a result, this is when the child first learns to trust another human. This is also the time when the basis of the child's ability for self-love and love of others is being strengthened. Like the close-up view of a tapestry, each development, or lack of it, has an important effect upon something else. At the early ages, the child's lack of physical coordination strengthens social and emotional development. This is because the child's need for care creates a close emotional bond between the child and the family. All of the

Figure 5-2. *Children learn to control the larger muscles in their arms before they can use their fingers skillfully. (Binney & Smith Inc.)*

individual coordination skills that are learned in infancy make possible other, more advanced developments.

During the first two years of life, coordination skills develop in about the same way for children all over the world. Like physical growth, coordination development progresses from head to toe (cephalo-caudal) and from general movements to fine finger movements (proximal distal). That development occurs in this way everywhere is seen as evidence of a "genetic blueprint" or plan that strongly influences the progression of development. However, environmental experiences such as freedom of movement, exercise, and rewards for increased coordination are also very important.

Illustration 5.2 shows how children normally develop coordination during the first 15 months of life. Table 5.2 provides a description of coordination development from birth to five years.

The child's control of the body is an important first step in learning to think. Also,

Illustration 5.2. *Coordination development during the first 15 months of life. (From Mary M. Shirley,* The First Two Years, *Institute of Child Welfare Monograph No. 7. Renewed copyright © 1961 by the University of Minnesota. Used with permission.)*

Table 5.2

Coordination Skills

Age	Activity
Newborn	Lifts head while on stomach and moves it from side to side while on back. Shows reflexive behaviors.
1 Month	Head still not self-supporting when held vertically. Stares at surroundings and can follow slow movement.
2 Months	Places hands together.
3 Months	Lifts chest while on stomach. Holds head steady when sitting (assisted) or held vertically. Grasps rattle, rolls over.
4 Months	Reaches for object, bears some weight on legs, can be pulled to sitting position without head lagging behind. Eyes follow more distant objects, plays with hands and clothing, sits with support.
6 Months	Feeds self a cracker, works to obtain a toy out of reach, passes object from hand to hand, drinks from a cup, sits by bending forward and using hands for support, can stand when helped. Tries to crawl (near 7 months).
8 Months	Plays pat-a-cake, makes thumb-finger grasp, gets into sitting position (without help), pulls self into standing position, walks holding onto furniture. Crawls with stomach on floor.
10 Months	Has accurate *pincer grasp* (with thumb and index finger) of small objects, may stand alone and take steps. Crawls on hands and knees.
12 Months	Plays ball, drinks from a cup, masters walking alone.
14 Months	Imitates housework, uses a spoon (some spilling), scribbles with crayon. Stacks a tower of two cubes, walks backwards.
16 Months	Can remove some clothes, walks up steps, goes down stairs creeping backwards (18 months).
20 Months	Helps with simple tasks, builds tower of four cubes. Kicks ball forward, throws ball overhand.
2 Years	Turns pages singly, imitates circular strokes with crayon. Puts on simple clothing, washes and dries hands. Builds tower of eight cubes, runs but falls in sudden turns. Climbs on chair to reach object, balances on one foot for one second. Jumps 12 inches, pedals a tricycle.

Continued on next page

Table 5.2 (Continued)

Age	Activity
3 Years	Buttons, dresses with supervision, copies a zero (0), picks the longer of two lines. Spills little from a spoon, pours well from a pitcher. Goes up and down stairs with one foot per step. Catches large ball with arms out straight.
4 Years	Dresses without supervision. Hops on one foot, catches a bounced ball, draws a person with three parts. Makes designs and crude letters. Does stunts on a tricycle, carries a cup of water without spilling. Eats with a fork and knife, rarely needs help to complete a meal.
5 Years	Catches small ball with elbows at sides, throws well. Gallops, marches in time to music, learns to ride a small two-wheeler. Beginning to draw a person with six parts, copies designs, letters, and numbers.

the individual skills of eye-hand coordination, grasping, crawling, standing, climbing, walking, and more allow the child to explore the world freely.

Your *pediatrician* (a physician who treats infants and young children) probably warned your parents to watch you closely as you became more able to move freely. As you began to crawl, stand, and walk you became ''an accident looking for a place to happen.'' You explored your surroundings excitedly and without fear. In doing so, you learned many things. The following is a list of some of the things you may have learned as a result of better *mobility* (ability to move) and coordination.

• Some things sink and other things float in the bathtub and toilet.
• It hurts to fall down.

• If you drop a spoon, it will make a fun noise and someone will come to pick it up so you can drop it again.
• If you squeeze a handful of peas, it feels funny and squirts through your fingers. The same is true of mashed potatoes. If you then rub this stuff into your hair, Mom and Dad get really excited.
• People pay attention to you when you turn the knobs on the television set.
• Standing, walking, and climbing feel like great accomplishments.

All of these experiences, and many more, are made possible by increased physical growth and coordination. Greater cognitive development (the ability to think) and social development also play a part.

As you learn of the various skills and when they are supposed to develop (Table 5.2), you

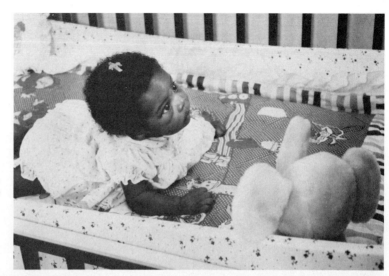

Figure 5-3. How might these experiences enrich a child's development?

USDA Photo

may wonder if a child you know is developing normally. It is fun to watch a child's development in this way. However, it is important to remember that children develop at different rates. Children may sit without support as early as four months of age, or as late as eight months. The average is seven months. Infants can be expected to crawl as early as six months and others as late as one year of age. These same kinds of individual differences also exist for other developments among children.

The ages for coordination developments given in this chapter are only approximate. Some normal children will be slower, and other normal children will be faster. But if a child's development differs widely from these or other averages for development, a

New York Convention & Visitors Bureau   *USDA Photo*

Figure 5-4. Children are unique in personality, but they are also unique in their rates of physical development.

physical checkup by a pediatrician is important and necessary. In such a case, a physical problem may be present.

QUESTIONS FOR GROWTH

1. Explain what is meant in this chapter when it is said, "The whole is greater than the sum of its parts."

2. How does physical growth influence other areas of child development?

3. Name and explain the two laws of developmental direction.

4. How do growth-rate patterns change from the prenatal stage to puberty?

5. How can physical coordination influence other areas of child development? Provide several examples.

6. Explain how your complete helplessness as an infant affected your development socially and emotionally.

7. Name five of the main coordination achievements that occur during the first five years of life, and tell at about what ages they occur.

8. Why is it that small differences between a certain child's development and a table of age averages of normal development are probably unimportant?

CHAPTER

6

Cognitive and Language Development

The word *cognitive* means the ability to think and know about things. *Cognitive development* refers to how this ability grows in human beings. As you read the following list of cognitive exercises, imagine that you are a young child again. Think about the questions and suggestions:

• How did it feel to suck your thumb?
• What did you hear when you dropped a spoon?
• What happened when a snow flake fell on your warm skin? What did it look like the moment it touched your skin? What happened next? Could you see and feel the change?
• What did it feel like to drink from a baby bottle? Imagine the weight of the bottle and how it changed. Do you remember the sounds and what the liquids look like as you drank?

• Remember all the details you can of a walk from your home to a friend's house.
• Imagine the way a circle, triangle, and square looked to you. Imagine the way a more complex shape, like a cube, looked.
• Picture and name several kinds of dogs that you knew about. Was it easy to tell the difference between a dog and a sheep?
• Think about how you would imitate something you saw someone do. Who did you imitate most? What kind of behavior did you choose to imitate?
• Imagine that you wanted to divide 12 sticks of gum evenly among 3 childhood friends. Examine your thinking and the symbols that you, as a child, might have used to solve this problem.

Many of these cognitive exercises are very simple for you now, at your state of development. Yet each skill was a remarkable accomplishment when you were a young child. To do any of the exercises required that you find ways to represent actions, events, and experiences in your own thinking. You had to create a *representation* (memory) of your various experiences; these impressions or images now remain available for you in your thinking. Words and math symbols (language) represent other learned meanings for you. This ability to store and use representations of experiences is necessary for cognitive development.

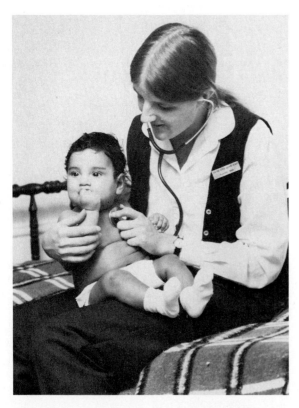

Figure 6-1. *In order to develop cognitive abilities, we must create a representation (memory) from our various experiences. What new sensations might this child be experiencing? (Visiting Nurse Service of New York)*

ASSIMILATION AND ACCOMMODATION

Jean Piaget was a Swiss psychologist who became interested in studying the ways in which children gain the ability to think. He theorized that cognitive growth came from *interacting with*—manipulating and exploring—the environment. Piaget believed that each of us comes to know about the world through two thought processes. These processes, assimilation and accommodation, are like opposite sides of a coin.

Assimilation means to use old ways of thinking to understand (to "take in") something new. People assimilate when they try to fit a new experience into what they already know. For example, as a child you showed assimilation in the following ways.

1. After learning to shake a rattle, you would shake new things that you grasped. You then grouped or classified (assimilated) the object as something which rattled or as something which did not rattle.
2. When you learned what the things in an aquarium looked like and that they are called fish, you tried to classify similar creatures seen swimming in water as fish.
3. When you learned that dogs have four legs, a tail, and are covered by hair, you then used the word dogs to refer to many creatures that fit that general description.

These are examples of how a young child tries to assimilate, or use old ways of thinking to understand new things. Of course, assimilation does not always work, as seen in the example about dogs.

When assimilation does not work, accommodation becomes important. *Accommodation* is creating a new way of thinking when old ways of thinking do not work. In accommodation, children often learn a new explanation or new definition. Or they may accept the fact that something works differently than they first thought.

Assimilation and accommodation go on constantly throughout life. The examples in Table 6.1 show how these two processes work together as children gain a better understanding of their world.

HOW COGNITIVE DEVELOPMENT PROGRESSES

Piaget's research indicated that children pass through four periods of cognitive development:

- Sensorimotor period
- Preoperational period
- Concrete operational period
- Formal operational period

Progression through these periods is produced by children's physical development as well as their environment. Having a rich and interesting environment to explore helps children to develop their cognitive abilities. Children learn best through active discovery of their environment.

Cognitive growth is gradual. All children move through all four periods in the same order, and no one "skips" one period to reach the next one faster. However, children move at their own speed. Therefore, the ages shown by each of the following periods of cognitive development are only approximate.

Table 6.1

Assimilation and Accommodation in Cognitive Development

Assimilation	*Accommodation*
An 18-month-old child goes to the zoo. She sees an animal with four legs, hair, and a short tail, and says, "Doggie!"	Dad says, "No, honey, it's called a bear. It has four legs, hair, and a tail, but it is much bigger than a doggie."
A one-year-old has learned to say "ball" when he sees a round object which can be rolled and tossed. One night the child looks at the full moon and says, "Ball."	Mom says, "No, that's the moon. It is round like a ball, but it is very big and way up in the sky."
At about the age of seven months, one child found a bug on the floor and ate it.	Mom tried to stop him but it was too late. Though it looked like something good to eat, the child accommodated two facts: 1. It did not taste good; and 2. Mom told him that bugs are not for eating.

Sensorimotor Period

Until about two years of age, children's main challenges are to gain greater control over their bodies and to learn from the things they see, hear, taste, smell, and touch. Because of the importance of the senses, this first state is called the *sensorimotor period*. At first (from birth to two months) children gain experience through simple reflexive movements such as grasping and sucking. They become more skilled at these activities during the first two months of life.

Between two and four months of age, children repeat simple behavior patterns over and over. They may begin to see that certain things they do have predictable outcomes (results). Children may repeatedly open and close their hands or scratch their fingers on their sheets. From repetitious actions, they learn more about the body and how it works.

Between four and eight months, children's behavior patterns are directed at surrounding

objects. They begin to reach out, grasp a rattle, and shake it or put it in the mouth. They might learn to kick their legs in bed to move a mobile toy that hangs above the head. Eye-hand coordination becomes much more skilled. Children become much better at seeing, reaching, grasping, and exploring objects.

Between 8 and 12 months of age, children begin to solve simple problems. They might pull a blanket with a toy on it. They may be reasoning that this motion is easier than crawling to get the toy. They will also move things to find something behind or under them. This is an important development, because it shows the children are becoming able to represent an object in their thinking when the object is out of sight. This important development is called *object permanence*. (Before, if an object is placed under a cloth or behind something else, young children act as though the object has ceased to exist.)

Between 18 and 24 months, children show even greater ability to represent objects and actions in their thinking. They observe an action and then imitate it at a later time. For example, one child of about two years of age watched his mother dust furniture. Later, he imitated the same action with a piece of paper.

Figure 6-2. The sensorimotor period: learning from taste, touch, smell, hearing, and sight (© Ron Meyer/ White Eyes Design)

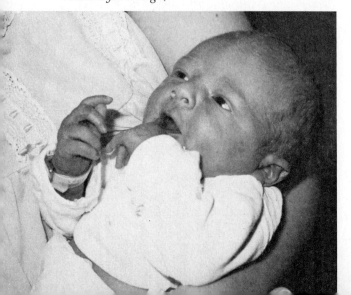

Preoperational Period

The *preoperational period* occurs between the ages of two and seven years. During this period the ability to speak and to understand language continues to grow. Children continue to learn names and meanings of many new symbols. (A *symbol* is something that represents something else.) Language development is occurring at a faster rate than at any other time in the life cycle. It is exciting to watch children experiment with language. Children are learning many more symbols such as numbers, letters of the alphabet, and shapes. They gain an understanding of more and less, longer and shorter, bigger and smaller, and much more.

The ability for symbolic play increases. In *symbolic play*, a stick might be treated as a sword or an airplane. In other words, the stick is used as a symbol of something else. A doll may be treated as a friend to whom the child tells a story. Play experiences are very important to cognitive growth in young children. Children in this period actually learn best by manipulating objects, exploring, and solving problems. They do not learn best by sitting still and listening.

By the age of two or three years, children are able to *classify* or group things. That is, children may put all of the red toys together or put all of the small, big, or long things together. Children can repeat two numbers and match shapes.

Figure 6-3. During the preoperational period, children learn best by exploring and manipulating objects. (March of Dimes Birth Defects Foundation)

Figure 6-4. This child is learning about colors and shapes as she looks at the picture book. Her skill at turning pages shows her increasing physical coordination.

Children are self-centered, or concerned mostly with themselves, during the preoperational period. They talk more about what they like or want, and what their feelings are. It is difficult for children to share during this time. This self-centeredness is called *egocentrism*; it is natural for children in the preoperational period. Children are more likely to see and understand other people's views and feelings as they gain more experience with others. Social experiences are necessary for children to learn to respect the views and feelings of other people.

Concrete Operational Period

Conservation is another major cognitive ability that is acquired around seven years of age. Conservation occurs during the *concrete operational period*. Conservation means that the child understands that liquids or solids can be changed in shape but remain the same volume or mass.

For example, when you were around five years of age, your parents might have shown you two round balls of clay which were the same size. If your parents had flattened one ball into a large, thin pie shape, you probably would have said that it was "more clay now." You probably would have said the same thing if your parents had rolled the ball into a long pretzel-like object. You had similar difficulties with conservation of liquids. If the water in a short, fat glass was poured into a tall, thin one, you might have said that there was more water in the tall, thin glass. By the age of seven, however, your cognitive abilities had probably grown to include an understanding of conservation. Learning

Figure 6-5. Creative play is not only fun. It also involves children in learning new skills and teaches them about sharing and working with others. (Future Homemakers of America)

about conservation is a big step because it is necessary for understanding many of the ideas in math and science.

The concrete operational period lasts from about 7 to 12 years of age. During this period, children begin to think in new and very complex ways. By this time, children are making increasing use of language and math symbols. They do this both to communicate and to learn more about their environment.

Formal Operational Period

Piaget's formal operational period represents the highest level of cognitive development. This is the period of cognitive development which, by now, you have achieved.

You probably entered the formal operational period at about the age of 12 years. By this time, you had become increasingly skilled at using your imagination and solving abstract problems. *Abstract problems* are those which involve ideas rather than concrete items (items which are present) such as water, sand, and pencils. You may have begun to think about how to solve the world's problems, how to end war, or ways to reduce crime. Perhaps you developed an interest in science fiction.

All of these thought activities require the ability to think and imagine things which are not concrete or present. Formal operational thought involves reasoning, "If these facts were true, then I could expect such results as . . ." Formal operational thinking can lead to creative problem solving in science, education, business, and all other areas of life.

LANGUAGE DEVELOPMENT

Can you imagine what it would be like to discover a world in which everyone spoke a language that you could not understand? It would be very hard for you to communicate even your most basic needs. To get along in such a world would require that you try to communicate in any way possible. Still, you would need the help of an *interpreter* (someone who could explain your meaning) and a language teacher.

This scene is actually drawn from reality: such was your situation when you were born. You could not speak or understand your culture's language. But the people around you interpreted your very basic communications, such as crying and smiling. They helped you to eventually learn very complex language skills. Language skills are a part of cognitive development.

HUMANS USE COMPLEX LANGUAGE

Noam Chomsky, a language specialist, theorized that human beings have a special, genetically based ability to develop very complex ways to communicate. While other animals such as whales or geese appear to communicate with one another, there is no evidence that they creatively use language in the complex ways that humans do.

A parrot may repeat exactly what it hears: "I want a cookie." Young children, however, will not only repeat what they have heard, but they then find other ways of saying the same thing. Like a parrot, a child may once have heard "I want a cookie." But unlike a parrot, a young child may say:

> "Me wants cookie!"
> "Cookie please."
> "Whaa! Whaa! Cookie!"
> "Cookie, daddy."
> "Mommy, cookie."
> "Cookie, cookie!"
> "Like cookie."
> "I want a cookie."

All of these statements are a young child's way of saying the same thing.

Young children work hard to learn their culture's language. They begin to apply a variety of rules of grammar, which they learn indirectly. Perhaps it is difficult for you to define the rules by which you form sentences from words; grammar is hard for many people. Yet, amazingly, people use rules of grammar to speak effectively, almost without conscious thought.

How Children Can Be Helped to Learn

Language in children seems almost to develop automatically, but it does not. There are many ways that parents and others help young children to develop language. When you were an infant, your parents listened to your sounds. When you made sounds, they showed happiness and excitement. They rewarded the many sounds you made, which then became the foundations for your later speech development. The rewards were natural ones, such as smiles, touches, hugs, kisses, and talking back to you. When these rewards happened after you made a sound, they strengthened your language development. Your parents and others also showed you how to talk by *modeling*, or giving examples of, their own speech for you to hear and imitate.

For language to develop normally, children must hear language and be rewarded for their attempts to use it. Parents need not be too demanding about the exact forms that

Figure 6-6. *How parents respond to their children's sounds plays a major role in language development. (USDA Photo)*

early language takes. Rather, language is often best strengthened when parents interpret and respond to what their young children are trying to say. Reading books and telling stories to children also encourages their language development.

Knowing what to expect during a child's language development is important for parents or anyone who cares for children. Infants start life with few vocal abilities beyond groaning, smacking the mouth, and crying. Within just a few years, though, children have developed the impressive ability to speak. Children, regardless of where they live and in what specific language culture they grow up in, acquire language in the same basic ways.

Human beings have an astonishing ability to learn and use language. You have learned to combine words in thousands of ways. It is even more impressive that you have chained these words together according to highly complex rules of grammar. Currently you may even be learning another language. We will now review the stages that you went through to learn your first language.

HOW LANGUAGE DEVELOPS

Language is a broad term used to refer to any form of communication. A person's actions, such as smiles, hugs, and hand signals, are visual forms of language. In this section we focus upon how children learn to understand and to use *oral*, or spoken language.

Language can be separated into two basic types: receptive and expressive. *Receptive language* refers to a person's ability to understand what others mean when they speak.

Figure 6-7. *Telling stories and reading to children is an enjoyable way to strengthen their language development and their interest in words. (Future Homemakers of America)*

This type of language development begins early in life, and it makes the other main type of language, expressive language, easier to learn. *Expressive language* refers to a person's ability to speak. In expressive language, the individual uses words to communicate countless meanings.

The Six Stages of Language Development

Overall language development progresses through about six stages. The first stage is extremely primitive, or basic. In later stages, children progress to very complex forms of speech.

The six stages occur during two major periods: the prespeech period and the language period. During the *prespeech period*, the child is unable to say words. In the *language period*, the child can say meaningful words. This period is said to begin with the child's very first meaningful word. Of course, the language period follows the prespeech period. We now describe the six stages of language development.

Stage 1: Crying. (Newborn to Two Months. Prespeech Period.) Infants are born with the sophisticated equipment needed for speaking. However, learning to speak requires further development. During the first few weeks after birth, most infants make few sounds other than crying, but they are very good at crying. As time passes, parents learn how to interpret different types of cries from their infants. Some cries indicate pain; others indicate boredom, hunger, or anger. Through their different styles of crying, infants are already communicating. Parents should listen for their infants' attempts to communicate and should care consistently for their needs of love, food, and warmth.

During this stage, the process of learning to vocalize in order to influence the surroundings begins. This process is also important for cognitive (thinking and reasoning) development.

Infants are also listening during this first stage of language development. Parents and others spend countless hours talking to infants. Around six weeks of age, an infant can tell the difference between very similar speech sounds. The infant can probably hear the difference between different intonations and/or stresses in word sounds, such as Pápa as opposed to Papá.

Stage 2: Cooing. (Two to Six Months. Prespeech Period.) At about two months, infants begin to make noises called *cooing*. These early sounds are the easiest for infants to make. The sounds are open vowels like "oooo" or "aaah."

The consonant sounds, such as "ccc," "bbb," and "ttt," require more skill with the lips, tongue, and gums or teeth to pronounce. These more difficult sounds occur in the next stage of language development.

Stage 3: Babbling. (Six to 12 Months. Prespeech Period.) By around the age of six months, babies have learned to use their lips, tongue, gums or teeth, and throat much better. They are able to make a much greater variety of sounds. In fact, infants are now able to make any sound used to speak any known language in the world.

Infants listen to their loved ones speak and begin to imitate their sounds during this stage. The people around the babies are delighted and reward the sounds with excitement, love, and affection. They talk even more to the babies. Actually, it is very hard to tell who is rewarding whom, because both the infants and the loved ones are responding to one another. This becomes like a game played between infants and their parents, and it is very important for language development. It helps to strengthen the tendency of children to imitate their parents. (See Illustration 6.1.)

During this stage, babies learn to imitate their parents' intonation, rhythm, and sound emphasis. The babies also alternate vowel and consonant sounds over and over. Many of the sounds not essential to the parents' language begin to lessen.

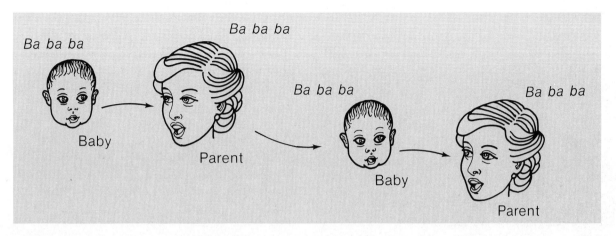

Illustration 6.1. *When the baby babbles, the parent babbles back. This fun and constructive game may continue for as long as the baby is cooperative.*

Babies' babbling (da da da, ba ba ba, etc.) begins to drift slowly in the direction of sounding like the parents talking. Often, the infants babble quietly when lying alone. Babies seem to have fun playing with the growing ability to make sounds.

Some babies progress faster than others in this sequence, and some babble more than others. However, all babies go through the same steps on the way to the next stage, in which the language period begins.

Stage 4: One Word. (Around First Birthday. Language Period.) It may be hard to tell exactly when a young child enters this stage. Babbling does not end suddenly, but at some point ''da da'' comes to mean Daddy and ''ma ma'' comes to mean Mommy. It probably takes several months for infants to start to use their first words, but then they begin to learn to say words more rapidly.

In this stage, children often use a single word to mean many different things. Such a word is called a *holophrase*. A child's parents

must figure out the meanings of these words depending upon where the child is at the time and how the child uses his or her face and voice to express the word.

Holophrase	Possible Meanings
''Mommy.''	• ''That is Mommy's (pointing at a diaper bag).'' • ''Mommy, come here!'' • ''That is my mommy (looking at her).''
''Potty.''	• ''I need to go potty.'' • ''There is the potty.'' • ''Oops, I just went potty.''
''Bye bye.''	• ''Can I go bye bye?'' • ''Did Mommy go bye bye?'' • ''I ate it, all gone.''

Clearly, the need for an interpreter is still great in this fourth stage. Children may use words that no one can understand. One child confused everyone. Whenever his family drove on a bridge across a river, he said "yegging." Later the family realized that "yegging" was the child's word for "going swimming."

Stage 5: Combining Two or Three Words. (Around Second Birthday. Language Period.) Children now begin to combine two or three words to make themselves better understood. Since they use only important words, they sound somewhat like a telegram reads, so an interpreter is still needed. For example, "Puppy go" could mean "The doggie is outside." "Daddy read" could mean "Please read me a story." "Linda eat cookie" could mean "I want a cookie."

Stage 6: Whole Sentences. (Between Three and Four Years. Language Period.) During this last stage, children continue to speak with sentences of greater and greater complexity. They also begin to ask questions.

Children between the ages of three and four years often experience difficulty as they try to talk in more complex ways. They have already learned some of the rules for choosing endings for words. A child might say "I goed to the store" or "I see the mouses." These are examples of a child working to use complex rules of grammar. In these cases, the child has accidentally misused a rule. These practices are normal and should be expected of all children.

Children may repeat sounds, stop, and then back up and start over again—and have trouble thinking at the same time. Language development is easier for children if their parents know that this will happen, that it is normal, and that patience is required. It is important that parents not become overly

concerned with such normal speech problems. Parents should not press children to think more carefully, and should not criticize them. Pushing too hard and criticizing tend to worsen the normal speech problems associated with language development.

Children gradually learn to pronounce the 44 separate sounds which make up our language. This is a challenging task. Children normally learn the pronunciation and use of vowel (a, e, i, o, and u) sounds within their first two years. The pronunciation of consonant sounds is more difficult and takes more

Figure 6-8. *Children who are hearing impaired may need special help. Here a therapist with a puppet helps to reinforce and teach language to a girl with a hearing impairment. (Photograph Courtesy of Better Hearing Institute.)*

time to learn. Illustration 6.2 shows the age ranges by which children normally master consonant sounds.

Sometimes children may have particular difficulty learning to pronounce various sounds. As a general rule, if a child's speech is very hard to understand at the age of three or three-and-a-half years, it is time for professional help. A speech therapist can help the child to speak more clearly.

Like millions of children before and after you, your language developed in an orderly way. Your interaction with loving and responsive parents and others helped you to learn your language. Table 6.2 lists the number of words that you had most likely learned

Table 6.2

Early Growth of Vocabulary in Children

Age (Years and Months)	Average Number of Words
0-8	0
0-10	1
1-0	3
1-3	19
1-6	22
1-9	118
2-0	272
2-6	446
3-0	896
3-6	1,222
4-0	1,540
4-6	1,870
5-0	2,072
5-6	2,289
6-0	2,562

Source: M. E. Smith, "An Investigation of the Development of the Sentence and the Extent of Vocabulary in Young Children." *University of Iowa Studies in Child Welfare,* 1926. Used with permission.

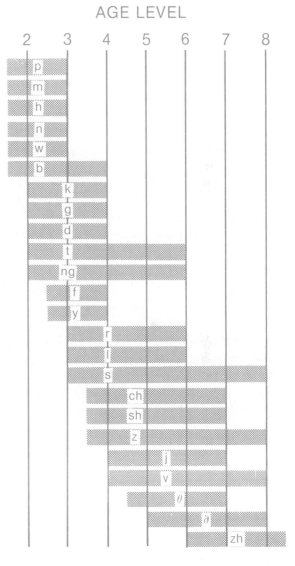

Illustration 6.2. *Estimates of average and upper age limits (in years) of normal consonant production. The bars start at the average age at which children can produce a particular consonant. The bars end at the age when about 90 percent of all children are normally producing the sounds. From E. K. Sander, "When Are Speech Sounds Learned?"* Journal of Speech and Hearing Disorders. *(From Templin, 1957; Wellman et al., 1931.) Used with permission.*

at various ages. By four years of age, you had probably learned most of the grammatical guidelines to normal speech. By the age of six years, you may have learned about 2,500 words!

Language development is a remarkable accomplishment. It is through language that humans have been able to learn and share knowledge across generations for countless centuries. A child's growing ability to use language represents a main avenue to future social and intellectual development.

QUESTIONS FOR GROWTH

1. What is cognitive development?

2. What is meant when we say that children create or have representations of their experiences?

3. Explain the ideas of assimilation and accommodation, and provide several examples of each.

4. Name the four periods of cognitive development, and identify some of the main cognitive achievements that occur in each period.

5. How is human language different from the ways that other animals communicate?

6. How do parents and others help young children to develop language?

7. Explain why it is said that language is a broad term.

8. What are the two basic types into which any language can be separated? What do these two terms mean?

9. How long does the prespeech period last?

10. Briefly describe each of the three stages in the prespeech period, and list about how long they last.

11. When does the language period begin, and what is the first stage of this period?

12. What is a holophrase? Provide two of your own examples of possible holophrases and what they might mean.

13. What are the last two stages of the language period, and about when do they begin?

14. How are parents advised to treat their children's early speech mistakes or problems?

15. What general rule can parents use to decide if a child needs professional help with language development?

CHAPTER

7

Social and Emotional Development

Newborn babies seem to be very self-centered. They cry when they are hungry or uncomfortable. If they are tired, they sleep regardless of who is around. If they need to eliminate bodily wastes, they do so in any place and at any time. While many people show their love for newborns, the infants are mostly concerned with their own needs.

Perhaps this description of newborn infants seems harsh, but it is the truth and parents must be ready to accept it. Many parents expect immediate love, affection, and friendship from their babies. These unrealistic expectations can lead to disappointment and frustration for parents. Realistic expectations, though, allow parents to love their newborn infants for what they are, and to look forward to the miraculous human developments soon to unfold.

Within just a few years, children learn to love others and to care more about what others think and feel. They start to make an effort to receive and give friendship, and begin to gain beliefs about right and wrong ways to treat people. Young children begin to try to help and protect animals and people and show concern when they are injured or in danger.

These examples are just part of the process of social and emotional development. *Social development* is a general term which refers to a child's growing ability to form relationships with others: to work, play, develop friendships, cooperate, and solve problems with others. *Emotions* are feelings that involve love, affection, joy, anger, fear, worry, jealousy, and more. *Emotional development* includes these feelings and behaviors and how children come to manage them. Social and emotional development are very closely related. One influences the other, and it is often hard to separate them.

Social and emotional development continues as children take on many of the values and beliefs of the people around them. This process continues throughout life as children learn their roles as playmate, student, friend, citizen, etc., on the road to adulthood.

THEORIES OF SOCIAL AND EMOTIONAL DEVELOPMENT

Two important theories which relate to social and emotional development are those of Abraham Maslow and Erik Erikson. As discussed in Chapter 4, Maslow felt that in order for children to develop healthy personalities, several basic needs must be met. These needs are, in the following order: physiological

Figure 7-1. *Children begin to learn about right ways and wrong ways to treat people and other living things at a young age. This is an important part of social and emotional development. (USDA Photo)*

needs, safety needs, belonging and love needs, and self-esteem needs. According to Maslow, if these basic needs are met, further personal growth through self-actualization can occur.

Erikson's psychological-social theory includes eight stages which span from infancy to adulthood:

- **Stage 1:** Infancy—Trust vs. Mistrust (Birth to 18 Months)
- **Stage 2:** Early childhood—Autonomy vs. Shame and Doubt (18 Months to 3 Years)
- **Stage 3:** Play age—Initiative vs. Guilt (3 Years to 6 Years)
- **Stage 4:** School age—Industry vs. Inferiority (6 Years to 12 Years)
- **Stage 5:** Adolescence—Identity vs. Role Confusion (12 Years to 18 Years)
- **Stage 6:** Young adulthood—Intimacy vs. Isolation (18 Years to 35 Years)
- **Stage 7:** Adulthood—Generativity vs. Self-absorption (35 Years to 60 Years)
- **Stage 8:** Old age—Integrity vs. Despair (60 Years and Older)

Each of these stages has the possibility for either success or failure. But Erikson believed that failure at an earlier stage could be compensated for by success at later stages. We now describe Erikson's explanation of his eight stages of emotional and social development.

Infancy—Trust vs. Mistrust

Erikson believed that if an infant's needs are met by a warm, caring, and consistent adult, the infant will learn to trust others. The quality of the interactions between the primary care giver and the infant is important. If the interactions are loving and responsive, trust is likely to result. However, if early needs are neglected, the infant may learn to mistrust others.

Early Childhood—Autonomy vs. Shame and Doubt

Children normally develop many coordination and cognitive abilities between the ages

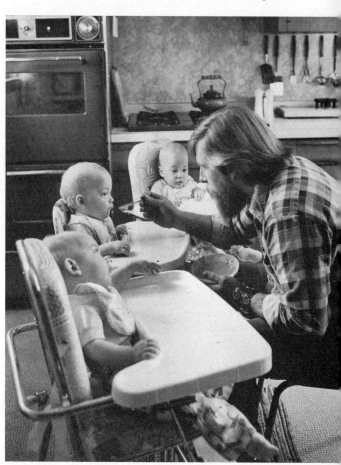

Figure 7-2. These infants are learning to trust others through the warm and loving care given to them by their father. (Abbott Laboratories)

of 18 months and 3 years. They usually learn to walk and talk. They establish themselves as being separate from their parents, and may bcome quite assertive. They want to try out all their new skills. If parents encourage their children to develop at their own pace within reasonable limits, children will become confident and independent (*autonomy*). However, if parents become overly restrictive or ignore this development, children may experience self-doubt and shame.

Figure 7-3. Children's natural eagerness to explore and learn helps them to develop self-confidence and independence.

Play Age—Initiative vs. Guilt

From 3 to 6 years of age, children exercise greater freedom of movement. *Initiative* means that children actively plan and try to accomplish things. They explore their environment more thoroughly. Language skills also develop to a high level, and children are able to use their imaginations extensively. With their increased ability to explore and experience, children also show initiative and are eager to learn. They initiate many activities on their own, and need many opportunities to play and discover their world. They eagerly want to do everything. If parents criticize or belittle these activities, children will develop a sense of *guilt*, a feeling of having done something wrong. If children are encouraged in their activities, they learn self-confidence and initiative.

School Age—Industry vs. Inferiority

From 6 to 12 years of age, children are very busy learning social skills and making or doing things with their peers. When parents praise and are supportive of their children's work and play projects, the children develop a sense of industry. *Industry* refers to activities and skills which require steady effort and busy application. If these activities are not valued or are criticized, children will develop a sense of *inferiority*, a feeling of being of less worth than other people.

Adolescence—Identity vs. Role Confusion

From 12 to 18 years, individuals face the task of experiencing many social activities and

Figure 7-4. Acceptance by peers becomes increasingly important to children during grade school. (HUD Photo by David Valdez)

selecting from many personal choices (education, work, recreation, morality). Through these choices, teenagers discover who they are and who they may become. If support is not given in making these decisions, teenagers may experience confusion about who they are.

Young Adulthood—Intimacy vs. Isolation

Once individuals have established their own identities, they are prepared to enter into *intimate* (close) and loving relationships with others. If young adults cannot become intimate with others for fear of losing their own identities, they may experience a sense of *isolation*, or apartness, from others.

Adulthood—Generativity vs. Self-Absorption

Those whose interests and concerns extend beyond themselves to others are said to have achieved *generativity*. Individuals who achieve generativity work to help others and improve the world, even if only in small ways. *Self-absorption* is a term which means the opposite of generativity. Self-absorption describes adults who remain self-centered—concerned only with satisfying their own wants and needs.

Late Adulthood—Integrity vs. Despair

In the later years of life, people look backward to assess or evaluate their accomplishments. They try to summarize what their life has meant to themselves and others. A feeling of *integrity* results when individuals are satisfifed with their efforts and would change little. A sense of despair is felt when people cannot be content with their life's efforts. *Despair* means that they feel unhappy or disgusted with their efforts and wish that they could have another chance.

SOCIAL AND EMOTIONAL DEVELOPMENT IN THE FIRST YEAR

Several important social and emotional developments occur during the first year of life. *Bonding* is the early formation of a relationship between infant and care giver. By about eight weeks of age, infants are seen to smile at other people. The social and emotional parts of bonding and smiling are hard to separate. Both emotions and social actions

Figure 7-5. During late adulthood, people often think about what their lives have meant to themselves and others. (Action)

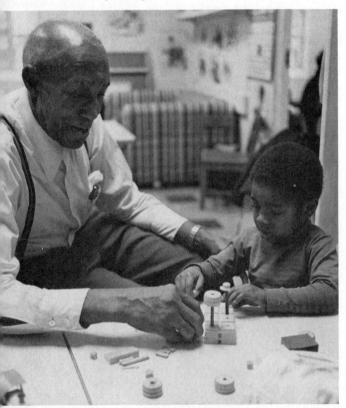

are involved in each case. Social development during the first year of life is summarized in Table 7.1.

Bonding

Emotional development appears to begin within the first hour after birth. This is a period in which infants are surprisingly alert and are likely to look intently at their parents' faces. Many parents find that the depth of their feelings for their newborn is increased when they can hold and be with their new infant immediately following birth. This is true also when they can do much of the infant care while they are still at the hospital. For these reasons, many hospitals now encourage fathers to be in the delivery room to be a part of their child's birth process. Parents are also encouraged to become much more involved in the infant's care at the hospital.

Most infants show a natural attraction toward their parents. This attraction is strengthened when parents provide the constant care and love necesary for life and normal growth. In this way, the images, sounds, and touches of parents become powerfully rewarding to their children. Children thus learn to care about their parents' presence and absence and to trust their environment. As time passes and many similar experiences occur, children learn to love their parents.

This process of developing love for another human is called bonding, or attachment, and it is essential to healthy development. Of course, bonding can also occur between children and care givers who are not their biological parents. All that is required for bonding is a consistent and caring relationship between child and care giver.

The basic building blocks for further emotional, social, and moral development are all laid during the bonding process. It is here that infants first learn to trust and love another human being.

Smiling

Smiling is one of the earliest positive responses of an infant. Research indicates that smiling in infants begins as a reflex within hours after birth.

During the *reflexive smiling phase*, infants'

Table 7.1

Social Development in the First Year of Life

Age	Activity
1 Week	Smiles spontaneously and in response to pleasant stimulation. Becomes excited and upset.
1 Month	Looks at others' faces and eyes. May smile at the voices of parents or strangers.
2 Months	Makes squawking and gurgling sounds called cooing. Cries in different ways to signal different needs. Laughs and smiles at people besides parents and siblings, and becomes quiet when held.
3 Months	Knows several people. May cry when primary care giver leaves, but not when other people do. May stop or begin to cry depending upon who holds the infant.
4 Months	Clearly responds to human sounds by turning head as if to look for the speaker. More sociable. Laughs while socializing. Interested in mirror image of self.
5 Months	May distinguish familiar from unfamiliar adults. Raises arms to signal desire to be held. Smiles and vocalizes to gain attention.
6 Months	Close emotional attachment to care giver. Plays games such as peek-a-boo. Responds to own name. May begin to imitate speech sounds near 7 months.
8 Months	Yells for attention. Shows fear of strangers and separation anxiety.
9 Months	Performs or plays for audience and repeats behavior if praised and applauded. Plays pat-a-cake, bye-bye, and ball games.
10 Months	Says first words (probably ''ma ma'' or ''da da''). Imitation improves. Understands meaning of the word ''no.'' Obeys some instructions. Seeks approval but does not always cooperate.
11 Months	Shows a sense of humor. Shows affection to humans and objects. Understands and plays simple games. Fears separation from care giver, strange places and people. Understands simple commands and says two or three words.

smiles are more of a physiological (physical) reaction to something than a social response. Smiles occur during feeding and sleeping, and in response to tickling or a high-pitched voice.

Around the eighth week of life, *nonselective social smiling* occurs. During this phase, infants are likely to smile at any person, regardless of whether or not they know the person. This may mean that infants have not yet developed the ability to identify the difference in human faces. It also suggests that the infants are happy to see someone (emotion) and behave in a way which is attractive to others (social development).

Figure 7-6. Smiling in infants is an early positive social response. (© Ron Meyer/White Eyes Design)

By around the age of 3½ months, infants enter the *selective social smiling phase*. Infants now smile at their parents and other family members and care givers. But when a stranger approaches, infants look concerned and do not smile. If a stranger comes too close too fast, infants may cry in protest. This *stranger anxiety* is a natural part of the bonding process and emotional and social development. Stranger anxiety is likely to reach a peak at about seven or eight months of age, and then it occurs less often.

CHILDHOOD EMOTIONS

Normally developing children show a full range of emotions. A very young child may move quickly from one intense emotional state to another. This sometimes confuses parents. As children grow and develop, they are able to exercise more control over their emotions. In other words, their emotional control matures. The following material describes some of the main emotions that you can expect to observe in children.

Anger

The amount of anger shown varies from individual to individual. Some children express anger frequently; others do not. Situations that commonly cause anger in children include physical restraint which limits what the child can do, and interfering with activities or plans. Infants may show anger due to physical discomfort or restrictions of movement. They may also become angry if they are ignored or if toys are taken away.

Figure 7-7. Childhood emotions can vary widely. Children experience all of the emotions that adults do. But children do not hide their emotions as much.

Preschoolers are angered by many of the same things that infants are. Because they are self-centered, they are especially likely to show anger if other children take or handle their possessions. Preschoolers are likely to fight with other children who interfere with their wants, activities, toys, or when they are asked to do things they do not wish to do.

Older children may become angry at some of the same things that preschoolers do. However, older children are more likely to become angry about criticism, nagging, teasing, or comparing them to other children in negative ways. Older children may become angry when they fail to achieve their own plans, or when their friends are unfairly punished or criticized.

Shyness

Stranger anxiety could also be called shyness. Older children may show their shyness by blushing, by talking very little, by nervous mannerisms, or by not looking directly at unfamiliar people.

Figure 7-8. Children often become shy when meeting Santa Claus for the first time! (© 1985 Joanne Meldrum)

Embarrassment

Embarrassment is similar to shyness in that it is a fear response to people. However, embarrassment differs in that it is the child's reaction to how others may judge him or her.

Embarrassment is not normally present in children until the age of five or six years. This is because feeling embarrassed requires the presence of social sensitivity to others' judgments and opinions. This sensitivity does not develop strongly until the age of five or six years.

Worry

Worry is a form of fear, but it is an imaginary fear. Worry is not produced directly by something in the environment. It requires a fair amount of intellectual development to worry about things which have not happened. Therefore, children do not begin to worry until about three years of age.

Young children normally worry about relationships with family and friends and about school problems. Children usually develop the intelligence to identify unrealistic concerns during early adolescence, and so worrying normally declines at that time.

Jealousy and Envy

Jealousy is a normal response to real, imagined, or threatened loss of affection. Envy is a similar emotion. Envy involves anger or resentment toward people because of the things they have. Children may show their jealousy through aggression or competing for attention. Envy may cause cheating and stealing.

Children vary in the amount of jealousy and envy they show. However, jealousy and envy appear with increased frequency at the ages of about three years and eleven years.

Grief

When children lose something they love, they experience grief, an intense, unpleasant emotion. Children who lose a parent, grandparent, pet, or friend may cry vigorously, show anger at the loss, or become depressed. Depressed children may withdraw from play and friends, lose appetite, and sleep poorly.

Joy and Delight

Joy and delight are important emotions for children to experience. Children normally experience these emotions over personal accomplishments (the infant climbing stairs or the preschooler winning a race), or by being pleasantly surprised or receiving a gift. Children show joy and delight by smiling and laughing.

Affection

Affection is an essential emotion for children to feel and demonstrate. This pleasant emotion is strengthened in children when they are given affection by those who love them. Children show their affection for others by cuddling, hugging, kissing, and stroking the person or things they care for. Children normally show affectionate behaviors to loved ones, friends, pets, and special toys.

Figure 7-9. *It's easy to spot the emotions of joy and delight in children. (USDA Photo)*

CHILDHOOD FEARS

Can you remember your own fears from early childhood? Perhaps you remember being afraid of being alone, strangers, bedtime, darkness, strange sounds, shadows, fictional characters (werewolves, vampires), and new places. These are some of the fears which commonly develop in children.

Infants react with fear naturally to loud noises, being dropped (a sudden loss of physical support), sudden changes in surroundings, or pain. These are experiences which reliably produce fear reactions in normal infants.

Children normally acquire other fears through their social development—through living and learning. Fears are different for each child, and there are several ways in

which children can learn them: association, imitation, and symbolic representation.

Association

In *association*, new fears are learned when previously unfeared things are connected with events which babies fear naturally. This basic form of learning can operate within the first months of life. For example, the infant who is placed in an overly hot bath may learn to fear bath time. The baby who is bitten by a dog or who receives a painful shot from a doctor may come to react fearfully at the sight of a dog or the mention of a visit to the

Figure 7-10. *Fear of strangers and new situations is common in childhood social development. (St. Jude Children's Research Hospital)*

doctor. Through a process called *generalization*, these fears can then spread to other similar situations. The baby could become fearful of all furry animals or of all people who wear white lab coats.

Imitation

Many fears are learned by observing other people act fearful. For example, parents can easily teach their children to fear spiders, darkness, or thunderstorms if they themselves show fearful reactions to these things. Learning fears through imitation usually begins before two years of age.

Symbolic Representation

As children grow in their ability to imagine and to learn from language and pictures, they also begin to acquire fears from sources such as frightening fairy tales, movies, or television programs. Children's imaginary fears appear to increase between the ages of three and five. They may fear witches, bears, or monsters which they may "see" in a shadow on the wall or "hear" in a branch rubbing against the side of the house.

Table 7.2 shows which fears tend to decrease and which fears increase between birth and six years of age.

Table 7.2

Common Childhood Fears

Age	Fear
Birth to 2 Years	Noise and things that produce noise Strange objects, situations, or people Pain Falling or loss of support
2 to 4 Years	Noise and things that produce noise Strange objects, situations, or people Animals
4 to 6 Years	Imaginary creatures Darkness Being made fun of Dreams Death Robbers Harm from accidents

Most experts advise parents and others to help children with their fears by providing security and support. Parents also should not demand that fears be overcome quickly or ridicule and deny the children's fears. This is good general advice. However, as we discuss later in this book, there are many details and specific procedures which can be used to help children cope with fears.

The ability to experience and show a wide range of emotions is an important part of being human. Feeling and expressing the emotions of joy and affection are an important part of personal and social development. These feelings and actions help to build relationships between people. Other emotions, such as anger, fear, embarrassment, and worry, can be harmful if they are not controlled to some degree.

Parents can do many things to help their children with emotional development. A variety of suggestions are discussed in Part D of this book. As you now know, helping children with emotional development also strengthens their social development.

THE ROLE OF PLAY

Young animals of all sorts, including humans, play much more than do adults. Play is more than fun; it also stimulates further development in many ways. Young children spend most of their time playing in one way or another. It is through this interaction with objects, themselves, and others that advancements in coordination, language, cognition, and other areas occur.

The many ways in which play contributes to general development are:

- Play helps to develop muscles.
- Play helps children learn how to form social relationships.
- Play provides children with chances to learn through manipulating and exploring things.
- Play can stimulate creativity and stimulate the imagination.
- Play can provide ways for children to release excess energy.
- Play and learning to play by rules help the development of morality.
- Play provides a setting for children to learn to communicate with others more skillfully.
- Play helps children learn how to cooperate to solve problems.
- Play provides children with a source of happiness and enjoyment which is generally very beneficial.

At the age of 2½ years, children have a great deal to learn about social relations with others. At this age, children are naturally self-centered. It will take many social experiences with other children and adults to learn new social skills. The important skills to be learned are initiating social contact, sharing people and materials, and resolving conflicts through learning to compromise with others. All of these social skills are strengthened through play.

Child's play may seem like "only play" to some people. However, play is a very important influence for all areas of child development. There are many differences in play skills at different ages.

Children at the age of 2½ years spend much of their time playing alone (*solitary play*), watching others (*onlooker*), or playing close to others and using similar materials (*parallel play*). Beginning social exchanges occur at this level as children imitate one another and indirectly share experiences. The children do not interact directly with one another very much.

At about three years of age, children's social interactions with one another are still likely to be short and infrequent. These early social contacts usually involve offering toys, playfully touching one another, or imitating various forms of behavior. With time, play becomes more social in nature. Play begins to include increasing amounts of *cooperative play* in which children "work" (play) together and each contributes to achieve some result.

Conflict often arises as children begin to interact more with others. Children are still self-centered. They also have difficulty solving frustrations and other problems with their limited vocabulary. Their time concepts are also limited, so a few minutes' wait for a toy may seem like hours to the three-year-old. All of this increases the likelihood of social conflicts.

Four- and five-year-olds learn that it is fun to play with others and to solve problems through compromising. Play groups in this age range may include two or three children; sometimes they are as large as six children. Children at these ages have better verbal, cognitive, and coordination skills. They are able to play together in more organized, imaginative, and active ways.

Still, four- and five-year-olds are likely to have trouble sharing, especially if a favorite toy is involved. They are likely to boast, boss others, and occasionally use hitting, pinching, and kicking to solve problems. Name calling and words related to bathroom functions are sometimes used to show anger toward other children. However, between four and five years, children spend more time in cooperative play.

Play and Social and Emotional Development

A special form of child's play involves imaginary friends. Children may develop imaginary friends at about three years of age. These children are normally well adjusted, so there is generally no cause for alarm about imaginary friends. As children grow older and enter school, such imaginary play decreases and play with other children increases.

The experience of play is important to children's sense of self-discovery. Through their play, young children can learn to start projects, explore, and create. Play also provides many opportunities for the development of social skills necessary to form friendships, to cooperate, and to solve personal problems. To play with others successfully requires that children begin to control emotions that can hurt the development of friendship, such as anger and jealousy. It is important that adults value children's play and not hurry them on to more adult tasks.

SEX ROLES

Have you ever wondered why little girls and boys come to behave differently? How many of these *sex-role differences* are truly necessary?

Could some of the traditional differences between boys and girls (and men and women) be restrictive and limit the potential for the healthy growth of both sexes?

Research has shown that many of the different ways in which boys and girls behave are learned. For example, adults treat newborn infants differently depending upon whether they believe the infants are boys or girls. One researcher found that visiting adults described an infant dressed in pink ("girl color") as darling, soft, and sweet. The same infant dressed in blue ("boy color") was described as solid, strong, and handsome. Sex roles are assigned to children and then strengthened by society in many ways.

Society is slowly learning that limiting children to rigid sex roles restricts their growth and potential as competent human beings. Letty Cotton Pogrebin, in *Growing Up Free*, reflected a more hopeful view for the developmental potential of both girls and boys. The following are based upon her suggestions.

• "All children should feel free to excel in any field and to fully enjoy the fruits of their performance."
• "Parents should help both girls and boys to strive freely, take pride in their accomplishments and be realistic about their failures."
• "Girls and boys should be encouraged to express themselves with originality and enthusiasm." They should be encouraged to strive, not to conform to prescribed sex roles, but to "make independent judgements based on facts, feelings, logic, pleasure, and consideration for others."

Children have learned their sex *stereotypes*, or traditional roles, in at least two different ways. First, children tend to imitate others who resemble themselves most closely. Parents, relatives, teachers, and others generally prompt and strengthen those behavior patterns traditionally assigned to the child's biological sex. For example, a little boy may be told that "Big boys don't cry" and be praised for being brave. A little girl may be told how important it is for her to stay clean and neat. She may then be praised for being such a "lovely young lady." These and similar traditional sex roles are restrictive and limit potential.

Another way in which sex roles appear to be acquired is related to cognitive development. Lawrence Kohlberg suggested that

Figure 7-11. Androgynous skills can lead to a happier and more competent life. For example, both boys and girls should learn homemaking skills such as cleaning and food preparation. (Fisher-Price Toys)

boys act like boys and girls act like girls because they organize their social world along sex lines. First children hear themselves labeled as boys or girls. When they know these labels, they then organize themselves around the labels on the basis of the behavior of others who are similarly labeled.

Differences do exist between the sexes beyond the most obvious biological features. Males, for example, normally have greater muscle strength and physical speed than do females. There are neurological differences as well. However, the differences between the sexes in a number of important areas have been greatly exaggerated. Members of both sexes can be helped to be generally competent human beings.

Competent, well-rounded people are able to combine the best of the traditional male and female roles and be flexible in expressing themselves. Such individuals may be said to be *androgynous*. The concept of androgyny is important to understanding present trends in the way our culture strengthens sex-role development. *Androgyny* is a term which refers to the ability to creatively combine characteristics of traditional male and female roles. An androgynous individual is often capable of expressing a full range of emotions and behaviors, depending upon the situation. Androgynous men and women, for example, may be somewhat unemotional and powerful while at work (traditionally male characteristics), yet they are able to be loving, caring, and express much emotion with their families (traditionally female characteristics).

Androgynous characteristics can lead to greater skills in living happy and successful lives. Parents are wise to encourage the following androgynous capabilities in their children, regardless of their sex:

- Express emotions.
- Give warmth and love.
- Love and care for children (nurturance).
- Develop physical potential (strength, agility, speed, stamina).
- Learn to compete successfully.
- Be reasonably assertive (stand up for one's own personal rights).

MORAL DEVELOPMENT

Most of us enjoy the company of people whom we can trust not to lie, steal, cheat, or hurt us in some way. These individuals, perhaps family and friends, show with their behavior that they live according to a moral code. A *moral code* is a set of rules that people follow in controlling their own behavior.

People have different personal rules, but the basis for sound moral development is the ability to understand how others feel when treated in a variety of ways and to care about other people. In other words, most successful social interactions are conducted in keeping with the idea of *social reciprocity*. This means that people treat others as they themselves wish to be treated. Or, simpler yet, if we treat each other in ways that we both like, we can be friends. This valuable ability depends on cognitive growth (the ability to think about another's feelings and rights), learning from loved ones and other authority figures, and the way children see others behave.

One important theory about moral development is that of Lawrence Kohlberg. Kohlberg, basing his theory upon Piaget's work in cognitive development, identified three levels of moral development.

Children who are younger than nine years are described as being at a *premoral level*. This means that they ordinarily make decisions about what is right or wrong based upon what is likely to be punished and what is likely to be rewarded. In other words, "If I'll get punished, it's bad; but if I get rewarded, it's good."

Kohlberg believed that in our society, children reach the next level, called *role conformity*, between the ages of 10 and 13. At this level, young people become concerned with living up to what is expected by people who are close to them. They may strive to be a good daughter, sister, or friend. At this level there is also concern for upholding laws and fulfilling duties or contracts which have been agreed upon.

The third level of moral development is called the *principled level*. Individuals may reach this high level of moral reasoning in adolescence or adulthood. Some people never reach this level. At the principled level of reasoning, individuals understand that people have a variety of values and opinions, and that these may change depending upon which group they belong to. However, some values, such as life and liberty, are viewed as being important no matter which group is considered. At the highest stage of this level of development, the individual has strong and broad views about justice, equality of human rights, and respect for others as individuals.

It would be a painful and unhappy world if people did not live by reasonable moral codes. Fortunately, many children learn and live by a moral code which is based upon a concern for the rights and well-being of others as well as themselves. It is the responsibility of parents and others in teaching roles to help young children to develop sound moral codes which they can use to make independent decisions later in life.

QUESTIONS FOR GROWTH

1. List the children's needs which must be met according to Maslow's theory of personality development.

2. Briefly explain Erikson's view of psychological-social development and tell what may be accomplished in each of the following stages: **(a)** infancy, **(b)** early childhood, **(c)** play age, **(d)** school age, and **(e)** adolescence.

3. Explain the meaning and importance of bonding in infants.

4. What are the three stages of smiling in infants? Describe how an infant would behave in each stage.

5. Name and describe five child emotions discussed in this chapter.

6. Name and explain three ways in which children may learn fears.

7. Name several fears which decrease with age and several which increase with age.

8. Describe several ways in which play can help a child's general development.

9. Explain how play activities can strengthen several specific social skills in children.

10. Name and explain several forms of play which children show as they develop.

11. Describe, in your own words, what sex roles are.

12. What is the meaning of the term *androgyny*?

13. Explain how you think an androgynous mother and father would behave and act towards their children.

14. Explain several ways that children learn their sex roles.

15. What is a moral code?

16. Name Kohlberg's three stages of moral development and explain how children think in each stage.

CHAPTER

8

Cognitive Influences in Learning

In this chapter, we explore the changing capabilities of children as they interact with and learn from their surroundings. Because of their changing capabilities, children generally gain different things from similar experiences as they grow and develop.

Perhaps you saw *Snow White* or *The Wizard of Oz* as a young child. If you saw one of these films when you were about six years old, you would have been in what is known as the preoperational period of cognitive development (refer to Chapter 6). By then you would have developed the language abilities necessary to remember and describe parts of the story and the characters that were important to you. You would have remembered many of these ideas and impressions for the rest of your life. But if you watched one of the movies again as a teenager, you would surely have learned different things. The additional learning would not be simply because you saw the movie twice, but because what you brought to the movie experience would have changed and grown.

As a teenager, you have entered the formal operational period of cognitive development. Now, for example, you can understand the moral lesson behind the Cowardly Lion's unnecessary pursuit of a badge of courage in *The Wizard of Oz*. Now you might recognize and think about the symbolism behind the Wicked Witch of the West, and so on. This is because you have changed cognitively. As a result, you now learn new things and think in different ways from how you did as a young child.

THEORY OF COGNITIVE DEVELOPMENT

Jean Piaget's ideas about cognitive development were introduced in Chapter 6. We now explore Piaget's theory in greater detail. We describe how an understanding of Piaget's theory can help parents to provide experiences for their children that make learning easier.

Recall that Piaget believed that cognitive growth (the ability to think and reason) develops as children interact with their surroundings. Learning is not a passive process in which children simply observe or receive knowledge. Instead, children taste, smell, push, pull, and in other ways sample and act upon their environment. It is this process that parents should *facilitate* (make easier). Parents can best do this when they are aware of each child's period of cognitive development.

Table 8.1 summarizes Piaget's periods of cognitive development. Each period is identified by age, and by the activities of children and parents which will help to bring about

Figure 8-1. Learning is a process which requires active involvement. (Florida Department of Commerce/ Division of Tourism)

further cognitive development. The years and months listed in Table 8.1 can be viewed as estimates. However, all children move through the four main periods of development in the same order indicated.

Table 8.1 provides information about the concrete operational and formal operational periods. However, these periods actually extend beyond the age ranges covered in this book. They are included in Table 8.1 so that you will be familiar with the last two periods of Piaget's theory.

PARENTAL ROLES IN COGNITIVE DEVELOPMENT

Parents can help to strengthen cognitive development in their infants and children in many ways. Two general and basic things that parents can do are:

1. Understand the cognitive periods that their children will pass through; and
2. Present various activities that are appropriate for each period.

Table 8.1 and the following material review these periods and suggest beneficial experiences which parents can arrange for their children to explore.

Sensorimotor Period

Refer to Table 8.1. Notice that the sensorimotor period (birth to two years) of development is divided into six subperiods. This is because a great deal of cognitive growth occurs in the first two years of life. Parents must respond to their infant's growing ability to

Table 8.1

Highlights of Piaget's Periods of Cognitive Development

Period	Child's Activity	Parent's Activity
Sensorimotor Period (Birth to 2 Years)		
Birth to 1 Month	Refines innate responses.	Responds to and stimulates the child's senses (sight, sound, taste, touch, smell).
1 to 4 Months	Repeats and refines actions which once occurred by chance.	Stimulates the senses through objects the child can interact with (rattles, bells, mobiles).
4 to 10 Months	Manipulates objects. Repeats actions by choice. Begins to develop object permanence.	Provides toys to handle, of various shapes, textures, colors. Partially hides a toy while child watches.
10 to 12 Months	Combines previous activities for new results. Imitation begins.	Provides toys (familiar dolls, balls, boxes). Encourages imitation.
12 to 18 Months	Experiments with objects to discover new uses. Locates an object with eyes and tracks it.	Provides experiences with water, sand, textures. Includes toys which can be manipulated to turn, roll, open, close.
18 to 24 Months	Practices deferred imitation. Applies old skills in new situations.	Provides opportunities to apply old skills to new experiences. Provides peer contact and interaction.

Continued on next page

Table 8.1 (Continued)

Period	Child's Activity	Parent's Activity
Preoperational (2 to 7 Years)	Language appears. Imaginative player, deferred imitation, egocentrism is common.	Provides dolls, cars, blocks, crayons, paste, paper, books, musical instruments, etc. Communicates at child's level or above. Provides experience with mass, liquid, and length informally. Encourages decision making: red or yellow shirt.
Concrete Operational (7 to 11 Years)	Applies simple logic to arrive at conclusions. Reasons deductively. Performs simple operations with physical objects. Conserves.	Provides opportunity to pursue areas of interest. Uses questions to understand child's reasoning processes but does not question too much.
Formal Operational (11 to 15 Years)	Reasons abstractly. Solves problems through inductive reasoning. Employs logical thought.	Proposes hypothetical problems to solve. Discusses ethical questions. Encourages personal decision making and problem solving.

Source: Based upon "Practical Parenting with Piaget," Thibault and McKee, *Young Children,* 1982. Used with permission.

experience and interact with the world in new ways.

Subperiod #1

During the first month of life, infants have very little coordinated physical behavior, but their senses are relatively advanced. Beneficial parental activities include lovingly stim-

ulating all of these senses during normal care-giving activities.

Subperiod #2

From one to four months of age, infants are still very uncoordinated, but they are learning to control their bodies by reaching out and acting upon the environment. Parents

Figure 8-2. Why is the parental role so important in a child's cognitive development? Could a lack of parental involvement limit a child's development? (March of Dimes Birth Defects Foundation)

can help development by providing objects to manipulate which stimulate infants' senses. Examples of such objects are bells, rattles, and other objects which move or make noise when they are touched. This helps infants to learn coordination and the ways they can influence or control their surroundings.

Subperiod #3

Between four and ten months, children become much more skilled at manipulating objects. Parents should continue to provide toys and harmless objects to manipulate and explore. (**NOTE: Any objects provided to infants should be larger than they could accidentally swallow.**) These objects should be of varied colors, shapes, and textures. Infants can be interested by differences in temperature as well, so they should have opportunities to touch cold and warm (**but not hot**) objects. Playing peek-a-boo—using objects or

parents who hide (or partially hide) behind things and then reappear in a moment—tends to fascinate infants. This game may help the development of object permanence during this subperiod.

Object permanence is achieved when children become aware that things—parents included—which are removed from sight, still exist in the world. To the child who has not yet developed the cognitive ability of object permanence, out of sight is out of the universe. Achievement of the object-permanence concept is important for intellectual, social, and emotional development.

Subperiod #4

Between 10 and 12 months, children combine previous activities with increasing skill and new results. Parents can make available toys, dolls, balls, boxes, and so on; children will then play in more complex ways. Children can now sit, creep, and crawl. Some may

Figure 8-3. Parents can help their child's cognitive development by providing a variety of new and interesting objects and environments to explore. (USDA Photo by Fred S. Witte)

begin to walk. Children's increased body control and imitative power allows them to hug and kiss their dolls and act out certain child-care activities with their dolls. Children may now play with balls by dropping or rolling them on the floor. Parents should also encourage children to *imitate* them (match their behavior) during this subperiod.

Subperiod #5

From 12 to 18 months of age, children grow in their ability to experiment with and find new uses for various objects. Parents can let their children play with water, sand, and other sense-responsive toys. So-called "busy boxes" are fascinating to children at this age—they can open little doors, turn dials, pull strings, and so on.

Subperiod #6

Between 18 and 24 months, children apply old skills to new situations. A major cognitive accomplishment during this subperiod is *deferred imitation*. This means that children watch someone do something and then remember the actions and imitate them sometime later. This is another important cognitive development, and much learning will occur in this way.

Parents should continue to provide many opportunities to practice or extend older skills to new experiences. Trips to new places help this process. Parents should also begin to provide more social experiences with other children. Peer contact now becomes very important for the development of many skills and abilities.

Preoperational Period

The preoperational period extends from two to seven years of age. Children master their language and begin to exercise their imaginations in remarkable ways during this period. Parents can do many things to strengthen cognitive development during these years. Certainly they can provide toys as before. Now, however, the emphasis can shift more in the direction of creative materials. Playthings may now include items which allow for individual expression, such as crayons, paste, paper, clay, books, and musical instruments.

Figure 8-4. *Creative play allows children to experiment with new materials and express their own interests and talents. (Fisher-Price Toys)*

Children in the preoperational period are egocentric. They think that everyone has the same thoughts, feelings, actions, and experiences that they do. Egocentric children have not gained the ability to see the world from another person's point of view.

Preoperational children also find it hard to understand concepts of time. The concepts of a week, month, and year have very little meaning for them. Only actual events which are experienced during any particular day have meaning. The parent may say, *''Right after breakfast* we will go to the beach'' or *''After your nap* we will go shopping.'' By referring to the events which children experience during their waking hours, parents can begin to strengthen their understanding of the meaning of time. Parents can also help their children to make comparisons between things. They can do this by showing differences and similarities in volume, mass, length, and weight.

Concrete Operational Period

The concrete operational period extends from 7 to 11 years of age. During this period, children learn to classify objects into categories, such as animals vs. plants, human vs. non-human, and so on. Parents should listen closely to their children and ask questions to stimulate them to think and reason. Parents should also continue to help them to compare differences and similarities between things.

As discussed in Chapter 6, children will learn the concept of conservation during this period. That is, they come to understand how objects can change in one dimension, such as shape, and yet remain the same in other dimensions, such as volume or weight.

Formal Operational Period

By about 11 or 12 years, children enter the formal operations period. Children are now able to think in logical ways, and this ability develops further with time and experience.

Now young people can think about conditions that do not exist and imagine what these conditions would be like. For example, what would it be like if we lived on another planet? Or what would life be like if everyone lived to be 200 years of age? Teenagers can now think about values and morals in abstract and mature ways.

Figure 8-5. Visits to a zoo or an aquarium are fun ways to strengthen the ability to classify things during the concrete operational period.

This final period is one which is achieved to various degrees. Some individuals experience much greater development in the formal operational period than do others.

TEACHING AND LEARNING SUGGESTIONS

Learning during the early years is very important to success in later life. The following are general suggestions which are useful to helping children learn. These suggestions are valuable for children of all ages and in all learning situations.

1. Keep it fun. Provide learning activities which are appropriate to the particular child's level of cognitive development. In this way, the child will learn while having fun. As Maria Montessori once said, ''Play is the child's work.''

If children are not enjoying and participating eagerly in a learning situation, it is a sign that they are being pushed too hard. This can make learning situations unpleasant and something which children may begin to avoid in the future. Young children have a natural desire to learn, to be curious, and to experiment with their environment. They are learning all the time.

2. Let children learn through actions. Children do not learn well by only sitting still and watching or listening. As Piaget and others have shown, children learn best by doing things. For example, children can be helped to learn colors by ''going hunting'' for certain colors rather than being drilled by flash cards of colors. The hunt could involve a trip to a room in the house or another location which is interesting and contains various colors. Children learn a sound basis for mathematics when they are building with blocks. It takes a lot of measuring, counting, balancing, and problem solving to create a structure.

3. Use activities which children can select and are interested in. Learning can be facilitated when using the materials most appropriate for children at various ages. It is good to provide a variety of possibilities and follow the children's lead to play and learn. Parents can present a variety of new things to do, such as playing with dolls, water, musical toys, and more, and let their children show them their interests. Activities which stimulate the senses will help young children learn. It is important to provide activities and materials that encourage creativity and problem-solving skills, and that do not have a right-or-wrong outcome. Children learn through trial and error and begin to view themselves as good problem solvers when they are given the freedom to experiment.

4. Strengthen feelings, attitudes, and interests as well as intellectual development. Society's expectations often tend to hurry children into *academic* or school learning before they are really ready. It is important to remember that all areas of development need time to mature, and each child has his or her own rate of development. Children also have their own special interests and abilities. If they are not given the opportunity to make choices and explore many new experiences, many of their individual talents may never be discovered.

5. Structure children's surroundings so they can learn. Parents should provide a stool at sinks, lower hooks and shelves, and provide children's furniture and utensils. Children

Figure 8-6. *Children need a wide variety of experiences in order to find their own special interests and talents.* *(Future Homemakers of America)*

will then be able to interact more effectively with their environment. These actions avoid frustration, increase chances of success, and strengthen feelings of self-esteem. Providing a place in the home where children can make messes and initiate projects without getting into trouble helps children to be creative.

6. Repeated practice is important to learning. Repetition is necessary for learning. However, boredom can be avoided by finding different ways in which the same intellectual skills can be practiced. For example,

"The Count" on *Sesame Street* was not content to count fingers. He counted elephants, popsicles, noses, and anything else that was fun to count. Practice is an essential part of learning many skills. Young children often delight in repeating a new experience over and over.

7. Remember that children have unique learning styles. Children approach learning situations differently. Some need encouragement; others plunge right in. Some children are very verbal when solving a problem, while others complete the task quietly. Many children involve their entire being in learning experience—they touch, taste, smell, jump, roll, and shout with excitement. Other children are more reserved as they interact with their environment. Each child will also differ in what he or she learns from each experience. When children are very young, parents cannot tell who has a talent for art, mechanics, or the medical field. That is why it is important to expose children to a wide variety of what life has to offer so that they can be better perpared to make their own decisons.

Cognitive development and other suggestions for learning do not occur in a vacuum. Other influences occur at the same time and are also critically important to learning. For example, children are greatly influenced by their growing ability to learn through observing and imitating.

OBSERVATIONAL LEARNING AND IMITATION

Many of us enjoy watching entertainers imitate well-known people. Have you ever imitated someone? Most certainly you have. In fact, your personality is a unique blend of the behaviors and attitudes that you have imitated from many others in your life. Other influences have also helped to make you a unique individual. But the ability to observe and imitate other people has been very important to your development.

Do other people imitate your behavior? They certainly do. Friends, brothers, sisters, or younger children who love and respect you have most likely imitated your behavior frequently.

Observational learning and imitation—observing and imitating others—are natural ways in which humans learn. This means that everyone has some responsibility to act in ways that not only benefit themselves, but which also benefit others who are sure to imitate them. This responsibility to *model*, or show, beneficial actions for others to observe and imitate grows as we grow.

If you choose to become a parent or teacher, you will have tremendous influence on children because of their tendency to observe and imitate you. At that level of development, you will have accepted the greatest responsibility for your own actions and those of the children who will imitate you. Perhaps, however, the same responsibility is held by anyone who will be watched by children.

Observational Learning

It appears that children begin to learn by observing (*observational learning*) as soon as they are born. Humans observe the world around them by seeing, hearing, feeling, tasting, touching, and smelling things. Newborn infants can do all of these things much better than we once thought.

When infants observe their world, one of the simplest ways they learn is by becoming familiar with things. This process of getting used to things is called *habituation*. Researchers have found that, at first, newborns react to a sound they have not heard before. Later, after they have heard the particular sound many times, they show less of a response to it. This means that habituation has occurred—they have become familiar with the sounds. However, when a slightly different, new sound is presented to the infants, they again show a reaction.

To develop normally, infants need to have the chance to observe their world. They must experience or observe many forms of stimulation during their waking times. Much evidence suggests that the absence of various forms of stimulation may lead to social, emotional, intellectual, and coordination retardation.

Parents are responsible for providing stimulation by talking, singing, holding, touching, and stroking their babies. Parents must also provide other kinds of stimulation for infants to see, feel, and hear, such as different colors, shapes, forms, toys, and sounds.

Children learn a great deal by observing and experiencing a stimulating environment (surroundings). Among the first and most interesting things for babies to observe are their parents.

If you can imagine yourself within the skin of a newborn infant, you will see the world very differently than you do now. Imagine that you are a newborn infant again and that you are seeing your parents and other humans for the very first time. You probably are amazed and fascinated by these large and (at first) unpredictable creatures. They make hundreds of strange noises, move about, and change their body positions in surprising ways. They even change the stuff on their bodies, which you later learn to call clothes. A very interesting part of their bodies is the flat portion (the face) of a round object (the head). Later you learn to name all the parts of the human face. You even learn that you have one, similar but different from everyone else's face.

As an infant, observing faces was fascinating to you. Noses, ears, eyebrows, mouths,

eyes, and wrinkles all moved and changed in different ways. Often, a warm and soft face came very close and rubbed against your own face, arms, and stomach. You noticed that the face made soft and soothing sounds when its mouth moved. You observed very closely and you learned amazing things. Weeks later, as your vision improved, you observed parents, brothers and sisters, or other relatives do many kinds of things. This process of observational learning is the same for all normally developing infants.

Bonding is another important early influence which might be viewed as a form of observational learning. Emotional bonding that

Figure 8-7. We've all learned many useful skills through observational learning and imitation. (© Ron Meyer/White Eyes Design)

occurs immediately after birth is expected to help normal emotional and personality development in the infant. Bonding is also thought to help parents develop stronger emotional bonds with their new child.

Imitation

Children not only observe the actions of others; they also imitate many of those actions. Imitation occurs when someone matches his or her own actions with those of another person, animal, or object. We all imitate others, but the tendency to learn and develop through imitation is most easily seen in infants and children.

When we talk or think about imitation, it is convenient to call the individual who is imitated, or who may be imitated, the model. Children imitate many people who model, or show, actions for them.

We do not know exactly when children begin to imitate others. Tiffany M. Field and her research team have demonstrated that children who are an average of 36 hours old can tell the differences between adult facial expressions showing happiness, sadness, and surprise. They have also provided evidence that young infants may imitate adult facial expressions at around this age.

It is reasonable to wait for more evidence before we make up our minds about exactly when imitation begins in infants. It is also reasonable to believe that it is possible for very young infants to imitate their loved ones. With this view, parents should be more aware of their actions as models and treat their infants in ways that cannot hurt, but might truly help, their development. For example, it would be sensible to try and model happy and affectionate behavior whenever possible, rather than sad or angry behavior.

Some people believe that the tendency for infants and children to imitate models is inherited genetically. They might argue that if imitation is observed in babies as few as 12 days following birth, then imitation cannot be a learned skill.

However, even if humans inherit a tendency to imitate others, it is wise for parents to strengthen their children's tendency to imitate them by reinforcement. Much evidence shows that when children are reinforced (rewarded) for imitating others, they imitate more often.

Children and adults tend to imitate people whom they love, respect, and admire. Those who are thought to be glamorous or powerful are also frequently imitated. Sometimes individuals imitate others whom they fear.

One of the major influences that parents have is through their role as a model. This process of child imitation of parental models is a very powerful one. It is important for parents to model quality behavior rather than unhealthy behavior. If parents model lying, stealing, cheating, and immature emotions, then their children are very likely to imitate these actions. See Illustration 8.1.

Healthful imitation is best brought about by parents who maintain a warm and loving relationship with their children. Healthful imitation is also strengthened when discipline remains *authoritative* in nature. This means that there are rules, that reasons for rules are explained, and that following rules is rewarded. Breaking rules, however, is dealt with in a loving but firm way.

Although infants may imitate some of their parents' behavior automatically, parents

Illustration 8.1. *The behavior that parents model for their children to see and hear is very powerful. Children normally do as their parents do—not as they say.*

must reinforce the imitation. In this way, the natural tendency to imitate is strengthened even more. This may sound difficult for parents, even mechanical, but it is not. Loving parents normally react with joyful praise, excitement, hugs, and kisses when their children imitate their facial movements, sounds, or other valuable activities. Much of the motivation to talk, walk, eat with utensils, become toilet trained, and much more, results from children's desires to imitate their loved ones.

Albert Bandura was interested in seeing if children would imitate forms of aggression modeled by adults. In his study, an adult took children (about three to six years old) to a room one at a time. Then the adult punched a large inflated doll in the nose and also hit it on the head with a toy hammer. The adult kicked the doll and threw it around the room and said, "Kick him! Pow!" Other children were taken to the same room one at a time to watch the adult play with the same toys in a gentle way.

Later, all of the children were allowed to be in the room alone. Bandura observed that the children who had aggressive models (hitting, kicking) often imitated the aggressive actions. The children who had observed the gentle, or nonaggressive, adult models were much less aggressive.

Other researchers have shown that children also imitate what they see in movies and on television. Child imitation of aggression and other undesirable actions seen in movies and television has become a major concern among informed parents and child educators. Televised violence and other problem behaviors, however, has not lessened. Therefore, the major responsibility for choosing and showing appropriate behavioral models to children, including in movies and television, remains with parent.

Vicarious Learning

Someone who is observed by a child may behave in a certain way that is either reinforced (rewarded) or punished. Children are influenced to imitate or not imitate by the consequences (results) they have seen others obtain. This is called *vicarious learning*. Children observe models and therefore learn. Children learn vicariously by observing consequences (punishment or reinforcement).

Vicarious learning has much to do with which behaviors children choose to imitate. For example, the young child who sees her older brother make his bed and be warmly praised by a parent is more likely to try to make her own bed. On the other hand, a child who sees another push a playmate down and take her toy to play with (reinforcement) is likely to imitate this behavior, too. However, if the child observes that aggression is not reinforced, but is mildly punished, the imitation is not so likely.

What infants and children observe and imitate is very influential to their development. It is thus essential for parents to understand the ways in which observational learning and imitation influence their education.

Figure 8-8. Why did this child know to pick up a telephone receiver and speak into it?

QUESTIONS FOR GROWTH

1. Explain how cognitive development could influence the way that you experienced the same movie, first as a child and then as a young adult.

2. What sorts of child activities did Piaget believe would strengthen cognitive development?

3. (a) Desribe several child activities which occur during the sensorimotor period. **(b)** Describe several things that parents can do to help cognitive development in the sensorimotor period.

4. (a) Describe several child activities which occur during the preoperational period. **(b)** Describe several things that parents can do to help cognitive development in the preoperational period.

5. (a) Describe several child activities which occur during the concrete operational period. **(b)** Describe several things that parents can do to help cognitive development in the concrete operational period.

6. (a) Describe several things that teenagers do in the formal operational period. **(b)** Describe several things that parents can do to help cognitive development in the formal operational period.

7. Name and explain three other teaching and learning suggestions which can strengthen cognitive development.

8. Explain why it is said that parents have a responsibility to model beneficial actions.

9. Tell when children seem to start learning by observing.

10. List the various ways in which children observe their world.

11. Explain the meaning of the term *habituation*.

12. What is imitation?

13. Explain what a model is.

14. When do children appear to begin imitating others?

15. Why is reinforcement an important part of imitation, and what other things influence who children may imitate?

16. What is authoritative discipline?

17. List several valuable things which children can learn through imitation.

18. Explain the meaning of vicarious learning, and provide two original examples of how vicarious learning might influence a child's imitation of others.

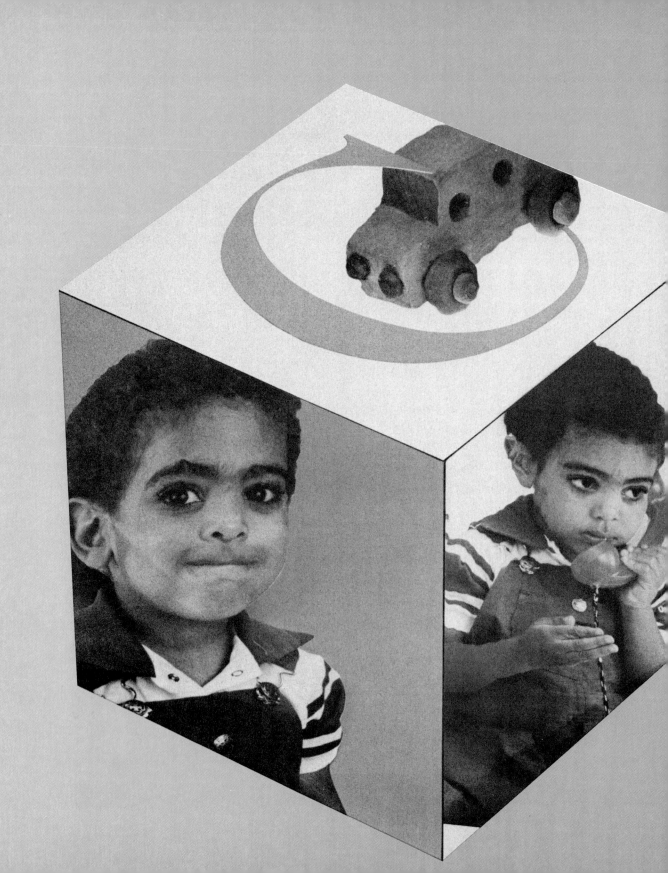

PART

C

PRINCIPLES OF TEACHING AND LEARNING

Providing consistent love and warmth is essential—but more is needed for quality parenting. In Part C we discuss the basic principles of teaching and learning which have a powerful influence upon a child's developing behavior and personality. These principles include respondent learning and operant learning. Informed parents and others who care for children often combine these principles into methods which can be used to teach children the great many skills they need for normal growth and development. In Part C we also describe the importance of using humane and effective discipline methods in parenting.

CHAPTER

9

Respondent Learning

Have you ever thought about why some children are afraid of water, while others love to go swimming? Have you ever noticed that some children approach animals eagerly, but others are afraid? Such differences in what children like and fear can be partially explained by *respondent learning*. Respondent learning has to do with how we are influenced when things we experience are associated, or paired together. For example, a sting and the sight of a bee may become associated. To understand how respondent learning can influence children it is necessary to discuss the reflex.

Reflexes are involuntary actions, such as sneezing, made in response to a stimulation of some nerve cells. Some of the reflexes that can be observed in newborn babies are the sucking reflex, the blink reflex, the pupilary reflex, and the startled reflex. These reflexes are inherited. They result from our genetic and biological makeup. Reflexes automatically help our bodies to stay healthy, and they normally serve other useful purposes. The behaviors observed in reflexes can also be called *respondent behaviors*.

RESPONDENT BEHAVIOR

Why is reflexive behavior called respondent behavior? A reflex is made up of two parts: a stimulus and a response. The respondent, or reflexive, behavior happens only after (in response to) a specific stimulus. Table 9.1 lists several respondent behaviors which are:

1. Physiological reactions which involve the body's smooth muscles or glands; and
2. Automatically produced by presenting a particular stimulus.

Table 9.1

How Respondent Behavior Operates

The Stimulus	*The Response* (*Respondent Behavior*)	*The Unlearned Reflex*
Nipple in the mouth	Sucking	The sucking reflex
Food in the mouth	Salivation (mouth waters), helping the swallowing and digestion of food	The salivary reflex
Light in the eye	Pupils (the black holes in the eyes) become smaller or larger, helping the infant to see	The pupilary reflex

---

THE UNLEARNED REFLEX

The unlearned reflex is the most basic kind of reflex. All of the reflexes shown in Table 9.1 are unlearned reflexes. An infant does not have to learn these respondent behaviors—sucking, salivating, or changing the size of the pupils in response to appropriate stimuli. (The term *stimuli* is the plural of stimulus.) The ability to do these things in response to the stimuli listed in Table 9.1 is genetically inherited. These behaviors are not learned; they are part of unlearned reflexes.

The unlearned reflex contains two parts. Table 9.1 illustrates that the unlearned stimulus of food in the mouth must be present to produce the unlearned response of salivation, and so on.

Each unlearned reflex has its threshold. The *threshold* is the amount of size or strength that the unlearned stimulus must have in order to produce its particular unlearned response. For example, a few drops of onion juice held near your eyes will not cause tears. But if you hold a whole teaspoonful of onion juice near your eyes, tears will probably start to flow. By increasing the amount of the unlearned stimulus of onion juice to a certain amount, the unlearned response of tears will finally be produced. The amount of onion juice necessary to produce tears is the threshold.

There are many unlearned reflexes which are very important to everyone. For example, food in your stomach (stimulus) produces digestive juices (response). When you become too cold (stimulus), you shiver (response). When you become too hot (stimulus), you perspire (response). If you were to step on a tack (stimulus), your foot would pull away without your thinking about it (response). We could describe many more unlearned reflexes. Can you think of some?

Although unlearned reflexes seem simple, even primitive, they are essential. Without many unlearned reflexes, normal development would not be possible. For example, a child would be seriously impaired if the body did not automatically adjust pupil size, withdraw from pain, or increase heart rate to supply greater blood flow when needed.

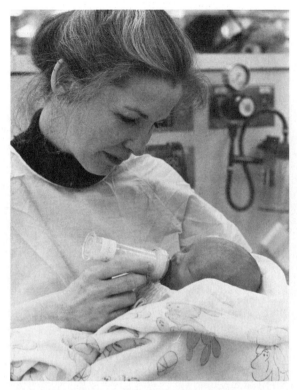

Figure 9-1. *What is the value of an unlearned reflex such as sucking? (March of Dimes Birth Defects Foundation)*

The Learned Reflex

Learned reflexes are acquired through experience. They are also necessary for development. In 1927, Ivan Pavlov, a Russian physiologist, published the results of his research in which he discovered the learned reflex.

Pavlov did his research on dogs. It is said that one day Pavlov noticed that his dogs salivated when they heard the footsteps of the person coming to feed them. It was easy to understand why the dogs would salivate when food was placed in their mouths; this is an unlearned reflex. But why did the dogs salivate to the sound of footsteps? Footsteps, certainly, are not unlearned stimuli for salivation.

Pavlov performed experiments to learn how dogs could learn to salivate to things other than food. As a result, he also discovered something important about how humans learn.

First Pavlov tested a stimulus to be certain that it did not cause salivation in the dogs. The stimulus tested was the sound of a bell. The sound of a bell was presented to the dogs, and salivation was measured. The sound did not cause salivation in the dogs. Because the bell did not cause a response, the bell was called a *neutral stimulus*.

Food, in the form of meat powder, was tested next. When meat powder was placed in a dog's mouth, it produced the unlearned reflex of salivation. The meat powder was the unlearned stimulus, and salivation was the unlearned response.

Pavlov's important discovery was that by pairing or associating a previously neutral stimulus (the bell) with an unlearned stimulus (food), a new reflex could be taught. After a number of such bell-food associations, the bell sound alone was capable of producing salivation in the dogs. The conclusion was that if such associations occur often enough, a new reflex could be *conditioned*, or created. The new reflex is a learned reflex, and can be conditioned in humans as well as in many other animals. The steps in Illustration 9.1 show how learned reflexes are created.

Pavlov found that the essential ingredient in producing a learned reflex is to associate a previously neutral stimulus with an unlearned stimulus. This form of learning is very important to human growth and development. Many beneficial things are learned

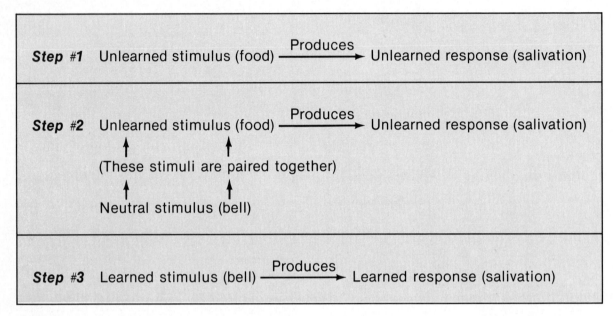

Step #1   Unlearned stimulus (food) ——Produces——▶ Unlearned response (salivation)

Step #2   Unlearned stimulus (food) ——Produces——▶ Unlearned response (salivation)

(These stimuli are paired together)

Neutral stimulus (bell)

Step #3   Learned stimulus (bell) ——Produces——▶ Learned response (salivation)

Illustration 9.1. *Steps in the development of a learned reflex.*

in this fashion. For example, people learn to desire and appreciate certain rewards, such as good grades, money, or praise. They learn to appropriately fear things that will hurt them, such as a hot stove or sharp knife. It is also true that things not so beneficial are learned in this manner, such as developing a fear of *all* dogs because of having been bitten once.

Parents who understand respondent learning will be in a much better position to help their children learn useful respondent behavior. They can also help children to avoid or unlearn respondent behavior that is not beneficial.

The following are some of the ways in which respondent learning influences human development. As you read, think about the ways that a caring parent could use this information to increase positive influences and reduce negative ones in a child.

LEARNING TO DISLIKE OR FEAR PREVIOUSLY NEUTRAL STIMULI

Respondent learning contributes to many learned emotional responses. Pain, for example, is an unlearned stimulus which can produce a variety of unlearned responses that are unpleasant to experience. Pain can cause adrenalin to be secreted into the blood, causing the heart to beat faster (to pound), and causing feelings like hot flashes, breathlessness, and momentary weakness. All of these are part of startle and fear reactions, which have to do with unpleasant emotions.

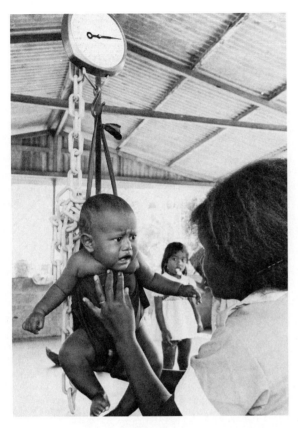

Figure 9-2. *Does this baby's expression indicate that he will look forward to visiting a doctor or nurse in the future? (UNICEF Photo)*

If a painful unlearned stimulus is associated with a previously neutral stimulus, the neutral stimulus can acquire some of the power of the painful unlearned stimulus. When this happens, the previously neutral stimulus becomes a learned stimulus. This stimulus will then produce startle or fear reactions when it is presented alone.

Many experiments have been conducted to demonstrate this form of respondent learning. In 1920, John B. Watson and Rosalie Rayner performed research to see how infants learned to fear things. Today, their research methods would be considered unacceptably inhumane and would not be allowed. Yet what Watson and Rayner learned can help parents understand, and perhaps avoid, the learning of unnecessary fears by their children.

The researchers' subject was an 11-month-old orphan named Albert. First, Albert was tested to see if he was fearful of a white rat, a rabbit, and a dog. Albert showed no fear of these animals. These animals were, therefore, neutral stimuli for the fear response.

The researchers next tested Albert's response to a loud noise by suddenly striking a steel bar. The loud noise frightened Albert and caused him to cry. The loud noise was demonstrated to be an unlearned stimulus capable of producing the unlearned response of fear.

Finally, Albert was shown a white rat. As he looked at the rat, the loud noise was sounded. After associating the neutral stimulus (the rat) with the unlearned stimulus (the noise) six times, Albert showed fear of the rat. The rat had become a learned stimulus capable of producing the fear responses of crying and crawling away.

Another important finding was that Albert's fears of the rat *generalized*, or spread, to other things that were similar. As a result, Albert also showed fear to previously neutral stimuli such as a dog, a man's hair, a fur coat, and a Santa Claus mask. This was an important finding, because to Albert these things had never been associated with the loud noise.

A more common example of generalization might be the small child who visited a doctor and was given a shot. Both the nurse and the doctor wore white coats. The child

previously feared stimuli, this process is called *respondent stimulus generalization*. Children may learn new fears in this fashion.

If you feel it was cruel and unfair to treat Albert in this way, you are right. Albert was adopted after this experiment, before he was helped to overcome his fears. Since that time, psychologists have learned that Albert could have been helped to lose his fears if the rat and other furry things were repeatedly shown to him without the loud sound. This process is called *respondent extinction*. In Albert's case, respondent extinction could have been accomplished by breaking the association of the unlearned stimulus (noise) with the learned stimulus (rat). The rat could again become a neutral stimulus for fear reactions.

It is likely that Albert lost his fears of animals as he grew up. But to our knowledge, no one knows for sure.

Children can learn to fear or dislike many things through the sort of respondent learning illustrated in Albert's case. Table 9.2 provides a few common examples of such fears that might be learned under normal circumstances.

Many fears appear to be learned through a similar process of association, even though the child has never experienced the pain of the unlearned stimulus. For example, children may only hear that something called a werewolf prowls around at night during the full moon and bites people. They may hear stories about other creatures such as ghosts and goblins that lurk in the dark. The association of fearful creatures and the night is enough to produce fear of the dark in most children. This is true even though the association is made through words alone. Notice

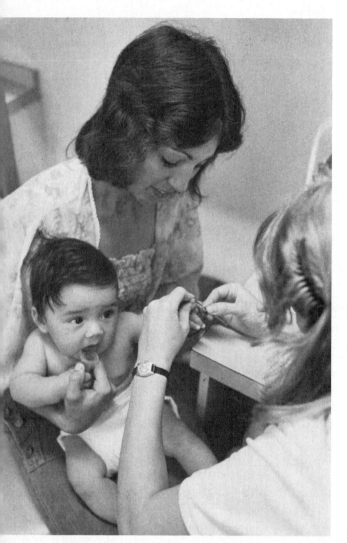

Figure 9-3. If this child's experience at the doctor's office is pleasant, it is likely that he will not fear doctors or health checkups. (USDA Photo)

became fearful of the office setting and the white coats. Later, the child also showed fear of the meat cutter at the grocery store, who wore a white coat. When new fears are acquired to new things which are similar to

Table 9.2

Respondent Learning of Fears

The Unlearned Stimulus	*The Neutral Stimuli*	*Learned Fears*
Pain from injection	Doctor's white coat, doctor's office	Fear of such settings
Infant is burned with bath water which is too hot	Water, bathtub, soap, and washcloth	Fear of bathtime and objects involved
Pain from soap in the eyes	Washcloth in the face	Fear of having face washed
Child is bitten by a dog	Presence of animal with long hair and tail	Child is fearful of all animals

that this learning is purely symbolic or cognitive. The children in these situations never directly experience pain from creatures fabled to lurk in the dark.

Respondent learning is not the only way that such fears can be acquired. The influence of cognitive development and children's growing ability to use their imagination also play important roles.

LEARNING NEW REWARDS

Just as children can learn new fears and dislikes through the process of association, they can also learn to like, appreciate, or want new things in a similar way. *Consequences* (things that happen immediately following a child's behavior) such as rewards can cause learning.

Some rewards for children are *unlearned rewards*. That is, infants like or value these rewards without learning to do so. Such

unlearned rewards are food, water, and warmth. When these rewards follow a child's behavior, they strengthen the behavior by making it happen more frequently in the future.

Other rewards are different in nature. They are called *learned rewards*. Something special has to happen for them to be liked or valued. Examples of learned rewards are kisses and hugs. Learned rewards, like unlearned rewards, also increase the frequency of the behavior they follow.

Smiles and praise are not unlearned rewards for a newborn infant. These rewards are learned. How do smiles, praise, and other forms of attention become rewarding to infants and children? The process appears to involve associations similar to those described by Pavlov. From the first days of life, infants experience the associations shown in Table 9.3, and many more.

The process of association shown in Table 9.3 also helps to create new rewards for older

Table 9.3

Learned Rewards

Unlearned Stimuli (Unlearned Rewards)	Neutral Stimuli	Learned Rewards (Capable of Strengthening the Behavior They Follow)
Food, water, warmth, removal of pain and discomfort, provision of toys and other new, rewarding experiences.	Smiles, praise, loving tones of voice	Smiles, praise, loving tones of voice

Figure 9-4. Smiles, praise and attention become learned rewards for children.

children. One five-year-old had a special love for a cabin he had visited for only one week per year for three years. He talked about the cabin with excitement and great pleasure. He had been to many buildings and houses in his life. But for some reason, thinking and talking about the cabin was the most rewarding subject of all. The cabin, of course, was a vacation home. It had acquired its extraordinary properties because it was associated with things which were already powerfully rewarding to the child: fishing, boating, swimming, catching frogs, delicious cookouts, and few restrictions on sweets. On a cold, dreary day, this child could probably reward himself by thinking about his favorite cabin, and obtain an emotional lift as well.

Attempting to Influence Through Association

Advertisers often try to influence the things that children find rewarding. They do this by associating a product (neutral stimulus) with other things known to be strongly rewarding to young children. Attempting to influence through association is also effective with older people. (See Illustration 9.2.)

Illustration 9.2. Adults as well as children learn new rewards through association.

Of course, some of the things that children are persuaded to find rewarding are good for them. For example, happy and attractive cartoon characters are often shown recommending that children brush their teeth, drink milk, or eat healthful fruits and vegetables. Other advertising associations may not create new rewards that are in the best interests of children. Ultimately, responsibility for guidance in such matters falls to parents.

Parents who understand respondent learning can help their children acquire healthful learned rewards, and avoid or help reduce unnecessary fears.

Figure 9-5. Parents can help their children to learn healthful rewards. (USDA Photo)

QUESTIONS FOR GROWTH

1. Name the two parts of a reflex.

2. Explain why reflexes are also called respondent behaviors.

3. Name several reflexes that can be observed in infants.

4. (a) Explain the meanings of the term *unlearned reflex*, and give examples of several unlearned reflexes. **(b)** Identify the unlearned stimulus and the unlearned responses in each of your examples.

5. Explain what it means when it is said that each reflex has its threshold.

6. Explain why Pavlov's findings are important.

7. In your own words, explain what a learned reflex is.

8. Describe how a learned fear was acquired by Albert.

9. (a) Explain what respondent stimulus generalization is, and provide several examples. **(b)** Explain how a similar learned fear could be cured. Use the term *respondent extinction* in your explanation.

10. Identify several common learned responses which children can easily acquire.

11. Review your own development, and identify an example of how you might have acquired a learned fear.

12. Explain what unlearned rewards are, and provide several common examples.

13. Explain the process of association in which children can learn to value new learned rewards.

14. Explain how advertising uses the process of association to create learned rewards for children.

CHAPTER

10

Operant Learning: Principles

Infants and children constantly "operate on," or change, their surroundings. They do this by grasping, pushing, pulling, twisting, and mouthing various things. There are also many other ways in which infants and children operate on their surroundings. They learn through these actions because the actions produce certain important *consequences*, or outcomes. Such actions are called *operant behavior*, and this type of learning is called *operant learning*.

Nearly any valuable skill that children learn can be influenced—positively or negatively—by the process of operant learning. Operant learning occurs with or without the presence of parents. However, parents influence their children's behavior through the principles (basic rules) of operant learning. This occurs whether or not the parents are aware of operant learning.

OPERANT LEARNING PRINCIPLES

Operant learning is a basic part of child development. The person who studies the principles of operant learning can become a more skillful teacher of children. In this chapter, we discuss five principles of operant learning:

1. Law of effect
2. Operant behavior
3. Positive reinforcement
4. Negative reinforcement
5. Extinction

LAW OF EFFECT

The *law of effect* is a very important principle in child rearing. It was first described by E. L. Thorndike in 1898. The law of effect is what operant learning is all about, because it states that many behaviors are influenced by their consequences. Consequences are the effects that a behavior produces.

Though you may have never heard of the law of the effect, you and all other people have experienced it countless times. To demonstrate this point, ask yourself why you do certain behaviors. Why do you:

• Put bread in the toaster?
• Turn on the water faucet?
• Turn up the thermostat in winter?
• Study for a test?
• Ask someone out on a date?
• Get a job?

Why don't you:

• Put your hand in a fire?
• Stick your fingers in a light socket?
• Walk across the street with your eyes closed?
• Insult your friends?
• Kick the biggest, meanest person in your neighborhood?

No doubt you are now thinking about the consequences or results of these behaviors. For example, you study (behavior) for a test in order to learn and to get a good grade (consequences). You don't put your hand in a fire (behavior) because you don't want to burn your hand (consequence).

The law of effect states that the occurrences of many behaviors are influenced by their consequences. In other words, what follows a behavior (rewards, punishments, or nothing) influences how often these behaviors are performed. For example, you may have a summer job so you can earn and save money for something you want. Today, we understand a great deal about what kinds of human behaviors are influenced by consequences, and how these influences occur.

OPERANT BEHAVIOR

Recall that *respondent behavior* is influenced by stimuli or things which occur before the behavior. For example, food placed in the mouth (stimulus) produces salivation (response). We now introduce another kind of behavior, called *operant behavior*. Operant behavior is influenced by the stimuli which follow the behavior, known as consequences. For example, Esta mows the neighbor's lawn (behavior) and is paid five dollars (consequence).

Table 10.1 lists a few examples of operant behaviors. All of these behaviors, and many more, are operant behaviors because the occurrences of all of them are influenced by consequences.

Operant behaviors are most often the things that people do to operate on or change the environment around them. Operant behaviors commonly involve our muscles, which help us to move around and manipulate things. Operant behaviors also include all of the sounds we make, our facial expressions, and our ways of thinking and solving problems. We do all of these things in certain ways, and certain consequences are produced.

Clearly, most of the important human behaviors are those which can be influenced by

---

Table 10.1

Examples of Operant Behaviors

Coordination

Moving the eyes	Riding a bike
Moving the head	Throwing a ball
Kicking feet and moving arms	Ice skating
Reaching and grasping	Playing an instrument
Creeping and crawling	Building with blocks
Standing and walking	Coloring
Jumping and running	Climbing

Social and Intellectual Activities

Crying	Learning to do mathematics
Smiling and laughing	Spelling and reading
Babbling	Making friends
Making wordlike sounds	Sharing
Saying words and sentences	Taking turns
Learning the numerals and the alphabet	Praising and helping others
Lying, cheating, and stealing	Swearing
Learning to control emotions	Hurting others

Self-Care

Dressing	Keeping living space clean
Brushing teeth	Taking care of possessions
Bathing	Learning to cross streets safely
Combing hair	Learning to ride a bike safely
Toileting	Eating good foods in proper amounts

---

consequences. The behaviors mentioned in Table 10.1 may seem small, but these small parts form a very complex and important whole. In operant learning, simple skills are combined to form complex accomplishments.

Consequences influence the operant behaviors of humans. But other factors also have great importance in the operant-learning outcome. An individual's heredity, physical and cognitive development, life's experiences, and environment all help to determine the influence of consequences upon behavior.

USDA Photo by Jack Schneider

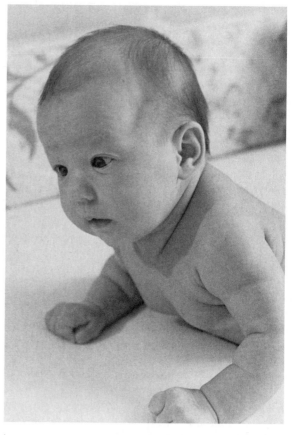

Figure 10-1. *What examples of operant behavior do you see in these photos? Coordination? Social and intellectual? Self-care?*

POSITIVE REINFORCEMENT

Positive reinforcement is another principle of operant learning. Positive reinforcement is the addition of something (a stimulus) following a behavior which increases the future frequency of that behavior.

It is sometimes hard to memorize the words in a definition. You might find it easier to memorize the diagram in Illustration 10.1,

and then produce a definition by describing what you see. With this diagram in mind, you might define positive reinforcement as follows.

1. First, the behavior happens.
2. Right after the behavior, something is added to the environment.
3. And, as a result, that behavior happens more often in the future.

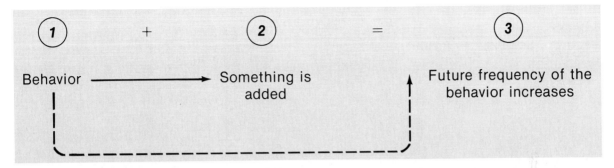

Illustration 10.1. How positive reinforcement occurs

Remember that positive reinforcement is a procedure in which all of these three things must happen. Without any one of these three things, we do not have an example of positive reinforcement.

Everyone has observed thousands of examples of positive reinforcement in daily life. Some examples that you might recognize are

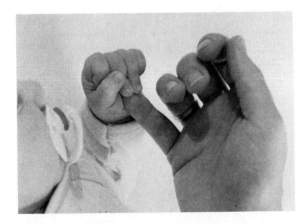

Figure 10.2. Positive reinforcement. The baby reaches and grasps a finger (behavior). The baby feels new sensations and the parent reacts with hugs and excitement. This causes the behavior to happen more often in the future. The baby reaches out to touch and explore her environment more frequently.

listed in Table 10.2. These examples should help you to understand the concept of positive reinforcement.

Each of the words in the term "positive reinforcement" has a common-sense meaning. The word *positive* can be related to mathematics and the positive or addition sign (+). In the examples in Table 10.2, something was *added* to the individuals' environment or experience after they behaved. The word *reinforcement* means that something is being strengthened. A tailor reinforces (strengthens) a hem. An engineer reinforces (strengthens) a bridge. And a parent can reinforce (strengthen) the future frequency of a child's behavior.

Mistaken Ideas about Positive Reinforcement

Positive reinforcement seems, at first, like a simple idea. However, many people misunderstand it. The following are some common mistakes that people make in thinking about positive reinforcement.

1. It is a mistake to think that positive reinforcement means adding or presenting

Table 10.2

Examples of Positive Reinforcement

Examples with Children

1 Behavior	2 A Stimulus is Added (the Reinforcer)	3 Future Frequency of Behavior Increases
An infant hears a dog bark and turns his head in the right direction.	The infant sees the dog.	The infant learns to look in the direction of sounds more accurately.
A two-month-old is hungry and cries.	Her father picks her up and feeds her.	The infant learns to cry for food.
An infant is held on his brother's lap. He looks up and smiles.	The brother hugs the infant and says, "That's a nice smile! I'm your brother."	The infant smiles more frequently in the future.
A five-month-old wiggles across the floor on her stomach.	She can now reach a bright toy she has been watching.	The infant learns to crawl more frequently in the future.
An eleven-month-old stands holding onto the arm of a chair. He lets go and takes his first step.	His parents, sister, and grandparents clap their hands, praise him, and show excitement.	The child learns to take steps more frequently in the future.
A three-year-old breaks her cookie in half and shares it with a friend.	Her babysitter praises her for sharing and pushes both children on the swings.	The child learns to share her treats more often in the future.
A five-year-old is helped to make his bed and clean his room first thing in the morning.	After he is done, his mother hugs and thanks him for doing such good work, and then gives him a good breakfast.	Helping to make his bed and clean his room occurs more frequently in the future.

Continued on next page

Table 10.2 (Continued)

	1 *Behavior*	*2* *A Stimulus is Added* *(the Reinforcer)*	*3* *Future Frequency of* *Behavior Increases*
Examples with Parents	A parent makes a funny face at a three-month-old.	The baby laughs and squeals happily.	The parent makes funny faces at the baby more often in the future.
	A parent praises his five-year-old for helping to clear the table.	The five-year-old brings more dishes to the sink.	The parent learns to praise his child more frequently in the future.
	A parent tells her daughter that she loves her.	The child hugs and kisses her mother.	The mother learns to say this more often in the future.

something following a behavior that you, yourself, like or think is good. In actuality, whatever is presented or added need not be ''good'' in any way. Positive reinforcement simply means adding or presenting something after a behavior occurs which increases the future frequency of that behavior.

Young children have explored closets, and the positive reinforcers (the stimuli) they have found and put in their mouths have been dirty socks or dead bugs. Even though we do not consider these things good, exploring such places happened more often in the future. Children have also misbehaved, their parents have yelled at them angrily, and the children still misbehaved in the same way more frequently in the future. These are examples of positive reinforcement.

A child may be praised or given money or a treat following some behavior, but the behavior may not increase in future frequency. For this child, money and treats may not be examples of positive reinforcement. Remember that all three parts of the definition must be present for positive reinforcement to occur.

2. It is a mistake to think that positive reinforcement only happens to child behaviors which are good or in some way positive. It is true that an effective parent or teacher will try to positively reinforce appropriate and valuable behavior. However, inappropriate behaviors can also be positively reinforced. This often happens by accident or when a parent does not understand how positive reinforcement works. For example, aggression may be positively reinforced when a child pushes another down and takes that child's toy. Temper tantrums may also be positively reinforced when a parent gives (adds) something the child wants in order to temporarily quiet the child.

3. It is a mistake to look for the effects of positive reinforcement in the immediate changes of a child's behavior. The effects of positive reinforcement are in the future.

Many parents feel that by giving a treat to a child who has tantrums, they are teaching the child to be calmer. However, positive reinforcement strengthens the future frequency of a behavior. A treat may quiet the child immediately. But the parents may notice later that day and the next that the child is having temper tantrums more frequently.

Identifying a Child's Positive Reinforcers

When talking about the consequence which is added and strengthens the behavior it follows, we can call it a *positive reinforcer*. Being held, being complimented, getting a toy, or seeing a dog may be examples of positive reinforcers.

Positive reinforcement is the three-part procedure which can strengthen operant behavior. A positive reinforcer is the thing which is added to the person's environment following a behavior and which strengthens its future occurrence. Skilled parents know which things will work as positive reinforcers with their child. If parents do not know their child's positive reinforcers, it could be argued that they do not know their child very well.

Unlearned positive reinforcers are the things that we all need to live. Such positive reinforcers are not hard to identify. Some unlearned positive reinforcers are food, liquid, warmth, and certain kinds of new and interesting things. Everyone's behavior is reinforced by these consequences.

Learned positive reinforcers are much more unique in their effectiveness. This is because each person learns a preference for different reinforcers. Some children will work very

hard to have an opportunity to go snake hunting. Some love to fish, play football, or paint. Other children love to eat sweets or vegetables, swim, or play with dolls. Some of these things are reinforcing to some children, but they are not reinforcing to all children. Learned positive reinforcers are often very special to the individual child. We now describe methods that may be used to identify a child's individual positive reinforcers.

Ask the Child

If a child can talk, ask what he or she likes. What are your favorite games? What are your favorite treats? What do you like to do when you can do anything you want? Who are your best playmates?

Answers to these and similar questions can help you to identify a certain child's possible positive reinforcers. This is not, however, a foolproof method, because people sometimes say one thing but do another. One child talked excitedly about riding horses, but was very fearful when brought near a horse. Asking children what their reinforcers are (what they like) is not a perfect approach. Yet it is still a useful method.

Observe the Child

A good way to identify a child's positive reinforcers is to watch the child's behavior. A researcher named David Premack found that if you watch the activities of children during their free time, you can discover their positive reinforcers. The activities that children (and everyone else) do most frequently *during free time* are their positive reinforcers.

It is important that you watch children during their free time to learn their reinforcers. If you watch a certain child during house-cleaning time, you might see the child taking out the trash and vacuuming the floor. You might then conclude that these activities are very reinforcing for this child. But if you watch during an afternoon of free time, you might find that the child does not clean anything. The child might spend the time looking at books, building with an erector set, or watching television. You would then conclude that these activities are probably more reinforcing to the child than is cleaning the house.

Premack's research led to the *Premack principle*. This principle states that if people are allowed to do an activity which they prefer (one they choose often during free time) immediately after they do an activity which they do not prefer (one they rarely choose during free time), the nonpreferred behavior will be positively reinforced. This principle has also been called "Grandma's Rule." Grandma's Rule helps people understand how to use the Premack principle, in common terms. Grandma's Rule states: "First you do what I want you to do—then you can do what you want to do."

The Sure Way to Identify Positive Reinforcers

The only sure way to know if you have identified a positive reinforcer for a certain child is to test it out. To do this, a behavior to be strengthened is counted for some time to see how often it occurs. When it is known how often the behavior normally occurs, the pos-

Figure 10-3. *Parents should learn their children's positive reinforcers and then use them. (South Dakota Tourism Photo)*

sible positive reinforcer can be tested. If something is added immediately following the behavior and the behavior happens more often in the future, then what was added is a positive reinforcer. For example, parents might praise their child for walking in the house, and then notice that the child's running in the house decreases and walking increases. For this child, praise is a positive reinforcer.

Guidelines for Using Positive Reinforcers

To strengthen a child's behavior through positive reinforcement, it is important to use the following guidelines.

1. Provide positive reinforcement immediately. Positive reinforcers work best when they are provided immediately after every target behavior.

2. Provide lots of reinforcement. Don't be shy or stingy with it. Give enough reinforcement to be effective. Show excitement with enthusiastic praise, hugs, and kisses.

3. Name the particular behavior you wish to strengthen during reinforcement. This helps the child to make the connection between his or her actions and the reinforcer.

4. Be consistent. For example, when parents decide to reinforce their baby's wordlike sounds with praise and excitement, they must do so whenever they can.

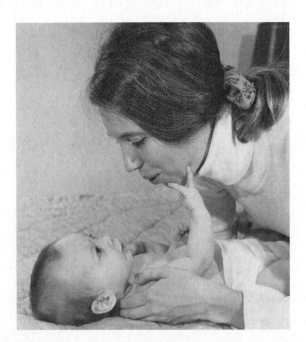

Figure 10-4. *Parents should be generous with their praise, a common positive reinforcer. (March of Dimes Birth Defects Foundation)*

5. Provide different combinations of reinforcers for the behaviors to be strengthened. By using many different positive reinforcers, parents can avoid problems with children losing interest in the reinforcers.

6. Much later, when a child's behavior has been thoroughly strengthened, parents can slowly begin to provide fewer reinforcers for the activity. The child who has learned to keep a room clean may not need praise every day. But occasional compliments and appreciation for the child's work will be important for many years to come.

NEGATIVE REINFORCEMENT

Negative reinforcement is the subtraction of something unpleasant following a behavior, which increases the future frequency of the behavior. For example, as a young child you may have noticed that a stone in your shoe was causing your foot to hurt. You removed the stone, and the pain stopped. In the future, you checked your shoes when your feet hurt. The definition of negative reinforcement can be diagrammed as shown in Illustration 10.2. The diagram shows that a behavior is followed by the subtraction of something unpleasant from the environment, and this makes the behavior happen more often in the future.

Recall that the particular stimulus which changes following the behavior is called a reinforcer. In the negative-reinforcement procedure, the unpleasant stimulus which is subtracted is called a *negative reinforcer.*

Table 10.3 includes some common examples of how negative reinforcement can strengthen both child and parent behavior.

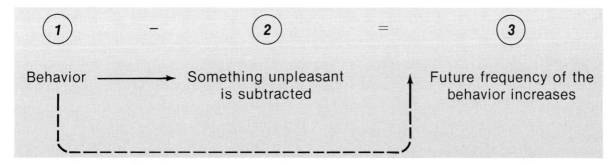

Illustration 10.2. *How negative reinforcement occurs*

Negative reinforcement, like positive reinforcement, is a form of operant learning that is a natural part of everyone's life. Children experience negative reinforcement in many ways, whether or not parents are aware of it. For example, children who cover their eyes or remove their hands from hot objects learn to do these things because unpleasant stimuli are removed as a result of their actions. In these examples, the reduced light (covering the eyes) or reduced heat (removing the hands from hot objects) reinforce certain actions. These examples show that valuable skills can be learned through negative reinforcement in very natural ways.

This does not mean, though, that negative reinforcement is a recommended technique for parents to use in teaching their children. It is generally not recommended. The problem with selecting negative reinforcement is that it involves the use of things that are unpleasant or painful to children. It is an error to associate unpleasant and painful things with normal teaching activities for children. Understanding how negative reinforcement works will help parents to identify its important influences in their

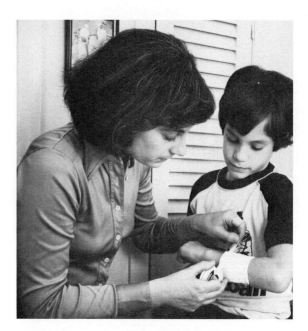

Figure 10.5. *An example of negative reinforcement. The child is hurt. He asks his mother for help, and the hurt is removed. As a result, the boy learns to ask his mother for help more often in the future. (Courtesy of Johnson & Johnson)*

child's development and learning. Parents can then work to control those influences in desirable directions.

Table 10.3

Examples of Negative Reinforcement

	1 Behavior	2 An Unpleasant Stimulus Is Subtracted (the Reinforcer)	3 Future Frequency of Behavior Increases
Examples with Children	An infant cries.	Dirty diapers are removed (subtracted).	The infant learns to cry for assistance.
	A child says his foot hurts.	Mom removes (subtracts) a stone from his shoe.	Asking mother for help occurs more frequently.
	A child lies about taking her friend's toy.	The threat of punishment is removed (subtracted).	The child learns to lie more frequently in the future.
	A child is playing in the hot sun.	The child moves under a tree and the heat is reduced (subtracted).	The child plays under the tree more often on hot days.
Examples with Parents	A parent changes his infant's dirty diaper.	The baby stops crying.	When the baby looks uncomfortable or cries, the parent checks the baby's diaper more frequently in the future.
	A parent spanks her child for misbehaving.	The child stops misbehaving.	The parent spanks her child for misbehavior more often in the future.
	A parent holds and rocks her infant in a rocking chair.	The infant soon stops fussing and goes to sleep.	The parent rocks the infant more frequently in the future.

When unpleasant and painful things are associated with teaching and learning, children often learn to escape and avoid the teacher or parent and the learning task. For example, parents who nag and threaten until their child helps to clean the kitchen will probably get the kitchen cleaned. However, they were unpleasant to their child until the child did what they requested, and then the parents stopped being unpleasant.

If this form of negative reinforcement is used often, the warm and friendly relationship between parents and children may be damaged. Also, children may not learn to willingly and happily do such work on their own, without nagging and threatening. This outcome is certainly not the goal of parenting. It is much better for parents to influence their children through positive reinforcement. In this case, the child would calmly be asked to help clean up the kitchen, and then would be praised warmly for helping.

Identifying a Child's Negative Reinforcers

Negative reinforcers are unpleasant or painful stimuli which can be subtracted (taken away) following a behavior in order to strengthen that behavior's future frequency. *Unlearned negative reinforcers* are things which are unpleasant or painful to everyone, without learning. Unlearned negative reinforcers include sickness; pain from pinches, hits, and burns; discomfort from too much noise and light; and unpleasant tastes and smells. These negative reinforcers are not hard to identify. Children will learn to do whatever removes or reduces these unpleasant things.

Learned negative reinforcers may be more difficult to identify. Learned negative reinforcers are those things that children learn to view as painful or unpleasant. Examples of learned negative reinforcers can be frowns, disapproval, criticism, and bad grades.

EXTINCTION

Extinction is another operant-learning principle. Extinction is the withholding of reinforcers following operant behavior, with the result that the behavior decreases in future frequency. For example, a three-year-old has a temper tantrum, but the parents ignore the child until the tantrum is stopped. Extinction is a technical word which lacks the warmth we prefer in terms applied to child development. Yet it is an important idea which parents and other care givers should understand so that the effects of extinction can benefit and not harm children.

Illustration 10.3 diagrams the definition of extinction. The diagram shows that when a behavior occurs and a reinforcer is withheld (not presented), the future frequency of that behavior decreases.

It is important to note that extinction affects everyone, not just children. People eventually do things less often that do not lead to reinforcement. Each of us has given up doing things that we once thought were a good idea but which were almost never reinforced.

Parents often identify behaviors in children which should be gently weakened and not

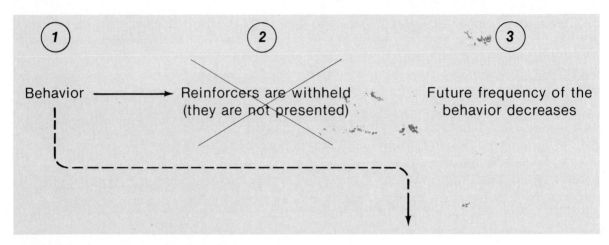

Illustration 10.3. How extinction occurs

strengthened, such as whining or temper tantrums. When such behaviors occur, the knowledgeable parent makes certain that reinforcers do not follow the inappropriate behavior. Extinction often works slowly, but it is a safe and humane method.

Parents who are unaware of how extinction works often accidentally weaken a child's desirable behaviors. It is a mistake to ignore and withhold positive reinforcers from babies who try to talk, crawl, walk, or feed themselves. It is also a mistake to ignore or withhold positive reinforcers from older children who help by doing chores, do their homework, show good manners, and act honestly. All of these behaviors should be positively reinforced.

Extinction sounds like a simple procedure, but a great deal of skill is required to use it wisely. In Chapter 12 we discuss in more detail the use of the extinction procedure to reduce undesirable behavior. We also discuss other operant-learning methods in Chapter 12.

QUESTIONS FOR GROWTH

1. Explain the meaning of the law of effect.

2. Explain what operant behavior is, and provide three examples of your own operant behavior.

3. Explain how human operant behavior is influenced.

4. (a) Write the definition of positive reinforcement. **(b)** Draw and explain the three-part diagram of positive reinforcement. **(c)** Provide two original examples of positive reinforcement of human behavior. Be sure to include all three parts of positive reinforcement in each of your examples.

5. Explain three mistaken ways to think about positive reinforcement.

6. Describe what a positive reinforcer is, and list ten possible examples.

7. Explain the difference between unlearned positive reinforcers and learned positive reinforcers, and provide three examples of each.

8. What is the most sure way to identify positive reinforcers?

9. List the six guidelines for using positive reinforcers.

10. (a) Write the definition of negative reinforcement. **(b)** Draw and explain the three-part diagram of negative reinforcement. **(c)** Provide two original examples of negative reinforcement of human behavior. Be sure to include all three parts of negative reinforcement in each of your examples.

11. Give two original examples of how children might learn something beneficial through negative reinforcement.

12. Explain why negative reinforcement is not generally recommended for use in teaching children.

13. Explain the difference between unlearned negative reinforcers and learned negative reinforcers, and provide three examples of each.

14. (a) Write the definition of extinction. **(b)** Draw and explain the three-part diagram of extinction. **(c)** Provide two original examples of extinction of human behavior. Be sure to include all three parts of extinction in each of your examples.

CHAPTER

11

Operant Learning: Methods

We introduced the basic principles of operant learning in Chapter 10. We explained how consequences influence human behavior. The principles (basic rules) of operant learning are an important part of parenting and teaching children. They are also important to understanding the focus of this chapter: the methods of teaching or strengthening operant behavior.

In this book, we often describe some of the ways in which small developments in children add up to valuable new accomplishments and abilities. In other words, the whole is greater than the sum of its parts. This chapter again illustrates that idea. We use the basic principles of operant learning (the parts) to describe valuable teaching and parenting methods (the whole).

Operant learning, as defined previously, results from operating on one's environment

and experiencing consequences. Every person's operant behavior is influenced by the consequences which follow. Basic principles of operant learning, such as reinforcement and extinction, can be combined in many ways to create new teaching methods that are effective with children.

DIFFERENTIAL REINFORCEMENT

Parents often wish to strengthen desirable behaviors in their children, and to weaken the less desirable ones. This can be achieved through the use of *differential reinforcement* without using punishment. To use differential reinforcement, a parent must provide reinforcement for desirable behaviors, but withhold reinforcers from less desirable behaviors. The following examples will help you to understand how differential reinforcement can be used.

Example #1

Sometimes a mother lies very close to her two-month-old son. They look at each other's face. When the baby is quiet and expressionless, the mother is also quiet and expressionless. As soon as her baby smiles or makes a sound, the mother immediately smiles, speaks affectionately, and cuddles her baby.

Figure 11-1. This father is differentially reinforcing happiness and social responsiveness in his infant. (© Ron Meyer/White Eyes Design)

By these responses, the mother is differentially reinforcing social responsiveness in the child. The child is thus likely to increase the frequency of smiles, expressions, and sounds.

It is important to notice in this example that the baby is also interacting with and influencing the mother. In other words, the baby is also differentially reinforcing the mother's social actions. Influence between parents and children is not a one-way process from parent to child; the child also influences the parent's behaviors.

Example #2

One set of parents worried that their six-year-old daughter whined too much. When the child wanted something, she often whined, cried, and complained until she got her way. The parents decided to teach the child that she would get what she wanted more often if she did not whine or complain.

The parents agreed to provide privileges—when possible and reasonable—whenever their daughter asked for a privilege in a normal, pleasant tone of voice. They agreed not to provide privileges when she whined, cried, or complained.

These parents used differential reinforcement to teach their daughter more pleasant and successful ways of obtaining the things she wanted. This is a valuable skill for anyone to learn.

DISCRIMINATION TRAINING

A big part of what a child must learn is how to *discriminate*, or tell the differences between people, places, and things. The infant learns the differences between light and dark, cold and hot, wet and dry, and big and little. The three-year-old may learn the differences between black and red, circles and triangles, and apples and oranges. Children learn thousands of discriminations, or differences, throughout their development.

Children show the discriminations they learn by behaving differently in the presence of different things. For example, a two-year-old child looks at her father and says "Daddy." She no longer says "Daddy" when looking at other men, as she might when she was younger. The child says the word "red" when asked the color of a red object. She does not answer "red" in the presence of other colors. In these examples, the child's behavior shows that she has learned to discirminate between one thing and others.

Parents can help their children to learn important discriminations by using the discrimination-training method. In *discrimination training*, parents reinforce correct responses to appropriate people, places, and things, but do not reinforce wrong responses to wrong stimuli. The following examples illustrate how discrimination training can be used.

Example #1

A white card and a black card are placed in front of a three-year-old. He is asked to point to the white card. He points to the black card. His mother quietly and calmly says, "No, *this* is the white card." She holds the white card up so her son can see it. (She may also hint that the white card is the same color as snow or milk.) The mother asks again, "Can you point to the white card?" The child points

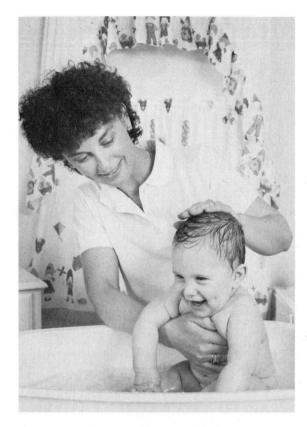

Figure 11-2. At bathtime a baby can learn to discriminate between wet and dry, and warm and cool. (Courtesy of Johnson & Johnson)

to the white card, and the mother praises the correct discrimination.

In discrimination training, the correct response to the white card is reinforced. The incorrect response to black or other colored cards is not reinforced.

Example #2

When a father is at the kitchen sink, his 15-month-old daughter often comes to him and makes grunting noises. The father knows that in the past this has meant that his daughter wanted a drink of water. He also knows that his daughter can easily say "waa." He holds the glass and says "waa-ter." When she says "waa," the father immediately praises her and says "That's right. You want waa-ter." He then gives his daughter a drink of water.

Later, the child comes to him near the sink and makes grunting sounds. The father says nothing and waits calmly. The child says "waa" and he immediately praises her. He lifts her in his arms and helps her to have a drink of water.

The child is learning that when she is thirsty, the correct behavior is to go to someone and say "waa." She is learning that making grunting sounds does not produce the reinforcers of water and praise. Later, her parents will help her learn to say "water."

Helpful Hints

When teaching children to discriminate between things, be sure to teach the simpler discriminations first. The more difficult ones can be taught later. In our Example #1, if the mother had tried to teach discriminations between yellow and gold, or red and pink, the differences would probably have been too small and difficult for the child. The child would have naturally made many errors, which would have frustrated both him and his mother. This could have turned the teaching/learning situation into something very unpleasant. Such an outcome is a mistake to be avoided at all costs. The same poor result could occur if too many discriminations were taught all at the same time (white, blue, black, yellow, green, brown, etc.). This

would also lead to an increase in unnecessary errors for the child and much frustration.

It is important to start by teaching a few easy discriminations. As these are learned, new ones should be introduced slowly so the child can learn them without too many errors.

When children are taught discriminations, they often generalize, or apply what they have learned to new situations. Sometimes these generalizations are helpful, and sometimes they are errors. It is natural for children to generalize what they have learned to new situations, and some errors should be expected.

The young child who has learned to say "doggie" when he sees a dog is also likely to say "doggie" when he sees a cat. When the differences between things seem small, generalizations can be expected. After all, both cats and dogs have hair, whiskers, four legs, and a tail. A child might rightly say, "What's the difference?" Such a generalization from dogs to cats can be viewed as an opportunity to use discrimination training to teach the differences between dogs and cats. Showing pictures of dogs and cats, or bringing an actual dog and cat side by side (provided they do not fight) can help to overcome the natural problem of generalization, and teach the close and difficult discriminations.

SHAPING

Shaping is an approach for teaching new skills or improving old ones. Shaping is done by teaching small improvements in a series of steps toward a goal or desired behavior. Each teaching step can be called an *approximation*,

Figure 11-3. *Discriminations can be taught during special occasions as well as in daily activities. (© Ron Meyer/White Eyes Design)*

because each step moves closer and closer to the desired behavior.

In shaping, the parent or other teacher differentially reinforces a series of steps to a desired behavior. This means that at any point in the shaping procedure, certain behaviors closer to the desired skills are rein-

forced. At the same time, behaviors further away from the desired behaviors are no longer reinforced.

The shaping procedure is a powerful and valuable one. Parents who use shaping skillfully avoid rushing or pushing their children. They allow the children to learn at their own pace. The following example shows how one skillful parent used shaping to help his daughter learn to say a new word.

Recall the father who was trying to teach his 15-month-old daughter to use words rather than grunt for a drink of water. The father used differential reinforcement. He praised and gave water for any "waa" sounds that his daughter made, but ignored other sounds. This was only a first step in what would be a series of steps. The father used shaping, a series of differential reinforcements towards some goal or desired behavior.

As the father listened to his daughter, he heard many sounds. What he chose to reinforce were sounds in the following steps, over a period of several weeks:

Step	Sound
#1	Waa
#2	Wa-wa
#3 ·	Wata
#4	Water (the desired behavior)

In studying these steps, remember that once taught, the steps further away from the desired behavior are no longer reinforced. Only the steps closer to the desired behavior receive praise and a drink of water. For example, if the child was at Step #2, "wa-wa" would be reinforced, but Step #1, "waa," would not be reinforced. However, when "wata," Step #3, was said, the father would quickly and happily provide reinforcement.

The four steps used in this example are just one of many ways that a child might learn to say "water." The challenge for parents is to slowly reinforce small steps in the direction of desired behaviors. At the same time,

the parents must extinguish behaviors that represent steps away from the goal. Parents can use shaping to help their children learn to draw, wash themselves, clean their rooms, and much more.

Shaping Guidelines

The following are guidelines for using the shaping method successfully.

1. Clearly identify the desired behavior.
2. Select a child's response which occurs frequently and is similar to the desired behavior.
3. Reinforce this first step toward the desired behavior immediately each time it occurs.
4. Watch for small improvements in the direction of the desired behavior, and reinforce them with enthusiasm when they occur.

Figure 11-4. In shaping, praise appropriate behavior enthusiastically.

5. When a new step is strong (frequent), extinguish earlier steps, but reinforce the newest one and any other improvements whenever they occur.

6. Repeat the process until the desired behavior is obtained.

Shaping requires a great deal of judgment on the part of the parent-teacher. Because it requires so much judgment, shaping may fail at times. When shaping does not seem to be working, there are several things to check before continuing.

• Be sure that the reinforcers used are effective for the particular child.

• Be sure that the reinforcers are given immediately each time the appropriate behavior occurs.

• Be sure that *small steps* are being required.

• Do not stop reinforcing steps toward the desired behavior.

• Do not require steps that are too large, or demand too many small steps too quickly.

• Do not try to reach a desired behavior before a child is developmentally capable.

When progress stops, check the possibilities just named. When the problem has been identified, start the shaping procedure over again and proceed more carefully.

BACKWARD CHAINING

Many skills that children need to learn are really a sequence of different actions, or progressive steps. To learn a complete skill requires that children learn 1) the individual actions, and 2) to do them in the proper order.

Whenever a certain skill is made up of a sequence of several or more behaviors, the skill is called a *chain of behaviors*. Getting dressed, making a sandwich, or going shopping can all be viewed as sequences or chains of behavior.

Backward chaining is a good method for teaching chains of behavior. In backward chaining, the last step in the chain is taught first. Most children find it reinforcing to finish a task. Therefore, by teaching the last step first, children are naturally reinforced immediately for their efforts. Teaching then continues with the second-to-the-last step, the third-to-the-last step, and so on. When the first step in the chain is taught, the children can easily perform all the steps in the chain of behavior and obtain success and praise. Both success and praise are normally powerful reinforcers for children (and adults).

The following example will help you to understand the backward-chaining procedure. As you read the example, notice that at first the child may be helped to do each of the required behaviors in a chain. This help is called *prompting*. Prompting a child to do the behaviors in a chain can speed up the learning process.

Prompting can take the form of instructions, physical assistance, or showing something to imitate. However, the prompt must eventually be removed. Removing prompts is called *fading*. In the following example, notice how the helpful prompts are slowly faded away until the child is performing each step in the chain alone. Let us examine how the backward-chaining procedure can be used to teach a young child to walk to school. Millions of parents have used this backward-chaining method naturally, without knowing the technical name for it.

As can be seen in Illustration 11.1, the route to six-year-old Sally's school may be broken down into six steps. To use backward chaining, you would start by walking Sally all the way to school and into her schoolroom on the first trip. On the next trip, if you felt Sally was ready, you could stop outside the schoolroom door and let her do Step #6 (entering the room) on her own. Next, if you judged Sally to be ready, you would let her do Steps #5 and #6 on her own. As teaching progressed, you would allow and encourage Sally to complete more of the steps alone. The sequence of accomplished steps would occur as follows:

- Step #6
- Steps #5 and #6
- Steps #4, #5, and #6
- Steps #3, #4, #5, and #6
- Steps #2, #3, #4, #5, and #6
- And finally, Steps #1 through #6.

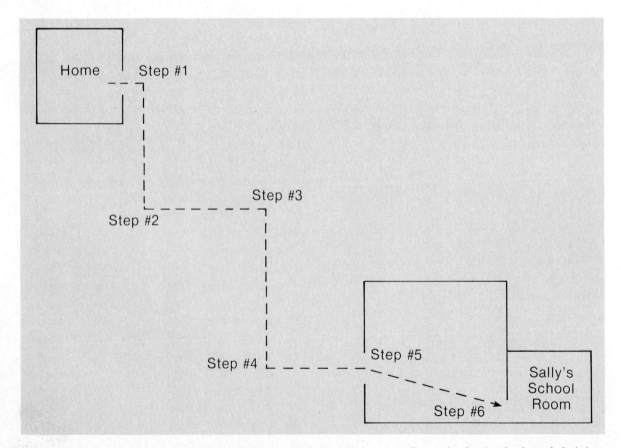

Illustration 11.1. *The six steps used by Sally's mother to teach her to walk to school using backward chaining. Teaching started at Step #6 and worked backward to Step #1.*

Some children will learn such a task rapidly. Other children will learn more slowly. Parents should tailor the speed of their teaching to the individual child's needs. Some children will need extra encouragement as their parents reduce their physical presence along the path. A few children may be hesitant to go alone. Skillful parents should recognize the hesitation and give what help is needed. They should praise and encourage the child, and slowly but firmly fade their assistance from each step as they become more sure of the child's growing ability.

Backward chaining is a good way to teach children to eat with a spoon, drink from a cup, and dress and undress. Parents can break these tasks into small steps and start to teach the last step first by using prompts, reinforcement, and then slowly fading their assistance. This approach is then repeated with each step until the whole chain of skills is learned.

SCHEDULES OF REINFORCEMENT

Parents and teachers have always noticed that some children rarely give up at things they try to do. Other children quit when the first thing goes wrong. The same behavior patterns can also be seen in teenagers and adults. Why do some people *persist* (keep on trying), and others give up and quit?

The answer to this question is not simple. Many things may cause children to persist at challenging tasks. Some children are born showing more action and energy than others. Parental encouragement, support, and modeling of persistence is important. It is also important to reinforce appropriate persistent behavior.

Schedules of reinforcement can be used to teach persistence. A schedule of reinforcement refers to how much one must do, or how long it must be done, before reinforcement is given or achieved. For example, perhaps you have to wash the dishes before you can leave the house with friends. This schedule of reinforcement may require washing 30 dishes (30 responses) before the reinforcement of leaving with friends. Maybe you have 20 math problems to do for homework. This means that you must do 20 things before you may watch television. Imagine that you have been asked to rake the yard for one hour. This means that you must work 60 minutes before you are reinforced with the freedom to do something more fun. These are examples of reinforcements for persistence.

What would happen if you asked a very young child to wash 30 dishes or do 20 math problems? The request is too much, and the child would probably quit long before the

Figure 11-5. Why do some children never give up? (USDA Photo by George Robinson)

tasks were done. A main goal of child rearing is to teach children greater and greater persistence at beneficial tasks. To help to reach this goal, parents need to understand two basic kinds of schedules of reinforcement: continuous reinforcement and intermittent reinforcement.

Continuous Reinforcement

Continuous reinforcement (CRF) means that reinforcement happens following each behavior. Each time you turn the ignition key, the car starts. Each time you answer the telephone ring, somebody talks to you. There are many other examples of continuous reinforcement in daily life.

People naturally prefer continuous reinforcement. After all, would you keep putting money in the vending machine if you only received a candy bar every third or fourth time? Would you want a car that requires six or eight tries before it starts?

CRF has two main advantages. First, everyone likes the continuous schedule best. Second, it is the best schedule for teaching new skills to someone.

An infant will learn to say ''DaDa'' more easily if each time it is said, Daddy reacts with praise and excitement. The father's response provides continuous reinforcement. A baby will learn to clap her hands more easily if each time she does, someone praises excitedly. A two-year-old will become toilet trained more rapidly if he is reinforced each time he uses the toilet. The child learning to do simple addition will do much better if, at first, each problem is checked and correct answers are praised immediately.

Even adults learn new skills better with CRF. The skilled teacher, coach, and employer understand this and give frequent praise and encouragement as we learn new skills.

CRF is the best schedule for teaching new behavior, but it is not a good schedule for *maintaining* some kinds of behaviors. It would be impossible to continue CRF forever for many behaviors. Can you imagine still being praised by your parents for each step you take?

Another problem is that people can become dependent upon CRF. Children are expected to become independent as they grow older. Children who are immature or overly dependent are generally demanding a schedule of continuous reinforcement for many things. The cause of this problem is not generally the CRF schedule itself; all children need CRF schedules to grow and develop normally. However, children also need to be *weaned*—parted or detached—from CRF schedules for skills that have been learned thoroughly.

If children are not helped gradually to work with less reinforcement, there may be problems. First, children may stop working when reinforcement is not immediately available for their efforts. These children are very likely to show low persistence. Second, children who are allowed to remain dependent on CRF are likely to show great emotion when they do not get what they want immediately. This is also true of adults who are dependent upon CRF schedules. For example, the adult who receives nothing after putting a coin in a vending machine is likely to show anger.

Some children become angry and tantrum whenever they cannot have a CRF schedule of reinforcement. A likely reason is that they still depend upon the CRF schedules which were started when they were younger.

Intermittent Reinforcement

Intermittent reinforcement is any situation in which more than one action or response is required before reinforcement. For example, a child might have to carry more than one handful of dishes into the kitchen before receiving the reinforcement of praise or thanks.

In Chapter 1, we discussed Yvonne Brackbill's experiment in which three- to four-month-old infants were praised and cuddled for smiling. The study showed that smiling was reinforced or strengthened in this natural manner. We now discuss the experiment as it relates to schedules of reinforcement.

Some of the infants were praised and cuddled on a CRF schedule—each time they smiled. Other infants were praised and cuddled on an intermittent schedule—after each fourth time they smiled. After the infants had experienced these schedules of reinforcement they all learned to smile more often. Then, for a short time, Brackbill used the operant-learning principle of extinction (withdrawal of reinforcement). The infants were no longer praised and cuddled for smiling. Can you guess which group of infants continued to smile the longest without reinforcement?

The infants whose smiles had been reinforced on an intermittent schedule smiled longer during extinction. They also smiled many more times than did the group of infants on a CRF schedule. This study demonstrated that intermittent reinforcement establishes a behavior more thoroughly. Therefore, the behavior will be shown longer when

Figure 11-6. *Learning new and demanding skills requires CRF at first. Later, this mother can move to intermittent reinforcement. (National Easter Seal Society, Inc.)*

the reinforcement is reduced. Intermittent reinforcement, then, is more likely to teach persistence than is CRF. The following is an example of how parents can teach persistence by moving from the CRF schedule to more and more intermittent reinforcement.

Each morning, a five-year-old was asked to pick up the toys and clothes in his bedroom and put them away. His father helped him and was careful not to require too much. During the first days, the father praised the child for each toy he picked up. Later, the father praised his child for every other toy. Later still, the father praised for every third or fourth toy his son picked up. After about two weeks, the father praised only the end result: the clean room. The father praised his son as soon as the room was done.

A few weeks later, the father sometimes delayed an hour or so before praising the child. Then the father sometimes missed praising the child's efforts every third day. However, he still checked to see that the room was clean. Eventually the father praised every second or third day. Reinforcement in the form of praise and compliments gradually became more intermittent, but the child continued to clean his room.

Even when the habit was established firmly, the father still found it necessary to check the room often. If the room was clean, he told his son how much he appreciated his good work. If the child had failed to clean the room, he would be told to do so. The frequency of room checks was then increased for a time.

In this example, the father was careful to reduce his reinforcement schedule. This necessary movement from CRF to intermittent reinforcement was done slowly but steadily. If reinforcement is reduced too rapidly, behaviors will weaken and, perhaps, stop completely. If reinforcement is not diminished at all, the child may become overly dependent upon CRF schedules.

Knowing when to move from CRF to intermittent reinforcement for learned behavior,

Figure 11-7. *This girl requires little reinforcement from other people to continue planting flowers. Her reinforcement comes naturally from her delight in gardening and watching things grow. (USDA Photo)*

and how quickly to move, is a matter of judgment. Parents and teachers can practice and learn how to make these decisions skillfully.

THE TOKEN SYSTEM

Sometimes children need a little extra help in learning how to do certain kinds of tasks. These tend to be self-care or work tasks that are time consuming or difficult. This is the sort of work that many children would prefer not to do. Also, the work is often made up of several smaller tasks. It is therefore easy for children to accidentally or purposely forget one or more of them.

If a task is not done, parents might become frustrated and angry. This sets the stage for nagging, criticizing, threatening, and punishment for not doing what is asked. Children can then learn to view relatively simple work responsibilities in very negative ways. They can become angry and resist work requests. They may even try not to do various jobs correctly or on time.

The *token system* can be a much more successful way for parents to teach their children to do work tasks. The token system is a way to motivate behavior by giving tokens for doing certain tasks. A *token* is a thing (stars, checkmarks, points, awards, grades, money) which stands for something else.

Someone may give you a small gift and say, "Take this as a token of my appreciation." The gift would have value for you because of what it stands for. Like a photograph of someone you love, the object itself has no great material value. Its value comes from what or whom it represents.

A token can represent love, respect, praise, or special recognition for accomplishments. Some tokens have buying power—they can be spent to obtain other things of value. As can be seen in Table 11.1, tokens are a very common part of our everyday lives. For example, we commonly work for, save, and spend money, one kind of token. Tokens can serve many useful functions.

• **Tokens can become reinforcers themselves.** When tokens are associated with praise and admiration, the tokens become powerful reinforcers. Tokens that an be used to purchase other valuable reinforcers also become powerful reinforcers. Either or both of these factors can work to make tokens valuable to children or adults.

• **Tokens provide something to see and count.** Children often enjoy collecting things and watching them grow in number. They

Table 11.1

Common Tokens and What They Can Buy

Tokens	What They Can Buy
Grocery-store coupons from the newspaper	Reduced prices on groceries and other items
Video-arcade or game-room tokens	Time playing different games
Checks and money orders	Almost anything
Cash	Almost anything
Points, stars	Almost anything a teacher or parent wishes to arrange

enjoy counting and playing with their special possessions.

• **Tokens can remind.** Token systems can function as helpful reminders to parents to consistently observe and reinforce their child's behaviors. Token systems can also remind children of the things they must do.

Tokens are a positive and pleasant way to motivate behavior. Parents are wise to choose positive ways to motivate children, rather than negative ways.

Guidelines for Starting a Token System

Using a simple token system is not hard, but it does require some planning and organization. The following guidelines are helpful in starting a token system.

1. Define the work to be done. Specify very clearly what is to be done or what a finished job looks like. Also provide a *deadline*, a time to finish the work. It is often a good idea to agree on a time that is acceptable to both child and parent. For young children, it is good to specify times for work completion in terms of the main events in their days. Such events may be a meal, right after school, or before or after a favorite television program.

2. Select the tokens. Points, checkmarks, stars, stickers, or money can work as tokens. Some parents do not wish to use money to motivate their child's work behavior. However, it is good to reconsider this position from time to time. It is true that volunteer work is much valued in our society. Children should be taught to volunteer their efforts,

without pay, in order to help their family and others. On the other hand, parents should also prepare their children to function as adults. Our economic system is really a large token system. It rewards work and initiative with money and other benefits. To do well in such a system, children must learn that both work and money have some value.

3. Back-up reinforcers should be identified. The things which can be purchased with tokens should be as varied as possible. In this way the tokens can have value no matter what the child wants to spend them for. It is also good to ask children what special things or privileges they would like to work for.

4. Explain the work, times, tokens, and back-up reinforcers. This should be done to increase the chances of success. It is good, at this time, to try to arrange the token system in a way which is agreeable to the child.

5. Make a chart or checklist. A chart or checklist reminds the child and the parents of jobs and deadlines, and allows for accurate record keeping. It also serves as a reminder of accomplishments.

6. Let the child sample the token system, at first, without working. With young children it is often helpful to ''walk'' them through the work to be done. First, the child should be shown the tasks to be done. Then, without work requirements, the tokens should be given to the child to spend. This will help the child to understand the connection between the work, tokens, and back-up reinforcements.

We now provide examples of two kinds of token systems in action.

Example #1

One set of parents decided that they would teach their four-year-old to hang up her night clothes and wash her face before breakfast. The parents installed hooks at the proper wall height for their child. A sturdy stool was placed at the bathroom sink for her use. They made a one-week chart to encurge the child and keep track of her progress, and made copies of the chart for future use.

On the first morning, the father excitedly showed the chart to the child and explained how it would work.

1. Each morning when she got up, the child would be reminded to hang up her night clothes and wash her face.

2. The parents would help her for the first few days, and then she could try it on her own.

3. As she finished doing each thing, a gold star would be placed on her chart. When the chart had both stars for the day, the child could go to breakfast.

On the first day, the father stayed with the child. As each of the tasks was finished, he immediately praised her and placed a gold star on the chart. See Illustration 11.2. After both stars were earned, the father hugged and kissed his child and they admired the stars. The mother was called, and she showed much excitement and praised

Task	Mon	Tues	Wed	Thur	Fri	Sat	Sun
	☆						
	☆						

Illustration 11.2. *How a token-system chart may look*

her child's work. She gave her daughter a hug and kiss, and they all went to breakfast.

During the next few days, the father reduced his assistance from the two tasks, and changed the reinforcement from CRF to two gold stars and praise after both of the jobs were completed. During the next few weeks, all assistance was withdrawn. The child was left to do the tasks on her own. Afterward, praise and good stars would still be given.

At about the third week, the little girl was encouraged to put her own gold stars on the chart. She really enjoyed doing this, but one of her parents still checked her work each morning before breakfast. After several more weeks, the parents praised her work every other day or so, but continued to check it daily. On one occasion the girl had forgotten to do her work. She was calmly but firmly reminded that the two chores had to be finished before breakfast.

Later, the little girl was told that she did not have to keep the chart unless she wanted to. She was praised for doing a wonderful job all on her own. By then, the parents were occasionally forgetting to check the work, but it was nearly always done before breakfast. The girl said she wanted to keep her chart, but after a few days she began to forget to put her stars up. The stars had become less important to her. A few times each week, the parents would tell their daughter how much they appreciated her work. They were feeling less of a need to check the work on a daily basis. But they did intermittently check and praise the child, about once or twice a week.

Example #2

Jaime, an eight-year-old, had recently made several requests to his parents to buy things

for him. It seemed there were many things he wanted. His parents decided that it was time their son learned to work and learn the value of money. They started by listing a variety of chores which they would genuinely appreciate help with. These chores were given an earning value for a kind of token system called a *work allowance*. The list of daily chores was as follows:

• Feed the dog—5¢ each day
• Empty the dishwasher and put the dishes away—15¢ each day
• Vacuum the family room—15¢ each day

On Saturdays, Jaime was expected to do the following:

• Vacuum his bedroom and dust the furniture—40¢
• Empty and replace the kitty litter—20¢

Jaime agreed to do the daily chores Monday through Friday, and to do the Saturday chores every Saturday. This meant that if all work was done well and on time, Jaime could earn $2.35 each week.

The child was not paid for all of his work activities, however. As usual, he was expected to make his bed and pick up his bedroom before breakfast. He also helped to set and clear the table at dinner, and he helped around the house in other small ways. These were the typical helpful things that Jaime had learned to do as part of his family.

But now, with the start of the work allowance, Jaime had some real jobs. He would work and be paid for them just like his older brother who babysat, raked yards, and shoveled walks around the neighborhood.

Jaime's parents indicated the times by which each job would have to be done, and discussed in detail how they were to be done. It was explained that, "as in any job," the work would need to be done on time and done well in order to be paid. In the beginning, a checklist was posted on the kitchen wall. The checklist functioned as a reminder to both the child and the parents.

During the first week, Jaime was paid at the end of each day. If he had been younger, the parents may have at first found it necessary to pay at the end of each job.

During the second week, Jaime and his parents agreed that it would be easier to make Wednesdays and Saturdays the paydays. Several weeks later, they agreed to have only one payday each week. Jaime requested that the payday be Friday, and so it was.

There could be many similar arrangements that would work well. The most important things in creating a work-allowance system are the following.

1. Work tasks, deadlines, times of payment, and amount of payment should be reasonable and agreeable to both parents and child.
2. In the beginning, there should be a checklist and schedule to remind both the child who must do the job and the parents who must check that it is done properly and on time.

It is very important to use a checklist until work habits are learned well and the parents' quality checks have become consistent. The checklist can be discontinued later on. However, it is necessary to intermittently check to see that the work is being done. Otherwise, work quality is likely to become a problem for most children.

3. Payment (reinforcement) should be very frequent in the beginning, and become more intermittent later. There is no need to ever completely end a work-allowance system. Older children can continue to be paid for other more mature jobs such as raking, doing the wash, painting, washing cars, and so on. The work allowance simply becomes more and more like the work-payment situations that adults seek to obtain.
4. Parents must see that work not finished on schedule is, nevertheless, finished. However, work not done on time or done very poorly should not earn pay.

Figure 11-8. Intermittent praise helps children to persevere at tasks. (USDA Photo by Marianne Pernold)

Remember that points, stars, or money are only one part of an effective approach to teaching work habits. The genuine praise and admiration from parents and other loved ones for jobs well done is also very important. All of these reinforcements can lead to feelings of self-pride and self-confidence in children.

QUESTIONS FOR GROWTH

1. Define differential reinforcement, and describe two original examples of its use.

2. (a) Explain the method of teaching discriminations. (b) Provide two original examples of how you would teach discriminations to children. (c) Name two common errors that occur in teaching discriminations.

3. Explain the meaning of generalization, and provide two of your own examples.

4. Define *shaping*, and provide two examples of how you could use shaping to teach new behaviors to children.

5. List and explain the six guidelines for using shaping successfully.

6. List and explain the three suggestions to follow when shaping fails.

7. Explain the method of backward chaining, and provide two original teaching examples.

8. Explain how prompting and fading may be used in backward chaining.

9. What is a schedule of reinforcement?

10. What are the differences between continuous reinforcement (CRF) and intermittent reinforcement?

11. Name two advantages and two disadvantages (long-term problems) of the CRF schedule.

12. How are children who are dependent upon CRF schedules likely to behave when reinforcement stops?

13. Explain how you would build persistence using both CRF and intermittent schedules.

14. (a) Explain what a token system is. (b) List several common examples of tokens. (c) Why might it be said that everyone works on a token system of some sort?

15. Describe four advantages of using a token system to encourage work behavior.

16. Design a token system for a child. Be sure to describe the behavior which is being encouraged.

CHAPTER

12

Discipline: Alternatives to Punishment

In parenting, *discipline* refers to the task of helping children to learn basic rules for self-conduct. The goal of discipline is not to have children follow rules simply because of what someone will do to them if they do not. Rather, the goal of successful discipline is to help children to accept and believe in beneficial rules for self-conduct.

Disciplining children is a complex process. Many factors need to be considered. In this chapter, we discuss parenting styles and effective discipline alternatives to punishment.

PARENTING STYLES

Diana Baumrind has researched several parenting styles and how they influence child behavior. These parenting styles are authoritarian, authoritative, and permissive.

Authoritarian parents tend to be very strict in their discipline of children. They often use their power to apply strong punishment. It has been found that parents who often use physical punishment and hostile language have children who show higher levels of aggression. This is especially true when fathers discipline in these ways. Authoritarian parents communicate less with their children, and do not encourage their children to express feelings when there is a conflict. Such parents are likely to demand great maturity of children. They rarely show their love in warm and tender ways.

Authoritative parents try to influence their children by setting limits and explaining their expectations. They use moderate discipline when necessary. Such parents communicate well and encourage verbal give-and-take. They often share with their children the reasons for their decisons. Authoritative parents are warm and loving to their children. They encourage individual initiative and self-esteem. They also encourage social responsibility and maturity.

Permissive parents are relatively warm toward their children, but they are not demanding or controlling. They rarely discipline or reinforce their children. They use weak demands for mature behavior. Permissive parents do not train their children to show independence and self-reliance.

Parents sometimes show a mixture of authoritarian, authoritative, and permissive approaches. A couple may show different styles: one parent may be permissive and the other authoritarian. Parents might also start with a permissive approach, not like the results, and then switch to a more authoritarian

Figure 12-1. Authoritative parents establish warm and loving ties within the family which encourage self-esteem and mutual respect. (H. Armstrong Roberts)

or authoritative style. Children may be confused by such mixtures of styles, which can result in problem behaviors.

Studies on parenting styles suggest that parents should show warmth and love as they encourage and reinforce independence, maturity, and responsibility. It is recommended that parents set and enforce limits consistently in loving but firm ways. These suggestions represent the authoritative parenting style. The authoritative style is one which can include a loving and considerate use of all of the discipline techniques that we discuss in this chapter.

DISCIPLINE ALTERNATIVES

Helping children to develop self-discipline is an important goal in parenting. Unfortunately, many people hold the mistaken view that discipline means punishment. Discipline means to help children learn basic rules for self-conduct. *Punishment* is a procedure in which something unpleasant is presented or positive reinforcers are removed following a behavior, and that behavior happens less often in the future. Sometimes parents need to use *very mild* forms of punishment in disciplining children. The use of punishment is discussed in Chapter 13. However, there are other excellent discipline methods which do not involve punishment at all.

A good definition of discipline is helping children to learn and accept basic rules for self-conduct. This broad definition allows for many discipline methods which do not involve unpleasant consequences. In this chapter, we examine good and effective alternatives which do not include punishment. But first, let us consider the reasons why parents sometimes overuse punishment and overlook the effective nonpunishment discipline methods soon to be described.

Reasons Why Some Parents Overuse Punishment

Parents who overuse punishment miss many opportunities to use mild but effective nonpunishment methods. As we discuss in the next chapter, there are many dangers in overusing punishment. There are many good reasons to avoid using punishment unless it is essential. We hope that the following list will help you to seriously consider using discipline alternatives rather than punishment with children.

1. Parents may overuse punishment because they are not aware of good discipline alternatives. People often parent the way they were raised. It is only recently that courses about teaching children have become available. Such courses teach parents how discipline alternatives may be used.

2. Parents may overuse punishment because they are not aware of the bad side effects when punishment is misused. Punishment can be risky. (Some damaging side effects are discussed in Chapter 13.) It is important to learn alternative methods of discipline.

3. Parents may overuse punishment because it appears easy to use. It *seems* easy to punish a child for misbehavior. Punishment *seems* to require less effort than other discipline approaches. However, alternative discipline methods require no more work than skillfully using punishment, and they avoid the unnecessary risks of punishment.

4. Parents may overuse punishment because they displace their anger and aggression. To *displace aggression* means to take anger out on someone who is not the cause of the anger. For example, someone whose feelings have been hurt by a close friend may take it out on someone else. The student who has received a bad grade may make hurtful remarks to family members. The parents who have argued may show anger at their children. Displaced aggression can happen to anyone, so parents should watch for it in their own behavior.

5. Parents may overuse punishment because they lose their tempers. Parents who are trying to teach children rules for conduct may become frustrated and angry when they do not see progress. Parents should learn to control their own tempers. They should also learn a wide range of effective teaching techniques which are less likely to cause physical or emotional harm to children.

6. Parents may overuse punishment because they expect too much from their children. It is important that parents learn what to expect in normal child development. They will then be more likely to understand the reasons for unpleasant but normal behaviors like crying by the infant or temper tantrums by the two-year-old.

7. Parents may overuse punishment because they fall into the punishment trap. Parents may get into the habit of using punishment too often. Children learn best when their behavior is immediately reinforced. This is also true of parents. When parents raise their voices, scold, or spank, children frequently stop what they are doing immediately. This quick control of a child's behavior is reinforcing to the parent. Therefore, parents can easily learn to raise their voices, scold, and spank much too often. This is the punishment trap. Parents can become trapped into using punishment too often because these

Figure 12-2. *Parents should learn what to expect in normal child development. This mother is not frustrated or angered by her newborn's crying, because she realizes that his behavior is normal. (March of Dimes Birth Defects Foundation)*

unpleasant consequences often show immediate results. Unfortunately, as parents begin to punish more, they normally begin to reinforce appropriate behavior less often. Parents who fall into the punishment trap treat their children in harmful ways.

In this section, we have discussed seven main reasons why parents overuse punishment. There are certainly more such reasons; maybe you can think of others. We now consider some common misbehaviors that children may show, and some effective discipline alternatives to punishment.

COMMON MISBEHAVIORS IN CHILDREN

All children show varying amounts of misbehaviors. Child behavior is normally considered inappropriate and in need of reduction

when it fits one or more of the following descriptions.

1. It may cause harm to the child or another person.
2. It is destructive.
3. It is too disruptive to others.
4. It interferes with the child's normal growth and development.

It is important not to be too demanding of children. But neither should parents ignore or overlook misbehavior during the early years. The early childhood years are normally the parents' time of maximum influence. It is during this time that children can most easily be helped to overcome behavior problems that later may bring them much trouble and unhappiness.

The following child behaviors are those which are generally viewed as inappropriate by parents, teachers, and others.

• Excessive verbal or physical aggression such as biting or hitting and other dangerous activities
• Excessive running, jumping, or climbing in portions of the home, school, or other places where reasonably controlled behavior is appropriate
• Excessively loud talking or shouting
• Purposefully destructive behavior
• Excessive "sassiness," or talking back
• Frequently refusing to follow instructions
• Frequent temper tantrums

Of course, some of these behaviors are appropriate under some circumstances. There is a difference between children running, shouting, and wrestling outdoors and acting the same way when visiting someone's home or in a classroom.

H. Armstrong Roberts

© Ron Meyer/White Eyes Design

H. Armstrong Roberts

Figure 12-3. All children show varying amounts of misbehavior. In each of these three cases, would you discipline the child? Or would your decisions depend upon the circumstances under which each behavior occurs?

Parents and other care givers must judge when a child's behavior is appropriate and when it is not. They should be concerned with weakening inappropriate behaviors. They should strengthen alternative behaviors such as walking calmly in the house, playing cooperatively with others, and following reasonable requests. Parents have to judge how often is too often, how long is too long, and how loud is too loud. Such decisions should be based on a respect for the child's individuality and an understanding of the requirements for normal development.

A young child should not be expected to always know what behavior is appropriate in a given situation. Therefore, the responsible parent should strengthen appropriate behavior as effectively and safely as possible. Very few parents argue that such decisions should be left to children. Even permissive parents will find themselves trying to eliminate some forms of their child's behavior because it is dangerous, interferes with learning, or is very annoying.

Keeping Track of Misbehaviors

Observation and measurement is an important part of effective discipline. Parents cannot be expected to measure everything their child does. However, when parents become concerned about their child's misbehavior, they should make close observations before taking steps to stop it.

Skilled parent-teachers will define the behavior problems. They may also do a *sequence analysis* (writing down what happens before, during, and right after the behavior), and count the frequency of occurrence over a period of time. These steps slow down the parents long enough to look at the problem in a calm, objective way. By taking the time to think and observe, parents can avoid losing their tempers and punishing needlessly. In this way, a better idea of the seriousness of the problem can be obtained. Parents can then identify a better way to help the child.

It is good to keep a written record of especially troublesome misbehaviors. For instance, if a child has violent temper tantrums, the parents might note the following observations.

• The tantrums normally, but not always, occur when the parents say "no" to the child.
• During the past week, the child had a tantrum at least once and sometimes twice per day.
• The tantrums last for about two to three minutes, during which time the child cries, screams, falls on the floor, and kicks vigorously.

By keeping a written record and continuing it after the start of a teaching approach, parents will be in a better position to know whether their attempts to solve the problems are working. Many parents stop their reasonable attempts only because they "feel" their efforts are ineffective. But if they keep records, they have a better basis for comparison.

Sometimes a certain discipline method will eliminate a problem in a day or two. Such an obvious change can be noticed by anyone. But many changes in behavior occur more gradually. To detect gradual change, parents should know, for example, that the misbehavior first occurred seven times a week but then slowly diminished to five, three, and finally zero times a week.

If parents fail to notice that nonpunishment methods are working slowly, they may needlessly use punishment. What if they notice that what they are doing is really having no effect or is having an undesirable effect? In this case, they could choose to change to a new method. If parents frequently measure their influence, they will learn which approaches work best for their child.

EFFECTIVE ALTERNATIVES TO PUNISHMENT

It is hard to imagine raising a child without the need to reduce behavior problems from time to time. But parents should resist any temptation to use punishment whenever children misbehave. In this section, we describe seven effective alternatives which should be considered before punishment.

Relabel the Behavior

Before trying to change a child's behavior, parents should consider whether it is really important that the behavior be reduced. Some behaviors may seem negative but are only natural consequences of growth. Is it all that bad if a baby plays with safe and unbreakable things such as a pan or imitation fruit? Is there really a problem if children sometimes suck their thumbs or refuse to eat something?

Parents should ask themselves if they have *labeled* (named) a behavior as bad only because it is annoying to them. Perhaps they are overly sensitive to little annoyances. They might be tired, ill, worried about something else, or in need of a little time away from child-care duties.

Parents may conclude that a certain behavior really is a problem. In other cases, they might conclude that a behavior is unimportant or even good. For example, they might *relabel* (rename) banging a pan as a sign of an exploratory nature. An older child's unique hairstyle might be relabeled as a sign of his or her individualism.

Another situation in which problem behavior may be relabeled is one in which a major change in a child's life produces temporary changes in behavior. A new baby in the family, starting school, or moving to a new house might require a period of adjustment for children. In such cases, "misbehavior" may be viewed as a natural reaction to something stressful. Parents should help children to deal

Figure 12-4. Sometimes misbehavior is caused by a new baby in the family, a move to a new home or school, family problems, or other circumstances. In such cases, understanding, not discipline, may be needed. (HUD Photo)

with such changes. If a misbehavior continues after a reasonable time, gentle discipline alternatives may be the answer.

Withholding Reinforcers

In Chapter 10, we introduced the idea of extinction—withholding, or failing to provide, reinforcers following operant behavior. The effect of this so-called *nonconsequence* is that the behavior weakens and occurs less often in the future. Withholding reinforcers is a gentle and often very effective way to reduce misbehaviors. Parents may choose to ignore and withhold other reinforcers from problem behaviors such as tantrums if these behaviors have become strong habits in their child.

Withholding reinforcers for such behaviors must be done consistently to be effective. Occasionally giving in to a tantrum after ignoring them will actually make tantrums harder to reduce in the future. Giving in is an example of intermittent reinforcement, which will build persistence in the behavior.

There are many common errors that parents sometimes make when trying to weaken misbehavior by withholding reinforcers. Imagine that a four-year-old is having one of his frequent temper tantrums over not getting something he wants. The following is a list of common errors that his parents might make during the temper tantrum.

1. Looking at the child
2. Talking to the child
3. Touching the child
4. Handing anything to the child
5. Moving closer to the child
6. Stopping what the parents are doing
7. Looking upset or making noises of impatience or annoyance

To effectively withhold reinforcers and reduce future temper tantrums, the parents must consistently avoid doing all of these things during the tantrums. Other people who might witness a tantrum must also withhold their reinforcers in order for the method to be successful.

Withholding reinforcers may fail for two additional reasons. First, if tantrums have normally been reinforced almost continuously (each time they occur), the child is likely to display a much bigger tantrum when ignored. Parents are often surprised by this and give in by reinforcing the bigger tantrum. This is unfortunate, because behavior maintained by continuous reinforcement (CRF) is normally weakened fairly quickly when reinforcers are withheld consistently. Second, if tantrums have been reinforced on an intermittent schedule (less than each time they occur), they can be expected to persist for a longer time when reinforcers are finally withheld. In this case, parents might lose patience and stop withholding reinforcers shortly before they would have seen success.

Withholding reinforcers sometimes works slowly, and so is not the best single approach for the following misbehaviors.

• Those which are dangerous
• Those which are destructive of materials or property
• Those which are so disruptive that ignoring them is impossible

Rearrangement

In some cases, eliminating a behavior might retard, or limit, development of important skills. For example, the child who is beginning to pull herself into a standing position to reach some objects is clearly learning from her efforts. It would be a mistake if, after struggling to her feet, her parents scolded her for reaching for an object. What may be delayed here is the act of standing.

In such a case, parents should choose *rearrangement* instead of punishment. A home can be rearranged and made childproof by removing fragile or unsafe objects. This will eliminate the need to consider discipline methods for normal exploratory behavior. Removed items can be replaced by others that are harmless but interesting enough to reward standing.

Rearranging a child's home will make it safer, and there will be less need for punishment. Some common methods for childproofing a home are shown in Box 12.1.

Other behavior problems may be caused by faulty schedules, and can be solved by rearranging the schedules. For example, the child who still needs an afternoon nap may become very irritable when these naps are stopped. The obvious way for parents to deal with this problem is to rearrange their schedules to suit the child's needs.

BOX 12.1

Suggestions for Childproofing the Home

- Fill unused electrical outlets with rubber inserts (available in many hardware stores).
- Pad sharp corners on furniture.
- Put safe baby gates at the top and bottom of stairways.
- Place cleaning supplies, medicines, sharp objects, and other dangerous materials in locations which cannot be reached by children.
- Place breakable and valuable objects in safe places until children learn not to damage things by accident.
- Choose toys that cannot be swallowed, that do not have sharp edges, and that are not coated with dangerous materials such as paint. Young children might accidentally swallow objects smaller than a golf ball.
- Place safety latches on drawers which, if pulled, could fall out onto a child.
- Keep pan and pot handles turned away from the front of the stove. Teach children to stay away from the stove.

Parents Should Examine Their Own Behavior

Imitation is a powerful influence in child development. Parents who shout or swear a lot, or who are physically aggressive, should not be surprised to see their children show the same behaviors. Children imitate many forms of undesirable behavior. To solve this type of problem, parents should examine and control their own behavior.

Satiation

Satiation means letting a child get tired of some behavior. Children often behave in a certain way to produce a new consequence which is reinforcing. Chances are good that if children are allowed to do the behavior repeatedly, it will lose its novelty and become boring. If the behavior only produces a simple but new result, the effects of satiation may be permanent.

Young children often love to play with dials, slam doors, or pound on pots and pans. Parents should discipline themselves to ignore these behaviors, *as long as they are safe.* It is likely that their children will soon satisfy their curiousity and then move on to explore other things. Of course, parents may not wish to use the satiation approach in all situations, such as in other people's homes.

Parents may accidentally turn children, who are only satisfying a temporary fascination, into "fanatics" who spend nearly all of their time playing with dials and the like. The problem is often that parents have accidentally reinforced the behavior through their immediate attention and mild scolding. Parents are then driven by great irritation to unnecessary forms of punishment. To allow satiation to work, parents must not provide any form of attention which might reinforce the activity. This even includes cross looks and scolding.

Reasoning

When parents *reason* with a child, they explain why the child should or should not behave in some way. The consequences of the behavior are described to the child in clear detail.

If reasoning works, it is because a *symbolic consequence* has been applied. Words are symbols. Therefore, to describe to a child what will happen if a certain behavior occurs is to present a symbolic consequence. The following are some examples of how parents might try to reason with children.

Behavior	Consequence
Share your toys.	It makes your friends happy and they will come to play with you again.
Pet the kitten gently.	The kitten likes this and may come to sit on your lap more often.
Do not throw sand at others.	It can get in their eyes and hurt them.
You must not go in the street without Mommy or Daddy.	A car might hit you and hurt you very badly.

Parents can try reasoning with children who are as young as two years. By this time, children have some understanding of the present and future. They also have some understanding of danger and the rights of others. Still, reasoning alone can be a weak approach with many young children. It may help to add *concrete illustrations* to symbolic consequences. For example, you might tell a child, "Do not play with the knife; it can cut you." This is a symbolic consequence. You might then show how the knife can cut some object, such as an orange. This is a concrete illustration. The younger the child, the more simple and concrete the reasoning should be.

Parents should praise children when they change their behavior in response to reasoning. Parents should also reason with their children when they are behaving appropriately. With this positive approach, the parents would praise the child for riding the bike in the driveway rather than in the street, while briefly reminding the child of the dangers of the street. It is best, though, not to overuse such reminders.

Sometimes, reasoning alone may not work or may even strengthen a problem behavior. Some parents might overuse the reasoning approach. The special attention—reasoning—which follows a misbehavior can be powerfully reinforcing. As a result, the more parents reason with a young child for misbehaving, the more the child may misbehave. This is especially likely if parents are busy with other things and their child has a hard time getting attention in appropriate ways.

Differential Reinforcement

Differential reinforcement is reinforcing good behavior and withholding reinforcers for inappropriate behavior. (Differential reinforcement was introduced in Chapter 11.) This is one of the most useful ways to discipline.

One way to use differential reinforcement is to reinforce any behavior other than the misbehavior which is to be reduced. Parents can check the child's behavior often. If the child is misbehaving, reinforcers (attention, treats) are withheld. If the child is doing something other than the misbehavior, reinforcers are provided generously.

This approach may work well for a variety of problems, but sometimes it will need to be changed in some way. The difficulty may be that the other behaviors may not be all that desirable either. For example, say that a parent wants to reduce crying in a toddler. Every so often, the parent seeks the child out when the child is not crying and praises him lovingly. Now suppose that the toddler is not crying, but is found under his bed pouting. This is clearly not a behavior to reinforce.

In such cases, parents must look for behaviors which *oppose*, or compete with, a specific misbehavior. Parents and teachers use this approach many times every day. A parent may praise a child for walking in the house but ignore running, or may read a story to a happy child but not to a whining one. Notice that the two behaviors in each category oppose or compete with each other. A child cannot both walk and run or be both happy and whining at the same time.

In disciplining children, it is very important to strengthen appropriate opposing behavior at the same time as you weaken inappropriate behavior. If walking in the house is strongly reinforced and therefore occurs more often, there is naturally less time available for running. If parents increase the frequency of their child's smiles, frowning and crying will naturally happen less often.

Guidelines for Using Differential Reinforcement

The following guidelines are important for using differential reinforcement skillfully.

1. Define the behaviors. Define the kind of opposing appropriate behavior which will be reinforced, and then identify actions that will not be reinforced.

2. Be consistent. If parents are not consistent about what they do and do not reinforce, the approach is likely to fail. Whenever possible, parents, teachers, relatives, and friends should work together as a team.

3. Reinforce frequently at first. In correcting misbehavior, parents are in effect teaching a new behavior pattern. Therefore, it is best to start with very frequent reinforcement. On the first day, it is good to look for appropriate behavior to reward every five minutes or so. As the child begins to behave more appropriately, parents can use longer intervals.

4. Reinforce powerfully. Use powerful reinforcers for appropriate behavior, and give them as often as possible at first. When the reinforcer is praise, it should be enthusiastic and descriptive. It is good to include reinforcers other than praise, such as letting the child call a favorite relative, talk, read, or play. Parents should learn which consequences are especially reinforcing to their children.

5. Reinforce immediately. Reinforcement works best when it is provided immediately following the desired behavior. Any delay will weaken this approach a great deal. This is especially true with young children.

Figure 12.5 With her attention and interest, this woman is reinforcing her granddaughter's appropriate behavior of playing with the truck outside the home rather than inside. (Action Photo by Susan Biddle)

Differential reinforcement requires time, but it offers parents a good chance of avoiding future unhappiness for the child and themselves. Through differential reinforcement, parents can positively discipline a misbehavior during its early stages. The approach can be used successfully to help solve a number of problems. The following are several examples.

Temper Tantrums. If the problem is temper tantrums, the goal is not to eliminate all displays of sadness, disappointment, or frustration. Sometimes it is natural to feel and express these emotions. While parents may not wish to praise these behaviors excessively, they should not hesitate to provide help or comfort.

Behaviors which parents should avoid reinforcing include screaming, throwing things, pounding or stomping on the floor, holding one's breath, and so on. Since these behaviors are distresing to watch and hard to ignore, they are often reinforced with attention in order to calm the child. This, of course, results in more tantrums. Ignoring tantrums may temporarily produce more dramatic tantrums than seen before, but this is often a sign that the child may soon give up tantrums. Parents should also look for times when children handle their frustrations in less emotional ways. Parents should praise these actions.

Not Following Instructions. Young children can easily learn to follow simple instructions if they are reinforced for doing so from the beginning. Parents can begin teaching during a child's first year by giving simple instructions such as "Come with me" or "Give it to me." Later on, instructions can be a little harder: "Come sit by me," "Bring me the book," or "Do what I do." By praising their children for promptly following instructions, parents can influence how the children will respond to future requests.

If a child does not follow instructions, parents can repeat the instructions. (But they should be careful not to reinforce opposition

with too much attention.) Then parents can physically help the child to follow the instructions. If the instructions are followed well, the child can be praised. During this process, no more help is given than is necessary, and help should be removed as soon as possible. The point is to reinforce following instructions, and not to reinforce the opposite. Of course, cheerfully following an instruction without any form of extra prompting should be reinforced strongly and with enthusiasm.

Bedtime Resistance. In some homes, the statement "It's time for bed" signals the beginning of a long and unpleasant struggle. Bed is not a very rewarding place for most young children unless they are very tired. Even then, some may protest to stay up, only to fall asleep on the couch.

To solve this problem, parents should firmly announce that it is time for bed, and cheerfully help the child (no more than necessary) to get ready. If the child is cooperative, parents might spend five minutes or so at the child's bedside, reading a story out loud or talking. If the child protests, cries, and resists the parents' attempts, the parents should carry on in a businesslike fashion, say "Good night," and take care not to reinforce this behavior. If parents consistently use this approach, most children should learn to go to bed reasonably well.

Some children have learned to struggle hard. If a child gets out of bed and wanders out of the bedroom, the parents can be firm but patient. It is important not to reinforce this behavior with extra conversation or snacks. Even scolding can function as a reinforcer. But, if as many times as the child gets up, the parents put the child back to bed without reinforcement of any kind, the child will soon give up the struggle. This method takes patience, but it is effective.

SUMMARY

The forms of discipline discussed in this chapter may not work in all situations, but the procedures should be very helpful in most. If a discipline method seems to be failing, think about the following points.

1. Are you using sufficiently powerful and immediate reinforcers?

2. Are you reinforcing often enough?

3. Are you reinforcing behavior which opposes or competes with the misbehavior?

4. Is the misbehavior really not being reinforced? Are others in the household reinforcing inappropriate behavior?

5. Do you scold, reason too often, or give annoyed looks? If so, you may be reinforcing misbehavior by your attention.

6. Are you sure the approach is failing? Have you counted misbehaviors for several days or weeks? Maybe progress is occurring very gradually.

Differential reinforcement and other forms of disciplining without punishment can be extremely effective. However, despite parents' best attempts, situations may arise which require some form of punishment. We discuss these matters in Chapter 13.

QUESTIONS FOR GROWTH

1. Discuss the three parenting styles. Explain why you would recommend one style over the others.

2. Give the definition of discipline which is recommended in the text.

3. Explain what punishment is and how it affects behavior.

4. Tell why punishment and discipline are not necessarily the same thing.

5. Explain why it is important to use discipline alternatives to punishment whenever possible.

6. Describe five of the reasons why parents frequently overuse punishment with children.

7. Tell what the punishment trap is. Explain how parents learn to overuse punishment through this trap.

8. List some of the common misbehaviors in children which may require discipline methods.

9. Explain why it is important for parents to keep track of behaviors that they wish to reduce through discipline methods.

10. Describe each of the following alternatives to punishment, and provide your own examples of how they could be used by parents: **(a)** relabel the behavior, **(b)** rearrangement, **(c)** parents examining their own behavior, **(d)** satiation, **(e)** reasoning, and **(f)** differential reinforcement.

11. Tell what is meant by strengthening opposing or competing behavior with differential reinforcement.

12. List and explain the guidelines for using the differential reinforcement procedure.

CHAPTER

13

Discipline Using Punishment

It is not easy to think about punishment without experiencing some negative emotion. For some, the idea of punishment brings thoughts of suffering, imprisonment, or worse. Of course, these ideas have no application or relationship to child discipline.

When we discuss the use of punishment with children, we are talking about *very mild* consequences which can be helpful to children. The use of such mild consequences is called punishment only because it weakens the behavior it follows. *Punishment, as we use the term, never stands for harsh and damaging treatment.* Instead, we discuss mild and logical consequences such as firmly telling a child why some action is wrong, having a child help to replace a purposely broken toy, or guiding a child to clean up some mess made in anger. See Box 13.1.

Actually, these can all be examples of punishment, but they are a very special and beneficial kind. Such consequences are sensible, mild, and very helpful for children to experience when loving parents use them consistently. These mild consequences can help children to learn and accept basic rules for self-conduct. Parents who use mild punishing consequences only when necessary, and who first consider using the discipline alternatives discussed in Chapter 12, normally are successful in disciplining.

HOW DOES PUNISHMENT WORK?

As mentioned earlier, punishment occurs whenever something is added or subtracted following a behavior, and this reduces the future frequency of that behavior. The most important thing to remember is that punishment reduces the future frequency of the behavior it follows. See Illustration 13.1. The

BOX 13.1

Logical Consequences in Discipline

Rudolf Dreikurs has written about effective discipline methods with children. He advises that parents set standards and limits and that consistency in discipline is all-important.

The powerful ways in which consequences can influence children's behavior is also recognized. However, Dreikurs advises parents that praise or disapproval should be directed only to the behavior and not to the child. This can be done by labeling the specific behaviors which are appropriate and inappropriate. The child is always shown respect as a person and is not labeled or judged as good or bad based upon the behavior.

Discipline should be firm, kind, and consistent. Furthermore, Dreikurs recommends the use of logical consequences in discipline. Logical consequences are a natural part of skilled parenting. Examples of logical consequences, which are naturally or sensibly related to misbehavior, are the following:

Behavior	Logical Consequence
A brother and sister are fighting over which television program to watch.	The parent calmly turns off the television and informs the children that when they can reach a decision without fighting, the television can be turned back on.
A five-year-old plays in a mud puddle and gets his shoes wet.	The parent tells the child that he cannot go outside again until his shoes are dry.
A child refuses to wear a short-sleeved light shirt on a warm day. He insists upon wearing a winter shirt.	The child becomes uncomfortably warm while playing.
A seven-year-old often refuses to come when called for supper.	Supper is put away when the family is finished eating. The child misses a meal and experiences hunger.
A young child runs into the street.	The child is restricted to the yard of house for a period of time.

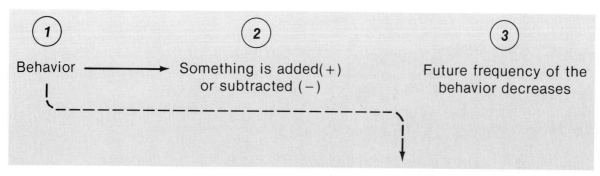

Illustration 13.1. A diagram of the definition of punishment

particular thing that is added or subtracted is called the *punisher*.

A common mistake is to think that punishment is the use of a certain kind of consequence. For example, is punishment being spanked, sat in a chair, or sent to a room? Many people would say that these consequences are punishers. However, in some situations they would be wrong. These and other consequences for behavior are examples of punishers *only* if they reduce the future frequency of the behavior they follow.

Another common mistake is to think that punishment is anything which is unpleasant to you personally. You may consider scolding to be a punishment because you dislike being scolded. But what if someone repeatedly scolds a child for running in the house, and as a result the child runs more often? This is actually an example of reinforcement, not punishment.

Examples of Common and Natural Punishments

Everyone has learned valuable lessons, without harm, through beneficial experiences

Figure 13-1. If this child plays too roughly with the cat's tail, she may soon face a natural punishment—and learn a valuable lesson about animals! (© Ron Meyer/White Eyes Design)

with punishment. Table 13.1 lists a variety of potentially punishing consequences which are common and natural throughout life. Re- member that the consequences are punishers only if they reduce the future frequency of the behaviors they follow.

Table 13.1

Common Behaviors and Potentially Punishing Consequences

Behavior	*Consequence*
A newborn scratches her own face	Pain
An infant puts his fingers in a flame	Pain
A young child climbs too high and falls	The "sudden stop" produces pain
A child plays in the snow without gloves	Her hands are very cold and sting
A child mistreats a valued toy	The toy breaks
A child eats something he is not supposed to	He gets sick and vomits
A preschooler becomes angry and throws toys	The teacher makes her pick up the toys and put them away
A child eats crackers in bed	The scratchy crumbs keep him awake
Someone does sloppy work in school	He receives a poor grade
An adult chooses to stay up very late at night	She feels tired and listless the next day
A sun worshipper stays in the sun too long	He is sunburned badly
A library book is returned late	A fine is charged
A teen eats the wrong foods	He looks unhealthy
Someone insults a friend	The friendship ends
Your father leaves the car lights on	The car battery is dead
Someone runs a red light	She receives a ticket and is fined
An individual smokes cigarettes	She develops a cough and loses ability to run and breathe effectively
A student goes to the movie rather than studying for a test	She fails the test
Your neighbors pay their income taxes late	The government fines them

Table 13.1 should help you to view punishment more objectively. It shows that experience with some forms of punishment is a natural and beneficial part of life.

THE DANGERS OF EXCESSIVE PUNISHMENT

The fact that children sometimes experience predictable punishing consequences does not, of itself, appear harmful. However, if punishment is inconsistent or overused in harsh and unskilled ways, it can have very undesirable or even dangerous effects. Punishment methods are very easy for parents to misuse or abuse. Therefore, a thorough understanding of these dangers is essential. The following are some of the risks of the excessive or unskilled use of punishment.

1. Children may come to dislike the person who punishes them. People, places, and things which are associated with painful or unpleasant feelings become viewed as painful or unpleasant. For example, if parents frequently spank their child, the child may begin to associate them with pain. How they look, the sound of their voices, or their physical closeness can become unpleasant to the child.

2. Children may develop strong fears and anxieties. The more often that harsh treatment is associated with a person, place, or thing, the more unpleasant these things may become to a child. In cases of extreme pain, often only one such experience will create new fears or dislikes of great intensity. For example, the child who is hurt by a classmate or an adult may become very fearful of that person.

Figure 13-2. Children who have been punished excessively may show signs of anxiety and fear. (© Ron Meyer/White Eyes Design)

3. Fears and anxieties produced through strong punishment can generalize to other people, places, or things. A child who is badly hurt by the father may become fearful of all men. A child who is often ridiculed and shamed in school may come to dislike all teachers, books, school, or organized learning in general.

4. Harsh punishment can produce fear and anxiety which interferes with learning. Children who are fearful or anxious have trouble focusing their attention well enough to learn at home and school. Such children may also show signs of fear and anxiety which make it hard for them to make friends and enjoy normal social development.

5. Children may learn to escape and avoid people, places, and things associated with excessive or harsh punishment. Parents who punish their child too often should not be surprised if the child does not remain warm and loving to them. There are many ways for a child to avoid an unpleasant parent, such as not talking and avoiding physical contact. These reactions can sometimes generalize to include all adults.

6. Children can adapt, or grow accustomed, to pain and other forms of punishment. When this occurs, punishment methods become completely ineffective. Out of desperation, the parent starts to punish a little harder, gets results, then eventually finds that even this fails to work. Unless a more appropriate way of reducing unwanted behavior is discovered, the punishments might cause physical damage. It is likely that this progression often plays a role in cases of child abuse. Child abuse is discussed later in this chapter.

7. If reinforcement and punishment are mixed together, pain and disapproval can become positive reinforcers to a child. Parents are in danger of creating this situation any time they punish a child and a short time later give powerful positive reinforcers. Every now and then, one parent's guilt feelings forced him to let his child stay up and watch television after a punishment. Another parent followed punishments with hugs and cookies. In each case, the child's behavior problem had been worsened; disapproval

was turned into a powerful positive reinforcer.

8. Excessive use of punishment (especially pain) may stimulate aggression in children. Pain has been found to produce aggression in animals. There is some evidence to suggest that some humans may behave in the same way. For example, the adult who hammers her own finger may be seen shouting at and even hitting or throwing the hammer. Children who have been punished excessively may become aggressive against their parents. Such aggression may become generalized and directed against innocent people or objects.

9. Children imitate the methods of punishment used by their parents. A very high proportion of parents who abuse their children were themselves abused when they were young. Children who see their parents consistently use physical punishment are likely to imitate the behavior in their own lives.

WHEN SHOULD PUNISHMENT BE USED?

As you have seen, the use of punishment involves many risks. Because of these risks, informed parents will be careful in their use of punishment. They will use punishment only when alternative discipline methods have failed. Such cases may involve children who are oppositional or who are extremely disruptive. *Oppositional children* refuse to follow nearly all reasonable requests or instructions. *Disruptive children* may run, scream, jump, climb, and purposely fall so often that they appear completely uncontrollable. These sorts of behavior problems may hurt family relationships and interfere with the child's normal development. It is important to remember, though, that these actions might result from a stress such as a birth in the family, going to school, or moving to a new home. It is always wise to look for such causes. Still, such actions should be reduced.

Another way in which informed parents will be careful in their use of punishment is that they will use punishment when behavior must be controlled quickly and other methods can be expected to work too slowly. Examples of such cases are children who repeatedly run into the street or who attack playmates in dangerous and hurtful ways.

Parenting involves making thousands of decisions about the best way to care for a child. Decisions about if, when, and how to use punishment require parents to have good knowledge, maturity, and self-control. If punishment must be used, the following general rules will help to increase its effectiveness and reduce risks.

- **Always use the least harmful form of punishment possible.** We will shortly review five different punishment methods. The first four methods are much less risky than the last. The least risky methods should always be considered first.
- **Take time to define and measure the behavior problem.** This is important in order for parents to objectively see the seriousness of the problem. Measurement also protects parents and children from techniques that can be seen not to work or to make behavior problems even worse.
- **Select one behavior at a time.** To avoid overusing punishment, it is important to not try to achieve too much too fast. For example, a child may hurt others frequently, run

almost constantly, and purposely destroy household objects. The skilled parent will have the patience to first control the aggression, then reduce the destructive behavior, and last work to reduce excessive running. In this way, a parent can consistently and mildly punish a forbidden activity and still avoid punishing too often.

- **Punishment should be given immediately following the inappropriate behavior.** Young children learn best when consequences for their behaviors are immediate. This is true of both reinforcement and punishment. If the consequences are immediate, they more quickly help children learn what not to do. Thus, the number of times that punishment will be needed is reduced.
- **Be consistent.** Research has shown that if punishment is inconsistently applied to inappropriate behaviors, the behaviors are likely to increase in frequency. If punishment must be used, use it every time the behavior occurs. Being consistent helps to reduce the number of times that punishment will be needed.
- **Use the punishment technique as skillfully as possible.** The physician who performs surgery follows a precise procedure. In the same way, punishment procedures are not simple. Harmful mistakes can be made if punishment methods are not used according to tested procedures. Precision in using punishment will reduce the number of times that punishment will be needed.
- **Never use punishment by itself.** After introducing punishment, differentially reinforce opposing or competing behavior. By combining the two techniques, the behavior will be reduced more quickly. If aggression is punished, cooperation and kindness

Figure 13-3. *Punishment should occur immediately after the inappropriate behavior. (© Alan Carey/The Image Works, Inc.)*

should be reinforced. If running into the street is punished, staying in the yard should be reinforced.

This dual approach has two advantages. First, if only punishment is used, parents cannot influence what will replace the behavior being reduced. Tantrums might be replaced by sulking, or aggression against toys might be directed against people. By using differential reinforcement, parents can influence which appropriate behaviors will replace the reduced misbehavior. Second,

the dual approach will eliminate the misbehavior much more rapidly. As a result, parents will have to punish much less often. Differential reinforcement reduces the need for punishment.

• **Know and avoid the common errors for each punishment method used.** Later in this chapter, we identify and discuss basic punishment methods. Each method can involve common mistakes which will hurt its effectiveness. By being aware of the common errors for each punishment method, parents can avoid such errors and reduce unnecessary risks to children. They can protect the loving relationship they enjoy with their children, and also reduce the number of times that punishment will be needed.

BOX 13.2

Child Abuse

It is estimated that between one-half million and one-and-one-half million children are physically abused by their parents or others each year in the United States. The true figures on child abuse in its many forms are not known. Child abuse can be *physical* in nature. In this case, children may suffer bruises, cuts, burns, broken bones, and even death. Child abuse can also be *emotional*. This occurs when parents are cold, rejecting, and unloving to their children. Parents may also blame and ridicule children to such an extent that the children show emotional damage. *Sexual abuse* occurs whenever adults initiate sexual contact with children.

Child neglect is another form of mistreatment of children. Parents who do not provide the essentials for healthy physical and mental development are neglectful. Such parents may not dress their child warmly in the winter, or may not provide their child with inoculation shots against common diseases. Neglectful parents may refuse to obtain help for speech or health problems, or may ignore the child's nutritional and hygienic needs.

PARENTS WHO ABUSE THEIR CHILDREN

Child abuse often grows out of discipline methods which are based primarily on physical punishment involving pain. Parents who rely on physical punishment normally do not know of other methods which are effective but do not risk physical and emotional damage. These parents may cause accidents which injure children.

Adults who abuse and neglect children were themselves very often abused and neglected as children. Abusive adults often have children with the expectation that the children will give them the love and respect that no one else has given them. These unreasonable expectations lead to strong feelings of rejection and anger in the parents when the children show unhappiness or misbehavior.

Continued on next page

Child Abuse (Continued)

Abusive and neglectful parents often show an inability to run an orderly, organized home. They are often—but not always—financially troubled, lack transportation, and do not have friends or family nearby to support them in times of trouble. Abusive and neglectful parents are often involved in heavy alcohol and drug use.

CHILDREN WHO ARE ABUSED OR NEGLECTED

Abused children often show physical signs such as scratches, cuts, bruises, or broken bones. Sexually abused children may bleed from their genitals or show irritation by scratching or rubbing their genitals. They may also show emotional problems. Abused children often seem uncomfortable around adults. They may show their discomfort by not speaking, avoiding eye contact, and withdrawing physically. However, children react differently. Some may become hyperactive and show extreme behavior problems.

Neglected children look neglected. They are likely to be dirty, poorly clothed, poorly fed, and show signs of needing medical care.

WHAT TO DO

Should you encounter a child whom you believe to be abused or neglected, it is important to take action. As we discussed earlier in this book, children have rights. Children are entrusted to the care of their parents, but they are not their parents' property. Children are helpless in the face of abuse and neglect. If their parents will not protect them, who will? People who discover or suspect abuse or neglect are morally obligated to report it to appropriate social welfare agencies. In many states, it is illegal not to report abuse or neglect.

Every community is served by a regional or county department of public welfare. A concerned citizen has the right and the obligation to call this agency should child neglect or abuse be suspected.

Should neglect or abuse be found, children are sometimes removed from the custody of their parents. Sometimes parents are legally prosecuted. Generally, however, the family receives counseling, parent training, babysitting services, and economic assistance to help the parents learn to provide better care for their children. It is clear, then, that those who report child abuse or neglect help the family as well as the children.

The last punishment method we discuss involves the use of pain to eliminate misbehavior. It is commonly called spanking. Spanking may be necessary in extreme situations where a young child is behaving in ways which may cause serious injury to self or others, and when other methods are not likely to work fast enough. However, spanking is a method which can have especially damaging results unless parents exercise very good judgment and skill.

Reprimands

A *reprimand* is a brief scolding showing clear disapproval. Parents and other care givers have always used reprimands. At first glance, reprimands may appear identical to the nonpunishment method of reasoning. However, reasoning does not involve the show of disapproval which is important to giving a reprimand.

Properly used, reprimands can be effective with many children. But reprimands can easily be misused with poor results. To use reprimands well, it is important to be very specific. This can be done by including three parts to any reprimand. The three parts of a reprimand are as follows.

1. Label the behavior that is unacceptable. Be sure to use very specific language.
2. Tell why the behavior is not acceptable.
3. Tell what the replacement behavior should be.

The following examples of reprimands contain all of these three parts.

Figure 13-4. *Every child has a right to a safe and loving environment. The lack of security may harm a child's ability to grow and develop properly. (© Mark Antman/The Image Works, Inc.)*

PUNISHMENT METHODS

The following five methods have all been tested carefully and found to be effective in eliminating inappropriate behaviors. The first four methods are the reprimand, response cost, overcorrection, and timeout. Any time that punishment is used, it can be misused, and therefore has the risks described earlier. However, the reprimand, response cost, overcorrection, and timeout are reasonably low-risk methods.

- Do not hit other children.
  That hurts others.
  Ask your friend for the toy.

- Do not run across the street.
  A car may be coming and you may be hurt.
  Stop at the street curb and hold my hand
  while we cross.

- Do not throw a ball in the house.
  Something might be broken.
  Go outside to throw a ball.

Rules to Follow When Giving Reprimands

There are several important rules to follow
in giving a reprimand. First, use a firm tone
of voice. It is necessary to show displeasure
at the misbehavior (not at the child), so use
a voice which is deeper and louder than
usual. During a reprimand, use strong emphasis on key words. But do not scream or
shout, since these actions normally interfere
with communication.

A second rule in using a reprimand is that
facial expressions should show displeasure.
This can be done by looking serious and star-
ing directly into the child's eyes.

Third, get the child's attention and make
physical contact during the reprimand. Calling across a room lacks effectiveness. Move
directly to the child, get down to the child's
eye level, and grasp the child's arms or
shoulders firmly during the reprimand.
Note: It is important not to shake or squeeze
the child. These actions can cause pain and
injury.

A fourth rule to follow in giving a reprimand is do not lecture. Parents who lose control may say too much. Provide only the brief
three-part reprimand. Too many words may

actually reinforce the inappropriate behavior, because children often misbehave for
attention.

Fifth, be consistent. When a behavior is
selected for reprimands, each occurence must
be reprimanded. Otherwise, the behavior
may actually increase in frequency.

The sixth rule is to physically stop dangerous behavior, and then reprimand. Sometimes misbehavior can lead to danger. In
such a case, especially with very young children, it is best to interrupt the behavior chain
as it begins to unfold. Examples of behaviors
to stop immediately are reaching for a hot
stove or pulling the arm back to throw something in the home.

Finally, back up the reprimands with
other punishment procedures when needed.
Sometimes reprimands alone will not reduce
undesirable behavior. When this happens,
it is important to first give the reprimand
and then provide another punishing consequence.

Common Errors in Using Reprimands

It is important to avoid making mistakes
when using reprimands. The following are
some of the common errors to avoid.

1. Becoming too negative, angry, or upset
during the reprimand. This can function to
reinforce some children's misbehavior.
2. Using too many words during the reprimand. Briefly label what behavior is unacceptable, tell why it is not acceptable, and
tell what the replacement behavior should
be. Too much talking may reinforce the
misbehavior.
3. Failing to show disapproval during the
reprimand. The reprimand should be de-

Figure 13-5. *There are six rules to follow when giving a reprimand. Which of those rules can you see in this picture? (H. Armstrong Roberts)*

livered firmly with a good measure of stern disapproval for the inappropriate behavior.
4. Failing to reinforce opposing or competing behavior. It is very easy for a parent to fall into the trap of reprimanding for inappropriate behavior, but not reinforcing appropriate behavior. This ineffective and damaging situation occurs when parents fall into the punishment trap which we discussed in Chapter 12.

5. Failing to measure the problem. Parents often do not know whether misbehavior is decreased as the result of reprimands. Parents must know the effect they are having on misbehavior in order to be successful.
6. Failing to back up the reprimand. If reprimands alone are not working, it is important to provide a reprimand followed by one of the other punishment methods described earlier in this chapter.

Response Cost

Response cost is a method in which a certain amount of reinforcers are lost following a behavior, and that behavior decreases in future frequency. Adult examples of response cost are fines for speeding or returning a library book late. Another example is being made to pay for items which you have broken in a store.

Response cost can be an effective, but mild, form of punishment with children. For example, if a child mistreats some reinforcing object (crayons, scissors, toys, books), the object can be immediately removed, or lost from use.

In one study, the problem was that children left their belongings lying around the house. When the children left an item where it was not supposed to be, the parents picked it up and placed it into a "Saturday box." This meant that the children lost the use of that item until Saturday. Many of the losses were important to the children, and they soon learned to look after their belongings. Since losing something not properly cared for is a common occurrence in life, this approach was an especially useful learning experience. Of course, it is important that children have special places to put their belongings.

Another case illustrates a related method called *bonus response cost*. In this method, a child is given a certain amount of tokens—points, extra minutes of some favorite activity, or money. It is explained to the child the tokens are available when the child works to reduce a problem behavior. It is also explained that every time the behavior occurs, a certain amount of tokens will be removed. This adds a positive element to the punishment procedure—new, delayed reinforcers

are available for trying to control a problem behavior. Of course, the misbehavior is immediately followed by a fine, or loss of some tokens.

One mother had tried everything to stop her six-year-old daughter from sucking her thumb. Earlier, it would probably have been best to relabel the thumbsucking as relatively harmless and ignore it. But over the years, the parents had thoroughly reinforced thumbsucking by giving a lot of attention to their daughter when she sucked her thumb. As a result, the little girl now sucked her thumb whenever she was not busy with her hands.

The mother decided to use bonus response cost. She put 25 pennies in a jar with the girl's name on it, and told her that she could keep the pennies that remained at bedtime. She also explained that whenever she saw the girl suck her thumb, she would remove a penny from the jar. The reinforcing power of the pennies was kept strong by frequent trips to the store, and praise for how well the girl was doing and how well she was earning pennies.

When thumbsucking occurred, the girl's parents did not act upset, as they had before. They simply called the girl's name and quietly let her observe them taking a penny from her jar. The girl was observed to fold her arms and sometimes sit on her hands during the first few days. These forms of self-control were not needed later when the thumbsucking habit was much weaker.

Another form of punishment can also be called response cost. It involves the loss of a specific privilege when a misbehavior occurs. Parents have long used—and misused—this method. To work well, the privilege must be taken away right after a misbehavior.

This is particularly true with young children. A loss of privilege should be experienced as soon after the misbehavior as possible. It is not very helpful to deny a trip to the movies on Friday afternoon for a misbehavior that occurred on Tuesday. It is also important to match the seriousness of the loss with the misbehavior. The loss of 30 minutes of television or an hour of riding a bicycle may be appropriate. However, such losses which span several days or a week usually cause problems and usually are not effective.

Common Errors in Using Response Cost

The following are some of the common errors to avoid when using response cost and related methods.

1. Failing to measure the problem. Without measuring the behavior, it will be difficult to know if the procedure is helping, hurting, or doing nothing. Also, the way to predict a child's loss due to fines is to measure the frequency of the misbehavior before the response cost.

2. Fining children until they owe parents. When tokens are lost, there is a danger that all tokens available can be lost. Many parents then begin negative counts—that is, ''You have minus 23 pennies.'' If this happens, the response-cost method is failing. The method should be readjusted or stopped. Bonus response cost helps to avoid the negative-fining problem, because only a specified amount of reinforcers are at risk.

3. Failing to reinforce opposing or competing behavior. Never use punishment without giving much reinforcement at later times for replacement behaviors. The parents using the ''Saturday box'' should have heavily praised the children when they were observed placing their belongings in appropriate spots. The mother using bonus response cost should have heavily praised her child for keeping her hands busy doing things other than thumbsucking.

4. Failing to provide fines immediately and every time the misbehavior occurs. Any delay in fines or failure to fine each time the misbehavior occurs may cause the method to fail.

Correction and Overcorrection

Correction is a reasonable and logical way to help children avoid repeating mistakes and to do many things properly. When children occasionally have accidents or forget to do things in proper ways, having them correct themselves is a good approach. The effort involved in cleaning up a spill, sweeping up dirt tracked into the house, or going back to shut a slammed door more quietly is a fairly mild consequence and can be effective.

Overcorrection is recommended when simple correction is not effective. *Overcorrection* means that more than one correction occurs following inappropriate behavior. The inappropriate behavior is actually overcorrected. For example, in correction a child would be asked to shut a door one time. In overcorrection, the child might be told to shut the door ten times.

One form of overcorrection is called *restitution*. Restitution overcorrection is good for times when a behavior produces a mess of some sort, such as a spill. In restitution overcorrection, more than just the spill being wiped up is required. The child may be asked

Figure 13-6. Restitution overcorrection. By being required to repair damage in the vegetable garden, these children are learning that the garden is not the place to play. (USDA Photo by Fred S. Witte)

to also wipe up the portion of the floor where small spatters fell.

Overcorrection can be used when occasional problem behavior is thought to be purposeful rather than accidental. Overcorrection can also be used when a misbehavior happens very often whether it is thought to be purposeful or not. For example, overcorrection could be used for a child who has trouble sitting still at the dinner table and thus "accidentally" spills things very often.

In situations where incorrect behavior does not leave a mess, *positive practice overcorrection* can be used. This method is useful for behaviors like excessive running in the house, jumping on the furniture, and slamming doors. When the incorrect behavior

occurs, the parent requires the child to practice the proper action several times. For example, a child who runs through the living room is told to go back and walk through the living room five times.

Common Errors in Using Correction and Overcorrection

The following errors are commonly made in the use of correction and overcorrection methods. These errors should be avoided.

1. Failing to measure the behavior problem. Measurement helps parents to know if these mild punishment methods are working.
2. Failing to reinforce opposing or competing behavior. Never use punishment without giving great amounts of reinforcement for appropriate behaviors.
3. Failing to use correction or overcorrection immediately and consistently for every occurrence of the misbehavior. Any delays between the misbehavior and the correction or overcorrection procedure, or any inconsistency, will decrease the effectiveness of the approach.
4. Failing to be firm and insist upon following instructions. Parents may need to physically help their child to follow instructions. The child who refuses to clean up a spilled glass of milk can be helped to wipe it up. However, it is important to remove the assistance as soon as possible.
5. Mixing positive reinforcement into the correction or overcorrection procedure. There should be no positive reinforcement involved in overcorrection. Parents should give the instructions and quietly see that they are carried out. Too much attention can be very

reinforcing to a child, so the instructions should be clear but not excessive. Any reinforcers could simply encourage the child to repeat the misbehavior in order to receive more attention.

Timeout

Timeout is the removal of someone from opportunities to obtain reinforcement for a period of time. In simpler terms, a child should be sent to a room to be alone for a short time. It is important that the room not contain things that the child will find reinforcing.

When timeout immediately and consistently follows an inappropriate behavior, its effects are normally very powerful. The future frequency of misbehavior is often reduced quickly. However, the timeout method is too strong for small behavior problems. Also, this method is generally not recommended for children younger than three years.

Timeout is appropriate for frequent misbehaviors such as tantrums, hurting others, mistreating pets, refusal to follow instructions, or other dangerous activities. Timeout may also be used for uncontrolled activities such as excessive running, jumping, falling, or shoving when other less severe methods have been skillfully tried with no success.

Timeout sounds simple to use, but it is actually quite complicated. It is an easy method to misuse. Using timeout properly requires good judgment and self-discipline on the part of parents.

Suppose that a parent is very concerned about how often his four-year-old is too aggressive with her brothers and other playmates. He has talked to his daughter about how others feel when they are hurt. He has also praised her frequently for playing nicely with others. However, these methods have not helped. The father is worried that the child will have social and school problems in the future if her excessive aggressiveness is not handled properly. We now examine how the guidelines for using timeout can be applied to this situation.

Guidelines for Using Timeout

The following guidelines for using timeout can be applied to the situation of the aggressive four-year-old.

Step #1: Aggression Is Defined. "The child hurts others by hitting, kicking, and scratching."

Step #2: Hitting, Kicking, and Scratching Are Measured. The father counts how often the aggressions occur. During this time, he continues to stop the aggression when it occurs, and he explains to his child why it is wrong. Measurement over a three-day period shows 7 aggressions during the first day, 15 aggressions the second day, and 9 aggressions the third day.

Step #3: The Proper Timeout Room Is Chosen. The room is a spare bedroom which does not contain anything enjoyable (reinforcing) or dangerous (such as poisons or sharp objects).

Step #4: The Duration of Timeout Is Chosen. The parent knows that timeout can be very effective over a duration of as little as 2 minutes for young children. For older children,

15 minutes is normally effective. The father chose 4 minutes for the timeout interval. He knew that 4 minutes can seem like a long time to a four-year-old. Generally, timeout periods of one minute per year of age of the child work well.

Step #5: A "Quiet Requirement" of One Minute Is Chosen. This means that during the last (fourth) minute, the child will have to be quiet, or she will have to remain in timeout until she has been quiet for one full minute. Even if timeout is set for 4 minutes, a child may cry or tantrum for 30 minutes. In this case, timeout would not end until after the 31st minute (the 31st minute fills the quiet requirement). The quiet requirement normally teaches children to sit quietly for timeout rather than crying or tantrumming for long periods. This quiet requirement is essential to ensure that possible crying or tantrumming is not reinforced by letting the child out of timeout.

Step #6: The Program Is Explained to the Child. The father tells his daughter what a good girl she is and how much he loves her. He then explains that there is one thing he must help her with. He explains clearly that she sometimes hurts people by hitting, kicking, and scratching, even though he has asked her not to do so. He then tells her that if she hits, kicks, or scratches others, she will have to go to a room and sit alone until she is told to come out. The father says no more at this point.

Step #7: Timeout Is Immediately and Consistently Used Whenever Aggression Occurs. The parent also works hard to reinforce opposing behavior such as sharing, smiling, saying kind things, and helping playmates. When the misbehavior occurs, the father says, "If you hurt people, you can't stay with us." He then takes her firmly by the arm and guides her to the timeout room. After the timeout period, he goes to the door and opens it, saying, "You can come out now if you like." He immediately leaves without saying more. Twenty minutes later, the child is playing well. The father hugs her and tells her how proud he is to see her playing without hurting others.

Common Errors in Using Timeout

The following are some of the errors to avoid when using timeout.

1. Failing to define and measure the problem behavior.

2. Failing to use timeout consistently and immediately following the behavior.

3. Selecting a poor timeout setting. The child should be left alone in a room that does not provide any reinforcers such as a radio, books, or toys.

4. Too much communication during the timeout method. Past the initial explanation, the only words used during timeout should be the labeling of the misbehavior and the permission to leave the timeout room. Extra words only risk the reinforcement of behavior that is supposed to be punished. Parents should not give in and provide lectures, warnings, or speak to the child when in the timeout room.

5. Failing to choose appropriate timeout intervals. A general rule of thumb is one minute of timeout per year of age. Timeout intervals should not exceed 15 minutes unless a child chooses a longer interval by misbehaving in timeout. The one-minute quiet requirement should also be strictly enforced before the child can leave the room. An alarm or timer should be set so that the child is not left in timeout for too long.

6. Failing to enforce the timeout procedure. Some parents give up this procedure because their strong-willed child refuses to cooperate. Some children will simply open the door and walk out of the timeout room. If strong-willed and oppositional children are successful in refusing timeout, they quickly learn that they, not their parents, control the household.

Children who refuse to stay in timeout can be taught to follow instructions by being fined (response cost) if they open the door, or by being placed back into timeout with the timer started over at zero and another minute added to the timeout interval. Another method is to combine a spanking with one or both of these suggestions. Some parents have considered placing outside locks on timeout rooms. This might frighten young children. It would be more appropriate to teach cildren to follow the simple instruction to stay in the timeout room.

7. Some people mistakenly feel that a properly conducted timeout method is cruel. Actually, the opposite is often true. Sometimes it is cruel *not to use* humane and effective timeout methods with children. Extreme and uncontrolled misbehavior can often seriously limit a child's chances for success and happiness. Most parents and teachers do not think it cruel to have children spend short times alone in order to weaken or eliminate serious misbehavior.

Spanking

Spanking is the most dangerous form of punishment. Spanking involves the use of pain to eliminate misbehavior. When misused, spanking will most rapidly produce those damaging side effects discussed at the beginning of this chapter. It is also true that the person who spanks can lose self-control and spank too hard or in areas of a child's body that are damaged easily.

NOTE: Spanking should never be considered lightly. Remember that one who spanks is inflicting physical pain on a child in an effort to influence the child's behavior. Under normal circumstances, there are very few child behavior problems which require this form of punishment. Many other methods can be used with effectiveness and much less risk.

The very few circumstances which might require spanking are those in which a young child repeatedly does something which could cause death or severe injury to the child or others. Such misbehavior must be stopped immediately to prevent great risk to the child or others. Spanking might also be considered after all other methods have failed to reduce extremely damaging behavior.

Examples of dangerous behaviors might be running into the street, excessive climbing, pounding on glass windows, playing with electrical outlets, or wandering to a cliff or riverbank during a picnic. If spanking is considered only for such infrequent circumstances, dangerous behavior can be weakened very rapidly.

To achieve such effectiveness without unnecessary risk to the child requires that spanking be administered in a very skillful and controlled way. **NOTE:** In our view, spanking should not be used with children younger than two years.

The Spanking Procedure

As you read over the following guidelines for spanking, remember that there are very few misbehaviors that require spanking.

1. Explain to the child why he or she must not do the particular behavior again. Tell the child that from now on the behavior will produce an immediate spanking.

2. The moment the misbehavior occurs, state firmly, ''When you do this (name the behavior), you will be spanked.'' Say no more. Then immediately provide the spanking.

- Spank immediately.
- The child should be held across the parent's knee, and spanked upon the high back of the thighs. This location is not likely to cause injuries.
- Spank only with one bare and open hand. Two or three slaps should be given with enough force to produce crying and stinging. This should only take several seconds. **NOTE:** Never spank harder than what will produce an unpleasant stinging sensation. Never use any tools such as a belt or cane.

3. When the spanking is finished, the child should be placed in timeout for an appropriate interval of time. Do not give any reinforcers such as more talk or apologetic hugs. If an ideal timeout location is not available, choose the best possibility. Withhold all attention, and be sure to include a one-minute quiet requirement. The timeout procedure is combined with the spanking to prevent the accidental mixture of reinforcers

with punishment. Also, timeout contributes its own power to reduce the behavior.

4. Later, always heavily reinforce appropriate behaviors which oppose the behavior that is punished.

Common Errors in Using Spanking

Several errors are common with the spanking procedure. These errors are likely to lead to an increase in the frequency of a misbehavior. They are also likely to lead to dangerous overuse of spanking.

1. As with other methods, the behavior to be punished should be clearly defined. Measures should be taken to monitor the effectiveness of the treatment.

2. Failing to spank immediately following each instance of the misbehavior. This inconsistency is likely to strengthen the problem behavior.

3. Failing to produce a stinging sensation. This is necessary because if spanking is not painful, many children may grow accustomed to the mild discomfort. Parents then attempt to spank a little harder. This cycle might continue and become dangerous to the child, as described earlier.

4. Spanking with objects other than the open bare hand. The open bare hand lets parents know how hard the spanking is, since they will feel stinging too. **NOTE:** A paddle, belt, cane, or switch does not provide such signals to the person who is spanking. This increases the possibility of using too much force. These objects can cause extreme pain and injury to the child, which is child abuse.

5. Failing to spank on a safe but sensitive part of the body. The high back of the thighs is a thickly muscled area of the body, yet is sensitive to the stinging produced by spanking. The hands and arms are not sensitive. The back is unprotected and too sensitive. The face, head, chest, and stomach are all very dangerous places to strike anyone. This should never be done to a child.

CASE STUDY

In this situation, a parent uses spanking to control the life-threatening behavior of running into the street.

It was a warm spring day. As the mother raked the lawn, her three-year-old wandered about the front yard. When the child moved toward the street, the mother stopped him and forcefully told him not to step over the curb and go into the street. She showed him the curb and the street and briefly explained her reasons for not going into the street. Within moments, however, the child again moved toward the street.

The second the child's foot crossed the curb, the mother loudly said, ''No! Stay out of the street!'' She told him that this was wrong and that she was going to spank him as a result. She then grasped him by the arm, knelt down, leaned the child across her knee, and spanked the back of his thighs forcefully three times with her open hand. This produced crying and obvious pain. She then placed him in an uninteresting room in the house for three minutes of timeout.

After the child had stopped crying and the timeout interval had passed, he was allowed back outside. The mother spoke to him every few minutes and praised him for staying out of the street and playing in the yard. She also explained as simply as possible the dangers of going in the street. She did this several times while the child played within the yard at a safe distance from the street.

During the next few days, the spanking had to be used twice before stepping into the street was completely eliminated. This mother had moved quickly and effectively to reduce the likelihood of tragedy. However, continued watching in such situations is always necessary, because even effectively punished behavior may happen again from time to time.

6. Accidentally mixing reinforcers with punishment. If spankings are followed by reinforcing attention, toys, or activities, the event of being spanked can become reinforcing. As a result, any behavior which produces spanking will increase dramatically. This can cause an excessive use of spankings and danger to the child as the behavior problems worsen.

7. Failing to differentially reinforce opposing or competing behavior. Whenever parents punish inappropriate behavior in any way, they must also select appropriate replacement behaviors to reinforce heavily.

SUMMARY

There is no single form of punishment that is most effective for all children and all behavior problems. Children are individuals. Parents must be sensitive to the overall effects of different discipline methods on each particular child.

It is necessary to achieve child-rearing goals through methods based mainly on reinforcement, not punishment. When mild punishment is required—and this shouldn't be often—parents should strive to punish effectively and in ways which do not damage their loving relationships with their children.

QUESTIONS FOR GROWTH

1. Define *punishment* and diagram its three parts.

2. Explain a most common mistake in thinking about what punishment is.

3. List three natural examples of punishment in peoples' lives.

4. Describe four dangers of using excessive punishment with children.

5. Tell how a parent can judge if punishment may be necessary to reduce certain misbehaviors.

6. Explain six general rules for using punishment methods correctly.

7. (a) Define *reprimand*. **(b)** Explain the three essential parts of a reprimand and provide one original example of a reprimand. **(c)** List and explain six common mistakes that parents make when giving reprimands.

8. (a) Define *response cost*. **(b)** Describe an original example of response cost with adults and one with children. **(c)** Explain bonus response cost. **(d)** List and explain four common errors that parents make when using response cost.

9. (a) Explain the correction procedure. **(b)** Explain the overcorrection procedure. **(c)** Provide one example each of how restitution and positive practice can be used with children. **(d)** List and explain five common errors that parents make in using overcorrection.

10. (a) Define *timeout*. **(b)** Tell when a parent might consider using timeout and for what kinds of behaviors. **(c)** Name and describe the seven steps which parents must take to use timeout effectively.

11. (a) Why is it said that spanking is the most dangerous form of punishment? **(b)** Tell when it may be appropriate for a parent to spank a child. **(c)** Describe the guidelines for parents to follow in order to spank effectively and safely. **(d)** Name and explain seven common errors in spanking.

PART

D

PRINCIPLES OF PARENTING

Part D consists of three chapters which will help you to better understand yourself as well as children. We focus upon goals and objectives in parenting; it is appropriate for parents and other care givers to think about the ways in which they wish to guide and influence children. We describe simple and informative ways to observe children. There is much about children that can be learned only through the close and intelligent observation of a child's behavior. We address an important parenting skill: self-control. Effective parenting often requires self-control to develop new good habits and to break poor ones.

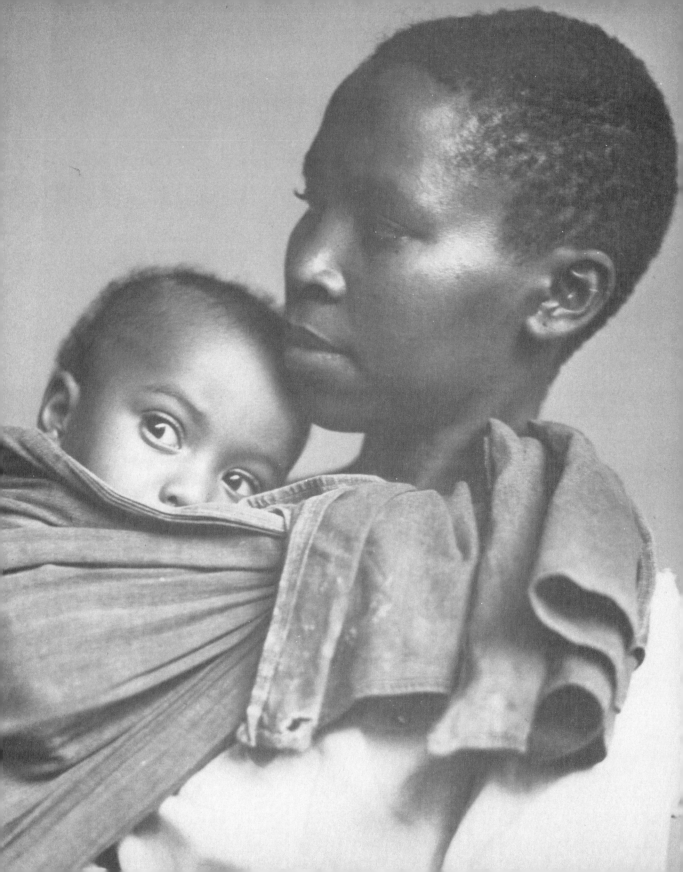

CHAPTER

14

Parenting Goals and Objectives

Child development is not a one-way process in which parents teach and children sit quietly and learn. Children learn actively on their own. They explore, play, and they break and make all sorts of things. Children's active involvement in learning can also be observed when they have learned to talk well enough to ask questions.

Still, parents have a major influence upon their children's development and learning. They influence through the many ways that they stimulate, teach, and guide their children. Of course, love and commitment are very important qualities in parenting. Combining these qualities with a good understanding of the ways to help children learn is another important step toward good parenting. Yet something might be missing. Though the love and commitment are present and the tools (learning principles) are available, the parents may have no plans for action. What general developments should they try to strengthen? How exactly will they achieve this?

Parents certainly want to help their children develop valuable skills and abilities. Parents should begin to think about which skills and abilities they would like to strengthen. This can be done by moving through three stages of thinking. Viewing behavior in this way is similar to using a microscope which has three settings, each setting with a different level of power.

On the first and least powerful setting, you can see only a general outline of what you are inspecting. Your view is far from clear. When you change to the second setting, you are rewarded by greater detail and clarity. The third and final setting is the most powerful. Now you can see and appreciate all of the details of the object under study.

When thinking about behaviors to teach, parents can use three similar levels of power and clarity. The first level or "setting" is called a *general goal*. Like the first setting of the microscope, general goals are simply general outlines or ideas. General goals specify behaviors to teach in very general or fuzzy ways. For example, a general goal would be to help a child become an honest person. General goals are a good first step, but they do not clearly identify which things to teach.

Behavioral goals represent a second level of clarity and power. To identify behavioral goals only requires that general goals be broken down into specific behaviors. What if the general goal is to help a child become an honest person? To achieve this will require that the parents teach the child to tell the truth, to keep his or her word, and to return lost property to rightful owners. Such behavioral goals thus identify specific behaviors for parents to teach to reach the general goal.

A *behavioral objective* is similar to the last, most powerful setting on a microscope. Behavioral objectives are very clear and specific.

Figure 14-1. From the moment of birth, parents have dreams for their children. Setting general goals can help the dreams come true. (Photo by Bob Ohr for The Christ Hospital)

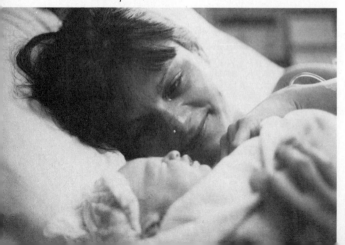

They state a) when or where the behavior (behavioral objective) should happen, b) how the behavior should be performed, and c) how to tell when the behavior is learned.

In the following material, we discuss these three levels of goals and objectives in greater detail.

GENERAL CHILD-REARING GOALS

We asked several hundred college students to write papers about their goals and objectives for parenting. Nearly all of the students enjoyed the exercise and thought that it was interesting and worthwhile. Even though many of the students were parents, the majority had never given much thought to parenting goals and objectives. They found that it was easiest to identify general parenting goals.

Parents should identify the general goals or ideas about what skills and abilities they would like to help their children develop. Individuals usually identify such goals based upon what they think must be learned in order to have a successful and rewarding life. The following are reasonable general parenting goals that have been identified by many people.

I hope my child will learn to—
   Be happy and cheerful.
   Be loving and affectionate.
   Communicate well with others.
   Be considerate of others' feelings.
   Avoid bad habits.
   Be an honest person.
   Be responsible.
   Develop good values and morals.

Take good care of his or her health and hygiene.

Respect the rights of others.

Know and stand up for his or her rights.

Be creative.

Appreciate nature and wildlife.

Develop a love and enjoyment of learning.

Control and show emotions appropriately.

Become good at making decisions and solving problems.

Do well in school and work.

Do well in athletics and other physical activities.

Can you think of other valuable general goals? Making your own list of general child-rearing goals is valuable because it stimulates thought about how you might help a child to develop in desirable directions. Such a list is only a beginning. A weakness of general goals is that they do not clearly and specifically identify which behaviors to teach. To be more specific about which behaviors to teach, parents will find it helpful to translate general goals into the more specific behavioral goals. Once general goals have been translated into behavioral goals, parents can easily see how they can help their children develop.

BEHAVIORAL GOALS

Identifying behavioral goals is not difficult. It is just a matter of practicing clear thinking. Translating general goals into specific behavioral goals involves a simple two-step process. First, identify the general goal which

Figure 14-2. People want their children to grow up to be capable and loving. Behavioral goals help in reaching these general goals.

is to be met. Second, identify the many specific behaviors that a child must learn in order to reach the general goal. The resulting list will contain the behavioral goals.

Example #1

First, state the general goal: I hope my child will learn to appreciate nature and wildlife. Next, state the behavioral goals: I will help my child learn to appreciate nature and wildlife by assisting in the following ways.

• Together, we will look at pictures and read books to learn where animals live and how they behave.
• We will go to woods and ponds to identify and watch animals.
• We will learn together about how plants and trees grow.
• We will grow, water, and care for some plants and flowers in our home.
• We will learn the names of common animals.

There are many more things that children can learn to develop an appreciation of nature and wildlife. The above list identifies just a few of many specific behavioral goals that will help to meet the general goal.

Example #2

State the general goal: I hope my child will be polite and considerate of other people's feelings. Next, state the behavioral goals: I will help my child to show politeness and consideration in the following ways.

• I will teach my child to share toys and treats with others.
• I will teach my child how to help others.
• I will explain how to say "I'm sorry" if others are hurt by my child's actions.
• I will help my child learn to take turns.
• I will teach my child when to say "please" and "thank you."
• I will help my child learn how other people feel when they are treated badly.

BEHAVIORAL OBJECTIVES

When specific behavioral goals are named, as in the previous examples, it is easier to think of specific ways to begin strengthening important skills and feelings. However, skilled parents often take their plans one step further. This next step involves setting behavioral objectives. Behavioral objectives help parents to think even more clearly about what to strengthen, when to strengthen it, and how to know if they are being successful.

Behavioral objectives include three important parts:

1. When, or under what conditions, the behavior should be performed
2. How the behavior should be performed
3. How to tell when the behavior is learned

To illustrate the clear thinking which occurs when a parenting progresses from general goals to behavioral goals and finally to behavioral objectives, think again of the two previous examples of setting behavioral goals.

Example #1

The first example had to do with teaching an appreciation for nature and wildlife. We now explain how to apply behavioral objectives to just one of the behavioral goals: teaching the names of common animals.

1. **The general goal:** I hope my child will learn to appreciate nature and wildlife.
2. **A behavioral goal:** I will help to teach an appreciation for nature and wildlife by assisting my child to learn the names of common animals.
3. **The behavioral objective:**
   • When to do it: When we are outdoors, looking out of a window, or looking at picture books.

Figure 14-3. This father is helping his child to develop an appreciation for animals. (National Easter Seal Society, Inc.)

• How to do it: The child will point to, name, or comment on the animals we observe. We will talk about the animals.
• How to tell when the behavior is learned: The child shows curiosity about animals and wants to discuss them, without being coaxed.

Example #2

The second example had to do with learning to be polite and considerate of other people's feelings. We will now apply specific behavioral objectives to this behavioral goal: teaching the child to share toys and treats with others.

1. The general goal is for the child to show politeness and consideration of others' feelings.
2. The behavioral goal is to teach the child to share toys and treats with others.
3. The behavioral objective is as follows:
• When to do it: When my child is with a friend and I give my child some treats.
• How to do it: The child will pleasantly ask the friend if she or he wants some treats, and then hand some to the friend.
• How to tell when the behavior is learned: My child frequently offers to share treats with friends without being reminded.

POSSIBLE CRITICISMS OF HAVING PARENTING GOALS AND OBJECTIVES

The following is a list of possible criticisms of having goals and objectives in parenting. These criticisms are aimed at common mistakes in parenting. It is good to think about such mistakes and consider how to avoid them.

1. ''Parents can overcontrol their children.'' By overcontrolling children, parents may take away their freedom to grow up and be individuals. It is true that unreasonable or excessive goals and objectives in parenting can be harmful. It is also harmful to have a total lack of parenting goals and objectives.

Overcontrolled children sometimes rebel through misbehavior. Other overcontrolled children have been taught to hold their anger and frustration inside them. This may result in becoming anxious and developing various physical problems such as headaches, tiredness, or stomach pains. Children may also

© Ron Meyer/White Eyes Design

USDA Photo by George Robinson

WORLD BANK PHOTO by Ray Whitlin

Figure 14-4. What goals are being taught through these activities?

become very dependent upon parents and be fearful of becoming independent. In these situations, parents have omitted the important goal of helping their children to become independent.

On the other hand, many parents have had too few consistent goals and objectives. Their children often have not been helped to learn the necessary social, self-control, and self-help skills needed to make and keep friends. They often have not learned to take responsibility for their own health and cleanliness,

and for the quality of their work in school. Such children fail to acquire skills and abilities needed to make wise personal choices in their lives. The parents of such children have not been responsible enough in setting parental goals and objectives. As a result, their children are undercontrolled and need more direction.

Reasonable parenting goals and objectives are important in helping children to grow towards responsible independence. Parents should not be excessive in the goals and

Figure 14-5. *It is not cold or unfeeling to set goals for a child, such as for independence, self-reliance, and social skills. Rather, setting goals increases a child's chances for success throughout life.*

objectives they set. Nor should they fail to set enough goals and objectives.

2. "Setting goals and objectives in parenting makes the approach sound cold, mechanical, and unloving." Love is a critically important part of parenting. Some people are much better at showing or giving love than others. However, having goals and objectives does not make parents unloving. Rather, parents who are both loving and warm and who have thought carefully about their goals and objectives simply increase their chances for success.

3. "Parents who set goals and objectives may push their children to grow up too fast." Anyone who is not familiar with child development can easily set unreasonable goals and objectives. However, the setting of goals and objectives, in itself, does not mean children will be pushed too hard. By learning about normal child development, parents can set reasonable goals and objectives. It is also important for parents to know that children sometimes develop at widely different rates, but are still developing normally. Therefore, parents should always be flexible with their goals and objectives.

4. "How can parents know what goals and objectives to select?" Some people criticize that it is not possible to know all of the important goals and objectives for parenting. However, it is not hard to identify many reasonable goals and objectives. Parents often get ideas for goals from what they believe children need to learn in order to be successful and well adjusted. Useful information about goals and objectives may also come from formally studying child development as well as countless personal experiences.

SUMMARY

In later chapters of this book, we discuss further how to achieve many behavioral goals and objectives with children. You will, therefore, have more opportunities to practice thinking about goals and objectives. As you have seen, the process of establishing parenting goals and objectives is not really hard or mysterious. Yet the process provides parents with many benefits.

QUESTIONS FOR GROWTH

1. Why is it important for parents to have general goals in child rearing?

2. List four general goals in parenting that you think are valuable.

3. Explain what a behavioral goal is and how it is different from a general goal.

4. Provide four examples of behavioral goals in parenting that you think are valuable.

5. Explain the three parts of a behavioral objective.

6. Select two behavioral goals that parents may wish to teach, and state them in three parts as behavioral objectives.

7. (a) Provide several criticisms that some may express about having goals and objectives in parenting. **(b)** Explain when these criticisms may be reasonable and when they may be unreasonable.

CHAPTER

15

Observing Children

What you read about in this book will come alive when you observe children. You can watch the infant play in a bath, see how well the three-month-old can control her hands, and watch the one-year-old stand and take faltering steps. You can hear and see the frustration of the two-year-old who cannot have his way, and listen to the three-year-old struggle to express herself. You can see and understand the child in a preschool classroom who is shy and afraid to join the other children. It is a joy to watch children growing. We can also learn a great deal by observing children.

By observing, we can see, feel, hear, and understand the similarities and differences among children that words alone cannot fully communicate. People who observe children nearly always grow in their ability to appreciate them. Many people think that watching children is the most pleasurable way to learn

about them. In fact, the good observer learns much that cannot be learned in any other way.

One student watched his 19-month-old nephew, Jimmy, play ball with his family in their front yard for 10 minutes. The student wrote down a record of what he observed. By taking the time to make the observations, the student gained a deep understanding of what is meant by the phrases ''age of discovery'' and ''seeing the world through a child's eyes.'' Jimmy excitedly explored the outdoors and was often surprised by what he found.

There are other reasons to observe children. Parents, teachers, and other professionals often observe children in order to learn specific things about them. Observations must be made in order to identify a certain child's level of development in any area (language, self-help, etc.). Direct observation

CASE STUDY

One student enjoyed watching his nephew, Jimmy, as Jimmy played in his yard. This is a record of what the student observed.

Jimmy is watching the others intently. He squats down and jumps a half inch in the air and nearly loses his balance. He recovers his balance and laughs loudly. Now he picks up a football one third his size and staggers to his father. He tries to throw the ball, but it only drops and rolls two feet along the ground. Jimmy laughs and squeals. His twelve-year-old sister takes a large plastic ball and gently throws it to him from two feet away. Jimmy catches the ball between his straight and open arms, and everyone praises him loudly and claps. Jimmy squeals and laughs and runs away with the ball.

He stops near a big kettle planter in the yard which is empty of flowers but full of dirt. He drops the ball and puts his hand in the planter and grabs a fistful of dirt. His mother says, "No, put it down." Jimmy stops and looks at her very seriously, his eyebrows lowered, and then looks back at the kettle. He steps away and throws the dirt on the ground. At that moment, a gust of wind blows. His hair is blown back, and Jimmy raises up on his toes with surprise. He laughs and acts like the wind took his breath away for a moment.

Jimmy then walks and runs to a stone walkway in the yard. The stones are old and sunken an inch and a half into the earth. Jimmy steps down onto one stone, first with one foot and then the other. He smiles and steps back up onto the lawn. Jimmy points at the stone and says something I cannot hear. He then steps down onto the stone and, with both feet together, bounces up and down several times. Jimmy then moves to a football, picks it up, cradles it in his arms, and runs 15 feet across the yard to the cement driveway. As he runs, he is suddenly startled and falls away from what has frightened him. Jimmy lays on the driveway with a frightened look on his face. Jimmy's father picks him up and says, "That's a water puddle." The father splashes his foot in the very shallow puddle. Jimmy imitates him and they both laugh loudly.

is also the best way to know what and how to teach a particular child. When starting to help a child develop, parents want to know how well they are doing. To do this requires that the child be carefully observed.

Many children show problem behaviors such as aggression, destructiveness, or hyperactivity. Observing these behaviors is the first step in deciding how serious they are and how best to help the children. In this chapter, we discuss how to make general observations, a timed running description, and a sequence analysis. We also describe ways to measure and graph the behaviors which are observed.

MAKING OBSERVATIONS

It is best to make and keep written records of observations of children. Written records are valuable for several reasons. First, it is very hard to remember all of the details that can happen during an observation session. Sometimes small, easily forgotten details can be very important. A second reason to keep written records is that it is possible to review the records as often as is needed. New things are often discovered about children by re-reading and rethinking old observations.

The Setting

When observing children, it is important to clearly describe the *setting*, the place where the behaviors occur. Judgments about children's behavior are very hard to make if the setting is unknown. For example, is it appropriate for a child of four years to run, scream, shout, throw things, and roll around? The

answer to this question depends, of course, on the setting. If the setting is a preschool classroom, the behavior is not generally appropriate. If the setting is a playground, the behavior is generally appropriate.

Is there reason for concern if, during an observation, a four-year-old sits quietly and does not talk or play with any of the other ten children in the room? Again, the answer to this question depends on the setting. If the observation was made during a 10-minute story time, there is no reason for being concerned about the behavior. Indeed, the behavior is desirable. If, however, the observation was made during a 50-minute play time, then there may be cause for concern. However, the shyness might be understandable if the observation was made during the child's first day in a new day-care center.

When identifying the setting in the written record, be sure to specify the following.

1. How old is the child? A child's age is very important when evaluating development. Much can be learned by comparing the activities of children at different ages.
2. Where is the child? State whether the child is at school, home, on the playground, in swimming class, etc. Be very specific. Sometimes it helps to diagram the setting in order to easily recall where toys, equipment, and activity areas were located.
3. What are the activities? Many activities may be occurring at once, or the child may be concentrating on only one. Some possible activities are rest time, play, listening to music, coloring, or listening to a story. Obviously, a child may be both coloring and listening to music at the same time.
4. Who is the child with? The child may be

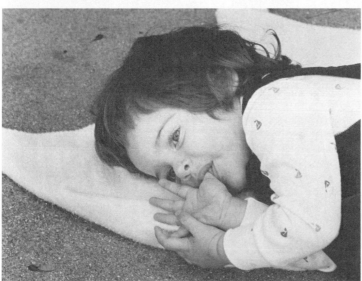

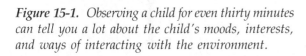

Figure 15-1. *Observing a child for even thirty minutes can tell you a lot about the child's moods, interests, and ways of interacting with the environment.*

with classmates (state how many), with one or both parents, with the teacher, babysitter, siblings, and so on.

Observing the Child

It is often helpful to structure observations so that they move from the general to the specific. First, concentrate on the whole picture—the general view. Describe everything you see that relates to the child. To do this requires that you have a watch, plenty of paper, a good pen, and time to observe. To record your observations, you might choose to write a timed running description or a sequence analysis. We describe these methods in the following material.

Children will often behave differently if they are not used to the observer's presence. Therefore, before starting serious observations, let them become adjusted to your presence. When observations are started, you may have to pleasantly but firmly tell children that you cannot talk with them until you are done. Even the most skilled observer cannot concentrate on several things at once. It is easier to make observations if you do only one thing: observe.

The Timed Running Description

The *timed running description* is a way to make initial observations. This is a good method to get a maximum of information. It is also a good way to get writer's cramp!

To do a running description, write everything that you see or hear that relates in any way to the child being observed. By using a stopwatch or clock with a sweep second-hand, it is possible to easily keep track of the passage of time by marking the approxi-mate minutes in the margins of your writing paper.

The purpose of the running description is to record as much information about the child as possible. Do not worry about penmanship, spelling, or punctuation while recording your observations. Such concerns will only interfere with the goal of recording as much information as possible. Rewrite the observation records after the observation session. In this way, you can make the records more readable and fill in any important details that might have been missed in the record.

Box 15.1 is a short example of a timed running description of a preschool child's behavior. Read and analyze the running description carefully to see what you can learn about the child.

The five-minute observation in Box 15.1 is packed with useful information. Take a moment to list some of the things that you learned from the observations. You might have observed the following.

1. Teddy changed his activities frequently. Little time was spent with any particular child or activity. Teddy changed his activities about five times within the five minutes, with less than a minute spent on any one activity.
2. Other children tended to avoid Teddy. They did not approach him, and they usually left soon after he came close.
3. Teddy knocked down blocks, threw crayons, and smashed toy cars together.
4. Teddy was frequently aggressive with other children.
5. The teacher did not talk with Teddy while he was not in trouble. But she did talk to or touch Teddy three times immediately after he had misbehaved.

BOX 15.1

A Timed Running Description

THE SETTING

Four-year-old Teddy is in a preschool class with one teacher and ten other children. It is free-play time, and the children can do as they wish. The teacher is circulating among the children as they play.

THE OBSERVATIONS

Minute One: Teddy is playing alone with a toy car. The nearest child is about five feet away. Teddy is playing roughly, smashing cars together and making crashing noises with his mouth. Teddy crawls rapidly to the other children who are playing together, and grabs one of their toys and crawls away with it. The teacher comes and talks to Teddy. She explains why it is unfair to treat friends that way. (About 30 seconds have passed so far.) Teddy smiles faintly. The teacher suggests that Teddy color something and then provides crayons and paper. (Another 30 seconds have now passed.)

Minute Two: The teacher goes to another group of playing children. Teddy takes all of the crayons from the box and begins to roll them around on a table. Another child walks by the table, and Teddy throws a crayon, hitting the other child in the back. The teacher moves to Teddy's side, kneels down, holds his arm, and talks to him about throwing crayons for about 15 seconds. Teddy smiles faintly.

Minute Three: The teacher leaves Teddy, who sits at the table and looks around the room watching what the other children are doing. Teddy continues to watch the children and the teacher as she works with them. Teddy joins another child who is playing blocks. Teddy laughs, talks loudly, and knocks down the other child's block house. The child is upset and leaves.

Minute Four: Teddy looks around the room at others playing. He is sitting on the floor. A little girl walks by and Teddy grabs at her feet. She laughs, jumps away, and moves across the room.

Minute Five: Teddy returns to the table and colors. Another child is now there coloring. Teddy watches her for a few seconds and then marks on her drawing. The child yells "No!" and the teacher intervenes. She takes Teddy aside and talks privately with him for about 20 seconds. She then has him apologize to the other child, and then the teacher leaves. She was with Teddy for a total of about 50 seconds during this minute. Teddy now stands alone and watches the other children and the teacher.

The Sequence Analysis

If a timed running description is rewritten in a different form—in a sequence analysis—other observations often become clear. A *sequence analysis* helps to see how certain consequences (reinforcement, extinction, or punishment) may be influencing a child's behavior. When observers know what they are looking for in a child, they can easily do the sequence analysis as they observe, instead of a timed running narrative.

In a sequence analysis, information about what a child does is detailed along with what happened immediately before the child's behavior and what happened right after the behavior. The child's experience is broken into the following parts, the ''ABCs'' of a sequence analysis.

A. The *antecedent* happenings (what happened before)
B. The child's *behavior* (exactly what was done)
C. The *consequence* (what happened after the behavior)

Box 15.2 is an example of how the timed running description of Teddy's behavior can be changed into a sequence analysis. Carefully read over Box 15.2. This sequence analysis may make you more aware of the following points.

• Misbehavior frequently occurred after Teddy was left alone.
• Misbehavior was closely followed by individual teacher attention and other children's reactions, which may have reinforced Teddy's negative behavior.
• Teddy spent so much time playing inappropriately that the teacher and other children had little time to interact with him while he was playing nicely.

This sequence analysis helps observers to see what misbehaviors were present, what appropriate play skills were absent, and when the teacher and children gave or did not give their attention to Teddy. Based upon these observations, you should already have ideas about how to strengthen Teddy's good play behavior and weaken some of his problem behaviors. The sequence analysis indicates that the teacher and other children provide more attention to Teddy's inappropriate play activities than to acceptable ones. This situation could be reversed in a number of ways.

HOW TO MEASURE SPECIFIC BEHAVIORS

Once general observations such as a running description and/or a sequence analysis have been made, more specific observations may be useful. These observations are so specific that they can be called measurements. Just as you may first generally determine that one object is heavier than another, you may also want to know exactly how much heavier it is. To do this with human behavior requires that the observer identify behavioral units of measure. In other words, the behavior or behaviors should be clearly identified. This is the first step in measuring behavior.

General observation showed Teddy to be a fairly aggressive child. He showed few positive ways of relating to his peers. In order to help Teddy improve his behavior, it is helpful to measure it. To actually measure his behavior, it is necessary to

BOX 15.2

A Sequence Analysis

	Antecedent	Behavior	Consequences
Minute One:	Teddy is alone playing roughly with the cars. The nearest child is five feet away.	Teddy crawls rapidly and grabs a toy from other children.	The teacher comes to Teddy and talks for about 30 seconds. He smiles faintly. She gives him crayons and paper to play with.
Minute Two:	The teacher leaves and in a few seconds another child walks by.	Teddy throws a crayon at the passing child.	The teacher comes to Teddy, holds his arm, and talks to him. He smiles faintly.
Minute Three:	The teacher leaves. Teddy watches other children and the teacher.	Teddy joins another child and knocks down the other's blocks.	The other child leaves.
Minute Four:	Teddy sits alone. In a few seconds, a girl walks near Teddy.	Teddy grabs at the girl's feet.	The little girl laughs and jumps away.
Minute Five:	A child is seated near Teddy at the coloring table.	Teddy marks the child's drawing.	The child says "No!" The teacher comes and talks to Teddy, and has him apologize.
	The teacher leaves.	Teddy stands and watches the other children and the teacher.	

clearly define aggressiveness. The behavior that is labeled as aggressive might include, in Teddy's case, hits, shoves, tripping others, throwing objects, and being destructive of property. Similar definitions could be identified for other aggressive behaviors should they seem likely to occur. Other aggressive behaviors might be pinching, scratching, biting, pulling hair, and so on.

Many times, like in the case of Teddy, it is also necessary to think clearly about the appropriate behaviors that need to be strengthened. Any good teacher will pay much attention to Teddy's appropriate behavior. Therefore, progress will eventually be identified not only as a reduction in the frequency of inappropriate behavior, but also as an increase in the frequency of appropriate play.

Teddy shows very little appropriate behavior. The parent or teacher should approach this problem by clarifying teaching goals and objectives for appropriate play. As discussed in Chapter 14, the first step is to identify a general goal. This might be to help Teddy learn to play more skillfully with other children. The next step is to specify and define each of the specific behavioral goals which represent skillful play. This exercise may proceed as follows.

Children who play skillfully with their peers:

• Share—let others have toys or crayons, etc.
• Take turns—wait for short periods of time for another child to use a toy, swing, or go down a slide.
• Help each other—cooperate to do something together for short periods of time.
• Call playmates by name.

In the following material, we describe several methods for measuring behavior. *Measurement* means that numbers are used to describe behaviors that have been observed.

The Frequency Count

Frequency counts are a very easy way to measure children's behavior. All that is required is to count the occurrence of the defined behavior. The behavior counted must have a very clear start and ending. It must also occur within roughly equal periods of time. For example, crying in a child may have a clear start and ending. But it may make little sense to count if crying lasts 3 minutes one time and 40 minutes the next. In this case, also timing the duration, or length, of crying would be helpful.

To compare frequencies among different days or observation sessions, the length of observation time and the child's surroundings should be similar. A child playing with one friend is likely to show different behaviors when playing with ten friends. Also, three aggressive behaviors in three minutes are much different from three in one hour.

Frequency counts can be used to measure many kinds of child behavior. If you wish to observe a child's vocal development, you could count the number of sounds she makes in each observation session. You might even count the number of certain types of sounds made, such as consonant or vowel sounds. To observe the development of walking, you might count the number of times a nine-month-old pulls herself to a standing position. Other child behaviors that can be easily counted include smiles, tantrums, toys picked up, blocks stacked, and so on.

Clearly, observations and frequency counts should not be limited to only problem behaviors.

Measuring Rates of Behavior

Sometimes, simple frequencies of behaviors do not tell much because the lengths of observation sessions are very different. When this happens, frequencies can be converted (changed) into rates of behavior. This can be done by dividing the total frequency by some unit of time:

$$\frac{\text{Response frequency}}{\text{Time}} = \text{Response rate}$$

For example, two-year-old Kim-Li smiled 20 times during the first 2-hour observation session:

$$\frac{20 \text{ smiles}}{2 \text{ hours}} = 10 \text{ smiles per hour}$$

One-year-old Jana took 90 steps during a 30-minute observation session:

$$\frac{90 \text{ steps}}{30 \text{ minutes}} = 3 \text{ steps per minute}$$

When frequency of behavior is converted to rates of behavior, observation sessions of different lengths can be compared.

Duration

Sometimes children do things that have clear starts and endings but that vary greatly in their *duration*—the amount of time they are

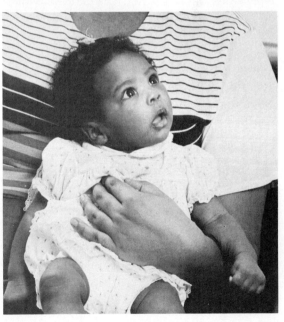

Figure 15-2. A baby's mood can change rapidly. Timing the duration of different behaviors can help parents to keep track of their children's development.

done. For example, in tantrums, how long do the tantrums last? In crying, the real question is, how long does the child cry? By using a stopwatch, the total time a child cries can be accumulated. If you try to measure crying, you will soon see the need to define crying carefully. For example, will you time a slight whimper? How long will the crying need to occur before you start the stopwatch? One mother kept track of her child's crying time. On days when the child did not have a nap, the mother observed that the child cried for longer durations. She concluded that her child was not ready to give up her noon-time nap.

Another parent, excited to see her child begin to stand up, timed the amount of time during the day that the child spent standing. It was enjoyable for her to see the development of standing in her eight-month-old child. The mother noticed that on days when some of the child's toys were placed high on tables and chairs, the child stood for longer durations of time. The parent began to purposely arrange toys to motivate her child to stand.

Percent Measures

Measures of behavior often make more sense when they are changed into percents. One father, for instance, wanted to teach his five-year-old daughter how to hit a ball with a bat. To measure progress, he counted the number of pitches and the number of hits. On the first day of practice, the child only hit 2 out of 10 pitches ($2 \div 10 = 0.20$ or 20 percent). She did not seem very interested in playing ball. On the second day, her father stood closer to her and used a larger plastic ball and a

fatter plastic bat. The child hit 15 out of 20 pitches ($15 \div 20 = 0.75$ or 75 percent). The girl became excited and wanted to play baseball with her father more often.

A mother was helping her son to do some addition problems. Each night he had a new worksheet with different amounts of problems. When his mother corrected the math papers, she found that he was only answering 50 percent correct. She decided to play a quiz game. She held up homemade flash cards and rewarded correct answers with pennies. She found that her son's homework scores increased to between 90 percent and 100 percent correct.

As the examples in this section illustrate, measuring a child's behavior can tell much about the child. Just as importantly, it can tell how effective certain teaching methods are with a particular child. Children are all different in many ways. Therefore, it is important for parents and teachers to adjust their teaching methods until they find out what works for each child.

MAKING A GRAPH

Once you have begun to measure a child's behavior, it is enjoyable and informative to have a picture of the measurements. This can be done by making a graph. A *graph* is formed by first making two lines that join each other. One line is the vertical (Y) line. The other is the horizontal (X) line. See Illustration 15.1.

The measures of behavior (frequency, duration, rate, or percent) are placed on the vertical line. The numbers of observation sessions are placed on the horizontal line. See Illustration 15.2.

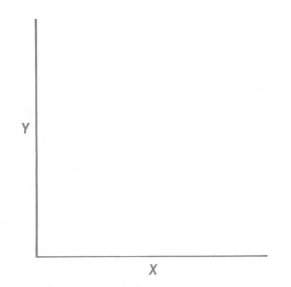

Illustration 15.1. The basic formation of a graph

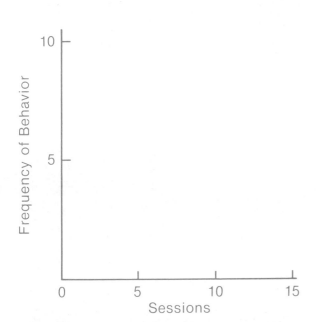

Illustration 15.2. Setting up a graph to measure observed frequencies of behavior

Once this is done, the measurements, or *data points*, can be added to the graph. Pretend you have observed a child, Teddy, in a play group for 20 minutes a day for 5 days. You have been watching how often he makes certain appropriate play responses (shares, takes turns, helps others, calls playmates by name). The following numbers are the total frequency counts for each observation session.

Session Number	Appropriate Play Behaviors
1	0
2	3
3	1
4	0
5	2

To plot these data on a graph, place a dark circle (●) directly over the appropriate session number on a parallel line with the number representing the frequency of behavior for that observation session. Then join the data points with a light line. See Illustration 15.3.

The graph in Illustration 15.3 shows Teddy's *baseline*, or beginning, play performance. There is obviously room for improvement.

Assume that you are Teddy's teacher. You decide to try to praise him whenever you see him sharing, taking turns, helping another child, or calling a playmate by name. Assume that you start this teaching approach on Session #6 and continue for the next five sessions. Each day, you plot the new data point to see if Teddy's play behavior is showing signs of improvement. Research has shown that your new graph is likely to be similar to that shown in Illustration 15.4.

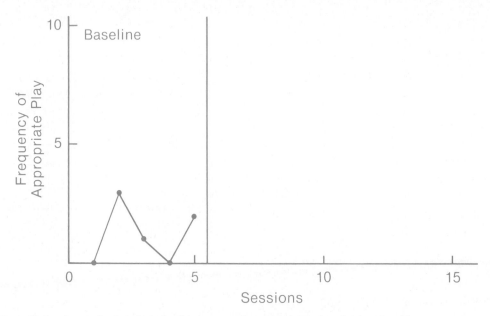

Illustration 15.3. A graph showing the frequency of appropriate play during baseline

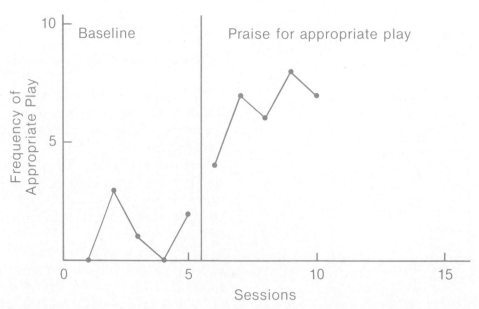

Illustration 15.4. A graph comparing Teddy's appropriate play during baseline and when he is praised for appropriate play

By graphing, you were able to see Teddy's baseline or beginning behavior. The baseline made you decide to try a new teaching approach. You started your new approach, positive reinforcement of appropriate play, on Session #6. The results encouraged you to continue. After several more sessions, you were sure that you were doing the right thing. If Teddy had not responded to your new method after several days (though sometimes it takes longer) the data would have encouraged you to try other methods that we discuss in this book.

SUMMARY

Skillful parents and teachers adjust their teaching approaches in light of facts—observations and measurement data—about how effective their approaches are. Measuring behavior, keeping records, observing, and sometimes making graphs are valuable skills needed by everyone who is involved with teaching children.

QUESTIONS FOR GROWTH

1. Describe some of the general benefits to be gained by observing children.

2. Tell several of the things you learned from the student's observation of Jimmy playing ball with his family.

3. Explain why it is important for teachers and parents to observe children.

4. Explain why describing the setting is an important first step to making observations.

5. Tell what a timed running description is. What are some advantages of using the timed running description?

6. Explain what was learned about Teddy's behavior as a result of the timed running description observation.

7. **(a)** Explain the main parts of a sequence analysis. **(b)** Tell what its advantages are over a timed running description. **(c)** Explain what was learned from the sequence analysis observation of Teddy's behavior.

8. Describe the first step in measuring behavior.

9. **(a)** List and explain each of the four basic measures of behavior. **(b)** Explain when it would be appropriate to use each of these measures.

10. Explain the value of graphing measures or data from observation.

CHAPTER

16

Self-Control

Self-control is the act of purposely motivating oneself to do or not to do some action. The term self-control is often used to talk about our attempts to do things that we find difficult or would rather not do. We also use the term self-control to describe our struggle not to do certain things.

Improving and maintaining the quality of our own behavior is what self-control is all about. If you are asked to look at your own efforts at self-control, you will easily notice a basic problem: It is much easier to tell others how to change their behavior than it is to control your own. All humans find it challenging to view themselves objectively and apply self-control.

The older we are, the greater self-control we are expected to have. Yet as we leave childhood and enter our teen and adult years, our powers of self-control may be most severely tested. In the teenage years, other

people try harder than ever to influence us. Acquaintances may or may not become our friends depending upon how we behave. It is difficult to exercise self-control with these types of influences.

By now you may spend more and more time away from parents or guardians. You have many decisions to make about things that may tempt you. How late will I stay out tonight? Will I brush my teeth? Will I smoke a cigarette? Will I drink alcohol, and if I do, how much? Will I put in the extra effort to really do well in band, athletics, or another activity? Will I schedule enough study time to do well in school? What foods will I choose to eat, and how much?

These are some of the kinds of self-control problems faced by both teenagers and adults. They are more advanced self-control problems, because consequences in the form of punishment or reinforcement are often not immediately available. This is what makes mature self-control so hard. The important consequences for many behaviors are delayed by days, weeks, or even years.

For example, eating certain foods may produce immediate pleasure, but over the course of time may cause an unattractive and unhealthy weight gain. Drinking too much alcohol may result in sickness the next day. Continued drinking may cause serious personal problems years into the future. The student who enjoys immediate pleasure instead of studying for a test may experience the unpleasant delayed consequence of failing the exam later. If you choose to smoke cigarettes, the immediate consequence may be acceptance by certain peers, but the delayed consequence is likely to be the loss of good health due to lung or heart disease.

Another challenge to self-control is to accept immediate inconveniences or unpleasant experiences in order to obtain future benefits. For instance, some may view studying or practicing the piano or a sport as an inconvenience. But putting in study or practice time can lead to great future rewards such as self-pride, peer acceptance, or perhaps a scholarship to college.

SELF-CONTROL IN PARENTING

Perhaps nowhere is the need for self-control greater than in parenting. The rewards for parenting are many, but the job is a very demanding one. Children do cry, whine, make messes, and require consistent care and attention. Parents have mood changes. There are times when they feel like doing certain things, and times when they do not. Parents

Figure 16-1. Parenting is very demanding: it requires patience and a sense of humor. Here, a woman juggles two of her jobs: removing weeds from farm equipment while holding her baby. (USDA Photo by Michelle Bogre)

become tired and bored of doing the same things over and over again. Some parents are more easily bored than others. Some are lazier than others in providing child care, and some have more trouble controlling their tempers.

The greatest demand for self-control in parenting comes from the fact that there are no supervisors or bosses to encourage good work. Who reminds and encourages parents to talk and play with their infant? Who suggests that parents watch for and reinforce

good behavior in their child whenever it occurs? Who tells parents to keep their baby
clean and in good health? Who reminds the
parents to avoid screaming at their child? In
most cases, the answer to all of these questions is *no one*—no one, that is, other than the
parents themselves.

To think about self-control in parenting,
we must first identify the behaviors that parents frequently struggle to control in themselves. You probably have observed many
parents with their children, and could easily write a list of parental behaviors in need
of change. You might start by making two
lists: one list of things that parents need to
start doing, and one of things that parents
need to stop doing. The lists in Box 16.1 are
certainly not complete. What things would
you like to add?

Figure 16-2. Who reminds parents to care for and
talk to their babies? (March of Dimes Birth Defects
Foundation)

BOX 16.1

Partial Lists for Parental Self-Control

Things to Start Doing	**Things to Stop Doing**
Praising	Swearing
Talking to a baby	Yelling
Hugging and kissing	Criticizing
Reading to a child	Hitting
Bathing children frequently	Jerking arms
Teaching new skills	Negative labeling
Playing with children	Making cruel remarks
Listening to children	Neglecting or ignoring children
Showing interest	Leaving young children alone
Being calm	Driving recklessly

Improving Self-Control in Parenting

Many of the items in Box 16.1 seem like common sense, but common sense may not be as common as we think. For parents to change a behavior in themselves, the first step is to recognize that it needs to be changed. Parents often have had no special training or preparation for their work. Therefore, they may not recognize their own behavior which is in need of change. Nor, sometimes, do they understand why the behavior needs to be changed. By studying child development, parents become much better at recognizing their own behaviors that need to be started or stopped.

A second step in improving self-control is that parents must look critically at themselves. Mature people accept that they are not perfect and can always improve themselves. Mature individuals are not afraid to see and accept themselves for what they really are. By contrast, immature people are often so fearful that they might not do well, or be respected or liked by others, that they refuse to recognize their own faults and imperfections. This is one reason why immature parents have great difficulty improving themselves through self-control.

The next step in improving self-control is understanding what is causing the self-control problem in the first place. This step is not always necessary, because people often control their problem behavior without understanding why it exists. Still, understanding why self-control is a problem is worth a try, because such understanding can definitely help.

Why Is Self-Control Difficult in Parenting?

The following are some common reasons why parents have trouble with behaviors that they either do too much or too little. You will see that many problems are caused by the ways that parents think about themselves and their behaviors.

1. "It's easier for me to do it myself than to teach my child to do it." This way of thinking focuses too much on immediate consequences. True, if parents start to teach their four-year-old how to make her bed, it will take a lot of the parents' time. But by taking the time and effort, the parents soon will not have to make the bed themselves. Also, and more importantly, the child will have learned one of the small skills which leads to self-care and independence.

2. "It's so boring to do many of the things involved in child rearing." Every job, including parenting, includes work that is repetitious, things that must be done over and over in much the same way. Sometimes people think that the "good life" does not involve such repetition. This line of thinking is wrong. Everyone, parents included, will be happier and more effective when they accept the fact that repetition is a part of life and is not really so terrible.

In parenting, repetition can easily be viewed as something new and challenging. Diaper changing can be seen as a time to help with language development or teaching cooperation. These parenting activities are certainly not boring or repetitious. Rolling a ball back and forth to a 12-month-old may be repetitious if a parent simply thinks about the ball rolling back and forth. But it is not repetitious or boring if the parent watches eye-hand coordination grow, along with the child's excitement over the new skill.

3. "I don't want to change!" Some parents are resistant to change. One mother recognized that she did not show affection often. She was not really affectionate in her relationship with her children. She was more businesslike and efficient in her approach. Although she knew that it was important for her to show her love more often, she said,

"But that's not me! I'm not the kind of person who does that!"

When people stubbornly refuse to try to change their own behavior, even when it will be beneficial to themselves and their loved ones, they are behaving irresponsibly. The psychologist who counseled the unaffectionate mother asked her to rephrase her statement about herself: "But that's not me! I'm the kind of person who stubbornly behaves the same way no matter what—even if it hurts me and the children I love!" After

Figure 16-3. As this father thinks about the benefits to his child's development, rolling the ball back and forth is anything but boring. (USDA Photo)

repeating this statement, the parent quickly realized how harmful her stubbornness could be.

4. "Parenting is frustrating!" Trying to teach children to feed or dress themselves can be very frustrating. Children take time to learn these things. Children may do especially well one day, only to do poorly the next.

One of the reasons that parents become frustrated is that they wrongly believe they must have quick success. They may think, "I have to have what I want now—I can't wait!" Or they may expect quick success because they simply haven't learned about what to expect in child development and learning.

Figure 16-4. Parents should be realistic—even the most cheerful children have bad days. (© Ron Meyer/ White Eyes Design)

Children do not always learn quickly, and when something is learned it does not always stay learned without further teaching. Mature parents accept these facts. When parents are more realistic in their expectations, they find that teaching and child rearing are less frustrating.

5. "I am fearful!" Immature parents often fail to work on self-control because of fear. Sometimes parents fear failure. They wrongly believe that they must succeed at everything they do, or else they will be miserable and shameful failures. Such people often avoid failure (in the short run) by not trying to do anything at all. They reason, "If I don't try, then I can't fail." In fact, everyone fails at many things, but this does not make anyone a failure as a human being.

Parents are sometimes fearful of rejection. One parent did not hug or kiss his five-year-old child because sometimes the child would push him away. The child really didn't mean anything bad by this act. He was simply involved in doing something and did not want to be interrupted. This parent had to learn to think more realistically about child development. He also had to recognize his oversensitivity to rejection. This was necessary in order to use self-control and begin to show his love more often.

Another parent feared rejection and loss of love so much that when her children misbehaved, she never disciplined them. As a result, her children had become destructive and disrespectful. This mother was extremely permissive because of her personal fears. When she finally recognized this as a problem, she began to use the effective methods of discipline described in Chapters 12 and 13. She continued to show her love during many other opportunities. She found that her children's behavior improved and that they continued to love her.

6. ''Sometimes I take my anger out on my child.'' Parents who have trouble controlling their tempers often learn that they are taking out their anger about something else on their children. This is called displaced aggression. It can happen to anyone who is not on guard for the problem.

Self-control for displaced-aggression problems is important. Parents must not only reduce their angry misbehavior toward their children. They also must learn to behave more effectively to solve the problems they are having with others. Children will benefit when their parents know and properly defend their personal rights in their relationships with others.

Parents can improve their own self-control by recognizing and working on any of the six problems just described. Sometimes these and other problems are serious enough to require professional help from a counselor or psychologist. Recognizing a need for help with such problems, and then seeking help, are not signs of weakness. These are signs of maturity and effective problem solving. They are also often the first steps toward self-control.

SELF-CONTROL TECHINQUES

In Chapter 15, we discussed defining, observing, measuring, and graphing a child's behavior. Those methods and the ones which follow are also useful in successful self-control. Read and think about the general steps to self-control listed in Box 16.2 before continuing.

Defining the Behavior

In order to change some behavior problem—either a child's or our own—it is first necessary to define the problem. To illustrate this,

---

BOX 16.2

General Steps to Self-Control

1. Recognize behavior which needs to be changed, and understand why.

2. Understand why you have found it difficult to change.

3. Develop a self-control strategy and work at it.

4. Review and revise.

assume that Alan, a teenager, is babysitting for his five-year-old cousin three times a week during the summer.

Imagine that Alan is slowly becoming dissatisfied with his performance. He might express his dissatisfaction in very general terms. "I lose my temper too often." "I'm just not patient enough with my young cousin." These are helpful beginning statements. But to help himself, Alan will need to be more clear and detailed in his description of the problem. For example, he might describe that he raises his voice or yells at his cousin too often. This is a better definition of the problem.

Measuring the Behavior

Measuring the behavior is often enough to change it. By measuring his problem behavior, Alan became motivated to change. He realized how often he raised his voice or yelled at his cousin. Alan's job now is to take advantage of that motivation and use it to help himself.

By noticing his yelling and noting it each time on a piece of paper, Illustration 16.1, Alan is actually providing himself with a mild punishing consequence. It is unpleasant for Alan to notice and record his problem behavior. However, the measurement is making Alan more aware of his behavior. As a result, he is noticing that his problem behavior is decreasing day by day.

To further reinforce his improving behavior, Alan drew a graph based on his tally sheet in Illustration 16.1. The graph was a visual way to reinforce his efforts. See Illustration 16.2. Like Alan, many people have

learned that self-measurement can be a very effective tool in self-improvement and self-control.

Illustration 16.1. *Alan's tally sheet for measuring his problem behavior*

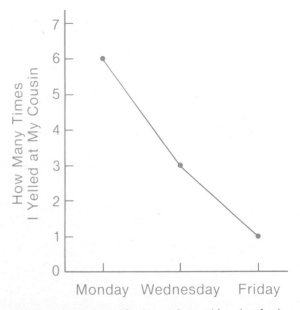

Illustration 16.2. *Alan's graph provides visual reinforcement for decreasing his undesirable behavior.*

Identifying Goals and Objectives

Sometimes measuring one's own behavior is not enough to improve it. Identifying goals and objectives may be what is needed to help improve self-control.

Assume that Alan's graph of his behavior appeared as in Illustration 16.3. In this case, measurement alone does not seem to be working to improve self-control. However, if Alan chooses to set small, easy-to-meet objectives such as one less yell per week, big improvements can be gained. The graph in Illustration 16.4 shows such a successful approach to self-control.

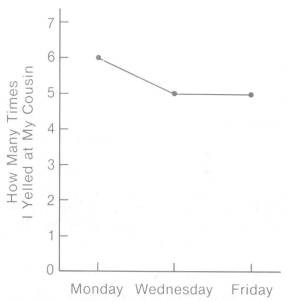

Illustration 16.3. *Measurement alone does not appear to be effective enough in improving Alan's self-control in this case.*

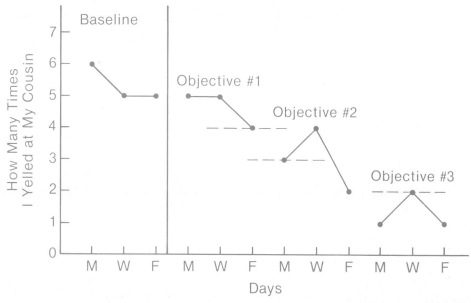

Illustration 16.4. *Graphing easy-to-meet objectives (the broken lines) to improve Alan's self-control*

Using Cues that Remind

Often someone wants to do the right thing but simply forgets about it. We have all forgotten books at home, missed meetings, or forgotten to exercise. In parenting, well-intentioned people can often increase their consistency at certain behaviors by giving themselves *cues*, or signals, as reminders. Cues are helpful in building self-control.

One parent wrote a schedule of daily activities for herself and her six-month-old baby. The schedule included naps, feeding, bathing, and play activities. The parent found that the schedule helped her to establish good basic habits. She was also able to remain flexible and change scheduled activities whenever it was wise to do so.

Other parents have posted small reminders in appropriate places. For example, there have been cases where young toddlers have fallen headfirst into toilets and, being too weak to get out, have drowned. One family posted signs saying ''Close the lid'' on the toilet. Another family placed warning cues near long flights of stairs or next to doors that older family members sometimes left open.

CONSEQUENCES AND SELF-CONTROL

Self-control is a challenge, because important consequences are often long-range ones. Parents who do not take the time to teach self-care skills to their child, for instance, may find in a few years that the child is too dependent upon them. The problem is that delayed consequences may not motivate people strongly enough. Skillful parents, though, will learn to provide themselves with important cues and motivating consequences more immediately. We discuss methods for doing this in the following sections.

Self-Reinforcement

One good method for learning self-control is to provide oneself with reinforcement. This is often necessary because, as discussed earlier, parents often have no one else to provide them with reinforcement.

Self-Praise

One easy reinforcing consequence that parents can provide for their own good behavior is self-praise. Almost everyone enjoys genuine praise from others. We have all worked a little harder or tried a little longer because someone has praised our efforts. Good self-control requires that we also learn to praise ourselves for the good things we do.

At first, some people think the idea of self-praise is silly. But when they think carefully, they soon see that they already praise themselves. When they make a good play in athletics, they think, ''Way to go!'' If they are in a play, they think, ''I played that scene beautifully!''

Self-praise is not strange or unusual. Those who are good at self-control use self-praise all the time.

Parents have no coach or audience to praise their good work. Because parents often are with their children alone, it is even more important that they get in the habit of praising themselves for good work. Parents can praise themselves in the following ways.

1. By labeling their appropriate behavior
2. By reviewing why their work is valuable (this can help to bring the future into the present)
3. By complimenting themselves heartily

Example #1. "I haven't lost my temper and yelled once today. I'm much more in control of my emotions, and I'm a better person for my children to imitate. Good for me! I'll keep it up. I really can improve my own behavior."

Example #2. "I read to my child twice today, just as I planned. That gave us some quiet and close time together, and will really help her language development. I'm doing well and feel like a responsible parent!"

Provide Self-Reinforcing Activities

Parents frequently help children to do things by providing reinforcing activities. Parents may, for example, tell their children that they must finish their meal before dessert. Or they may tell children that first they must do their homework before they can play.

Adults may not have others to provide reinforcing activities. They must provide the activities themselves. Parents might provide themselves with special treats and privileges for meeting their own self-control goals. The parent who has praised his son's good behaviors may provide himself with reinforcing consequences by, for example, reading a great book or calling a special friend. A parent who has followed a time-consuming child-training procedure for several days might make arrangements to go out to eat or to see a movie. These kinds of

self-reinforcement activities are an important part of self-control.

Seek Reinforcement from Others

There is nothing wrong with sharing personal goals, work projects, and progress with friends and loved ones. People who truly care about us are truly happy about our progress. They show their care in the things they say and do. These are important reinforcing consequences, and they help to motivate all of us.

Parents can describe their self-control projects and progress to friends and loved ones. Showing a graph of improvement to others will often give them a reason to provide genuine praise and encouragement.

Figure 16-5. Parents should share their successes as well as their concerns and fears with each other.

Self-Punishment

Parents can use *self-punishment* as a method to improve self-control. The same guidelines which apply to the use of punishment with children also apply to adults' use of self-punishment. Punishment should be as mild as can be effective. Alternative appropriate behavior should be reinforced frequently. The rule is to never punish inappropriate behavior without, at later times, reinforcing appropriate activities. Self-punishment should be used only in those situations where other appropriate and well-tried methods have failed.

The Self-Reprimand

The reprimand technique described in Chapter 13 is mild, yet frequently effective in self-control. The reprimand consists of three parts.

1. Labeling the inappropriate behavior
2. Telling why the behavior is wrong
3. Stating the right way to behave

When giving *self-reprimands*, people reprimand themselves. It is important that they focus their full attention upon what they are saying to themselves. It is also important that the statements be somewhat scolding. However, self-reprimands should only describe behavior and consequences. They should not include insulting or disrespectful attacks on one's own personality. Examples of self-reprimands are shown in Table 16.1.

Response Cost

Response cost is the loss of a certain amount of reinforcers following some misbehavior. Frequently, the result is that the misbehavior will happen less often in the future. Parents who do something they consider wrong can

Table 16.1

Examples of Self-Reprimands

The Behavior	Why It Is Wrong	The Proper Behavior
I lost control and screamed.	When I scream, my children will learn not to listen to me, and they will probably learn to scream at others.	I must speak firmly and use the timeout, overcorrection, the reprimand, or response cost when my child misbehaves.
I became too angry and slapped by child.	When I lose my control and hit, I could seriously hurt my child. Also, my child may get used to being hit and learn to hit others.	Before I strike out, I must stop myself and consider the use of timeout, overcorrection, the reprimand, or response cost.

use response cost on themselves. Response cost is a mild form of punishment.

One parent observed that he often criticized his child and rarely praised her. As a consequence, his daughter began to seek his company less and less. The father decided that each time he criticized, he would put one dollar in a jar. The dollar was the response cost. The lost money would then be sent to a charity.

Another parent was concerned over her habit of swearing in front of her five-year-old child. Her child had begun to imitate her, often swearing in front of other people. As a mild self-punishment and a reminder to control her own language, the parent decided to give up some of a favorite activity when she swore with her child present. In the evening, after the child was in bed, the mother often watched her favorite programs on television. She decided to give up watching 15 minutes of a favorite program for each time she swore around her child.

Overcorrection

Parents can also use the mild self-punishment method of overcorrection. They do this by overpracticing an appropriate activity immediately after undesirable behavior.

One father occasionally failed to close the front-yard gate when he let his two-year-old play in the yard. Whenever this happened, he practiced closing the gate 15 times. This was his use of overcorrection.

Another parent sometimes left dangerous items out where her toddler could get them. She noticed that she also sometimes failed to turn the handles of pans toward the back of the stove. She became concerned that the toddler would be injured by her carelessness.

She decided to use overcorrection. Whenever she found a dangerous item lying around, she put it away ten times. If she forgot to turn the pot handles toward the back of the stove, she also practiced this action repeatedly. By practicing these movements during overcorrection, they soon became more automatic. The home became a safer place for the child.

Self-Punishing Thoughts

If a self-control problem is serious enough and other approaches have failed, self-punishing thoughts may be effective. The use of self-punishing thoughts requires that a clear, unpleasant mental picture be constructed. This image should represent what could happen as a result of the parent's undesirable actions. Parents can think of the image immediately following each of their own inappropriate behaviors.

Example #1. The father of a 16-month-old toddler became concerned about his tendency to leave a baby gate open at the top of the basement stairs. The child could be seriously injured if he fell. Still, the father would occasionally forget to close the gate.

The parent decided that, in the future, whenever the gate was left open, he would imagine seeing his child falling down the stairs. He also imagined what the horrifying event would sound like. These images were based on possible reality. They were so powerful that the parent learned to stop leaving the baby gate open.

Example #2. One parent had the habit of becoming frustrated with her stubborn two-year-old. At these times, she would often grab the child's arm and jerk it powerfully.

The mother realized that this was a dangerous thing to do and decided to stop the habit. To do so, she thought about the real dangers involved. It is very possible to dislocate a young child's shoulder by jerking on the arms.

The parent decided that the next time she was tempted or actually did jerk her child's arm, she would stop immediately and think about what might happen. She thought of a clear image of how it would feel to injure her child, and what the child would see, hear, and feel. She also thought about how it would feel to take the child to the hospital. In this case, thinking such thoughts whenever she was even tempted to jerk the child's arm was enough to break her bad habit. Self-punishing thoughts can be used to punish ideas or thoughts that may come before inappropriate actions. They can also be used as punishment following such actions, should they occur.

COMBINING SELF-CONTROL TECHNIQUES

As in disciplining children, one technique is generally not enough for establishing parental self-control. The goal of self-control is to increase one's motivation to do or not to do certain things in parenting. Another goal, of equal importance, is increasing competent actions combined with an increased sense of personal pride.

With these goals in mind, the best form of self-control is positive reinforcement. Should positive reinforcement alone be ineffective, it can be combined with mild forms of punishment. However, punishment should be

Figure 16-6. Participating with other families in community support groups can help parents as they share experiences. (March of Dimes Birth Defects Foundation)

used only when other well-tried methods have failed.

Parents may find that some of their attempts at self-control are unsuccessful. If the problems involve neglectful or harsh treatment of a child, parents should not stop their efforts to gain self-control. In such cases, parents should immediately seek professional assistance from counselors, psychologists, or other programs available in their community.

QUESTIONS FOR GROWTH

1. Explain the meaning of the term self-control.

2. Tell some of the things that may challenge a person's self-control during the teen years.

3. Explain how the timing of many consequences for behavior can make self-control difficult.

4. Tell, in your own words, why self-control can be especially challenging for a parent.

5. Name some things that parents may often struggle not to do and to do more often.

6. List the three general steps to improving self-control.

7. List and explain six ways of thinking and feeling that can hurt parents' self-control.

8. Provide specific definitions for the behaviors described by the following general statements: **(a)** ''I'm just too hot-headed.'' **(b)** ''I'm just not patient enough.'' **(c)** ''I'm a lazy parent.''

9. Select some specific behavior that someone might wish to improve through self-control and then do the following: **(a)** Make up a tally sheet of how frequently the behavior may have happened over the last seven days. **(b)** Make a graph of the data.

10. Explain why it is important to measure and graph self-control data.

11. Explain how you might use setting goals and objectives in small steps to improve a self-control problem.

12. Provide three original examples of how a parent could use cues that remind to improve self-control.

13. Provide four original examples of how parents could use self-reinforcement to improve self-control.

14. Identify three ways that parents could get others to reinforce their improvements in self-control.

15. Name each form of self-punishment explored in this chapter and provide one original example of each.

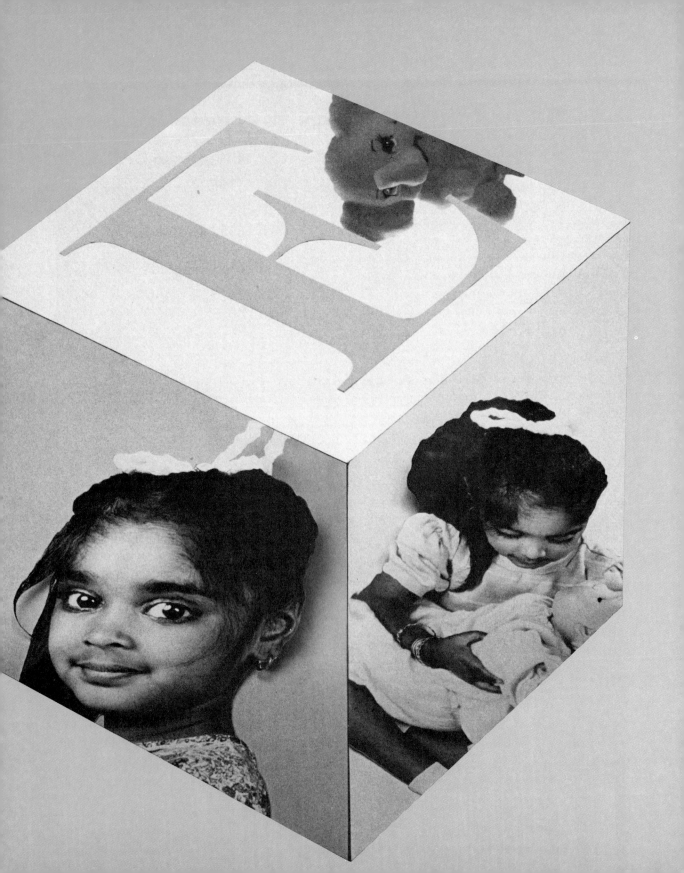

PART

E

PRINCIPLES OF PARENTING AND TEACHING AT WORK

I n Part E, we apply important information and concepts of child development to actual teaching situations with children. The parenting and teaching examples are illustrations of methods that can be used in countless other teaching goals. The examples provide a basis for personal creativity in teaching children. In the chapters in Part E, we focus our attention on three specific children: Jimmy, Maria, and Richard. We share in their parenting from infancy through first grade. Although these children are each unique, you will see that their parents may use similar teaching methods, personalized for the needs of each child and family.

CHAPTER

17

Strengthening Happiness
(Birth to Two Years)

Many things which influence our happiness are not under our control. We have no control, for example, over the loss of loved ones due to death. We all have disappointments and sadness which we cannot control. On the other hand, we can take many steps to make happiness more likely. We can seek love, trust, and encouragement, and learn the many skills necessary to meet life's demands. In other words, we can *foster*, or strengthen, happiness in ourselves. Parents can also foster happiness in their children.

Most parents understand that they can influence the happiness of their children, and they wish to do so. In fact, one of the most frequently identified parenting goals is "to have a happy child." Effective parents strengthen their children's actions and skills which make happiness more likely, easier to achieve, and easier to maintain. In this chapter, we discuss how to foster happiness in infants and toddlers. (Children are usually called infants during their first year. They may be called toddlers during their second year.) We also identify reasonable expectations about happiness in infants and toddlers.

HAPPINESS AND LEARNING

Helping children to be happy can affect their future in very important ways. Psychologist Elizabeth Hurlock wrote about studies that show how early happiness affects later adjustments. These were some of Hurlock's conclusions.

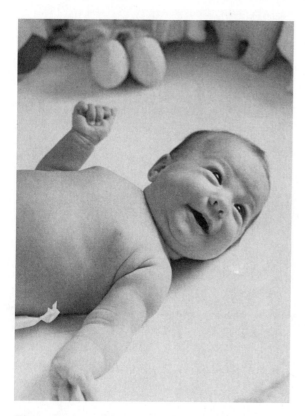

Figure 17-1. Helping a child to be happy is a common parental goal.

• Happy children are generally healthy and energetic. Unhappiness reduces children's strength and energy, and hurts their general physical well-being.
• Happy children focus their energy on purposeful activities. Unhappy children waste their energy in excessive daydreaming and self-pity.
• Happiness provides a source of motivation to do things; unhappiness reduces motivation.
• Happy children handle frustrations more calmly than unhappy children. Happy children try to understand why they feel frustrated. Unhappy children are more likely to respond to frustration with temper outbursts.
• Happiness encourages social contacts and involvement in social activities. Unhappiness can cause children to be withdrawn.
• With repeated experiences, happiness becomes a habit. Unhappiness develops into a habit in the same way.
• A happy childhood does not guarantee adult success, but it does provide a basis for adult success. Unhappiness provides a basis for failure.

There are some general factors which strengthen happiness in children. Happiness is strengthened when parents are generally

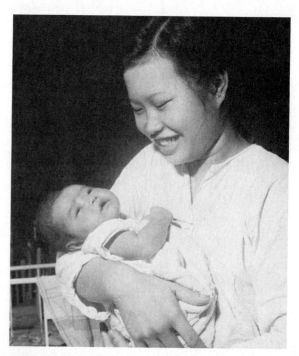

Figure 17-2. Most parents realize that their own happiness is an important influence on their child's happiness. (UNICEF PHOTO/Ling)

happy, and when children are given opportunities to experience success. Happiness is strengthened when children receive praise and recognition for what they do. It also helps when parents provide quality time to their children by talking and listening to them and being physically close.

Play is another factor in strengthening happiness. The value of play cannot be overemphasized. Children learn a great deal from it. Play stimulates happiness, and happiness stimulates play.

Happy children approach new situations in a happy manner. This is called generalization. In generalization, behaviors developed to deal with one situation are used to cope with new situations. Children are born with certain differences (health, sleep patterns, irritability) that clearly influence personality development. However, the generalization of learned attitudes and behaviors to different situations is also an important factor.

Figure 17-3. Happy children like to socialize and play. (© Ron Meyer/White Eyes Design)

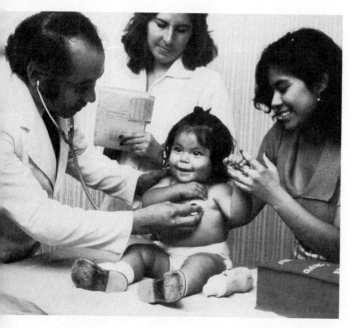

Figure 17-4. Children who are happy approach new situations with ease. (Photo Courtesy of IBM Corporation)

HAPPY CHILDREN, HAPPY PARENTS

A happy child makes life a lot easier and more pleasant for parents, brothers, and sisters. Most people, children as well as adults, respond more favorably to happy people.

But some parents are unrealistic in their expectations of a child's happiness. They sometimes mistakenly think that crying is a form of rejection, rage, or hatred directed against the parents. Such mistaken views can make parents depressed and angry. These strong feelings can even lead to child abuse.

It is important for parents to know that normal happy children do cry and show anger and sadness. Crying is a normal and healthy response. Periods of crying and fretfulness are an inevitable part of infancy and toddlerhood.

HAPPINESS AND UNHAPPINESS IN INFANTS

From birth, infants differ in how happy and contented they are. As infants develop, great differences in the amount of time they spend crying or contented still exist. Some of these differences are caused by the infant care methods used by parents. Other factors include digestive problems and physical health.

Crying in young infants is a valuable and important activity. A certain amount of crying actually helps to strengthen lungs and muscles. Though few people enjoy listening to infants cry, crying is also an important form of early communication. Crying signals that the infant is in need of care. Crying helps to motivate parents to assist in any way they can.

When babies cry, parents can assume that they are unhappy about something. An infant may be hungry, thirsty, cold, stinging from the discomfort of a dirty diaper, frightened, or sick. In the normal and healthy newborn, crying is reflexive. If various forms of pain or discomfort occur, the infant will cry.

Crying during the first two weeks of life may occur at unpredictable times and for no known reason. The amount of crying is likely to decrease during the third week of life. By the third or fourth month, crying should decrease still more. This reduction in crying time is more likely to occur when parents have taken care of the infant's basic needs.

If an infant spends a great deal of time crying, it is important that the parents report the problem to their pediatrician.

ENCOURAGING HAPPINESS

It is essential that from the very beginning of life infants be lovingly talked to, held, and cuddled. Research has shown that infants who receive such loving care as well as adequate food, warmth, and cleanliness are generally happy. In other words, babies are more likely to be contented if their basic needs are met.

Recall from earlier discussions that Maslow and Erikson both emphasized the importance of fulfilling an infant's basic biological, safety, and security needs. When these needs are provided by parents, the infant's social and emotional development is strengthened in essential ways.

Although happy and unhappy expressions and sounds begin as reflexes in infants, they soon show operant tendencies. This means that consequences begin to influence the frequencies of happy and unhappy behavior. The Brackbill study, which demonstrated the reinforcement of smiling in infants, was an illustration of this. It showed that parents can strengthen happy behavior in infants by responding to happy behavior in reinforcing ways whenever it occurs.

NOTE: Do not misunderstand the meaning of this recommendation to reinforce happy behavior. It does not mean that an infant's unhappy behavior should be ignored. Parents should not ignore crying newborns and young infants. Parents do not ''spoil'' infants by caring for them when they cry.

The evidence indicates that such care actually leads to more healthy and contented infants.

Skilled parents give special care whenever their infant is distressed. They also look for opportunities to lovingly respond to smiles and happy sounds. Recall that very young infants appear to imitate the facial expressions of their parents. This emphasizes the importance of parents showing their own happiness to their infant.

The idea of encouraging happiness in infants is based on the following observations.

1. Crying is not the only way that infants communicate their needs. It is only the loudest way.
2. Babies quickly learn how to control their parents, not only by crying, but also by smiling and making happy sounds.
3. By listening for noncrying sounds and reinforcing them early, parents can teach their babies to often communicate in happy and pleasant ways.

THREE FAMILIES' EXPERIENCES IN STRENGTHENING HAPPINESS

When Jimmy was brought home from the hospital after birth, his parents found that he normally slept about four hours and then would awaken and cry to be fed. Maria's parents noticed the same thing with their new daughter. Both Jimmy and Maria cried often, but they were easy to calm and make happy.

Richard was a premature infant. His parents noticed that he awakened about every three hours for his feeding. Much of Richard's waking time was spent crying and

Figure 17-5. Unhappiness in newborns and young infants should not be ignored.

fretting. His parents found it difficult to help him to be content.

The following are some examples of the ways that these three families strengthened happiness in their children.

Strengthening Happiness through Feeding and Care Routines

Jimmy's parents developed a feeding and care routine which increased their chances

of reinforcing Jimmy's happy behavior when he awoke. They were aware that Jimmy tended to awaken for feeding about every four hours in the weeks after birth. When the feeding hour drew near, the parents listened more carefully to the small signs that Jimmy was waking up. Jimmy, like most babies, did not immediately wake up and cry loudly. Instead, he would make quiet grunts, groans, gurgles, and sucking noises. These were the signs that Jimmy was close to his feeding time.

Jimmy's mother would then go to him while calling his name lovingly. She picked him up gently and talked to him as she moved to change his diaper. After this, she took Jimmy to a rocking chair and nursed him. Jimmy ate hungrily while his mother rocked, talked, hummed, and sometimes sang to him. Every few minutes, she would place him over her shoulder and pat or rub his back. Sometimes he would burp some air that he had swallowed while nursing.

When Jimmy was done nursing, he often watched his mother's face as she smiled and talked to him. He watched it very closely. Occasionally he would smile, and his mother would respond with even more enthusiasm. But slowly his eyes would grow heavy and close for short periods of time. Eventually, Jimmy would fall asleep.

Jimmy's mother used a feeding routine which fulfilled his needs in a calming way. She provided the immediate reinforcement of her voice and physical presence for non-crying vocalizations. She provided the unlearned reinforcers of food, warmth, and loving care while Jimmy was contented. This helped Jimmy to learn more contented behaviors.

There were times when Jimmy cried when he awoke, but that did not bother his mother. She went to him as usual and gave all of the loving care that he needed. However, sometimes when Jimmy awakened and began to cry, his mother could tell that he would be quiet in a few seconds. In these cases, she would wait and go to him when he became quieter. She did this so that Jimmy would not learn to use crying as the only way to get her attention.

Teaching Infants to Call for Their Parents Using Noncrying Sounds

Like Jimmy, Maria often made noncrying sounds when she awoke for her feedings. Noncrying sounds included vowel and sucking sounds as well as quiet grunts and groans. At first, Maria's parents had to listen carefully to hear these sounds. Maria's mother and father fed her with a bottle rather than nursing. When they could hear her awakening sounds, they placed a bottle in a pan of hot water to warm, and then they cared for her in the same way that Jimmy's mother cared for him.

Maria's father enjoyed sharing the feedings with his wife. It was a special time for him to be close with his new daughter. Sometimes Maria would cry when she awakened, and her parents would go to her. As the weeks passed, Maria began to make a greater range of different noncrying sounds as she awakened. By around six and seven weeks, her sounds had grown much louder and she was cooing. She was making vowel sounds and mixing them with little squeals and gurgling sounds. Maria's parents reinforced such sounds whenever they could, because they enjoyed hearing them. They also knew that these vocalizations were an important step toward the day when Maria would say her first word.

Maria's parents were very skillful at teaching her to call and jabber in happy ways. To do this, they used the idea of moving from continuous reinforcement (CRF) to intermittent reinforcement.

In the beginning, the parents went to Maria as soon as they heard her awakening sounds. When Maria had learned to call for her parents in this way, they changed their approach slightly. The parents began to pause outside of her door and wait an extra 20 or 30 seconds before entering. They would listen carefully for reasonably loud and happy sounds. When they heard the sounds, they would enter immediately, softly calling Maria's name. Maria's parents were shaping louder and louder vocalizations with their attention.

Later, Maria's parents began to pause for longer intervals at her door to listen for happy sounds. They were careful not to wait too long, which would have caused Maria to become frustrated and cry. However, sometimes Maria would cry for her meal. The parents would wait for a short lull and then go to her in the usual way. If Maria did not show a lull in her crying in a minute or two, they simply picked her up and prepared for her feeding.

Maria soon learned to coo and make other sounds louder and for longer periods of time. It began to appear as though Maria was calling for her parents to come and feed her without crying.

Strengthening Smiles and Happy Sounds at Other Times

Richard's early infancy was much different from Jimmy's and Maria's. Richard was a fretful baby. As is often true of premature babies, Richard did not develop consistent sleeping habits. He frequently cried, and his parents found it difficult to comfort him. After feeding, they would often walk around with him over their shoulders. At these times, they rubbed and patted his back and tried to comfort him in any way they could. Eventually, he would go to sleep.

Even though Richard was fussy at times, there were plenty of opportunities for his parents to reinforce happiness. For example, on one afternoon the father had just finished changing Richard's diapers. The father paused and bent low with his face close to Richard's. Richard watched his father's face very intently, and then he smiled a bright and toothless grin. His father laughed and kissed Richard's stomach with a big smack. Richard squealed with delight. His little arms and legs thrashed with excitement. In a few seconds, Richard watched his father's face intently and calmly once again. Soon Richard made a cooing noise. His father again responded with affection and excitement.

The father's actions produced smiles in Richard. Then the father reinforced the smiles with more stimulating and enjoyable actions. As the two played, the father was learning what to do to make Richard laugh and smile. Richard was learning what to do to make his father continue his playfulness. Richard was learning to play with his father's reactions as he would with a new

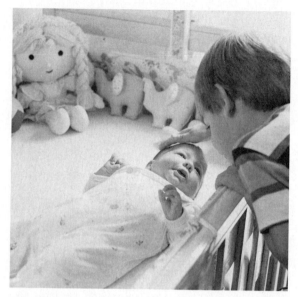

Figure 17-6. What is the value of reinforcing happy sounds in infants?

and responsive toy. Richard was learning about happy social relationships.

DEALING WITH UNHAPPINESS

So far we have only talked about what to do to increase happy behavior. We now will explore the valuable but sometimes distressing behaviors of crying, whining, and temper tantrums.

Crying

As mentioned before, crying begins in the infant as a valuable reflex. In young infants, crying is properly reduced by fulfilling the infant's needs. For young infants who cry a lot, parents can normally expect some relief by about the age of three or four months.

By this time, perhaps due to greater physical maturity, infants often begin to spend less time crying. However, some babies continue to cry a great deal until they are six months and older.

The *healthy* baby who is about four months old and still cries excessively is probably showing a learned behavior. If this is the case, it is important to discuss the problem with a pediatrician. Infants beyond this age will naturally cry or fuss when sick or in pain, or when they are frightened or tired. Infants will also become upset when their movement is restricted, when they lose a toy, or when something they are trying to do ends in failure.

By about four months, parents may gain greater ability to judge their infant's cries. A sensitive parent learns to tell the difference between distress crying due to pain or discomfort, and crying due to tiredness or boredom. At this time, parents may need to decide when they will reinforce their child's crying with attention and special care.

The most frequent infant cry is the *rhythmical cry*. This is the type of cry that infants show when they are hungry. They will also rhythmically cry in one of two other kinds of crying. An *angry cry* is shown by crying with greater loudness, in louder blasts. This is caused by forcing more air through the vocal cords. A *pained cry* is indicated by a long wail followed by a breath hold, then another long wail and a breath hold, and so on.

Excessive Bedtime Crying

When Richard came home from the hospital, he did not sleep consistently. He was very colicky. *Colic* is a word used to indicate that an infant has trouble digesting food. Colicky infants often cry and fuss because they have stomach pains or discomfort. When the pediatrician changed Richard's food formula, Richard seemed to have fewer digestive problems. However, he was still fussy after eating.

Richard's parents had always had difficulty in getting him to sleep as a young infant. Sometimes a wind-up music box helped to soothe Richard to sleep. But he often fussed and cried. His parents would properly try to comfort him by rocking him and walking with him until he quieted. When they laid Richard down, he would often cry loudly until they picked him up again.

Richard's sleeping had improved somewhat by the time he was eight months old. His health was good. By then, his parents had become convinced that he had learned to be dependent upon their constant attention before he would sleep. In order for Richard to sleep, one of his parents would have to remain in his room for about half an hour as he slowly dozed off. If the parent would try to leave the room before he was asleep, Richard screamed and cried. Richard was crying for attention.

Richard's parents decided that it was time to teach Richard to go to bed without excessive crying. They prepared him for bed as usual, and hugged and kissed him goodnight. They then left the room and closed the door. As usual, Richard began to cry loudly. This time, however, the parents did not go back into the room to pick Richard up. Though it was hard for them to do, they let Richard cry until he went to sleep. They were using the extinction method by withholding reinforcement from crying at bedtime.

Richard cried and fussed for nearly an hour before falling to sleep. Over the next ten bedtimes, Richard cried for shorter intervals before falling to sleep. Finally, on the eleventh time, Richard smiled at his mother and quietly went to sleep.

Richard's parents reviewed how he had learned to cry for so long at bedtimes. Some things became very clear. When he was younger, Richard's physical problems had caused him to cry after feedings. His parents naturally picked him up from bed to comfort him hundreds of times. *This was right and proper.* But his parents also realized that their attention to Richard's crying had strengthened his crying.

Later, as the parents noticed that Richard's health had improved, they had often tried to put Richard to bed and "let him cry it out." At first, they would wait for ten minutes or so, and then give in and pick him up. Later, they tried to wait 15 and sometimes 20 minutes before going into the room to comfort Richard. Sometimes they would wait for 30 minutes before going in to comfort him.

By these actions, Richard's parents had taught Richard to cry with greater perseverance by slowly making reinforcement (their attention) more and more intermittent. The parents were thankful that their pediatrician had encouraged them to be firm and use extinction for Richard's unnecessary bedtime crying. The extinction method gradually worked. Bedtime now became a much more pleasant event for both Richard and his parents.

Parents of a healthy three- to four-month-old infant can normally prevent excessive bedtime crying by gaining confidence in their infant's general health and well-being. They can make sure that the infant is well fed, the diaper is clean, there are no signs of sickness or physical problems, and there is a comfortable room temperature. Once these things are assured, parents can hug and kiss the infant and firmly put the child to bed. They should not return until the child has gone to sleep, unless something unusual occurs which may indicate a dangerous or threatening situation.

OTHER FACTORS INFLUENCING HAPPINESS

Many factors can influence the happiness of infants and toddlers. Some of these factors can be controlled by parents, and others cannot. We now discuss various factors that can influence the happiness of children, and provide suggestions for how parents can help.

The Deprivation Trap

Deprivation is a situation in which someone's basic needs are not met. For example, an infant who is hungry and cold is deprived of food and warmth. Deprivation causes unhappiness.

The first step toward having a contented baby is to anticipate and fulfill the baby's needs (sleep, feeding, diapers, etc.). However, these needs will change with growth and development. Parents must remain sensitive to their baby's new requirements. Otherwise, the infant may become deprived and will then naturally cry and fuss. The *deprivation trap* occurs when parents just as naturally tend to these needs, and accidentally reinforce fussiness and crying.

NOTE: This is not to suggest that parents should leave an infant to cry when the infant is hungry, cold, damp, or tired. When these problems arise, parents must solve them. But these problems need not arise very often. By being sensitive to an infant's changing needs, parents can avoid a major source of unhappiness—that of deprivation.

Teething

The discomfort of teething is a natural source of unhappiness which may begin as early as three or four months. Babies usually get their first tooth at about seven months of age. Children will grow 20 teeth during their first 2½ years, and this is bound to cause discomfort and fussiness.

Teething may cause an infant to awaken and cry at night, and lose appetite. Teething infants may develop a tendency to chew nearly anything. Parents can help by massaging their infant's gums and providing rubber teething rings.

Frustrations

Frustrations are another source of unhappiness in an infant's life. Frustrations arise when the infant begins to move around. Infants will start to reach various places in order to obtain and manipulate objects. Imagine the eleven-month-old who pulls herself up to a couch, and steps carefully along it to a nearby table. She reaches for an object, only to lose balance and fall to the carpeted floor on her padded bottom. The child will probably cry—not because she hurt herself, but because she is frustrated. She has made a long and difficult chain of actions for the purpose of reaching an object. After all of that work, she nearly had the object in her hand, only to fall. How frustrating!

Unsuccessful attempts to do things are likely to happen when a child's coordination is improving but is not yet good enough for the child to do many things perfectly. It is natural for infants and toddlers to experience the unhappy emotions of frustration and disappointment. Young children may also become unhappy when they struggle and at first fail to communicate verbally.

Parents should be sympathetic to such problems. However, too much concern probably reinforces crying and tantrums, and does little to teach better coordination and language skills. Parents are advised not to punish or try to stop natural displays of frustration. Instead, parents should let the displays run their course without any heavy reinforcement. Naturally, as children become

Figure 17-7. To reduce frustrations, clothing and the environment should be geared to the baby's comfort and ease. (HUD Photo)

more skillful, they will have fewer reasons to feel frustrated.

The environment itself sometimes reinforces failure-produced emotional behavior. One 18-month-old was pulling a toy duck on wheels around the house. She was having a great time as the duck squawked and its wings flapped. Then the child rounded a turn in the kitchen, and the cord attached to the duck became stuck under the refrigerator. The toddler was suddenly stopped. She pulled again and again without success to release the cord. All of a sudden, she let out a loud, angry shout and pulled with all of her might. The cord was jerked free, and the child went off happily with the toy duck. The refrigerator, cord, and toy duck had worked together to teach her two general things: meet force with force, and show anger while doing it. The release of the toy was the reinforcer in this natural learning situation.

This example shows one way in which the child's environment may automatically teach unhappy reactions. There are few things that parents can do about such situations. However, the home should not unnecessarily limit the infant's activities and cause frustration or anger. The infant's clothing should be comfortable. It should not interfere with crawling and walking. Parents should provide toys which do not break easily and which are appropriate for the child's age. Parents should also explain to and show young children how to do things that they find difficult.

Fears and Hurts

Other unavoidable sources of childhood unhappiness involve fears caused by startling sights and sounds. At around six months of age, there are also fears of strange places, strange people, and separation from parents. Unhappiness also comes from the many hurts that children will experience while growing up, such as soap in the eyes, a pinched finger, or a hard fall. These fearful or painful events are almost certain to make normal children cry.

Of course, parents should comfort children when they are hurt or frightened. However, parents should be careful not to overreact with great concern over very small and harmless mishaps. Judgments as to when and how much to comfort require maturity and sensitivity on the part of parents.

Conflicts from Growing Independence

Around six months of age, infants begin to show a growing tendency toward independence. They may insist upon holding their own bottles, or may struggle against being held at times. Infants may stubbornly crawl to forbidden places or try to pursue forbidden activities. Such growing independence is perfectly natural. Unless they are potentially unsafe, activities toward independence should be encouraged.

Conflicts between parents and children, due to growing independence, will increase during the first two or three years of life. When a conflict arises, parents must carefully consider why they do or do not wish to allow a certain activity. It is good to let children show independence when they can do so safely. But if parents feel that they must limit the child's behavior, then it is important to stand firm and not pay attention to crying or tantrums.

As described in Chapter 12, much can be done to avoid such conflicts between parents and child. Safety gates can be placed across dangerous stairways. Dangerous or fragile items can be put away. Other necessary limitations can be enforced with consistency.

Sickness and Its Effects

Children who go through a period of sickness or discomfort due to injury or surgery will likely cry, fuss, or whine a great deal. At such times, parents feel great sympathy and will do anything they can to make their child more comfortable. After all, the parents' most basic responsibility is to preserve the health and life of the child.

But parents must also understand that in caring for their sick child, they will be providing many positive reinforcers. Reinforcers strengthen the behavior they follow. Since sick children cry and whine a lot, crying and whining might be heavily reinforced. When the sickness lessens or the injury heals, the child may continue to expect extra attention. The child may continue to cry and whine in order to get it.

Fortunately, the behavior problems which often follow extended sickness are not hard to improve. But efforts to improve such behaviors are best made soon after the child has become healthy again. If parents continue to reinforce the child's illness-related behaviors, the behaviors may become very difficult to change. Eventually, professional assistance may be necessary.

To avoid encouraging behavior problems, parents should carefully identify when their child becomes well. Then they can treat their child as a normally healthy person who no

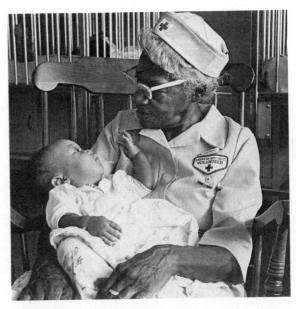

Figure 17-8. *Infants who are ill need extra attention. After the illness passes, parents and other care givers should work to reduce the typical behavior problems that may result. (American Red Cross)*

longer has a good reason to act overly dependent.

SUMMARY

In this chapter, we have described some of the main factors which influence happiness and unhappiness in infants and toddlers. Strengthening happiness in infants is extremely valuable, and parents can play an important role in these influences.

QUESTIONS FOR GROWTH

1. Explain four of the ways that happiness influences behavior, as described by Elizabeth Hurlock.

2. Explain how crying in infants can be a valuable activity.

3. Discuss what is meant by this statement: "Happy and unhappy expressions and sounds soon show operant tendencies."

4. What is one common way to strengthen happy behavior in newborns?

5. Explain why parents should not ignore crying in newborns and young infants.

6. Describe the sounds that babies normally make as they begin to awaken for a feeding.

7. At about what age might a normal and healthy baby who cries be showing a learned habit?

8. Explain how the deprivation trap can cause parents to teach their infants to be unhappy.

9. How can teething influence an infant's happy behavior?

10. Discuss how frustration can affect happiness in infants and toddlers.

11. Explain how a child's growing independence can influence happy behavior.

12. **(a)** How is sickness likely to affect behavior in infants and toddlers? **(b)** How can parents avoid encouraging behavior problems after a child's sickness?

CHAPTER

18

Strengthening Happiness
(Two to Seven Years)

Children between the ages of two to seven years are changing in dramatic ways. During these ages, children are in the preoperational period of cognitive development. Their abilities to think, imagine, and understand grow markedly during this period. These developments can influence happiness and unhappiness in important ways.

When children enter preschool, kindergarten, and grade school, they must cope with more time away from home. They are asked to join with unfamiliar children and make friends, and get to know new adults. Children between the ages of two and seven are still egocentric; they show self-centered attitudes. This can make it hard at times to play happily and cooperatively with friends or siblings. Young children also develop the language to say and understand things which can build friendships or which can hurt feelings.

Most young children are happy, energetic, and enthusiastic about life. They approach experiences with eagerness and curiousity. However, as they grow and develop, they begin to cope with unhappy experiences as well. Many children face painful losses due to death. They may be fortunate and not lose a loved one to death. But they will almost certainly lose someone they know, or perhaps a pet. A death is an unhappy event. But with proper guidance, children can learn to accept it and avoid unnecessary stress and fear.

Other painful losses are related to our mobile society. Children can become unhappy about moving away from their homes, friends, neighborhoods, and schools. The uncertainties and stresses of becoming familiar with a new environment and new friends can also cause unhappiness.

Another form of unhappiness may involve the divorce of a child's parents. Divorce rates are roughly 50 percent. Approximately one-third of American children experience the divorce of their parents. Children's abilities to think and understand grow in early childhood. Yet they still need special help to deal with divorce. Preoperational children are likely to think in self-centered ways about the divorce. They may feel responsible for and guilty about the divorce. They do not realize that it is something over which they have no control.

During early childhood, children are normally happy and energetic. They often show their happiness during play and social interactions with parents and others. Strengthening happiness in early childhood involves providing love, encouagement, respect, and comfort in times of trouble. Yet it is still important for parents to reinforce happy behaviors and attitudes when they are observed. Parents and others should continue to model (show) happy actions whenever they reasonably can.

The need for parents of young children to have and use basic guidance and counseling skills becomes increasingly important. Parents must still use or manage consequences to influence child behavior. However, they must also become more skillful at influencing through talking. Ineffective or poor communication may build anger, resentment, loneliness, and unhappiness. Effective communication, though, can influence behavior in positive directions. It can increase respect, self-esteem, and happiness.

Figure 18-1. Children are normally happy and enthusiastic.

MODELING HAPPINESS

Children normally watch their parents very closely, and they imitate their behavior. Therefore, to increase the chances that children will show outward signs of happiness, parents should show these signs themselves. Outward evidence of happiness may involve expressing optimism, dancing, singing, smiling, and laughing. Other signs are whistling, humming, "playing around," and telling jokes or funny stories.

Expressing pleasure is another way for parents to communicate happiness to children. Thousands of things make adults happy, but they sometimes enjoy the happiness privately. It is often helpful to invite children into this private world of happiness by showing and explaining it. Parents can easily label things they find pleasurable. In so doing, they can model their happiness for their children. This is not difficult. Parents need only think of whatever gives them pleasure—nature, a painting, music—and show and explain these sources of happiness to their children.

Parents should also try to show happiness about who they are, what they have done in life, and what they look forward to doing. Children have a better chance at self-esteem and happiness when they see their parents value themselves and show happiness with their lives. Parents can show their enjoyment of friends and family by sharing happy occasions such as birthdays and holidays. In this way, children can gain a sense of being an important and valued part of something larger than themselves.

When children show signs of imitation or of developing their own unique, happy personalities, parents should reinforce them with delight, praise, and encouragement. Such reinforcement strengthens these behaviors and increases self-esteem.

REASONABLE EXPECTATIONS ABOUT HAPPINESS

No one is happy all of the time. If parents always appeared happy, they would communicate an unrealistic view of the world. To never show unhappiness would suggest that parents are perfect, all-knowing, all-powerful, and without personal problems. If children learn to expect life to unfold in this way, they are likely to become sadly disappointed. They may even view themselves as inadequate.

If parents show their happiness often, it is also reasonable for them to show mature reactions to disappointments and unhappiness. Children learn to *cope*, or deal with, problems when their parents show ways of resolving their own unhappiness. For example, a friend of Maria's mother was killed in a car accident. Maria was five years old when she found her mother crying over her loss. Her mother explained why she was sad, and said that she would miss her friend very much. Later, she talked with Maria about the good times she and her friend had shared together. She even managed to smile a little about how fortunate she was to have had such a good friend.

Parents who are unhappy about personal shortcomings can sometimes share their feelings with their children. Richard's mother shared that something had not gone well for her at work one day and that she was unhappy about it. However, Richard's mother then showed optimism. She discussed a way to cope with her problems. She explained that she would try to do better next time, and would write herself notes as a reminder to get things done on time. While the mother showed her unhappiness about a problem, she modeled an appropriate problem-solving strategy. She also modeled self-forgiveness, an important quality for children to learn.

When parents occasionally share unhappy feelings, they show their natural human reactions to common difficulties. They also help children to learn how to solve personal problems and regain happiness.

HAPPINESS IN PRESCHOOL AND SCHOOL-AGE CHILDREN

Children entering school face a variety of new experiences, some of which may be stressful. A *stressful experience* is one which places demands upon children to change or adapt to a new situation. They must learn to interact with many other children and with teachers. This is happening at a time in development when children are becoming more socially sensitive. Their growing concern about how they are treated by, and compared to, others can easily lead to times of both happiness and unhappiness.

Preschoolers, kindergarteners, and first graders may be proud and happy when they are accepted by others. They may also be hurt to the point of tears when other children show rejection through insults, ridicule, or physical aggression. Children must start to

Figure 18-2. The pride and happiness that children feel when they are accepted by others contribute to greater self-confidence and self-esteem. (HUD Photo)

deal with the fact that there are others who are faster, stronger, better looking, more popular, or smarter. In kindergarten and first grade, teachers will have higher expectations and stricter rules. They may begin to use more powerful forms of disapproval for inappropriate behavior. Hopefully, there will also be plentiful rewards for good behavior.

Parents should not concentrate on unhappiness and ignore happiness in children. Parents who are too busy to give attention to anything but unhappiness in a child risk teaching that unhappiness is the only way to get attention. It is important to reinforce expressions of joy and happiness in children. Parents can also help children to deal with the new kinds of unhappiness that may come from school and other social experiences.

Many possible sources of unhappiness may enter a preschool or school-aged child's life. There are several general approaches that parents can use to help in such situations. Some of these techniques are based upon familiar principles of teaching and learning. Other techniques relate more to successful methods of communication between adults and children.

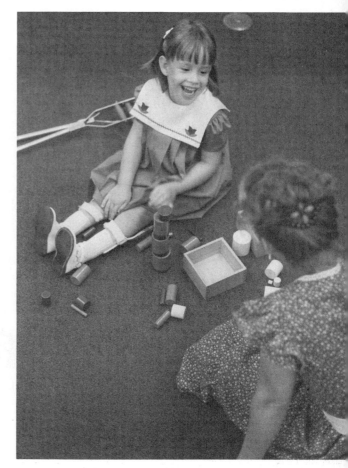

Figure 18-3. Parents can help children to deal with potential unhappiness by modeling happy behavior and encouraging a positive outlook. (March of Dimes Birth Defects Foundation)

HELPING CHILDREN TO DEAL WITH UNHAPPINESS

Parents who use effective communication skills can help others in many ways. Those who can communicate skillfully will experience benefits with their friends as well as children. Parents who can talk and listen to children and show a real concern, acceptance, and understanding of a child's unhappiness are on the right track.

A child's unhappiness sometimes occurs because of conflict with parents. Sometimes parents have to say no, or must discuss their child's behaviors that need improvement. In these situations, parents should emphasize the positive rather than the negative. **NOTE:** It is very important to not attack or negatively label a child's personality or character. Such statements lower a child's self-esteem and cause anger, resentment, and unhappiness. The following statements are mistakes that attack a child's personality or character.

- "You are a bad child."
- "You are a lazy person."
- "You are so disorganized."
- "You never listen to anything."
- "You can't be trusted."

When parents communicate to children in such ways, there is a danger that the children will begin to believe the negative labels. Not only might the children develop a negative view of themselves, but they may also begin to believe the negative labels and behave accordingly. For example, a child who has often been told she can't be trusted may begin to lie and steal more than before.

Instead of attacking a child's personality, it is much better to do the following.

1. Label the inappropriate behavior (not the child).
2. Tell why the behavior is inappropriate.
3. Tell the appropriate thing to do the next time.

These steps will help in listening and communicating more effectively with children. Good communication increases happiness shared between people who care about each other.

The form of criticism described in the three steps just named is called a reprimand. The reprimand avoids attacking the child, because only the behavior is described, not the child. Reprimands are often effective, but sometimes other discipline approaches are

also needed. It is possible to combine the reprimand with other effective discipline methods which do not cause unnecessary amounts of unhappiness for children.

Avoiding Unhappiness Due to Power Struggles

Sometimes children react negatively to their parents' requests to do things. When possible, it is good to resolve such conflicts without using parental power or force. This approach helps to avoid *power struggles*, situations of conflict in which someone has to lose and someone has to win. The following steps are a way to avoid power struggles between parents and children.

Step #1. Define the specific problem or behavior.
Step #2. Suggest possible solutions.
Step #3. Discuss the possible good and bad points of each possible solution.
Step #4. Decide on a plan that is acceptable to both the parents and the child.
Step #5. Try out the solution.
Step #6. Evaluate how the solution worked, and improve it if necessary.

By following these steps, problems can be solved in ways that make both parents and children happy winners. For example, one six-year-old and his five-year-old sister often argued over which television programs to choose. Their mother defined the problem (arguing over television programs) which was causing unhappiness in the family. They all discussed possible solutions to the problem. They decided that the children should take turns choosing television programs.

For a time, the solution seemed to work well. The family discussed how enjoyable it was to have no arguments over use of the television. However, arguments started happening again. At this point, the mother decided to use a logical consequence. She firmly told the children that, from now on, the television would simply be turned off when they fought. She said that it could be turned back on when they found a solution for the disagreement. This helped to control the problem, and gave the children experience in problem solving. When the children could not agree on whose turn it was to choose a program, they would flip a coin and settle the matter that way.

Sharpening Listening Skills

Parents should sharpen their listening skills to avoid power struggles and unhappy outcomes for themselves and their children. To *listen effectively* means to pay close, concentrated attention to what another is saying. The person who listens effectively will also pay attention to communication which is not verbal. *Nonverbal communication* is feelings which are not expressed in words. This includes tone of voice, gestures, and facial expressions.

Good listening skills alone can often prevent misunderstandings, anger, and much unhappiness. Parents who listen effectively have a better chance to understand their child's feelings.

The following are suggestions which will help you to become an effective listener. This skill can improve your relationships with children and others.

1. Be supportive—do not criticize. Show children that you care about them and their feelings. Children want to know that their thoughts and feelings have value. They learn this when parents and others show respect for their thoughts and feelings and appear genuinely interested. Showing eye contact, touching, nodding, and saying ''I see'' or ''I understand'' are important.

2. Set a good example. Try not to become upset or show shock at things that children may say. Stay calm.

3. Look into the other person's eyes. Consistent eye contact tells children that you want to understand and that you are paying attention. This may encourage them to talk and share their feelings more openly. By watching children's eyes and faces, you may be able to tell if they understand what you say and how they feel about it.

Figure 18-4. Good parents work on their listening skills. Even after a long day at work, this mother is still pleased to listen to her daughter.

4. Give your total attention. It is important to take the time to listen to what children are saying. Turn off the television or radio; put down your book or newspaper. Paying attention is a key to good listening. It will communicate that the children's thoughts are important and that you are interested.

5. Repeat main ideas. Repeat aloud the main ideas that children express. When you do this, you reflect or mirror back important information. This lets children know that you are really listening and that you care. You might say, "So your feelings are hurt" or "I can tell that it really frightened you."

Putting Listening Skills to Work

Richard, age seven, was upset about several things that had happened to him one day. Richard looked very unhappy to his father, who had just come home from work. We examine how Richard communicated his unhappiness. We also describe how his father first felt about Richard's feelings. In the following story, what you read in parentheses ( ) represents the father's accidental misunderstanding of the importance of the events.

Richard had fought with a friend in school. (It was a minor fight, no one was hurt, and this sort of thing did not happen often to Richard.) Richard and his mother had found a lost puppy in the snow. They brought it home and cared for it until its joyful owners were found. (But this was best for the puppy, and it was never really Richard's in the first place.) Also, the older neighborhood children were playing street hockey. They would not let Richard play because he did not know how to play and did not have a hockey stick. (But these things happen from time to time.

Before long, the other children will play a game that you can also play.)

Richard sadly said, "Today was really rotten!" The father suddenly realized that the events which were not as important in his eyes were of major importance to Richard. The father realized that the events should not be dismissed so lightly.

Richard and his father went for a walk in the snow. The father said, "When bad things happen, we can easily forget the good things that have happened, and the good things that will happen in the future." Richard asked, "But what if nothing good ever happens again?" His father admitted that that was possible, but not at all likely.

As they walked, they talked about the fight with Richard's friend. Richard said that his friend was much smaller, and so Richard was careful not to hurt him. The father praised Richard for being considerate and thoughtful in that way. He also mentioned that he, himself, always tried to talk out a problem rather than fighting. If talking did not help, he said he would just walk away or ignore the person. Richard asked, "But what if somebody chases you and hits you?" They both agreed that there were times when it was necessary to defend oneself. But they also agreed that Richard's fight at school was a different situation.

Richard and his father discussed the puppy. Richard had been very sad to see it leave with its owners. But with his father's help, Richard began to feel happier. His father told him that it was good to have rescued the puppy from the snow and to have looked for its owners. Of course Richard would feel sad, but the puppy was happy to be back with its family.

They talked about how much a hockey stick would cost and where they could buy one. They decided that Richard could use some of the money he had gotten for his birthday. His father offered to help by donating one-half of the cost. Richard asked his father if he would teach him how to play hockey, and his father agreed excitedly.

During the short walk, Richard and his father had learned about themselves and each other. They had discussed ways to solve problems, and ways to look at sad events. Richard's father had modeled an optimistic view of life. Because he had started to use effective listening skills, both he and his son returned to their home happier and with a closer relationship.

UNHAPPINESS DUE TO DIVORCE

It is estimated that since 1970, the divorce rate has been at about 50 percent. *Divorce* is the legal ending of a marriage. Divorce occurs between the husband and wife. However, when children are involved, the effect upon them is great.

It is often hard for parents to talk openly with their children about a divorce. Both parents may feel anger and hurt. But it is very important that, at first, they cooperate with each other to help their children to deal with the divorce. Caring and honest discussions with children are essential to help them with this task.

Without such discussions, children are likely to misjudge what is happening between their parents. It is common for children to feel that they have done something to split up their parents. They may also think

that there is something which they can do which will save their parents' marriage. Such beliefs are almost never the truth. However, it takes good communication to help children understand and believe that they are not at fault. If parents avoid discussing the divorce with the children, the children are likely to feel even greater stress and anxiety.

Divorce is difficult for both parents and children. The life of a divorced parent who must work and rear children alone is likely to be more stressful and demanding than for happily married parents. Often, the divorced parent must do all of the child-rearing tasks and face many financial problems. The individual must make many tough decisions without the social and emotional support of a caring mate.

Although the trend may be changing, the mother in the divorce is normally given legal custody of the children by a court judge. Legal *custody* means that one parent keeps the main responsibility for rearing the children and looking after their welfare. Therefore, divorced mothers are likely to feel the pressures of single parenthood most strongly. The divorced father, though, also has pressures, even though he may not be given custody of the children. The father is generally faced with child-support payments. He also has his own set of stresses due to not being part of his children's everyday lives.

While divorce has many disadvantages, there are cases when it can have important benefits. For example, divorce can have a positive influence upon children if parents were continually fighting while they were married. Other cases are when there has been violence or abuse, or when alcoholism or drug abuse has not been treatable.

Another possible benefit of divorce is that parents may try to put their time with their children to better use (quality time). This can provide greater warmth and emotional support for growth than the children experienced before the divorce.

If possible, parents who are divorcing should talk with their children together about what is going to happen. During these talks, it is important that parents do not criticize or place blame on each other while talking to the children. Children defend their parents no matter how bad the situation has been. Even though the parents' feelings toward each other have changed, the children still feel the need to love and be loved by both of the parents. Blaming in front of children nearly always has negative effects. Blaming tends to encourage children to take sides and increase their involvement in the parents' problems. Parents might discuss some of their differences with older children, but they should avoid making one parent seem at fault for the divorce.

It is important that children hear that both parents still love them. They also need to hear that they have in no way caused the divorce. Coping with a divorce can take a long time for both parents and children. Therefore, parents should encourage continued communication with their children. Parents and children may require the professional help of a psychologist or counselor before, during, and after the parents' separation. This extra help is certainly needed if children become very depressed, show great anxiety, or withdraw from favorite activities and loved ones.

Parents must continually reassure their children that both parents still love them

very much and will not abandon them. Children should be assured that they will continue to see both the mother and father, if this is true. Children have difficulty understanding divorce. The idea of their parents not living together may threaten their feelings of security and trust.

Parents must tailor their discussions to the levels of understanding of which their children are capable. When Maria was five years old, her parents decided to divorce. Her parents understood the importance of communicating effectively about the divorce to Maria. They had the maturity and self-control to sit together and list the kinds of things that they should discuss with Maria. Some of the things that they discussed with Maria are shown in Box 18.1. The items in Box 18.1 are necessary for any child of divorcing parents.

In the weeks and months before and after the divorce, Maria's parents talked with her about the divorce from time to time. At first, Maria was very sad that her parents would be divorced. In time, she accepted the fact that her family would never be the same. Maria appeared to adapt to her new way of life reasonably well.

Maria's parents found some children's books which deal with the topic of divorce. Both parents found it helpful to read the books to Maria, and then discuss the books.

The risks from divorce for children are high. Therefore, adults have the responsibility to choose their mate carefully. Adults must work to keep their families healthy and loving for their own and their children's growth and development. It is important for parents to realize the effects of divorce on their children and to put time and effort into helping their children adjust.

BOX 18.1

Main Points to Discuss with Children about a Divorce

The following material is based upon Arthur Bodin's suggestions found in Peter Keller's and Lawrence Ritt's manual, *Innovations in Clinical Practice: A Sourcebook.*

- ''We are going to get a divorce.''
- The word divorce should be explained.
- ''You did not cause our divorce.''
- ''You couldn't have prevented our divorce.''
- ''We are still your Mommy and your Daddy.''
- ''We both still love you very much.'' (This cannot be emphasized enough.)
- ''We will always love you.''
- ''You do not have to choose between us.''
- The new living arrangements should be explained.
- It must be explained that the parent who is moving out is not leaving the child.
- If it is true, explain that the child will spend some time with both parents.
- ''Mommy and Daddy may still continue to have some arguments.''
- ''We don't want you to take sides with either one of us.''
- ''Mommy and Daddy need to talk more about the divorce. You might need to talk about it too. We'll always be ready to listen and talk with you.''
- ''Sometimes you may feel upset and confused and be sad, hurt, or angry. Please don't keep these feelings to yourself. We want to know how you are feeling.''
- ''It's all right to tell your friends that we are getting a divorce. It's not a secret.''

UNHAPPINESS DUE TO DEATH

Emotionally healthy people do not want to die. Nor do they wish to see others die. However, death is as much a part of life as birth is. Children should be helped to cope with the fact that all living things will die. It is not sensible or healthy to view death as a horrible thing. This view is not accurate, and it interferes with the enjoyment of a happy and productive life.

How Children View Death

The ways that children think about death are influenced by their levels of cognitive development. Children think differently from adults. Very young children think that dead people can hear, see, taste, and feel things. Before about five years of age, children may think that dead people are simply living in another place. Later, children may think of death as a person deserting them or just being gone away for a little while. Before the age of seven years, children believe that death is reversible, and that things that have died can come back to life. At around eight years, most children see death as being permanent.

Young children do not understand that death happens to everyone. However, by about seven years, most children understand that death is a fact of life.

Helping Children to Cope with Death

It is important to bring up the topic of death when children are young. Death should be discussed at a level that children can understand. There are many opportunities to do this. For example, during one year in five-year-old Jimmy's home, a cat, several goldfish, and a bird died.

Jimmy's parents helped him to understand the death of these animals by telling him the truth in simple terms. When they talked about the bird, they explained that the bird was dead and would not come back to life. They said that it was sad that the bird had died, but it was wonderful that it was born and was able to fly and be happy during its life. Jimmy's parents showed some sadness about the bird's death, but they didn't cry or act as though it were a tragedy.

In the fall, Jimmy's parents showed him the leaves on the ground and talked about how the leaves grew and how they died. Jimmy asked if someday he would die, and his parents answered that he would. But they also told Jimmy that young children are normally very healthy and can look forward to growing very old before they die.

Jimmy's grandfather died when Jimmy was five. Jimmy's parents explained his death in a straightforward way.

Jimmy: "Grandpa is dead?"

Parent: "Yes, Grandpa is dead. He doesn't eat or breathe or talk or walk anymore."

Jimmy: "He can't play with me anymore?"

Parent: "No, honey, only live people can play. Grandpa got to play a lot when he was alive, but Grandpa died and he can't play anymore."

Jimmy: "Will he ever come to see us again?"

Parent: "No. Only live people can come and visit us."

Jimmy: "But why? Doesn't he love us? Is that why he won't come back?"

Parent: "Grandpa loved us all very much, but he can't come back. He didn't want to die and leave us. But everyone will die someday."

Jimmy: "Will you die, too?"

Parent: "Yes, honey, but it probably won't happen for a very long time. We never know for sure when we will die, but I'll probably live until you're all grown up. Most people don't die until they're very old."

Jimmy: "I wish Grandpa could come back. I'll miss him."

Parent: "We all loved Grandpa very much. We'll all miss him."

Figure 18-5. Pets can help children to learn about and accept the cycle of life. (© Ron Meyer/White Eyes Design)

At first, Jimmy acted like he did not feel badly about the loss of his grandfather. This is a normal reaction in young children. Later, however, Jimmy began to ask questions. He asked more questions than many children might. Other parents may need to help their children to have a similar conversation as Jimmy's. Other children may not be quite so willing to ask questions as openly as Jimmy did. This is another example of how parenting requires good communication skills.

Parents must be prepared to answer difficult questions. Some common questions that children ask have to do with the parent's deaths and what will happen to them if their parents die. Parents must be ready with an honest yet reassuring answer to such questions.

Jimmy went to his grandfather's funeral. His parents did not force him to do anything that he seemed afraid to do. They continued to answer Jimmy's questions openly and honestly. They did not hide their own sadness over his grandfather's death.

Jimmy soon got over the sadness from the loss of his grandfather, and seemed to be his old self again. Jimmy and his family still talked about Grandpa from time to time, and they enjoyed the good memories.

SUMMARY

All of us experience unhappy events in our lives. This is a part of living. It is important for parents to help their children learn to deal with unhappiness in honest and supporting ways. However, most children approach life in a positive and enthusiastic manner. Encouraging happiness in children is rewarding to both parents and children.

QUESTIONS FOR GROWTH

1. Name the period of cognitive development that children are in between the ages of two to seven years.

2. Explain how entering school presents possibilities for happiness and unhappiness in children.

3. Explain several ways in which you could model happiness for a child.

4. Why is it important for parents to occasionally show their unhappiness to their children?

5. Explain the problem that parents may face if they *only* pay attention to unhappiness in their children, and ignore happiness.

6. (a) Describe some ways that parents may mistakenly attack their child's personality or character. **(b)** Tell what harm this may do.

7. Identify the three steps in giving a reprimand properly.

8. Describe some of the ways that parents can avoid power struggles with their children.

9. List the steps involved in developing better listening skills.

10. Explain how children at different ages think about death.

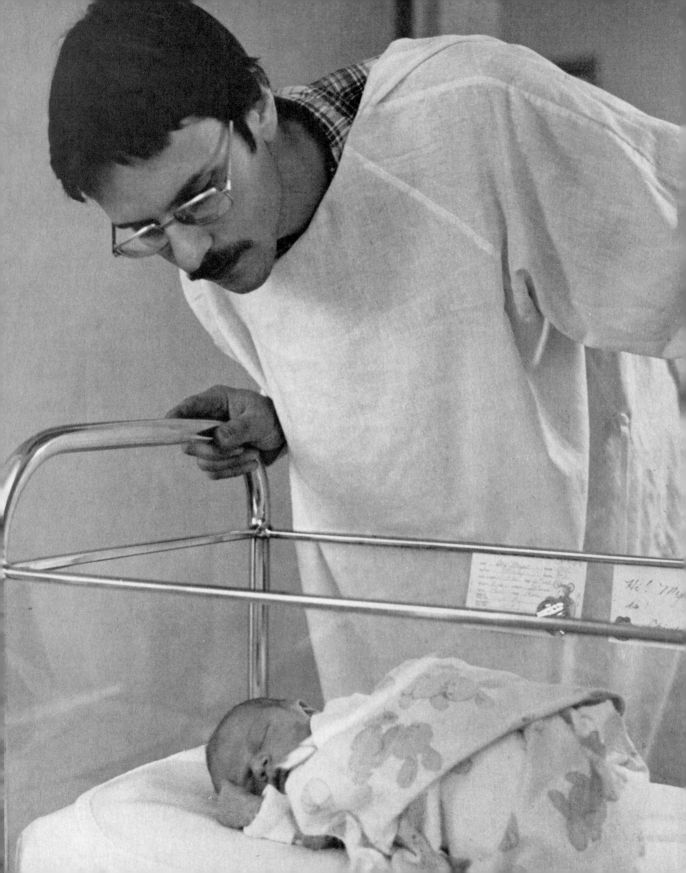

CHAPTER

19

Strengthening Coordinated Movement (Birth to Two Years)

Newborn babies have surprisingly advanced sensory abilities. That is, they can hear, see, taste, feel, and smell their world. Just as surprisingly, in contrast, is newborns' nearly total lack of physical coordination. Physical coordination refers to the ability to control one's muscles to move the body in skillful ways.

From birth to two years of age, humans normally achieve control over bodily movements. They learn from things seen, heard, tasted, smelled, and touched. Some of the early coordination achievements do not sound important by themselves. However, the development of eye-hand coordination, sitting, and crawling set the stage for other, more complex learning experiences.

In this chapter, we discuss the role of parents and others in strengthening coordination development in children from birth to two years. All of the developments which we discuss have importance. You will recognize that many of these skills will develop on their own, without special attention from parents. Yet the parents' attention and help can strengthen a child's development of coordination.

THE ROLE OF PARENTS IN DEVELOPING COORDINATION

It is useful for parents to understand the ways in which they may help, rather than limit, their baby's coordination development. In this chapter, we discuss ways in which parents can assist their child's normal development. **NOTE:** We do not suggest that parents try to push, press, or speed up normal development.

Watching and helping an infant to gain better coordinated movement is an exciting experience. Closely involved parents will see their infant's attempts to learn. Parents will notice personal mannerisms, small signs of progress, and growing responsiveness and affection.

The development of muscular coordination is influenced by the following factors.

- Genetics
- Biological maturation (delays or spurts of growth)
- The child's basic body build
- The child's general health
- Nutrition
- The child's environment

Parental influence is also a major factor. To some extent, development of all coordination skills depends upon providing opportunities for learning and development. Infants may differ by as much as two, four, or more months as to when they will learn to roll over, sit, stand, and walk. Different levels of nerve development, muscle development, and bone strength will account for some of the differences. Yet each baby's environment and parental relationships will also be influential.

Parents can provide infants with a variety of learning experiences. The suggestions in this chapter involve giving praise and physical help. We also recommend other reinforcement methods such as shaping and continuous reinforcement (CRF). Parents must observe coordination development and judge when to provide more or reduce reinforcement.

WHAT AN INFANT CAN DO FROM BIRTH

The early weeks of life are sometimes mistakenly viewed as a time when parents need only provide their infants with warmth, food, love, and cleanliness. New infants do usually just eat, look around for a while, and go back to sleep. However, infants already have some physical abilities which parents can help them to develop.

Newborns can see. They probably do not see color, and they are unable to focus their vision on objects at various distances. But newborns will look intently at bright objects. After a few days, their eyes will follow a moving light with short, jerky head motions. Newborns can also hear, taste, smell, and feel different textures.

Muscular development progresses in a definite pattern. Infants first learn to control their large muscles, starting at the head and shoulders. Later, the control extends down the body to the legs and feet. The muscles in the trunk of the body become coordinated before the more distant ones in the arms, hands, and fingers.

Figure 19-1. *What items in this child's environment will encourage her physical and mental growth?*

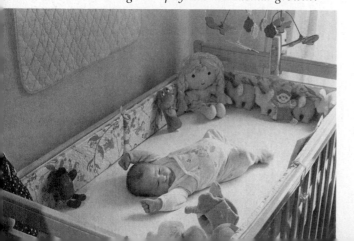

Newborns are soon able to raise and turn their heads when they are placed on their stomachs. They also show small creeping movements when in this position. If newborns are held upright with their feet against a surface, they will support some of their own weight. They will also make small, reflexive stepping movements. There are many other things that newborns can do. It is important to remember, though, that each infant is different. Individual variations will occur from baby to baby.

The suggestions in this chapter are arranged in the general order that they can be applied. However, parents can help with many of these goals at the same time. Success will depend, to a great degree, upon the parents' skill and the infant's readiness.

WHEN TO START HELPING

Table 19.1 is a developmental table which can guide parents in deciding when to start helping certain developments. Developmental tables show the order and probable times in which some coordinated movements generally develop. While the order of early coordination development applies to nearly all babies, the ages vary. Individual differences in timing may range from several weeks to several months.

Developmental tables cannot tell parents exactly when to start teaching any specific skill, because no two babies are the same. While the time to start various teaching methods will depend on the infant, parents can be prepared. For example, a developmental table may state that an infant is likely to shake a rattle which is placed in the hand at four months. But this does not mean that parents must wait until four months; parents can place a rattle into their infant's hand much earlier. By helping in this way, parents can help the learning of steps that must come before grasping and shaking the rattle. Nor should parents be concerned if their infant does not shake a rattle at four months of age.

Parents can arrange their infant's environment (surroundings) so that reinforcers are waiting for the infant's earliest tries at various skills. To *enrich the environment* means to provide the infant with interesting objects to reach for and view. When such reinforcers are available, infants are able to learn at their own pace.

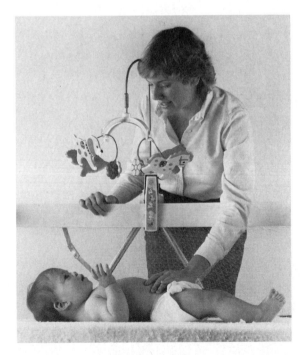

Figure 19-2. Parents can creatively enrich a baby's environment by providing changing "scenery" for the baby to enjoy. (Fisher-Price, Division of Quaker Oats Company)

Table 19.1

Average Coordination Abilities from Birth to Two Years

Age	Activity
Newborn	Lifts head while on stomach. Moves head from side to side while on back.
1 Month	Stares at surroundings and can follow slow movement. Still cannot support own head when held vertically.
2 Months	Places hands together.
3 Months	Lifts chest while on stomach. Can hold head up when helped to sit. Grasps a rattle.
4 Months	Reaches for objects. Eyes follow more distant objects. Plays with hands and clothing. Sits with support. Can roll over.
6 Months	Feeds self a cracker. Works to obtain a toy out of reach. Passes objects from hand to hand. Sips from a cup. Sits bending forward, using hands for support. Tries to crawl (around seven months).
8 Months	Plays pat-a-cake. Can grasp things between thumb and finger. Sits without support. Pulls self to standing position, walks holding onto furniture. Crawls with stomach on the floor.
10 Months	Accurate pincher grasp (thumb and first finger) of small objects. May stand alone and take steps. Crawls on hands and knees.
12 Months	Plays ball. Masters walking alone.
14 Months	Initiates housework. Scribbles with crayons. Stacks a tower of two cubes. Walks backward and manages own cup.
16 Months	Can remove some clothes. Walks up stairs. Goes down stairs creeping backward (about 18 months).
20 Months	Helps with simple tasks. Builds a tower of four blocks. Kicks ball, throws ball overhand. Uses spoon with little spilling.
2 Years	Turns pages singly. Imitates circular strokes with crayon. Puts on simple clothing. Washes and dries hands. Builds tower of eight blocks. Runs but falls in sudden turns, climbs on chair to reach an object. Balances on one foot for one second. Jumps twelve inches, pedals a tricycle.

The only way to know if an infant is ready to benefit from certain experiences is to try them out and see how the infant responds. If the infant responds with interest, delight, and signs of trying and improvement, the parents are probably right on target. Parents must learn to watch carefully for small improvements in the skills they are trying to teach.

Parents must also be patient. Learning does not always increase slowly and steadily. Learning may reach a temporary stopping point. Learning may also slip backward for a time, or may progress in leaps and bounds.

Strengthening Eye Coordination

Newborns have some basic abilities to see, as discussed earlier. However, learning to control the eyes and head in coordinated ways is a complex task. It involves biological readiness and a rich source of stimulation and reinforcement for proper development.

Eye coordination is necessary for the future development of eye-hand coordination. Eye-hand coordination, in turn, is important for early exploration and manipulation of the environment.

Visual stimulation is essential. The natural reinforcers for alert and skillful looking are seeing new and interesting things. If reinforcing sights are not present, infants' looking responses will occur less and less. Coordinated eye and head control will probably suffer. Studies have shown that babies who are exposed to many different sights, sounds, and objects to touch are generally more alert and responsive.

One of the most interesting things that infants can watch is a human face. When

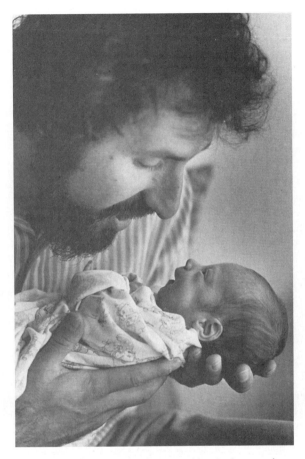

Figure 19-3. Infants are fascinated by the human face. (© Mark Antman/The Image Works)

parents spend time with infants in eye-to-eye contact, infants move their eyes in order to watch facial expressions change. This is a natural and enjoyable way to encourage visual development.

Jimmy's mother provided him with many bright and colorful things to see. She built a small mobile which would rotate slowly when a crank was turned. She then suspended a variety of interesting pictures and light objects from the mobile. She laid

Jimmy within about two feet of it and turned the crank. Jimmy stared with fascination as each of the reinforcing sights slowly moved by. Jimmy's mother had found a fun way to help Jimmy's development of eye coordination.

Providing interesting and new sights not only helps an infant's eye coordination. It also makes further learning easier. In addition, it makes the infant more pleasing to other children and adults who can provide and enjoy rich visual and social experiences.

Environmental enrichment is the earliest and easiest form of teaching that parents can use. Parents can make sure that infants' surroundings include many interesting objects. The objects should be of various colors, sizes, and shapes—stuffed animals, brightly colored stickers on the crib, mobiles, and so on. There is no need to spend a lot of money. Common household items and bright pictures from magazines work nicely. However, many initially reinforcing sights will become boring once an infant is familiar with them. Parents can save the reinforcing powers of various objects by changing their location from time to time, and by rotating them in and out of storage every few days.

Parents should also change infants' locations during waking times. Infants should be carried to different rooms in the home, driven in the car in an infant seat, and taken along on errands. In good weather, infants should be taken outdoors.

What infants gain from these experiences will depend upon their level of visual development. Infants can see at different distances, and can focus on objects depending upon their level of development. Color vision should be present at about two months of

Figure 19-4. New scenery and new experiences help children to develop intellectually, physically, and emotionally.

age. By around four months, an infant should be able to focus on both near and far objects almost as well as an adult can. Regardless of the level of development, though, infants should experience many different environments as long as they remain safe and comfortable.

Maria's parents played a useful game to improve her visual coordination. As early as Maria's first week of life, her parents showed her large objects held about 12 inches from her eyes. As Maria looked intently at an object, her parents slowly moved it from the left to the right. They moved it slowly enough so that Maria could follow it easily with her eyes. When her eyes had followed the object to the end of its movement, they immediately praised and stroked her. They also helped Maria to feel the objects with her hands and, if she wanted, with her mouth. Some of the objects made a noise, so Maria's parents would sound the noise also. The parents gradually made the game more complex, as appropriate to Maria's level of development. The important thing about this or any other way to help development is to keep it fun and at a level where the infant can be successful.

Strengthening Eye-Hand Coordination

Eye-hand coordination refers to an infant's ability to look at an object and then accurately reach out and touch it. This is not as easy as it sounds. Imagine the infant's field of vision. In it are two things which move about, occasionally disappearing from view. The infant's task is to learn how to accurately direct these things to touch and grasp whatever he or she sees. These things are, of course, the infant's hands.

The eye-hand coordination learning process begins in the first months of a baby's life. For instance, an infant's hands repeatedly find each other and also the infant's face and mouth. With infants, sucking is a strong reinforcing activity. Therefore, this activity strengthens the development of those coordinated hand movements that bring the hands or fingers to the mouth very early in life.

Parents should provide reinforcers for their child's first tries at reaching and grasping. A variety of safe but interesting objects and toys should be within easy sight and grasp range during the early months of life.

It is good for parents to help an infant to touch these objects. Around three months, infants will start to reach out for some of the things they see. These first clumsy reaches, and infants' fascination with sights, sounds,

and textures, are more than play activities. They are also learning activities. The toys used are not only toys, but also very important learning aids.

Suppose that three-month-old Richard is lying on his back. A string of brightly colored bells is suspended slightly above his chest and within easy reach. His hands move to and fro in short, jerky motions. Most of these clumsy movements do not touch the bells. Therefore, the movements are weakened because they are not reinforced. Suddenly, Richard's hand moves out and strikes several bells. At that moment, several important things happen. Richard feels his hands strike the bells, he hears them jingle, and he sees them move. Each of these consequences, separately, would be good reinforcers. Taken together, along with his parents praise and physical affection, they powerfully strengthen Richard's coordinated reaching and manipulation. If reinforcers are often present, infants will make rapid progress. If reinforcers are mostly absent, eye-hand coordination will be slowed. Also slowed will be more advanced coordination, self-care skills, and exploratory behaviors.

To strengthen eye-hand coordination, parents can play a game similar to the one used to aid simple eye coordination. This game can begin shortly before the third month, or whenever an infant appears ready to benefit from the experience. Richard's parents chose a large toy—the reinforcer—which Richard would watch intently and try to touch. Richard's parents took the following steps.

1. They held the object very still, about nine inches in front of Richard's face.
2. They reinforced any early responses that

Figure 19-5. *Eye-hand coordination: Babies will reach for interesting objects. Parents should provide reinforcement to encourage these actions. (© Ron Meyer/White Eyes Design)*

came fairly close to the toy by guiding Richard's hand to the toy. Richard's parents praised him for a good reach. They also let him hear any noise they could make with the toy, such as squeaking or rattling.

3. As Richard began to reach more and more accurately, his parents reduced their assistance. Much later, they started to use smaller objects. Slowly, they moved the objects a little farther away from Richard. His parents were careful to proceed gradually and in small steps. This avoided having Richard miss the object too often and experience too few reinforcers. If Richard was frustrated too often, he might begin to cry in protest.

4. After Richard had mastered reaching for nonmoving objects, his parents started to move an object very slowly to Richard's right and left. Richard would try to catch it. This task involved a more advanced form of eye-hand coordination. Richard's parents were careful to increase the difficulty of the task slowly. They used small steps so that Richard could be reinforced with success at each level.

Infants generally learn to grasp accurately between the ages of four and six months. By around eight months, infants are probably able to manipulate small objects, such as finger foods, with the index finger and thumb.

Helping to Raise the Head and Strengthen the Neck and Shoulders

Infants can normally raise their heads when they are lying on their stomachs. However, infants can be taught to lift the head more often, for longer intervals, and with greater control. This form of exercise will strengthen the neck, back, shoulders, and arms. This allows infants to visually explore the environment with greater ease. Later, infants will more easily develop the ability to roll over, creep, crawl, and to some extent to sit up and pull to a standing position.

By around two or three months of age, many babies can lift their heads and chests off the floor. This seemed like a reasonable goal to Jimmy's parents. As a step toward achieving it, they placed Jimmy on his stomach with interesting objects in front of him several times each day. They then played with Jimmy in the following ways.

1. With Jimmy on his stomach, they showed him a favorite toy. When he was watching it intently, they slowly raised the toy until Jimmy raised his head slightly. If he did not raise his head, his parents checked to be sure that the object interested him. They sometimes lifted Jimmy's head slightly in order to teach him the game. Later, they reduced their assistance until he lifted his head on his own.

2. Jimmy's parents immediately praised him and helped him to touch and fondle the toy when he lifted his head.

3. As he became stronger, they tried waiting for Jimmy to hold his head up a few seconds longer before praising him. Later, they waited for him to lift his head even higher.

This short and playful exercise can be fun for both the infant and the parents. It is important, though, to not overtire the infant. It takes a lot of effort for a young infant to lift the head. Jimmy's parents tried two short sessions each day, and they did not require too much too soon.

Helping an Infant Learn to Roll Over

Infants generally roll over between two and five months of age. Maria began to push forcefully against the floor with her arms at about 3½ months. Her parents started to help her learn to roll over. Maria's parents kept the game enjoyable. They would stop each session before Maria showed signs of boredom, tiredness, or unhappiness.

Maria's parents started by teaching her to roll from her stomach to her back. They placed Maria on her stomach on a padded surface, the carpeted floor. Then the parents placed Maria stomach-down on a pillow so that she was propped on her side at about a 30-degree angle. They then gently and slowly helped Maria to roll off the pillow onto her back. They immediately cuddled her and praised her. Sometimes they gave her a favorite toy for a few minutes.

As Maria became stronger at pushing herself off the pillow, her parents slowly reduced their assistance. When Maria could roll off the pillow without any help, Maria's parents lowered the height of the pillow slightly. They then repeated the teaching procedure at that level. As Maria mastered the skill, her parents gradually progressed to a lower height until she could roll over while lying flat on the floor.

This same teaching method could be used to teach Maria to roll from her back to her stomach. But this is a harder skill to learn, and Maria's parents did not hurry her. They were careful to use small, easy steps so that Maria would not become frightened. This approach is a form of backward chaining with prompting and fading. Not only did Maria learn to roll over, she also enjoyed the close and positive interaction with her parents.

Strengthening Creeping

Creeping is the ability to inch forward while lying on the stomach. Creeping requires a fair amount of strength and coordination. It occurs before crawling, the more efficient means of moving on all fours. Attempts to

creep are likely to occur shortly before five-and-a-half months.

Most parents naturally let their infants have some amount of time on the stomach on the floor, surrounded by favorite toys. Playpens are convenient for short periods when parents are unable to watch a baby closely. But playpens should not be overused. They limit an infant's ability to learn to creep and explore the environment.

Creeping is an important activity for overall development. Sooner or later, a reinforcing toy will be just out of reach. The infant will stretch and struggle, and will finally make the moves necessary to move forward and reach the toy. When this happens, the environment has reinforced the beginning of creeping. Parents can strengthen creeping by first placing toys just barely out of reach. As their infant progresses, parents can slowly increase the distance of the toys from the infant. Creeping will also be helped by the traction provided by a carpeted floor. It is more difficult to creep on a slick surface, such as linoleum.

Once Maria learned to creep on her stomach, she spent much of her time trying to creep up on her cat, named Muffet. Muffet never seemed to move away any farther or faster than necessary to avoid being caught by Maria. As the days and weeks passed, Maria learned to move faster. Muffet learned to make the necessary adjustments to stay out of reach. Sometimes Muffet would misjudge. Then Maria's efforts were reinforced when she touched Muffet and watched her run.

Maria could crawl nicely at the age of eight months. Her parents believe that Maria's game with Muffet had helped her in this

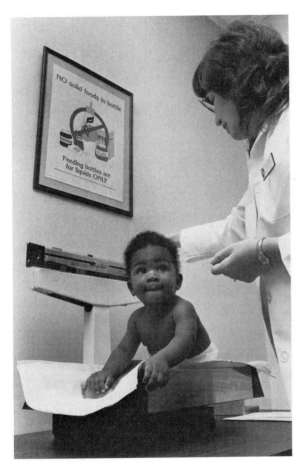

Figure 19-6. Each baby develops at a different rate. Regular medical checkups can reassure parents that their child is progressing normally. (USDA Photo)

coordination development. Luckily, Muffet was patient and extremely gentle, so Maria never suffered scratches or fright.

Maria was also helped by the fact that her parents clothed her in ways that did not interfere with creeping and crawling. They were aware that dresses and nightgowns could get in the way of creeping and crawling.

Strengthening Standing

What motivates most children to stand up between nine months and one year of age? Why do they bother? There are many reasons, including imitation of others around them and the home environment.

Almost everyone around a baby stands and walks. Imitation is a powerful force in learning. Therefore, it is likely that imitating others is one reason why children try to stand and walk.

In addition, a variety of new and tempting reinforcers await babies when they pull themselves to a standing position. One reinforcer is praise and excitement from parents and others when babies try to stand. There are also an endless variety of common household items which fascinate infants and reinforce their attempts to stand and climb.

As with almost all coordination skills, the development of standing is related directly to infants' tendencies to explore their environment. As a general rule, unless there is a danger, parents should avoid scolding infants for struggling to their feet and reaching for something. In the beginning, these actions require a huge effort. Punishment could easily have a slowing influence on this development.

Of course, there will be times when infants will reach for dangerous or fragile objects. Instead of punishing infants for forbidden exploration, parents can childproof the home. Toilet-seat covers should be kept down, gates should be placed across stairways, and medicines and poisons should be locked away. Parents should also put away anything fragile or dangerous. After their infant has learned to stand with ease, parents can return some of the stored objects, one or two at a time. They can then teach their infant to handle the objects properly or to stay away from them. It is normal and healthy for infants to be curious about their environment. It is the parents' responsibility to keep the environment safe.

To encourage standing, parents can put some toys on low tables, chairs, or a couch. When such desirable items are placed on surfaces above the floor, children tend to stand up much more often. Whenever infants try to stand, they should be praised enthusiastically.

Painful falls can discourage standing. Therefore, it is important to place toys and other reinforcers in carpeted areas until an infant becomes more skilled. Parents can also reduce painful falls in uncarpeted areas by using no-slip throw rugs. Parents should be on guard against roughly playing brothers and sisters, or pets which could knock the infant to the floor.

Some parents have hesitated to encourage their healthy and willing infants to stand out of fear that it could damage their bones. But it is not true that weak bones, bow legs, and the like result when healthy babies are encouraged to stand and support their own weight whenever they are ready. *Rickets* (a lack of vitamin D), or perhaps forcing an infant to stand when the infant cannot, may lead to bone-structure problems. Informed and responsible parents can easily avoid such problems.

Many babies learn to stand unsupported by about ten months of age. Some take as long as 14 months. When Maria showed enough strength to stand while holding on to something, her parents tried the following game. For a few sessions each day, Maria's parents stood her on her feet and provided her with balancing support. Then, while telling her to stand up, they slowly released their support of her. They released their support clearly, so Maria could see them doing so. They released their support for only about one second, and then caught her before she started to fall. They praised Maria and were sure not to let her fall. They also kept the sessions very short and enjoyable to avoid tiring her.

Maria became more and more skillful at balancing for short times. Her parents then increased their nonsupport to two, three, and finally four seconds. As time went by, Maria's parents praised only her more balanced and longer stands.

Helping Children to Walk

Most children begin to walk unsupported between 11 and 15 months. Before this occurs, they spend much time walking about while hanging onto tables, chairs, and so on. To help his development of walking, Richard's parents did the following.

1. They stood Richard in front of a couch or padded chair. They placed a favorite toy about one step to one side and out of his reach.

2. While verbally encouraging him to walk to the toy, Richard's parents helped him to take a step. When he stepped, they praised him and let him play with the toy briefly. As Richard gained in skill, his parents gradually moved the toy farther away from him. They reduced their assistance slowly.

Richard's parents also helped him to walk very short distances around the house. They slowly reduced their assistance as he walked more and more on his own. They stood behind Richard and supported him under his shoulders as he walked toward a desired object or person. From this position they could rock Richard's body to the left while nudging his right foot forward with theirs, and vice versa. In the meantime, Richard's arms were free for balancing. Later, to reduce their assistance, they moved their support from under Richard's shoulders to the outside of his shoulders. Still later, Richard's parents went from using their whole hands to just the tips of their fingers and then, finally, just one finger.

At first, Richard's parents helped him across short distances by praising nearly every step. As he became able to walk this distance with a very small amount of assistance, they began to extend the distance by one or two feet at a time. Gradually, Richard became able to walk alone with little difficulty. Richard's parents were careful not to tire or frustrate him.

When starting to help unsupported walking, it is important to praise nearly every step. Children should also receive praise and encouragement as parents slowly reduce their assistance. As children become able to walk farther, the amount of praise should also be reduced. Praise should begin to occur only for longer and longer sequences.

As Richard became skillful enough to walk unaided in his home without falling, his parents allowed him to experience walking elsewhere. Richard tried walking on different surfaces—grass, leaves, dirt, and sand. Richard's parents let him try out the many reinforcers which exist outdoors. They watched as he rustled through crisp fall leaves, tottered across uneven ground, and kicked happily through sand.

Such experiences are enjoyable to parents as well as children, and they lead to greater coordination and further learning. Parents and others who are involved with very young children can easily identify many other coordination goals toward which they can provide skillful and loving assistance.

Figure 19-7. *As children learn to walk, their world expands tremendously. (© Ron Meyer/White Eyes Design)*

QUESTIONS FOR GROWTH

1. Name six factors which influence the development of muscular coordination in infants.

2. Discuss the differences in newborns' ability to sense their world as compared to their ability to make coordinated movements.

3. Explain how parents may judge when to start various teaching methods to strengthen coordination.

4. How can reinforcement and a visually stimulating environment strengthen an infant's eye coordination?

5. Explain what can be done to help improve infants' eye-hand coordination skills.

6. (a) What can parents do to help their infant to raise the head with greater strength and control? **(b)** What future coordination abilities can this achievement help?

7. Describe some things that parents can do to help their infant learn to creep.

8. Explain how parents can arrange the home to make it easier for their infant to learn to stand up.

9. Name some of the natural reinforcers which can strengthen standing in infants.

10. How can parents protect their infants and toddlers from unnecessary punishment while learning to stand?

11. Name some of the teaching mistakes that parents should avoid when strengthening coordination.

12. Explain some of the things that you could do to strengthen walking in a child.

CHAPTER
20

Strengthening Coordinated Movement
(Two to Seven Years)

Hwong, age twelve, was a very kind and sensitive person. Although he was big for his age, he never picked on smaller or weaker kids. Hwong was warm and gentle with everyone, and was a very bright student. Though he was a little shy, he liked to help others with their schoolwork. Hwong was also a good musician. He worked hard to master the violin, piano, and organ.

However, Hwong's physical coordination in sports was very poor. One reason for this might have been his genetic or biological makeup. Another likely reason, though, was Hwong's lack of experience, from early on, with those activities which sharpen coordination skills.

Hwong was especially quiet in gym class. He seemed to be uncomfortable and fearful. He could not tumble or swim, and he was confused and clumsy when playing touch football, basketball, and baseball. Other kids began to tease Hwong without mercy. They watched his every move and made jokes and laughed at him.

Finally, Hwong stopped going to gym classes reliably. When he did go, he usually said he had a headache, or a cold, or a sore ankle. He always apologized to the coach for not feeling well. It is not hard to imagine how Hwong must have felt about his lack of skill at sports, and why he tried to avoid gym class. Yet, it is most likely that his coordination problems could have been prevented at an early age.

Coordinated movement normally develops in a fairly predictable pattern in the first two years of life. Between two to seven years, development is less predictable. Yet an enormous number of small and large muscle skills are mastered during these years. Even the small skills are important and lead to further coordination development. See Table 20.1.

During the ages of two to seven, some developments still occur in fixed sequences. For example, children can normally stand on one foot at about two years. They can normally walk down stairs, alternating feet, at about three years. They can run, stop, and turn skillfully at about four years.

Many other coordination skills appear at widely differing ages. Some children can turn a somersault at three years. Others may learn in a first-grade gym class. Some children may learn to ice skate when they are five, while many learn in junior high school. Some skills may never be learned at all. Many adults do not know how to swim, do a cartwheel, dance, shoot a basket, or throw a baseball.

WHY IS PHYSICAL COORDINATION SO IMPORTANT?

You may be thinking, "So what if a child does not learn how to hit a ball with a stick?" Or "Why is it so important that someone learn to jump rope?" The fact is, such abilities are important for further development. Their

Table 20.1

Average Coordination Abilities (Two to Seven Years)

Age	Activities
2 Years	Turns pages singly, imitates circular strokes with crayon. Puts on simple clothing, washes and dries hands. Builds tower of eight blocks. Runs but falls in sudden turns, climbs on chair to reach an object. Balances on one foot for one second, jumps twelve inches, pedals a tricycle.
3 Years	Buttons, dresses with supervision. Copies a zero (0), picks the longer of two lines. Balances on one foot for five seconds. Pours well from a pitcher. Goes up and down stairs with one foot per step. Catches a large ball with arms out straight.
4 Years	Balances on one foot for ten seconds, hops on one foot. Catches a bounced ball, catches a ball with bent elbows. Draws a person with three parts, cuts on a line with scissors. Makes designs and crude letters. Does stunts on a tricycle. Eats with a fork and knife, rarely needs help to complete meals.
5 Years	Catches a small ball with elbows at sides, throws well. Skips with both feet, marches in time to music. Learns to ride a small bicycle. Draws a person with six parts. Copies designs, letters, numbers.
6 to 7 Years	All areas of coordination development become more skilled. Children may grow in their ability to use coordination in play, organized athletics, music, and matters of self-care.

importance goes well beyond the specific skills involved.

A major reason for being concerned with the development of physical skills is that children, like Hwong, can suffer if they are unnecesssarily clumsy. Unusual awkwardness in a child of four years or more can make it hard to find friends. Much of a young child's early social life revolves around play and games. Therefore, a child is often judged by playmates according to his or her level of skill in play and games.

The common observation that children can be very cruel to one another is shown in their treatment of those who are physically awkward. The child who stumbles and falls may be laughed at. The one who runs slowly is often left behind. Later, when children are old enough for team games, the awkward child may be rejected or chosen last. Such ridicule and rejection can be embarrassing and hurtful to a child.

Physically awkward children may become very withdrawn and timid. A steady diet of social rejection can easily cause a child to feel inadequate. Sadly, such children may generalize their feelings of inadequacy even to situations which require no physical competence. They may refuse to join in any activity which resembles a game. They may avoid activities which are important to their social and intellectual development. Children who have met with rejection from peers because of clumsiness may show a tendency to "freeze" in any performance situation. Thus, a child's emotional reaction to past experiences can interfere not only with coordinated behavior, but also with learning in other areas.

Figure 20-1. Why is it important to develop physical skills and coordination?

There is much that parents can do to reduce the likelihood of such an outcome for their child. But there is no guarantee that the child will not experience problems. For example, an adequately coordinated six-year-old who plays with older, more physically skilled children may look clumsy by comparison. Also, factors such as genes, rate of growth, and basic body build will influence the development of a child's coordination.

There is a somewhat positive view of the tough ways in which children treat those who are less skilled. With good parental guidance and support, occasional peer

Figure 20-2. Meeting physical challenges can give a child poise and self-confidence. (Pocono Mountains Vacation Bureau)

able to transfer these skills to other activities such as skating, dancing, or tennis. The child's feelings of accomplishment may also stimulate interest in other difficult tasks.

Children who successfully explore the capabilities of their own bodies may come to better appreciate and preserve their health in later years. People who help adults to solve alcohol and drug problems stress the importance of teaching children to value their health and physical well-being. These people feel that this is one way to help avoid future drug-abuse problems.

rejection may help to make a child more sensitive to other people's feelings. Still, caring parents will certainly want to help their child to become well coordinated.

Perhaps the most important benefit of co-ordination learning is that other, less obvious abilities may be learned at the same time. This is called *incidental learning.* For example, a child who learns to throw, catch, and hit a ball not only learns these skills, but is also likely to be included in ball games where other important lessons can be learned. The older child may learn to cooperate with teammates, to follow game rules, and to both win and lose with grace.

Incidental learning occurs in many ways. A child who learns gymnastic skills may also learn to watch the teacher carefully and follow instructions. The physical exercise will benefit muscle development and graceful, coordinated body control. The child may be

Figure 20-3. Team sports teach sharing, appreciation of others' skills, and how to win and lose graciously. (USDA Photo by Larry Rana)

The challenge for parents is to help their child to develop natural coordination abilities in interesting and enjoyable ways. A common mistake, which should be avoided, is pushing a child to do too much. Instead, parents can enjoyably stimulate their child's interest in many things. They can encourage and help strengthen advanced coordination skills in the direction of their child's greater interests.

The coordination skills discussed in this chapter are examples of many that young children may be helped to pursue. These skills are not presented as being essential for normal coordination development. However, certain advantages of each skill are discussed.

GUIDELINES FOR TEACHING ADVANCED COORDINATION

Children learn many coordinated physical movements without intensive teaching. A special effort is normally not needed to teach a child to turn a light switch on and off, for example. The child will likely imitate the parents' behavior. Then, the immediate reinforcer of the light going on or off will automatically teach the behavior. In the same way, children learn that pushing a ball makes it roll, and turning a door knob opens the door. However, while much learning occurs naturally, some coordinated skills are not so sure to develop. Such skills are generally the very complex ones. Their development can be strengthened by good teaching approaches.

Complex coordination skills are best taught when reinforcers are combined with both encouragement and positive suggestions. Children are very likely to imitate what parents

or teachers do. This emphasizes the importance of demonstrations—showing how to play catch with a large ball, shoot baskets, skip, or draw pictures. Parents should start teaching at an appropriate level for each child. One of the principles of good teaching, no matter what the task, is to start at a level where a child is able to experience the reinforcer of success.

Parents must also avoid causing tension or nervousness in their child about not being

Figure 20-4. Good teaching approaches combined with encouragement can help children to enjoy success in developing coordinated skills. (March of Dimes Birth Defects Foundation)

successful. These emotions can result from ridicule, criticism, or too much punishment. Such emotions can also be caused by asking children to do tasks which are too difficult. Tension and nervousness often block, or interfere with, the performance of coordinated behavior. These emotions can cause a child to become frustrated and quit.

The following information includes specific suggestions for strengthening a variety of coordination skills, such as:

- Small muscle skills (coloring, painting)
- Catching a ball
- Running and galloping
- Riding a tricycle
- Climbing
- Hitting a ball with a bat
- Shooting baskets
- Riding a bicycle

These skills are much more important than they appear at first glance, because such skills result in further coordination learning.

Small Muscle Skills

Small muscle skills allow children to use their arms, hands, and fingers well. During the first two years of life, children learn how to grasp and handle toys, interesting objects, and food. These abilities improve with time and practice.

Around the age of two years, children can begin to learn greater small muscle control if they are given opportunities and encouragement to play with crayons. Richard's mother sometimes sat with him and played with crayons. She provided blank sheets of

Figure 20-5. Complex skills are learned through imitation and repetition. (© Ron Meyer/White Eyes Design)

paper, different colors of crayons, and herself as a model. For many sessions they just scribbled and had fun with the many colors and color combinations. Richard's artwork was often hung up on the refrigerator for others to see and praise.

Richard and his mother sometimes colored large pictures. The mother knew that Richard could not yet color only within the lines, and so she simply encouraged his experimentation. Richard admired his mother's pictures, and over time his coloring within the lines of pictures began to improve.

Richard's mother also provided opportunities to use watercolors and finger paints. Richard especially liked finger painting, and his parents hung up several of his paintings for everyone to enjoy. Richard liked to create new things. As he did, many of the valuable small muscle skills needed for learning to draw, print, and many other things continued to develop.

Catching a Ball

Children can toss a ball a very short distance at about one year of age. They should be given many opportunities to practice this skill early. When Jimmy was about seven or eight months old, his mother started playing with him by rolling a large, soft ball back and forth between the two of them on the floor.

Jimmy could be expected to catch a large ball in the air at about three years. But his parents began a simpler version of this activity when he was about one year old. They used a ball about ten inches in diameter, and light enough not to hurt if it should strike the face. At first, the game of catch closely resembled handing the ball back and forth between Jimmy and his parents. As Jimmy's catching and throwing skills increased, his parents began to slowly increase the distance between them. When Jimmy became more skilled, his parents used a slightly smaller ball.

Foam-rubber balls are excellent for teaching children how to catch. Children can learn to catch balls thrown faster from greater distances if these balls are used rather than regular basketballs and footballs. Regular balls are harder to handle, and they can hurt children. When children are hurt or miss too many catches, it is only natural for them to learn to dislike playing ball.

Running and Galloping

Young children should be encouraged to experiment with movement and action in many ways, such as through running and galloping. In informal and uncontrolled play, children gain in their abilities to control countless body movements.

Maria's mother often took her to parks and playgrounds. Maria sometimes met other children in these places, and they would play on the equipment and run, jump, and chase one another. This free play helped to strengthen Maria's muscles and improve her coordination.

Maria's mother often played with her in their yard. They sometimes played chase. The mother was sure to run slow enough to be frequently caught by Maria. One day the mother helped Maria to learn how to gallop like a horse. She showed how to run and yet keep the same leg in front of the other. Maria enjoyed the fun of galloping and making noises like a horse.

Riding a Tricycle

Riding a tricycle (a three-wheeled bike) is easily learned at about two or three years. However, the construction of the tricycle should be good enough so that a child does not have to pedal with great strength. Maria's parents helped her by assisting the alternating thrusts of her legs. They gently pushed down on her thighs until she learned the rhythm involved. Her parents then slowly reduced their assistance, and off Maria went on the tricycle. Maria's parents were sure to praise small improvements as they occurred. However, making the tricycle go was reinforcing enough to keep Maria practicing. On the other hand, if Maria had shown no interest in riding the tricycle, her parents would have waited and tried again later.

Climbing

Children will learn many climbing skills without direct teaching. Between the ages of one and two, children normally will learn to climb onto and off of chairs, creep up and down stairs, and eventually walk up and down them. Richard tried to climb anything which was near and climbable. His parents worried that he would fall and get hurt, so they did set some limits on what he could do. Yet they also valued the strength and coordination which Richard was gaining through climbing. His parents enjoyed his pride and excitement after he climbed over some small obstacle.

Parents should try to limit climbing to relatively safe areas. One way to do this is to take children to parks which have swings, slides, and the like. If there is room, it is also good to have a combination swing and jungle-gym set in the family's yard. Richard had such a set, and his back yard became the neighborhood ''recreation center.'' This was good, because Richard was helped to learn social skills such as sharing and taking turns. Also, as older children played on the equipment,

Richard improved his own coordination skills through imitation.

Hitting a Ball with a Bat

Many parents wait until their child is about seven before helping the child learn to swing a baseball bat. These parents wait about four years longer than is necessary. Jimmy's parents taught him how to hit a ball when he was three. They did not start with a regular bat and ball. Regular bats are too long and heavy for young children. Regular baseballs are too small to hit easily, and they hurt if they hit the body. Instead, Jimmy's parents bought a lightweight plastic bat, about four inches in diameter, and a large plastic ball. With such equipment, even a small child can manage to hit a slowly pitched ball and watch it travel in the air.

Jimmy was thrilled when he hit the ball, and his parents showed their excitement, too. At first, Jimmy's mother stood close and pitched very slowly. Later, as Jimmy's skills increased, she moved farther away in small steps.

Jimmy soon became very skilled with the large plastic bat and ball. His parents then changed to a smaller plastic bat and ball which more closely resembled regular ones. At age seven years, Jimmy was strong enough to handle a regular bat and ball. He easily made the change and maintained good batting accuracy because of his early learning.

Shooting Baskets

A strong child of six can only barely get a regular basketball to a hoop 12 feet above the ground. However, parents can use plastic balls and miniature basketball hoops. The backboards and hoops are about four feet above the floor. This allows a very young child to enjoy the excitement of shooting a basket. Maria shot baskets in the playroom with her parents' help when she was about two. Maria enjoyed this so much that she asked visitors to shoot baskets with her.

Of course, it is not essential to buy a toy basketball hoop. Maria's parents could just as easily have interested her in a game of shooting the ball at an empty wastebasket.

Many outside backboards are designed to attach to a pole. These backboards can easily be lowered until older children can enjoy success. Later, as children's strength and accuracy increase, the height of the backboard can slowly be raised.

Riding a Bicycle

Most children are able to ride a bicycle (two-wheeler) at about five or six years without too much help. But there are several ways that parents can assist in the learning of this skill. First, it is important to buy a bike of the appropriate size. A child should be able to straddle the seat with both feet on the ground. Next, a strong pair of adjustable training wheels can be installed. In the beginning, the training wheels can be adjusted so that the bicycle is supported in a stable, upright position.

When Richard's parents began, only a few short periods of assistance were required to get him moving on his own. Some children will need more help. Others will ride off immediately without assistance. All children, however, will benefit from helpful hints. Parents should describe and show how to go

into a turn without falling and what to do if the bike does start to tip. Richard's parents helped him to practice turns until he could do well without falling. This helped to reduce the chances of bad falls. As Richard gained in skill, his parents raised the training wheels in gradual degrees. This did not teach Richard to ride totally without training wheels, but it did help him to learn to control the bike and his body.

When Richard's parents felt that he had learned good control of his bicycle with training wheels, they asked him if he would like to try it without the training wheels. Richard was excited and willing. Because he had

Figure 20-6. *Parents should be sure that children understand safety rules before allowing access to any bicycle or scooter. (Radio Steel & Mfg. Co.)*

already learned most of the necessary skills, only about 15 minutes of assistance were required. Richard's mother jogged along beside him and steadied the bike as he pedaled. Slowly, she reduced her assistance. She began to let go for short periods, and then longer ones. However, she continued to run alongside to prevent bad falls until Richard had mastered the skill.

Many people do not view learning to ride a two-wheeler as an important event. However, we suggest that it is. The excitement shown by parents and others is similar to that shown when a child first walks. Riding a bike makes independent social development possible. Bike-riding children can now join older children whose play often involves bicycles. Children who ride bikes can expand their exploration territory. Whenever and wherever parents feel a bike-riding child can go, the child is likely to go.

NOTE: Richard's parents were careful to consider safety when dealing with this new independence. There is no exact age at which a child should be allowed to ride a bike in the street, or ride to school. Children always say, ''I can do it, I'll be careful.'' However, responsible parents should rely upon their own judgment. Their child's life is at risk, and young children normally have little understanding of the dangers involved.

The best and perhaps only way to judge a child's ability to ride safely in traffic is to ride with the child. When parents do this, they can teach safety through demonstrations, reminders, and praise for safe bicycle operation. Safety rules will depend largely upon the traffic conditions the child will encounter. Parents should place limits on bike riding. A partial list may include the specific limits where the bike can be ridden, staying close to the curb, and looking carefully before crossing the road. Other limits should include stopping and walking across intersections, and stopping at all stop signs. Parents must use caution and good judgment to decide whether or not their child is ready to ride alone.

Parents must set very high standards of safety for bike riding. They should not allow their child to ride alone until they repeatedly observe that the child meets the standards. Even then, parents should watch whenever they can, and continue their praise for proper bicycling. If rules are broken, it is appropriate to restrict the use of the bicycle until parents and the child can ride together for further teaching.

Teaching Other Complex Skills

A great deal of skill is needed to teach complex abilities. Swimming, gymnastics, and especially musical instruments are often best taught by experienced teachers. Good teachers break the complex skills into smaller skills which can be taught separately. Once all of the parts are learned, they can be combined to form the desired skill. The skilled swimming teacher who uses this method would instruct the child as follows.

1. Sit on the edge of the pool and kick feet in the water.
2. Sit on the edge of the pool and blow bubbles into the water held in the teacher's cupped hands.
3. Lie on the stomach at the edge of the pool and blow bubbles into the water.

4. Hold onto the side of the pool and kick in the water.

5. Hold onto a float board and kick across the pool both on the stomach and on the back.

6. Practice jumping into the shallow end.

7. Practice the "dog paddle" with the teacher giving support. This support is then slowly reduced and eliminated.

8. Dog paddle from three to five feet out in the shallow end of the pool to the side of the pool.

9. Extend the distance of the dog paddle in small steps.

Figure 20-7. *These girls may or may not grow up to be dancers, but they are learning valuable lessons in self-discipline, social adjustment, and meeting physical challenges. (H. Armstrong Roberts)*

The exact order may change somewhat depending upon the particular teacher and child. However, the steps are an example of how a complex skill can be broken into small parts and then combined. A similar approach may be used to teach a child how to button, snap, zip, and tie clothing. After each individual part is learned, the skills are combined to form the complex skill of getting dressed.

Another complex skill that many parents hope their child will learn is playing a musical instrument. Good-quality teaching is essential but may be difficult to find. Parents should shop around for a good teacher. It helps to talk to other parents whose children are progressing well. Student progress is probably the best evidence of a teacher's skill.

Parents should talk with possible music teachers and find out if they try to make learning fun. Parents should ask how the teachers teach. Do they use praise, token systems of some sort, or perhaps a child's favorite songs as part of the teaching approach? Are the teachers concerned with changing their approaches to fit each child's needs? Parents should go with the child to some lessons and see if a teacher is actually doing the things which the teacher and parents discussed.

Home practice, praise, and modeling are also very important. Some parents show their interest and involvement by playing an instrument themselves. Parents can show appreciation by listening to and outwardly enjoying music often. They can also listen to music that features their own child's instrument.

When parents demonstrate their own musical values, modeling and imitation have a chance to work. While a musical instrument may be more easily learned at younger ages, it is never too late to learn. Some parents have taken their role as a model seriously enough to start taking lessons themselves. One father slowly learned to play the piano by having his seven-year-old son, who was taking lessons, teach him. This unique approach put the child in the role of the teacher. This added a new dimension of responsibility and reward to the child's musical activities.

SUMMARY

Learning a coordination skill influences development in other areas, such as social adjustment and intellectual development. In addition, when children master their environment and gain control over their own bodies, they have met one of the greatest challenges of childhood. Parents more than anyone else, have the opportunity to help children develop their physical coordination.

QUESTIONS FOR GROWTH

1. Explain how coordination problems can influence a child's personality.

2. Name four coordination skills that may develop at widely varying times, or perhaps not at all.

3. Explain the reasons why it is important to learn a variety of seemingly unimportant skills such as running, jumping, throwing a ball, or batting.

4. Discuss how awkwardness in children four years and older can influence their social development.

5. Describe the kinds of incidental learning that can occur when children learn a variety of coordination skills.

6. Explain the general suggestions for best teaching complicated coordination skills.

7. Explain how you might help a young child learn to play catch with a ball.

8. How might you help a young child to play tennis?

9. Explain how you might help a child learn to shoot baskets.

10. Tell the age at which most children learn to handle a two-wheel bike.

11. What can parents do to start helping their children to deal with various degrees of "tippiness" with their bikes?

12. When can parents consider removing safety wheels from their children's bikes?

13. Describe the concerns and considerations involved in giving children permission to ride their bikes alone.

14. What is recommended that parents do if they observe their children making dangerous bicycle-riding errors in traffic?

15. Explain how very complex coordinated activities can be taught in pieces and then recombined. Provide an original teaching example with your explanation.

CHAPTER

21

Strengthening Language
(Birth to Seven Years)

The process of language development in children is fascinating. Communication skills are essential in everyday life. Language progress is strengthened when infants and young children interact with others through the sounds they make. The word *interact* means that communication works both ways. Parents and their children grow to understand one another through their expressions, movements, physical contact, and the sounds they make.

Infants in the early part of the prespeech period (birth to one year) make many sounds. Their parents answer (interact) with their own language as well as repeating the infant's sounds. Parents, in this way, help infants and young children to exercise their natural language abilities.

Parents are encouraged to look for meaning in infants' and children's sounds. Re-searchers believe that parents should pay less attention to their young child's form ("cooka") of communication. Instead, they should pay more attention to the meaning ("I want a cookie."). Of course, prespeech infants require much translation of the meaning of their sounds. Infants are able to make many different kinds of sounds. Yet young children in the language period (starting at about one year) also require translation of meaning, especially in the first three years of life.

Infants and young children really work to acquire language. They experiment with sound and word combinations. Although we do not fully understand how, they learn to use complex grammar rules. They will be less frustrated in this effort when parents try to understand their meaning rather than concentrating on form.

Another factor important for language development seems to be the range of language experiences. Children have a wide range of experiences when interacting with responsive adults. Quality language interactions can occur when children communicate with several adults. This appears to be more beneficial than language interactions with only one adult or other children.

Children also appear to benefit when their parents use a less directive pattern of communication. In other words, they benefit when parents often follow the children's lead in conversation. By allowing children more of a chance to control language interaction, parents can look for meaning in what is said. Parents can then respond. They might provide agreement, questions, or more information. This process is similar to what occurs

Figure 21-1. Although we do not fully understand how, children learn complex rules of grammar and become able to communicate abstract and concrete thoughts and ideas. (Action)

when parents reinforce exploration and manipulation of the environment.

Parents can simplify their language to suit the particular child's level of language development. As the child's ability to speak and understand grows, parents naturally start to speak to the child in more complex ways.

STRENGTHENING LANGUAGE DURING THE PRESPEECH PERIOD

Children are born with the ability for language. But there are limits to how rapidly language can be acquired. In general, language development can be expected if an infant is given two kinds of language stimulation. One, parents must talk to their infant so the infant can hear and become familiar with language. Two, parents must respond when their infant makes sounds. Language capabilities are heavily dependent upon inherited ability. But parents must provide an environment which is responsive to their infant's early vocalizations (sounds).

During the first two months, infants normally make nearly all of the sounds necessary to speak any of the world's languages. Loving parents are responsive to these sounds. They will coo or babble back when an infant coos or babbles. Parents will smile, laugh, touch, and praise their vocalizing infant. These sorts of responses are very reinforcing for language development.

Parents and infants develop a give-and-take relationship in language development. After a time, infants start to make the sounds of their parents' language more often. These sounds occur because the infants are becoming more skilled at imitating their parents.

Parents also respond with more enthusiasm to those infant sounds which are more like language. The sounds that parents make become more important to infants as they become more attached to their parents. Infants eventually seem to find it reinforcing to make their parents' sounds themselves.

Helping Infants to Talk

There are no exact ages at which all infants will benefit from the language-development suggestions which follow. The information and tables presented in Chapter 6 provide a rough guide. Yet every child is different. Some infants are much slower or faster in their language development, yet are still within the normal ranges.

Our suggestions for helping infants to develop language are not meant to be used as formal procedures. The suggestions can be used in natural and relaxed interactions between parents and infants. Each day provides parents with opportunities to play with their infants in ways which will help them learn. Opportunities arise while playing with toys, bathing, shopping, changing diapers, and on outings, to name a few. The following are specific suggestions for strengthening language development in infants.

- Talk to infants
- Help infants to imitate sounds
- Help the understanding of simple words
- Help infants to say words

Talking to Infants

Parents' voices appear to fascinate newborns. Newborns will look at their parents' faces.

Figure 21-2. Parents who frequently talk to their infants give them a head start in language skills. (March of Dimes Birth Defects Foundation)

Upon hearing the parents' voices, newborns will look even more closely. This is especially true if the parents speak in a higher than normal tone.

When parents speak, they provide a model for their infant to imitate. Shortly following birth, infants can hear well enough to notice small differences in sounds. Therefore, parents should talk to their infant right from the beginning. Probably no other language-development method should receive more emphasis.

Some parents say that they feel funny talking to someone who does not talk back. But it is important that they talk to their infant anyway. Of course, there will be some quiet times. But parents should never run out of perfectly natural things to say to their infant. They can talk about how much they love the infant. They can talk about the infant's new family. They can tell the infant what they are doing at the moment, and what they plan to do later. Parents should talk in a pleasant and expressive tone. This talking can occur during diaper changes, playing, feeding, bathing, cuddling, and so on.

An infant's listening experiences can be enriched with other sounds. The radio, television, stereo, or noises from outdoors provide listening experiences. However, these sounds cannot be a substitute for human language. Human language is both stimulating and responsive to the infant's vocalizations.

A wide variety of early sound experiences—especially a parent's voice—helps infants to learn the differences between sounds which make up human speech. This ability is essential for understanding language and eventually speaking it.

Helping Infants to Imitate Sounds

Infants must learn to imitate the sounds that parents and others around them make. This is essential for infants to learn to say words. During the first six months, parents should often react to their infants' sounds by making the same sounds back to them.

It appears that infants may imitate sounds naturally. However, parents strengthen this tendency by showing their infant how to imitate. For example, one day Richard said "Ma." His mother playfully said back to him, "Ma." Suddenly Richard said "Ma" back again. This was the imitation that his mother had been waiting for. She enthusiastically praised and cuddled him for his effort. Richard and his mother played this game often with increasing success.

At about six months, Richard began to repeat consonants followed by vowel sounds. This is called *babbling*. Richard often lay alone and babbled by himself. It seemed as if he was playing and experimenting with the sound combinations. Watching this, Richard's parents commented that it was almost like he was learning to talk on his own. It is true that Richard was an active participant in his own language development. However, his parents had helped with this accomplishment. They would continue to help future language developments in important ways.

Babbling becomes a more accurate form of imitation. That is, it slowly drifts closer to adult speech patterns. By around eight months, Richard even used many of the tone patterns normally associated with exclamations, protests, and questions. These had been learned from the expressive language that Richard's parents used with him. At about this time, Richard began to babble and imitate sounds less often. This surprised and concerned his parents. But their pediatrician said this was a common occurrence. This quiet time appears to come before the infant's first meaningful word. However, Richard's language development was a little slow. He did not say his first meaningful word until about 15 months of age. Richard's parents were patient. They kept talking, and continued to respond when babbling and imitations did occur.

Helping the Understanding of Simple Words

When Maria was about 3½ months old, her grandmother told her parents about a favorite teaching game. In the game, Maria was carried near a common object and asked, for example, ''Where's the light—light—light?'' Maria's grandmother helped her to point and look more closely at the light. Her grandmother happily said, ''There's the light! That's right, the light, light!'' They played the game frequently for short periods. They started with things which were large, interesting, and especially meaningful to Maria. Such things included her bottle, her family, pets, and household objects. Later, they included parts of the body. Maria's grandmother and parents started with only a few things that had short, simple names. They played the game in a relaxed and playful manner.

From time to time, Maria's parents would ask, for example, ''Where's the light?'' They did not give assistance because they wanted to see if Maria would show learning by finding the light on her own. Soon, Maria would show evidence of learning by looking at the object. Later, she would point to the object. Maria slowly began to identify more things in her environment when her parents said the words. Her parents were patient. They added words slowly, one or two at a time. They were delighted to see the evidence that Maria was learning.

This teaching method has the advantage of easily adding words to an infant's understanding. Also, research suggests that when children learn the meaning of a word first, it is easier for them to say the word.

Helping Infants to Say Words

Infants show large differences in the speed of their speech development. However, somewhere between 8 and 13 months, parents can expect to hear their infant's first meaningful word. This word is likely to be ''Mama'' or ''Dada'' because parents are so important to infants. Also, these words consist of repeated single syllables. They are relatively easy to say. Other first words may be ''me,'' ''no,'' the names of pets, brothers or sisters, or ''bye bye.''

As in Richard's case, babies normally start to babble wordlike sounds which do not mean anything in particular. Richard did this at eight months, but it may occur as early as six months. When this happens, it is important for parents to provide meaning to their child's sounds. The baby who says ''mom-mom-mom'' or ''da-da-da'' or ''ba-ba-ba'' may or may not be calling the parents or asking for a bottle. However, parents should find and demonstrate the appropriate meaning to these sounds. For example, if a baby says ''da-da-da,'' the father can hold the baby and say, ''Yes, I'm da-da-da. Dada.'' This kind of help is powerful in language development. If an infant says ''ba-ba-ba,'' the parent could hold up a bottle and say, ''Here's the bottle.''

Jimmy's parents always tried to say the names of the people who Jimmy saw. They also named the things they showed or gave to him. They called themselves by their names (Mommy, Daddy) as they went to him. They demonstrated the meaning of words to Jimmy by showing him bright pictures and labeling (naming) the objects in them. They labeled objects with short, simple words and phrases.

It is important to show large and realistic pictures that look like the real objects. This is more likely to help infants make the connection between the picture and the real thing. Pictures have the advantage of showing many things that are not seen ordinarily—lions, horses, trains, and the like. Of course, it is good for infants to see and experience the real things whenever possible.

Parents should continue to play imitation games and strengthen any attempts to imitate with praise and hugs. Infants will gradually learn to imitate sounds and words. Then parents can help them to label and ask for many things with reasonable ease. This is simple to do. First, the parents must get the infant's attention. The parents then stand

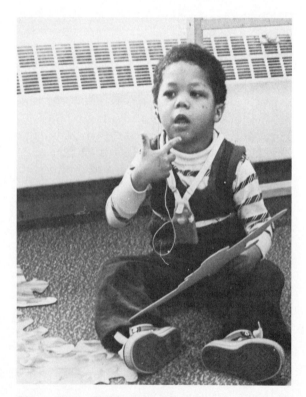

Figure 21-3. *Children learn language through hearing, remembering, and then repeating sounds. (Photograph Courtesy of Better Hearing Institute)*

a short distance away and say, for example, "Mama." When the infant says "Mama," or someting similar, the mother should go to the infant and say, "Yes, I'm Mama," and praise and hug the child. Later, parents can show their baby an object and say its name. When the baby imitates the word, the parents should praise and help the baby to handle and explore the object. This game helps infants to label interesting things and to use words to obtain them.

Sometimes parents can show an object without saying anything to see if their baby will say the appropriate name. If the baby does, the parents should show their enthusiasm. However, patience is very important. The infant may not say the meaningful word again right away. It may be a while before the infant uses the word again without assistance. But as more and more words are learned in this way, the infant will learn other new words more quickly. The more the infant learns during this period, the more the infant will learn in the future.

STRENGTHENING LANGUAGE DURING THE LANGUAGE PERIOD

The language period (starting at about one year of age) is an exciting time of child development. Parents will hear their baby's very first meaningful word during this period. Then, slowly, the child will learn to pronounce words more clearly and accurately. The child will learn to combine words into short phrases and then into sentences. While these skills continue to improve, a child will learn to use about 2,500 words in very complex ways by the age of 6 years.

Other language-related abilities such as math and reading are also learned during the language period. But in this chapter, we focus on the development and understanding of speech.

An interesting fact is that parents tend to talk to their young children in very special and similar ways. This is true even of parents from different countries. It is possible that many parents naturally understand and provide what their children need for good language development.

How to Talk to Young Children

Earlier in this chapter, we mentioned that parents normally change their language to suit their child's abilities. As the child's language abilities improve, parents begin to speak in more complex ways to the child. It is very important that parents alter their language to match the child's growing abilities. Most parents seem to do this naturally, without special training.

Parents speak a special form of *baby talk* to their young child. Baby talk, as we use the term, does not mean silly or senseless talk that fails to communicate. Rather, baby talk means that parents adapt their language to make it most understandable to their young child. For example, parents speak in clearer and simpler ways to their one-year-old than they do to their three-year-old.

The following are some of the ways that parents adapt their language to the special needs of the young child.

• Using exaggerated and different tones. This means that parents use wide ranges of higher and deeper voice tones. This makes language more expressive in meaning.

• The use of a high-pitched voice. Infants and young children appear to pay more attention to pitches of voice which are higher than normal.

• Whispering. By whispering occasionally, parents can add emphasis to what they say. The change in voice gets a young child's attention.

• Using short sentences. This practice can greatly simplify communication.

• Simplifying grammar. Parents are likely to say "Baby laugh" rather than "The baby is laughing." Of course, this practice should be reduced as the child grows.

• Avoiding first- and second-person pronouns. Parents are likely to avoid the use of *I* and *you* when talking to young children. For example, parents might say "Miguel is happy" or "Mommy like that." This form of language is easier for young children to understand.

• More repetition, paraphrasing (saying the same thing in different ways), and questions. With these methods, parents can strengthen a child's understanding.

• Use of special words such as "tummy" and "potty."

• The language focuses on the here and now. Talk is about things or people which are present in the environment during the conversation.

As parents communicate with their young child, they are more concerned with the meaning of sounds rather than the form, or structure. The child will naturally learn rules of grammar during normal development.

As children appear to understand, parents should gradually use more natural ways of speaking. Otherwise, children may continue to speak in immature ways. If this should happen, parents should not panic and try to push their children too hard. Instead, they should slowly and easily begin to shape their language in more complex ways. This should be done in small steps.

Parents should be aware that many sounds are hard for young children to pronounce. It is important for parents to encourage children to experiment with language, rather than expecting correct pronunciation. Language development continues over a long period of time.

Improving Pronunciation of Difficult Words

Shaping can be used to help improve the *pronunciation* (ways to make the sounds) of large words. Parents can do this by breaking such words into smaller parts. When the parts are learned separately, they can then be combined to form an accurately pronounced word. This is the same approach used to strengthen advanced coordination skills.

When Maria was three, she still called hamburgers "hand-a-bur-gers." Her parents had accidentally reinforced this mispronunciation by smiling and laughing lovingly. They first thought it was cute, so they even started to use Maria's word back to her. It was then a challenge to help Maria to say "hamburger" properly. Maria's parents did a very skillful job. They used no punishment or ridicule. Nor did they repeatedly correct her. Instead,

they played a game. Now and then Maria's parents would cheerfully say to her, "Can you say ham?" Laughing, Maria would easily say, "Ham." Her parents would react with much praise and excitement. The next question was, "Can you say burger?" Maria would again playfully imitate, and much praise followed. After a while, she was asked to repeat both parts of the word, in order, with shorter and shorter intervals between them.

Maria's Imitations	Parents' Responses
"Ham......burger."	"Good, honey!"
"Ham.....burger."	"That's right!"
"Ham....burger."	"That's much better!"
"Ham..burger."	"Excellent!"
"Hamburger."	"You did it! Hooray! Let's go get a hamburger!"

Maria's parents continued to praise her for saying the word so well until the pronunciation was fully learned. They also continued to use the correct pronunciation themselves.

Maria, at age five, asked the name of her favorite pet fish. The real scientific name was *plecostomus*. Maria wanted to say the name. In only two short sessions, she learned how to say it, from the same method used to teach her to say "hamburger." Maria's delight at learning to say such a big and hard word was obvious. In the days that followed, she said her new word often.

Helping Children to Say Phrases and Sentences

Around two years of age, children begin to combine words. As the number of word combinations increases, children begin to speak according to complex rules of grammar. Amazingly, children do this without ever having studied a grammar book. Although this process occurs naturally, parents can help when their children reach the age of two. At this point, parents should begin to pay some attention to form. Of course, parents should still adapt their language to a child's level of understanding. But there are other ways in which parents can help.

Reading stories to children is a very rewarding activity that can continue throughout childhood. Reading books at the appropriate level is important and enriches a child's language experiences. When a child shows interest, parents can read books that have illustrated stories. It is not necessary to read everything that is written on a page. Parents can also simplify some of the words and sentences at first.

Sometimes children have favorite stories which they like to hear again and again. When parents read these, they can be sure that their child's level of interest and motivation to learn are high. It is important to point out and label action pictures (running, jumping, swimming), because these are hard to learn. Parents should question their child from time to time about the pictures. What do the pictures show? What do they have to do with the story? Parents should also be patient and let the child question and talk. In this way, the child can often control the direction of conversation. Parents should respond with enthusiasm to their child's questions and comments.

Reading to a child is not only a good opportunity to help language development. It is also a time when parents can reinforce sitting still and paying attention. However, the sessions should not be so long that the child becomes bored or tired. Another benefit of reading to a child is that the activity can strengthen the close and loving relationship between parents and child.

Figure 21-4. Reading to children is an enriching language activity that can continue throughout childhood. (Future Homemakers of America)

Figure 21-5. *Putting sounds, pictures, and letters together aids in development of language skills. (Photo Courtesy of Kinder-Care Learning Centers, Inc.)*

First, a child will learn to say the nouns that label people, places, and things. The child will then slowly learn how to describe them more thoroughly. This process is fairly difficult and requires an understanding of complex and related concepts. Noun-verb phrases such as "Doggie barks" or "Mommy sings" represent actions which exist only for a short time. Therefore, these are difficult to learn. Repetition and actual demonstrations of barking or singing, for example, will help learning.

It is good to involve children in the actions which are labeled as laughing, running, jumping, and so on. The same approach can be used when illustrating adverbs, such as "barking loudly." Adjectives are also difficult to learn. Parents should try to explain or show exactly what is meant by "cold water," "pretty flower," or "large ball." This will require much repetition, imitation, and experience.

Parents can naturally use two special techniques to help their child to learn to say phrases and sentences. One of these techniques is called *expansion*. Expansion involves restating a child's simple statements in more complex ways. A child's first words will stand for single things which are important to the child, such as water. Later on, though, the child will begin to use a single word in place of a sentence. As explained in Chapter 6, this is called a holophrase. A holophrase is a single word which is used by young children to say several different things. For example, "Mommy" might mean "Pick me up," "Look at me," or "I'm hungry." When a child says a word or perhaps two in combination, parents can try to figure out what the child is trying to communicate. The parents should then quickly restate it in a proper sentence. This is the expansion technique. In expansion, the parents interpret the meaning of a child's sounds or words. The parents then expand them into proper grammatical form. The child's meaning is not changed in any way.

Jimmy	Jimmy's Parents
"Cookie."	"You want a cookie."
"Go potty."	"You have to go potty."
"I eat."	"Yes, you are eating."
"Kitty run."	"The kitty ran away."
"Happy Momma."	"Yes, Momma is very happy."

The expansion method has two benefits. First, parents can reinforce their child's beginning speech with an immediate reply. Second, the reply serves as a model for the child to imitate in the future and exposes the child to more language.

It is important that parents understand exactly what a child's words mean before expanding them. For example, the expansion "That is your ball" would be wrong if a child was looking at the moon and said "ball."

A second technique which can be used by parents to help their child learn to say phrases and sentences is called *extension*. As in expansion, parents identify the child's meaning and restate it in a more correct form. In extension, though, a new but related idea is introduced.

Jimmy	Jimmy's Parents
"Cookie."	"Mommy bought the cookies at the grocery store."
"Go potty."	"Yes, you go potty in the bathroom."
"I eat."	"When you eat your meat and vegetables, you grow big like Mommy and Daddy."
"Kitty run."	"The kitty can run, jump, and climb trees."
"Happy Momma."	"You make me very happy when you talk."

Like expansions, extensions reinforce what a child has said, and provide new sentences to imitate. Extensions also provide new ideas which are associated with words. By frequently extending the things a child says, parents can teach the relationships between new ideas and words.

The methods of expansion and extension are good, but as with any approach, they can be overused. If parents were to expand or extend everything their child said, the child might lose interest in listening. As always, it is important for parents to be sensitive to how their child is reacting to them.

Another way for parents to encourage language development is to ask questions of their child. This can stimulate children to think and practice talking. Often a question may produce an answer which can then be expanded or extended. Such questions are "Where did Daddy go?" and "Where do bears live?" These questions serve as ways to stimulate speech and to teach new words and ideas. Often parents can ask questions which stimulate their child's imagination. For example, "What if you could fly?" "Why do cats climb trees?"

Questioning a child can also be overdone. Too many questions may cause a child to become annoyed and refuse to answer. However, questions can also be very reinforcing. Therefore, parents should be careful not to question their child only during times when the child is not speaking. Otherwise, the child might be heavily reinforced for silence.

Correcting Speech Errors

When children first learn to talk, they will make many errors. When they start to use words together, children may sometimes say them in the wrong order ("train choo-choo"). They may use the wrong word endings ("I felled down"). These are normal signs that children are experimenting with language. Sometimes they will misuse the rules. However, these are really signs of learning, and should not be viewed negatively.

Children often stop in the middle of a sentence and go back to the beginning to try again. They stammer and repeat certain words. These problems often occur when children get excited; their thoughts seem to race ahead of their ability to speak. They will also make statements which seem to make no sense until parents discover their meanings. For example, Maria talked about someone scaring her ears. This was her first try at saying that loud sounds frightened her.

Our language system is very complicated, and it is normal for some of these speech errors to continue until children are five or six years old. After all, it is very hard to organize thoughts and then, using proper grammar, communicate them through words. If you are trying to learn to speak a foreign language well, you will easily understand these difficulties.

Parents should not use disapproval to eliminate speech problems. Bad stuttering and stammering in older children often seem to be the result of this approach. The approach of using disapproval to influence speech is almost certain to cause more problems than it solves. Punishment for errors in speech can cause children anxiety about possible errors. This anxiety will interfere with the proper development of speech. Parents should also avoid showing their disappointment and impatience.

The following are some examples of parental behavior which should be avoided.

1. When the child pauses, the parent impatiently finishes the sentence.

2. When the child stutters, the parent interrupts and says, ''Stop and think about what you are going to say.'' The parent then makes the child begin again.

3. The parent shows signs of disappointment or disapproval whenever the child makes speech errors.

4. The parent tries to discourage immature speech by laughing or making fun of the child.

5. The parent pays more attention to speech errors than to developing language. This actually reinforces errors with attention, and weakens better speech through extinction.

What if a child has difficulties with certain phrases or word combinations? The parents can plan to use these phrases or word combinations at some later time (not right after the error). The child can then hear the correct way, imitate it, and be praised for the effort. This can be done without any mention of the child's error. Immediate correction should be used sparingly and done in a pleasant and warm way. The goal is for the child to remain confident and enjoy learning from the occasional correction. Children should be praised for any reasonable attempt to imitate the correction.

Parents should avoid discussing the child's speech difficulties in front of the child. It is important to remember that we all have our good and bad days. Parents can take advantage of their children's good days to strenthen language development. They should also be patient and understanding that language development goes through many stages.

SUMMARY

In a loving and reinforcing home, a normal child will experiment with and practice using language. The child will slowly but surely improve. By the age of three or four, the child may ask dozens of questions and make many more statements each day. But the child still has a long way to go. The average adult's speaking vocabulary is roughly 12,000 to 13,000 words. It is thus important for parents to continue to model correct language. Parents must also frequently reinforce their child's growing ability to communicate through words.

Figure 21-6. Even children who have mastered the basics of language skills still have a lot to learn. Creative play with puppets is one way to encourage the development of a better vocabulary.

QUESTIONS FOR GROWTH

1. (a) What is the prespeech period, and what time interval does it cover? **(b)** Describe the language abilities of the infant in the first two months of life.

2. (a) Tell the manner, style, or mood that parents should use when strengthening language in their infants. **(b)** Name some of the situations in which parents can help strengthen language in their infants.

3. What advice would you give to parents who say that they feel funny talking to someone who doesn't talk back?

4. List some of the ways that you would enrich an infant's listening experience, and explain why this enrichment is important.

5. Describe the imitation game that can help infants learn to imitate their parents' sounds.

6. (a) About when can parents expect their infants to babble? **(b)** Explain why babbling can be viewed as a form of imitation.

7. How might you help to increase an infant's understanding of the meaning of some simple words?

8. Which words are likely to be said first by infants?

9. Explain how, at about six months, parents can help their infants to say their first words.

10. What is the language period, and what time period does it cover?

11. Tell roughly how many words children will learn by six years of age.

12. Describe some of the ways that parents adapt their language to the needs of a young child.

13. Explain a method that parents can use to help children pronounce difficult words.

14. Name some general things that parents can do to help their children learn to say phrases and sentences.

15. Why is it important to correctly interpret a child's holophrase before expanding or extending the word?

16. Explain expansion, and provide an original example of how parents might use this technique.

17. Explain extension, and provide an original example of how parents might use this technique.

18. Name two ways in which expansion and extension can improve language development.

19. Explain what can happen if extension or expansion are overused.

20. How can questions be used to help language development, and how can questions be misused?

21. Describe some of the common errors that children make while learning to talk.

22. Tell how old children may be and still show normal problems with speech.

23. Describe one method that parents should avoid when trying to improve speech problems.

24. Describe one positive approach to correcting speech errors in children.

CHAPTER

22

Strengthening Self-Care
(Birth to Two Years)

Newborns are totally without the ability to care for themselves. Without help, newborns cannot survive. However, within the first two years, children can be expected to learn to feed themselves and help in dressing themselves. Around two years, children can be taught to signal when they have to go to the bathroom, and perhaps toilet training can begin.

The importance of these early forms of self-care goes well beyond simple self-care. Children who experience success during their early learning and who receive loving encouragement and praise will strive to learn more. Success in learning to care for themselves helps children to gain feelings of mastery and independence. These feelings can lay the foundations for accomplishment and independence in later years.

There are many other small but important developments that can be considered part of self-care. For example, learning to reach, grasp, crawl and walk, and talk all have something to do with self-care. Clearly, teaching self-care is one of the parents' major responsibilities.

TEACHING SELF-CARE

Teaching self-care involves slowly but consistently requiring improvement. Parents should assist children and then reduce assistance (prompting and fading). They must also build perseverence by slowly reducing the frequency of reinforcement.

Parents can often use the technique of backward chaining to teach self-care. Recall

Figure 22-1. *Although newborns are totally without the ability to care for themselves, by the age of three most children can feed themselves easily. (USDA Photo)*

that this is a simple but powerful way to teach behaviors which require a certain sequence of actions. Backward chaining and many more teaching techniques can be used to teach the self-care skills described in this chapter and Chapter 23. In this chapter, we focus our attention upon several important self-care developments which occur during the first two years of life.

Introducing Semisolid Foods

During the first months of life, infants drink milk from their mother's breasts, or they drink formula (a milk substitute) from a bottle. There are advantages and disadvantages to each method. For example, breast feeding is very convenient in that no preparation of

formula is required. However, it may be inconvenient if the mother's schedule does not allow her to always be available to her infant. Feeding formula from a bottle allows more flexibility for the parents—especially, of course, the mother. However, preparing the formula can be time consuming. Today there is much discussion about the health benefits to the baby of breast feeding vs. bottle feeding. Many people support breast feeding. Yet it is helpful to know that happy and well-adjusted children have been fed in both ways. Mothers should discuss both feeding methods with their pediatricians and choose the method with which they are most comfortable.

Some pediatricians recommend starting infants on solid foods between two and four months. Some recommend waiting until about five or six months. Parents should work with their pediatrician to determine the particular infant's needs. Infants may have different needs due to their general health and digestive systems.

The reason for feeding infants and children is not just to satisfy hunger. Food must also provide good nutrition. Good nutrition means selecting foods which contain the vitamins, minerals, proteins, and fats which help the child to grow and stay healthy. Good nutrition is essential to both physical and intellectual development.

Changing an infant's diet from liquids (mother's milk or formula) to semisolid (blended liquid and solid) food can take time. The infant's only food for many weeks has been liquids. There is a great difference in texture, taste, and consistency between liquids and semisolid food. The infant may at first reject semisolid food. Also, the

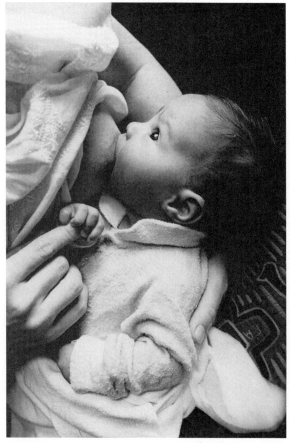

© Joel Gordon 1975

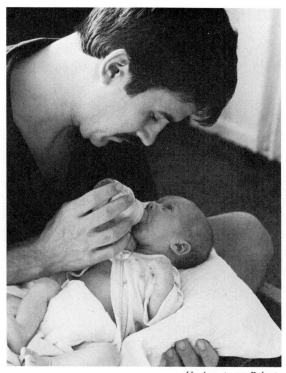

H. Armstrong Roberts

Figure 22-2. Both breast feeding and bottle feeding have advantages and disadvantages.

infant is often very hungry at mealtime and is in no mood for time-consuming new experiences.

Infants must learn to use the lips and tongue in new ways before they can swallow semisolid food. This skill is usually learned at about three months of age. Before this time, most semisolid food placed in a baby's mouth will come back out, because the tongue's natural motion ejects it. This is something an infant cannot help, so parents need to be patient.

Maria's parents were very successful at helping her to accept semisolid food. At first, they presented semisolid food near the end of the meal. In this way, Maria was not so hungry. Therefore, she did not cry for her bottle. However, she was still a little hungry and remained interested in eating.

Maria's parents, in her sight, tasted her semisolid food and expressed great delight. This may have helped Maria to imitate them. They then placed a tiny amount of food on a small, shallow spoon and put it in her mouth. At first, Maria looked a little surprised by this new experience. Her parents praised her warmly and gave her back the bottle as a reinforcement for eating from the spoon.

Maria was not rushed or pushed in this process. Her parents gave her only one or two small spoonfuls during the first meals. They did not "force feed" her, but they did praise any of her attempts to cooperate. Later, as Maria showed signs of liking the food, they began to provide greater amounts. As Maria became more skillful and willing to eat from the spoon, semisolid food was given closer to the start of the meal. Maria's parents then continued to slowly increase the number of spoonfuls they gave her at each meal. The whole process took several weeks.

With this approach, the taste and textures of semisolid foods became more reinforcing. They became associated with the removal of hunger. Swallowing the food also reinforced the correct movements of Maria's lips and tongue. As she made the movements and swallowed the food, these complex muscle actions were reinforced and thus learned.

Taste Preferences

Individual food preferences can greatly influence proper nutrition. It is therefore important for infants to learn to enjoy well-balanced meals and a wide variety of flavors. There is evidence that some tastes are naturally preferred by infants. However, taste preferences can be greatly influenced by one's environment and personal experiences. After all, some people of the world learn to love all sorts of foods—seal blubber, squid, monkey, insects, and even hamburgers!

The parents' best opportunity to influence their child's taste preferences is early, well before the child begins self-feeding. Parents should introduce a variety of fruits, cereals, vegetables, meats, and dairy products. The infant's diet, however, should be reviewed and approved by the pediatrician. Puddings, cookies, cakes, and candy have little nutritional value. These could easily be replaced in the child's diet by fruits. Again, the pediatrician should suggest the order and timing of introducing new foods.

There are often a few foods that an infant will refuse to eat. Parents might substitute other foods of comparable nutritional value. Or parents might choose to let the infant indicate which foods he or she wants. The parents might find that over time the infant naturally chooses a balanced diet. Many infants do.

On the other hand, an infant might consistently reject some very valuable foods such as fish or vegetables. In such a case, the parents should try to teach the child to enjoy these foods. Infants can be helped to enjoy foods which are necessary for good health throughout life.

Parents can try to associate a disliked food with another reinforcer. Jimmy did not like chicken, but he would eat applesauce and carrots very happily. It is safe to assume that applesauce and carrots were reinforcers for Jimmy when he was hungry. Jimmy's parents would first give him a small taste of chicken then praise him excitedly and quickly give hime some carrots or applesauce.

Some parents have tried mixing nonpreferred foods with reinforcing ones in the hope of fooling their infant. Many have reported little success with this approach. When two foods are blended, a different flavor results which may be unpleasant to the infant.

Jimmy's parents presented disliked foods in small amounts at first. They also introduced them early (but not at the start) in the meal to take advantage of Jimmy's hunger. They first gave him one very small bite of chicken, immediately followed by a small bite of carrots or applesauce. Later, they offered two small bites of chicken for one bite of preferred food, and finally three bites to one. Jimmy's parents were satisfied with this progress. They did not go beyond the level of three to one for a long time.

Drinking from a Cup

There are several reasons to start teaching a child to drink from a cup by around one year of age. Many babies seem less interested in sucking on a bottle or breast by around six or seven months. This can be a natural time to start weaning. Weaning refers to the process of helping an infant to give up drinking from a breast or bottle and begin drinking from a cup. If babies are allowed to drink only from a breast or bottle throughout their first year, they may grow more attached to it. They might then resist drinking from a cup. This is especially likely if the bottle or breast is used to quiet crying or fretting. This also occurs if parents normally allow the infant to take the bottle to bed. It is tempting to let an older baby lie in the crib and drink a bottle before falling asleep. However, the milk left in an infant's mouth during sleep

can decay developing teeth. Also, infants may, through association, become dependent upon the bottle to fall asleep easily. Such children may remain dependent on the bottle for up to two years or longer. This may cause them to drink too much milk at a time when they need other valuable foods and a balanced diet.

Teaching an infant to drink from a cup can be a challenge. A hungry infant will be unable to swallow much milk from the cup. Therefore, the infant will find drinking from a cup frustrating as compared to sucking. In addition, the sight of the bottle or breast and the feel of the nipple in the mouth are very reinforcing. They have become associated with the removal of hunger. The cup has no such advantage. The cup will have to acquire its own reinforcing qualities slowly.

Parents may be tempted to present the cup at the start of a meal. They think that if the baby is hungry, the baby will try harder to drink from it. However, the infant is likely to become frustrated and upset at not being able to swallow the milk. If parents then give the bottle or breast to soothe the baby, future rejections of the cup are reinforced.

Jimmy's mother began to offer him a swallow or two of breast milk in a cup each day. She waited until he had begun to slow his sucking to a fairly relaxed rate. At this point, Jimmy's mother gave him a sip from the cup and praised him happily. She then immediately let him finish his normal feeding. The praise and the quick return to normal feeding were both reinforcers which slowly strengthened Jimmy's desire to drink from a cup.

Jimmy's mother was careful not to demand too much too quickly. In the beginning, a sip or two from the cup each day were enough.

Some parents make the mistake of getting mad at an infant who spills or drools milk. Jimmy's mother was very patient and loving.

Jimmy was soon willing to take drinks from the cup. He had learned to swallow reasonably well. His mother then began to present the cup earlier in the meal. She also began to put more milk into the cup. But she was sure to move in small steps. She did not require Jimmy to take too much milk from the cup too soon.

To complete the weaning, Jimmy's mother let him take more and more of the meal from the cup. Finally, breast feeding was simply omitted.

The pediatrician should be asked before starting to wean an infant. In breast feeding, the mother's milk production is a factor which increases the need of discussion with a physician.

Teaching How to Handle a Cup

Infants who drink on their own from a cup have taken an important step in the area of self-help. Self-feeding is a very basic and valuable accomplishment on the way to becoming an independent human being. This accomplishment, like all others, can be a source of pride for young children and can lay the foundation for future successes.

Backward chaining is recommended for teaching an infant to handle a cup during drinking. Backward chaining is an operant-learning method which was introduced in Chapter 11. The last step in a sequence of behaviors is taught first in backward chaining. This allows children to be immediately reinforced for their efforts.

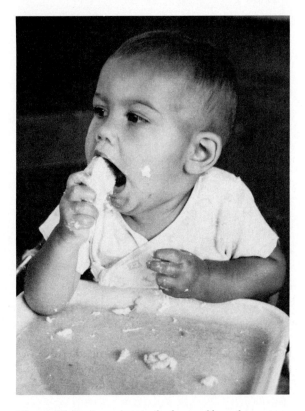

Figure 22-3. Learning to feed oneself can be a messy experience, as this seven-month-old shows. Parents should be patient. (©Mark Antman/The Image Works)

Most babies can learn to use a spoon by about 14 months. Drinking from a cup is a little easier because it does not require such fine muscle coordination, and is learned at about 12 to 14 months. Therefore, parents are wise to teach their baby to handle a cup before they work on spoon management. Teaching may begin at about 11 months or when the baby seems to have the necessary coordination to learn.

To teach her to handle a cup, Maria's parents began with an easy-to-grasp cup with two handles. They used the backward-chaining method. They started with the last of five steps first. Maria's parents helped her tip the cup enough to drink from it (Step #5). Later, they began to pause with the cup touching her lips and wait for her to help tip it. When Maria helped, they praised her. The milk in her mouth also reinforced her efforts to tip the cup skillfully. Maria's parents slowly removed their assistance from Step #5 until Maria could do it on her own.

Next, they moved the cup to within an inch of Maria's mouth (Step #4) and helped her to move the cup to her lips. As she became more skillful, they reduced their assistance with Step #4. Soon Maria could do Steps #4 and #5 by herself.

Her parents next worked on Step #3, which was placing the cup at about one half the distance from the high-chair table to Maria's lips. They reduced their assistance. They continued to praise greater skill until Maria could do Steps #3, #4, and #5 alone.

Step #2 involved holding the cup about two inches above the high-chair table. Step #1 was the beginning of the sequence. The cup was placed on the high-chair table for Maria to lift up and raise to her lips. Finally, Maria could reach out, grasp her cup, raise it to her mouth, and drink without spilling—sometimes. Maria's parents were very patient with her as she learned the skill more thoroughly. To avoid big spills, they continued to provide only a quarter cup of liquid at a time.

Strengthening Cooperation During Bathing and Dressing

Richard, age 13 months, was being washed in the tub. His father held up the washcloth in front of him and said, "This is a washcloth. See the washcloth?" He then held up and named the soap. "Let's put the soap on the washcloth," he said. The father placed the cloth in Richard's right hand and the soap in the left hand. He held Richard's hands and helped him to rub the cloth and soap together. The father could tell that Richard was cooperating, and said, "Rubbing the soap on the washcloth! Good! Look at how well you are rubbing the soap on the washcloth." The father continued to help, smile, and praise Richard for a few seconds longer. Then he removed his hands and watched Richard make small rubbing motions with the soap. Richard's father praised him excitedly. He then asked, "Can you say soap?" Richard laughed and said, "Oop," and his father praised and hugged him enthusiastically.

Richard's father said, "Can you wash your tummy?" and guided Richard's hands and washcloth to his stomach. He lightly moved Richard's arms so the washcloth rubbed his stomach. The father removed his hand and watched for a cooperative moment. Richard rubbed the washcloth on his stomach three times, and his father again praised happily. "Yes, you are washing your tummy, good boy! Look at you wash your tummy!" He then asked, "Can you say wash?" After Richard said, "Waas," his father praised him again.

A lot is happening in this example. Richard's father labeled common objects and actions, and praised Richard for trying to imitate. The father knew these words would help Richard to follow instructions later. He also asked Richard to do things. He first assisted the behavior, reduced his assistance, and praised Richard for continuing on his own. By reinforcing early instruction-following, Richard's father was making it more likely that Richard would follow future requests.

Learning to dress and undress oneself is an important self-care accomplishment which strengthens independence. Children can normally remove some of their own clothes by about 16 months of age. By about two years, they may be able to put on simple clothing. Children can often fully dress themselves without supervision by about four years. The

Figure 22-4. Even very young infants can be encouraged to cooperate during bath time. The wide-eyed child looking on is also learning important lessons in self-care and independence. (© Ron Meyer/White Eyes Design)

process of helping children to manage their own clothes is a long one which can begin quite early in simple ways.

Maria's father was preparing the 14-month-old for bed. He said, "Let's take off your socks." He pulled one sock almost off, leaving it dangling around Maria's toes. He said, "Pull your sock off, honey." Maria grasped the stocking, but nothing happened. The father said, "Pull it hard," and nudged his daughter's hand lightly. Maria pulled, and off came the sock. Her father exclaimed, "Good pull! Great! You pulled your sock off!" He then repeated the procedure with the other sock. He pulled it almost off and then let the child start with the last and easiest movement.

Maria's father was using backward chaining. Over a number of sessions, he gradually left more of the sock on Maria's foot and helped her to pull it off in small steps. The father then reduced his assistance and praised Maria for following instructions.

Several weeks later, Maria's mother was helping her to put on her pajama top. She helped Maria to place her arm through the right armhole. She then pulled the sleeve almost all of the way on. But Maria's mother stopped when Maria's hand was still in the sleeve but well past the elbow. She asked Maria, "Can you push? Push your hand out of the sleeve." At first, she helped Maria by pushing lightly against her elbow so that Maria's hand slipped through the sleeve. She then praised Maria for her small assistance. Soon Maria began to push harder, and her mother began to reduce her assistance. She continued, though, to praise Maria's effort. Maria's mother used a similar last-step-first approach to teach Maria to pull up her pajama bottoms. The mother helped to put the bottoms on, but let Maria pull them up the last two or three inches. Slowly, Maria was able to do more and more on her own.

Maria would be two years old before she could put on her pajamas by herself. Her parents were both very patient, and were comfortable with her progress. They knew that there are many small movements involved in putting on clothing, and that much time is needed to learn the motions. Maria's parents gave gentle instructions, assisted behavior, and gave praise. They even thanked Maria. This was a fine way to encourage politeness through early modeling.

SUMMARY

When children learn the self-care skills of self-feeding, washing, dressing, and more during their first two years, they grow more independent. This history of learning to do for themselves encourages future self-care accomplishments. It also strengthens other important areas of development, such as social, emotional, and intellectual development.

QUESTIONS FOR GROWTH

1. Explain why the move to semisolid foods can be difficult for infants.

2. What might you do to help an infant learn to eat semisolid foods?

3. Explain why parents may wish to help their infants to like certain foods.

4. Explain how parents might help infants to learn to eat a nutritious food which the infants do not like.

5. Describe several reasons why it is good to start to teach an infant to drink from a cup before one year of age.

6. Explain how you might help an infant learn to drink from a cup.

7. (a) Explain why infants normally manage drinking from a cup before they can learn to use a spoon skillfully. **(b)** What kind of cup is recommended for teaching an infant to drink from a cup?

8. Describe how the backward-chaining approach can be used to teach an infant to handle a cup.

9. Explain how you might teach a young child to wash himself or herself.

10. Describe two examples of how parents can teach their young children to put on or remove simple clothing.

CHAPTER

23

Strengthening Self-Care
(Two to Seven Years)

One general goal in parenting is to help children learn to behave independently. It is hoped that children will eventually behave independently not for constant praise and attention, but for feelings of accomplishment and pride. If a variety of reinforcers is often associated with a child's self-care behavior early in life, self-care activities can themselves become reinforcing.

Parents should continue to praise their children from time to time. But when self-care behaviors occur without constant praise and attention, children are becoming more independent. By this stage, children are showing some amount of responsibility and pride in their achievements.

Most two-year-olds normally have learned many of the basics of self-care, such as self-feeding, walking, communicating basic wants, removing clothing, and more. From

two to six years, children learn more complex self-care tasks. They begin to take more responsibility for themselves. This can lead to the development of *self-esteem* or *self-pride*—a sense of value and worth in oneself. Children who have good self-esteem are generally happier and are socially better adjusted. They are more likely to apply themselves to new and challenging tasks. Parents can thus strengthen both self-care and self-esteem in their children at the same time.

In this chapter, we describe the methods for teaching self-care skills that normally should be learned between the ages of two to seven years. We apply the methods to a few major self-care skills. However, the teaching methods we discuss can be applied to a large number of self-care goals.

In Box 23.1, we list many specific self-care skills to be developed in the young child. The

BOX 23.1

Self-Care Tasks Learned by Seven Years of Age

Eating

Using a butter knife, fork, spoon
Pouring liquid into a glass
Making a sandwich
Pouring cereal and milk into a bowl
Peeling carrots, potatoes, etc.

Dressing

Buttoning, snapping, zipping, tying
Putting on and taking off shirts, sweaters, pants, dresses, boots, shoes, socks, mittens

Personal Hygiene

Washing face and hands
Brushing teeth
Taking a bath
Washing hair
Combing and brushing hair

Caring for Personal Belongings

Placing clothes in the hamper
Making the bed
Helping to clear the table
Picking up and putting away toys, books, etc.
Hanging up clothes or folding them and putting them in drawers

Personal Information

Knowing own name, address, and telephone number
Knowing how to answer the telephone and use it for emergencies

Concepts of Time

Knowing days of the week
Understanding before, after, long ago
Understanding yesterday, today, and tomorrow
Familiarity with clocks
Learning the months of the year

Safety

Crossing low-traffic streets with and without the assistance of traffic lights
Following safety rules when bike riding

Going about the Neighborhood without Supervision

Telling parents where he or she is going
Staying within limits
Coming when called
Walking to school or the bus stop

Figure 23-1. *Why do self-care skills contribute to the development of self-confidence and self-esteem?*

list in Box 23.1 is certainly not complete. You are encouraged to identify other self-care skills. Reviewing the list will help you to realize the size and complexity of the tasks which lie before parents and children.

TOILET TRAINING

Toilet training involves teaching children to want to use the bathroom, to recognize their urges to go to the bathroom, and to master the self-help skills necessary in using a toilet. It was once thought that toilet training had a great influence on a developing child's personality and even on his or her adult personality. This theory has lost much of its support. Many experiences that occur before, during, and after toilet training are just as likely to have an important influence. Toilet training is a complex and demanding teaching task. Yet it is just another of the many self-care skills which parents must help their children to learn.

It is very important to wait until children are ready to benefit from toilet training. The results of harsh or too-early toilet training can be bad. Children show their readiness by staying dry for several hours at a time. They may urinate a lot at one time rather than trickling small amounts frequently. They may try to imitate others in toileting. Children may also show signs that they know when they are about to urinate. Children are likely to show these signs of readiness sometime after two years of age.

Toilet training is sometimes difficult because of children's long-standing habit of urinating and defecating whenever and wherever they want. Not only must new and complex skills be taught, but old and easy habits must be eliminated.

Jimmy's parents approached toilet training by first being sure that he showed signs of readiness. Next, they agreed upon the importance of being patient. They decided to show no frustration over the accidents which were sure to occur. They both recognized the importance of using a positive approach to toilet training. Jimmy's parents used the following general method.

1. They started toilet training at a time when parents and child could focus their attention on the skill. They chose a time which was free of events such as vacations, trips, and holidays. Such events tend to cause parents to be inconsistent in their training. Consistency is essential for successful toilet training.

2. They determined when Jimmy was most likely to urinate. They recorded his urination times for a few days.

3. They placed Jimmy on a special toilet called a potty chair shortly before the expected times of urination. While in the bathroom, they tried to make the time short (about three to five minutes) and pleasant. Jimmy's parents normally sang, talked, or read to him.

4. When Jimmy did urinate or defecate in the toilet, his parents expressed their delight with his success. They praised Jimmy when he was done and then provided a few minutes of a reinforcing activity.

5. Jimmy's parents encouraged him to let them know when he needed to go. Jimmy's parents gave him frequent special praise on occasions when he indicated his need to "go potty."

6. When accidents happened, they calmly and casually told Jimmy, "You had an accident." They then helped him to wash and change himself.

7. After Jimmy was going to the toilet on his own for several weeks, his parents slowly reduced reinforcers such as praise and attention. They were careful, though, to not completely eliminate reinforcers for quite a while.

This method slowly and steadily allowed Jimmy to learn the skill. His parents kept the sessions in the bathroom short and entertaining. They did not give reinforcement when he was not successful on the toilet. But they did not make a big fuss when Jimmy had an accident, because this attention could be reinforcing. They would calmly state that he had an accident, and had him finish on the potty chair. Then Jimmy was helped to wash

himself and change his clothes. Though Jimmy's parents were consistent, they did not rush or push him.

The general guidelines that Jimmy's parents used are very effective. Jimmy learned toileting skills at a reasonable speed. If he had not learned, his parents should first have reviewed their method. If they felt they were doing a good job, they should have talked to the pediatrician. Sometimes a child has physical problems which make it difficult to become toilet trained.

Parents should know that toileting skills are often lost for a time when children experience stress. This is common in families where a divorce, a death, or a change in residence has occurred. Parents must be patient during such times and not show anger or frustration. Toilet training can be started again later.

USING A BUTTER KNIFE

Maria's mother began to teach her to spread butter with a knife at about three years. Her mother made the task as easy as possible. She used toasted bread, which will not tear easily, and soft butter. She provided a small, dull butter knife that Maria could handle without danger.

Maria sat in a high-seated chair at the table. Her mother placed the toast in front of her, and scooped up some butter with the knife. She began to spread it on the toast. The mother described what she was doing: "See how I spread the butter on your toast?" She buttered about two thirds of the toast. Then she said, "Now you spread butter on your toast." She placed the knife in Maria's hand

and guided it to the butter. She scooped some of the butter onto the knife, and helped Maria to spread it on the bare corner of the toast. Maria's mother praised her for cooperating and let her eat the toast.

After many such meals, Maria's mother reduced her assistance. She slowly left more and more of the toast unbuttered for Maria to complete. Finally, Maria could complete the whole process on her own.

POURING LIQUID INTO A GLASS

When Jimmy was two and a half, his father began to teach him to pour liquids. He started by using a small, plastic pitcher with a handle, and a heavy, plastic cup. The cup worked well because it did not tip when Jimmy started to pour liquid into it.

Jimmy's parents kept the pitcher, filled with his favorite drinks, in the refrigerator. When Jimmy wanted a drink, his parents pushed a kitchen chair to the sink. They placed both the pitcher and the cup in the sink. They helped Jimmy to stand on the chair. With the cup upright in the sink, they told him, "Pour your drink." Jimmy's parents helped him to grasp the pitcher by the handle and pour his drink. They then praised him and then gave him another reinforcer—the drink.

As Jimmy poured more by himself, accidents sometimes happened. Jimmy's parents praised him when he did not spill or when he spilled only a small amount. They ignored big spills. However, if Jimmy's parents judged that he spilled because of carelessness rather than lack of skill, they did comment. Calmly and politely, they said, "Oops, you

spilled too much that time." They then poured what remained in the cup back into the pitcher, and let Jimmy try again.

Having to wait for the drink and the added work of pouring again helped to weaken careless behavior and strengthen more skilled pouring. When Jimmy began to pour with hardly ever a spill, his parents let him pour on the counter or table. They were careful and patient to not become angry at his unskilled attempts to pour by himself.

Figure 23-2. Children who watch food preparation will soon be eager to try it themselves. (© Ron Meyer/ White Eyes Design)

MAKING A SANDWICH

Richard's parents began to teach him to make a sandwich when he was about four. They started with peanut butter, using a brand that spread easily. Richard could already butter his bread, so he was ready to learn quickly. At lunchtime, Richard's father called Richard to the kitchen and described what he was doing. "I'm going to make some peanut-butter sandwiches for lunch. First, I'll get the bread from the box. Then I'll get the peanut butter from the cupboard and a knife from the drawer." Richard and his father gathered these items on the table within Richard's reach.

As Richard's father made the sandwich, he explained exactly what he was doing, step by step. He then encouraged Richard to try one himself. When Richard imitated, he praised him. He gave a little help when Richard started to look confused, so that Richard would not become frustrated. Richard and his father then ate their sandwiches (reinforcers), and the father talked happily about what a good job Richard had done.

As time went by, Richard's father let him get the bread on his own, and then both the bread and the knife. Finally, he let Richard get the bread, knife, and peanut butter. When Richard made his first sandwich completely by himself, his father excitedly praised him and asked for a bite. He said it was the best peanut-butter sandwich he had ever tasted.

Richard's parents encouraged him to help with other food-preparation activities. This helped Richard to become more independent in the future.

BUTTONING

When Maria was about three years old, her parents began to teach her to button clothes. They started by using large buttons and buttonholes which were loose enough for the buttons to slide through easily.

Maria's parents stood behind her and helped her to grasp the outside edge of a sweater button. Maria held the button with her left thumb and forefinger, her thumb on the underside. Then her parents helped her to hold the outside edge of the buttonhole between the right thumb and forefinger. The forefinger went on the inside (underside) of the shirt, and the thumb spread the buttonhole. Maria's parents helped her to push the button through the hole with the left hand. Her right thumb and forefinger grasped the tip of the button and pulled it through the buttonhole. Maria's left hand was then free to help pull the cloth over the top of the button. Then the button was completely through the hole and locked in place. This complex task took weeks to learn. Maria's parents were patient and praised all good attempts.

For practice sessions, parents can provide patches of material equipped with big buttons and buttonholes. A similar approach can be used for teaching other dressing skills such as handling snaps, zippers, and hooks. There are also dolls which are designed to help children practice these skills.

PUTTING ON PANTS

Jimmy's parents began to teach him to put on his pants when he was about two years old. They used a loose pair of pants which required no zipping or buttoning. They began by sitting beside Jimmy and saying, ''Let's put your pants on.'' They helped him to put both feet through the legs. They then prompted him to stand up and pull his pants up just over his buttocks. Next, they helped him to grasp the front of the pants with one hand and the back with the other. They said, ''Pull up your pants.'' They helped, if necessary, and praised his cooperation.

Jimmy seemed to prefer to pull up from the sides, rather than from the front and back. This method would be inconvenient later on, when Jimmy had to pull his pants over his bottom. Therefore, his parents encouraged him to pull from at least close to the front and the back of the pants.

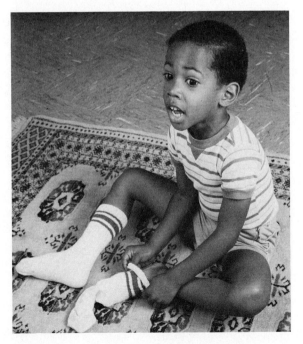

Figure 23-3. *This four-year-old can accomplish many of the tasks involved in dressing.*

Jimmy's parents were using the first step in a backward chain. Jimmy was pulling his pants up from just below the waist. He soon was doing this with no problem. Jimmy's parents then started to raise his pants to just under his buttocks. Using the same pattern as for the last step, they helped Jimmy to learn to pull his pants up from just below his bottom. They helped if necessary, then reduced their help, and happily praised Jimmy's good efforts.

The parents gradually moved to the point where his pants were left lying on the floor with Jimmy's feet in the pant legs. He soon learned to pull the pants all the way up. Next, his parents helped Jimmy to put one foot completely into the leg, leaving the other foot only partially in the other leg. Jimmy learned to do the rest. His parents guided him at first, and then reduced their assistance. Jimmy gradually learned to put on his pants by himself. His parents handed him the pants and said, ''Put on your pants.'' Jimmy then inserted both legs, stood up, and pulled his pants up around his waist.

This backward-chaining approach can be adapted to teach a child to put on other types of clothing. It is important to move slowly and keep the teaching sessions short and enjoyable.

TYING SHOELACES

Learning to tie shoelaces is a very difficult task. Children can start learning at about four-and-a-half years. But some children may not do well until around six years. Before beginning, Maria's mother spent some time thinking about how she tied her own shoelaces. She was surprised at how much she did without thinking.

Maria's mother started to teach her with a thin rope. She placed the rope under Maria's leg. It was long enough to be wrapped around the leg and tied on the top. She also used a similar rope for her leg so she could show Maria the many steps involved in tying a bow. Later, after Maria learned to tie a bow with the thin rope, she could try the same method with a shoelace. Since the rope was longer and thicker than the shoelace, it was easier for Maria to handle at first.

Maria's mother used these steps in teaching how to tie shoelaces.

Step #1. Sit alongside the child, each with a tying rope underneath one leg and holding the ends in each hand.

Step #2. Guide the child's hands and show her how to make an X over the top of her leg with the rope ends. Practice and praise this step several times until the child does it well.

Figure 23-4. Tying shoelaces is difficult work for children's short, small fingers.

Step #3. Teach the child to take the rope end which crosses the top of the X, pass it underneath the bottom rope, and pull it tight around the leg. Have the child practice this until she can do it with ease.

Step #4. Teach her to make a loop with one of the rope ends. Practice and praise this step thoroughly. At this point, go back over the first four steps and make sure the child can go through them on her own.

Step #5. While the child holds the loop in one hand, help her to wrap the other rope end around her thumb and the loop, and push it through, using her index finger to form the other half of the bow and pulling it tight.

Once these skills are learned and practiced, children know and understand the mechanics of tying a bow. The next step is to help them learn to tie a shoelace. This will require still more effort.

Maria's mother helped by letting Maria take her shoe off her foot and hold it in her lap. In this way, it was much easier for Maria to see and handle the shoelace. This stage of teaching was still a challenge, so Maria's mother worked with her in short sessions over several more days. Maria was very successful and happily showed others her new accomplishment. Of course, she received lots of praise for learning such a difficult skill.

The recent use of shoe straps that stick and unstick easily is very helpful to young children. However, children still need to learn to tie shoelaces.

BRUSHING THE TEETH

When children are about 18 to 20 months old, it is good to build the habit of brushing the teeth after each meal. This skill can be taught through modeling and imitation. After each meal, Maria's father let Maria watch him brush his teeth. He explained what he was doing and why. He then let Maria have a try with a child-size toothbrush and tasty toothpaste. Most young children like to brush their teeth, but it helps to use a flavor of toothpaste that they enjoy.

Maria's father provided a strong stool in the bathroom so Maria could reach the sink and mirror. He stood behind Maria and helped her to squeeze the toothpaste onto her brush. He then told her to brush up and down and very lightly assisted her. He often stopped helping and then praised Maria for brushing on her own.

The father showed Maria where the toothpaste and toothbrush were kept. He helped her to put them where they belonged. Next, they looked at Maria's white teeth in the mirror. Her father praised her for taking such good care of them.

The toothpaste and brush were kept where Maria could reach them and put them away, using the stool. The father consistently took interest in how Maria brushed her teeth during the next several weeks. Soon, Maria grew more and more skilled and independent at brushing her teeth.

PUTTING AWAY BELONGINGS

Jimmy began to learn to put away his belongings when he was about 18 months old. At this early age, his parent's goals were very small, but still important. They were teaching Jimmy to follow instructions and to know where things belonged. When Jimmy was about two years old, his parents began to work more on teaching perseverance in picking up and putting away personal belongings. This was good training for Jimmy's future.

Jimmy's parents arranged his room so that there was a place for everything. They provided low bookshelves for books, a box for toys, a small hamper for dirty clothes, and several low hooks for clothing. They helped Jimmy by drawing pictures of his belongings and placing them next to where they should be put away.

Once or twice each day, when several toys had gathered in Jimmy's room, his parents would cheerfully tell him that it was time to put his toys away. They demonstrated by picking up several items and putting them where they belonged. They labeled what they were doing. "The doll goes in the toy box." Or "The book goes on the shelf."

Jimmy's parents watched for and praised his imitations. If he did not imitate, they guided him to an item. They then told him to pick it up and where to put it. If necessary, they physically helped him. Jimmy did not resist, and seemed to enjoy the game. If he had resisted, his parents would have helped him along firmly.

In the beginning, Jimmy's parents praised any form of cooperation. They were especially praising when he imitated them on his own. They quickly finished the rest of the job themselves, and thanked him for helping. They told him how nice his room looked with everything in its place. Next, Jimmy was provided with a special activity or treat as an added reinforcement for finishing.

As Jimmy grew older, he became less dependent upon reinforcement and instructions. His parents slowly added tasks, such as putting his dirty clothes in the hamper when he changed for bed. When helping him dress for the day, they asked Jimmy to hang up his pajamas on a hook in the closet. By starting this teaching early and keeping it up, Jimmy's parents were helping him to grow in responsibility and independence.

MAKING A BED

Making a bed is a big job for a young child. By four or four-and-a-half years, children should be able to learn most of the steps involved. With help and encouragement, they should be able to make a bed by the time they enter kindergarten. This is a major step in children's independently rising and preparing themselves for the day.

It is good to teach making a bed in the morning, before breakfast. Praise and going to breakfast are both powerful and natural consequences for finishing the job. Also, parents will be encouraging the habit of doing things right away rather than putting them off.

The steps involved in making a bed should be explained to the child. First, the pillow must be taken off, and the sheet and blankets are pulled up to the head of the bed. Next, the pillow is placed near the center of the head of the bed. Finally, the bedspread is pulled over the pillow, tucked in, and straightened so that it hangs evenly. It is important that parents do not expect perfection. At first, wrinkles or a crooked edge should not be of concern. Improvements can be expected and encouraged, but only in small steps over a long period of time.

Richard's mother started by standing beside him by the head of the bed. She asked him to take the pillow off and set it nearby. She praised his move briefly and then said, "Let's pull the sheet up tight on this side of the bed." She waited for Richard to grasp the sheet and start to pull. She then helped to pull it the rest of the way. Richard's mother moved slowly so that he could watch. Together, they went through all of the steps to make the bed on both sides. The mother then praised Richard for his efforts.

Richard's mother was sure to keep this time together happy and enjoyable. They talked and laughed, and the mother showed her genuine appreciation. She gradually let Richard take over more of the job. She did this by using backward chaining. Soon Richard was pulling up the bedspread by himself. Next, the mother removed her assistance from the pillow, blankets, and sheet.

When the mother felt Richard was ready, she let him make the bed while she was out of the room. She told him she would get breakfast ready while he made his bed. She soon returned to check the job, praised him, and happily walked with him to breakfast. The mother was careful not to be too demanding. The fact that Richard was cooperating and trying to make his bed was a fine accomplishment. Slowly, over the weeks, she identified and praised improvements. More improvements occurred over time.

TEACHING SELF-CARE SEQUENCES

Teaching children how to care for themselves is one thing. Getting them to care for themselves *on their own* and *at the right time* is quite another thing. At first, children depend upon instructions. But if they are to become responsible in later years, they must learn to care for themselves without being told. This can be done by teaching self-care sequences.

When parents first say, "Wash your hands," their child probably does nothing. This instruction, or *signal*, has not yet acquired the power to produce hand washing. The child will learn to respond to these words with repeated instruction, assistance, and reinforcement for cooperation. Self-care sequences involve 1) the instruction, 2) the child's self-care behavior, and 3) the reinforcement of the child's behavior. Parents can eventually help their children to do things without always giving verbal instructions. Children can be taught to respond to other appropriate signals, such as various times or events in the day. Good rules for self-care specify a signal or time (before breakfast), a behavior (wash your face), and a reinforcing consequence (before you can go out to play). Such sequences of self-care are described in Box 23.2.

Children will learn responsible habits if parents consistently repeat, enforce, and reinforce the three-part rules for self-care sequences. Natural daily events will replace direct instructions as signals for actions.

BOX 23.2

Common Self-Care Sequences

Signal	Behavior	Reinforcement
When you get up in the morning	Get dressed and make your bed	Before you come to breakfast
When you come home	Change your clothes	Before you go out to play
When I call you to eat	Wash your hands	Before coming to dinner
When we finish eating	Help clean off the table	Before going out to play
When I say it's time for bed	Put on your pajamas	Before I read you a story

Figure 23-5. *Teaching children to care for themselves is a long-term project. Involving children in such necessary tasks as selecting the family groceries can encourage them to take an interest in preparing their own healthful foods.*

TEACHING CHILDREN TO PREPARE FOR SCHOOL

Around age five, children are normally ready to learn a series of self-care activities that end with being ready to go to school on time. Children at this age can often do each activity separately. When several self-care tasks are combined, though, young children lose their concentration and often waste time. This can be very frustrating to parents. Parents may be tempted to lose their tempers and shout at or punish their children. Giving

in to their tempers only complicates the problems. The morning routine soon becomes an unpleasant daily struggle.

Richard's parents had this problem. Five-year-old Richard could easily handle every self-care task involved in being ready to leave for school on time. Yet he could not seem to do all of the tasks together and on time. All his parents wanted was for Richard to prepare himself for school in the morning. They did not understand why he could not do these tasks in the morning. Each morning was filled with Richard's crying, whining, and protesting. His parents, in turn, talked loudly and angrily, and the day began unpleasantly for everyone. What had begun as a basic teaching problem became a threat to the general well-being of the family.

After much discussion, Richard's parents realized that they were expecting too much from him too fast. Getting ready for school is a complex series of activities for a five-year-old. This ability requires time and motivation to develop. It is made more difficult by the fact that many people, including Richard and his parents, tend to be more short tempered in the mornings, and often are rushed.

Richard's parents identified the specific activities that Richard had to complete. He had to brush his teeth and wash his face, brush his hair, dress, make his bed and hang up his pajamas. Richard's parents judged that 30 minutes was enough time for these tasks. They thought that if he would follow the same series of activities every day, it would soon become a habit. They designed a chart of clear drawings to help everyone remember the order of activities. They hung up copies of the chart so Richard would have frequent reminders. The chart is shown in Illustration 23.1.

Richard's parents knew that it is best for tooth brushing to be done after breakfast. But they temporarily reversed the order so that breakfast could be used as a powerful reinforcer. Richard needed powerful reinforcers for learning his morning series of self-help activities. The longer Richard took to get ready for school in the morning, the longer he had to wait for breakfast. To a hungry child, breakfast is a strong encouragement to work efficiently.

Richard also had a strong interest in money. It was decided that he would receive five cents each morning that he finished his work on time. The father was at first against paying his son for a required task. But the mother mentioned that when she was a child, she sometimes received money for doing certain tasks. She pointed out that she ''had turned out all right.'' Richard's father wisely decided not to argue the point. He was willing to try using money as a reinforcer in order to solve the morning problems.

On the first morning of the reinforcement system, the mother gently awakened Richard. When he was wide awake, she cheerfully explained his morning tasks as though they were a game. She explained the activities chart to Richard and taped it to his door. Next, he was shown an egg timer which would be left in his room. Richard's mother said that if he could get ready for school before the timer rang, she would give him five cents and then they would eat breakfast. She told Richard to do everything shown on the chart, and to call her as soon as he was done. At first, Richard protested. But his mother ignored this and cheerfully repeated the rules. She then set the timer for 30 minutes and left Richard's room.

In 23 minutes, Richard called for his mother. He was done in record time! There had been no scolding or nagging. A stick-on star for the day was placed by each item on the chart. Richard was hugged and sincerely praised. His mother gave him five cents and asked him to join the family for breakfast.

During the next few weeks, Richard independently reduced his time to 18 to 20 minutes. He even began to set the timer himself. After a month, they stopped using the

	Mon	Tue	Wed	Thur	Fri	Sat	Sun
1.	☆						
2. 	☆						
3. 	☆						
4. 	☆						
5. 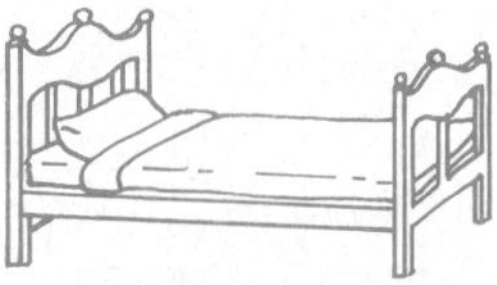	☆						
6. 	☆						

Illustration 23.1. A morning self-help chart

timer. A short time later, the chart and the stars were discontinued. After two months, the five-cents reinforcement was omitted. Richard was proudly told that he was a big boy now and could get ready for school all on his own. By this time, Richard was used to his "income" and enjoyed buying small things at the store. He was happy when his allowance was continued for helping to clear the dinner dishes each evening.

If Richard did not finish preparing for school on time, his parents stated their disappointment calmly, just once. They then prompted him through his tasks with as few words as possible, and breakfast was delayed until Richard finished. Happily, this did not happen often. Richard soon established the habit of preparing himself for school on time. He had only needed some motivation to do the tasks on time.

SHOULD PARENTS USE FOOD AND MONEY AS REINFORCERS

The most natural form of reinforcement for children is the praise and admiration they receive from loved ones and others. There is much scientific evidence that the skillful use of praise can be a very good motivational force for children. Reinforcers such as toys or common household objects that children can obtain as they learn to creep, crawl, walk, and climb are very valuable ones. These reinforcers have always motivated children to learn new things. Other reinforcing consequences which have been well researched are the many activities which children enjoy, such as outside play, television, and playing with toys. These activities, of course, vary

from child to child. These reinforcing consequences have often been useful in teaching procedures. We do not hesitate to recommend their skillful use.

When teaching self-care skills to children, parents sometimes consider using food or money as a reinforcer. In the last teaching example in this chapter, Richard's parents used both food (breakfast) and money (five cents) to teach him to prepare himself for school on time. We feel that this was a reasonable teaching approach, because Richard had not learned this important skill through other means. Also, the levels of frustration in the family had increased to the point of causing yelling and punishment.

Richard's parents finally and wisely chose a more positive approach—the work allowance combined with breakfast, ample praise and a visually reinforcing chart (Illustration 23.1). This broad mixture of reinforcers was very successful for them. The parents did not use meals as reinforcers for other teaching goals. But they did continue to use the work allowance for other chores. Since this worked so well with Richard, they felt that it was a natural and beneficial way to parent.

Everyone eats food and has some money. But should these things be used to teach children? There is no simple answer to this question. Experts argue for and against such an approach. Currently, there is no convincing scientific evidence to help solve the debate.

The majority of professionals do not support the use of giving food as a reward for good behavior in normally developing children. It is felt that food could become too important to children and lead to overeating and unhealthy weight gains.

Food has often been used as a reinforcer to help hard-to-motivate retarded children. This is appropriate. However, its frequent and widespread use with normally developing children is hard to defend at this time.

The use of money as a reinforcer for children also creates disagreement among professionals. It is suggested that children who are paid to do things may become too dependent upon money. Some believe that children may lose the motivation to do all things that they are not paid to do. However, the facts are that many healthy and well-adjusted adults were paid money for doing chores as children, and others were not. Clear scientific findings are not yet available to help settle this issue. Parents, then, must judge for themselves and their children.

Many professionals believe that using money as a reinforcer to strengthen work-like behavior is beneficial. They observe that in our society we are expected to work, earn money, and use it wisely. They also feel that it is important to balance a desire for money among other important things, experiences, opportunities, and values in life.

To do this, they argue, requires that children have experiences which slowly help them to have realistic ideas about money, and appropriate ways to earn and spend it. Experience is also needed to learn what money can buy—and the important things that money cannot buy. Most parents would agree that too great a love for money *or* a total disregard for its benefits can lead to much unhappiness.

Parents must use their own judgment to help their children to achieve healthy attitudes about money. This is just one of the many self-care skills which children will need in preparation for their future.

QUESTIONS FOR GROWTH

1. List ten specific self-care skills which, if learned, will strengthen independent self-care.

2. Describe some of the undesirable problems which can result from poor toilet training.

3. Explain how parents can tell when their young children are ready for toilet training.

4. Describe the main points of the toilet-training approach based upon reinforcement methods.

5. Explain how you would begin to teach a three-year-old to use a butter knife.

6. Describe how a three-year-old could be taught to pour liquids into a glass.

7. Tell what you would do to teach a four-year-old to make a sandwich.

8. Describe a way to teach children how to button buttons.

9. What are some things that parents can do to teach children to tie shoelaces?

10. How might you help a child to learn to keep his or her bedroom clean?

11. Explain how parents can begin to teach their children to do self-care activities without being told.

12. Describe the problem which Richard's parents faced in motivating him to prepare himself for school in a reasonable amount of time. How did they solve the problem?

13. Explain how you feel about using food and money as reinforcers to motivate work activities in children.

CHAPTER

24

Helping Children to Cope With Fears
(Birth to Two Years)

A reasonable goal is to raise children who are not careless and who have a healthy respect for real dangers. But children should not be troubled by excessive and unnecessary fears. The human emotion of fear can be valuable in some situations, but harmful in others. Fears of real dangers help us to protect our lives and health. However, unrealistic fears benefit no one.

Infants who remain fearful of harmless new people, strange places, or noisy toys may not grow independent enough to explore. Because of unrealistic fears, they may miss a wide variety of important experiences. Unnecessary fears which continue throughout childhood may even produce physical problems. Such fears have been known to cause stuttering, nervous tics, and stomach, heart, or breathing problems.

Events such as loud noises, sudden loss of support (being dropped), sudden changes in surroundings, or pain are likely to produce fear reactions in babies. These things may cause babies to cry, gasp, become stiff, and thrash their arms. These are unlearned fear reactions which are normal for infants. Yet the events which produce these normal fears can be involved in the process of learning new, unnecessary fears.

In this chapter, we discuss how parents and others can help infants between birth to two years to cope with fears. Much of the information in this chapter can also be applied to Chapter 25, which deals with fears in children between the ages of two to seven.

COGNITIVE INFLUENCES IN FEAR DEVELOPMENT

Parents will feel less alarmed over their children's fears when they understand how fears develop. This understanding will also help them when they work to reduce fears in their children. As discussed in Chapter 9, children may learn new fears in several ways.

• By association—Neutral stimuli become associated with things that are feared naturally (unlearned fears).
• By imitation—A child watches other people act fearfully.
• By symbolic representation—A child remembers stories, pictures, or movie images of monsters or "bad" people.

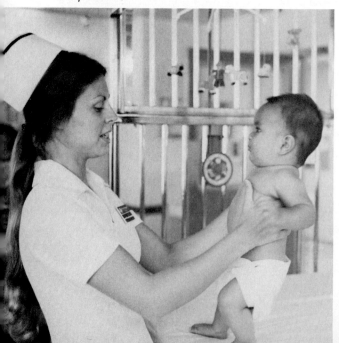

Figure 24-1. Sudden changes in routines and surroundings can produce fear in babies. (The Greyhound Corporation)

Children do not think like adults do. Infants and young children are egocentric, or self-centered. That is, their views of the world are very personal. They naturally relate what they see and hear to their own thoughts, needs, and insecurities. Infants and young children also experience growth in their ability to use their imaginations. Some perfectly normal children even develop imaginary friends.

The combination of egocentrism and a growing imagination makes it very easy for children to believe that sounds in the night relate directly to them. For example, they may imagine that a monster or wild animal is hiding in their closet or coming to get them. These fears are not silly or unreasonable. Young children have not lived through enough experiences to realistically judge how likely it is that a bear or dragon would be in their closet. If you think about it, you will realize that much learning is required before one can logically rule out that possibility. These are ways in which a child's cognitive development (what he or she knows or does not know about the world) can stimulate or limit certain fears.

GUIDELINES FOR ELIMINATING FEARS

Parents must learn to recognize and change behaviors which reflect fear in order to help children overcome unnecessary fears. Babies between birth and two years of age may show fear in several natural ways. They may cry, scream, tremble, hide their faces, or try to crawl or run away. They may go to great lengths to avoid or escape from a person, place, or object. This is one reason why unnecessary fears continue. Avoidance or escape causes a form of negative reinforcement of fear behaviors. That is, fearful actions which remove the feared object or situation are strengthened.

Babies who are allowed to escape from a feared but harmless object may never learn that the object is harmless. Parents must increase babies' exposure to harmless but feared objects. Parents must stay calm and help their babies to relax during this process.

In so doing, parents can demonstrate their own lack of fear and reinforce their infants' fearlessness.

A researcher named Mary C. Jones first used this method in 1924 with a child named Peter. The boy, who was nearly three, was very fearful of small, furry animals. Jones chose to try to eliminate Peter's fear of a white rabbit.

For treatment, Jones took Peter to a room to play with several other children who did not fear the rabbit. The rabbit was present

Figure 24-2. When children are exposed to feared objects, parents should stay calm and show their own lack of fear.

in the room, a long distance away from where Peter played. Occasionally, Peter's friends would go over to the rabbit and pet and feed it. Peter watched them with interest. There was more such play each day for seven days. Every day the rabbit was placed closer to the play area. By the seventh day, Peter was able to touch the rabbit without fear, just like his friends.

The major factors involved in curing Peter's fears were as follows.

1. Fearless behavior was demonstrated by playmates whom Peter could imitate.

2. The rabbit was placed first at a comfortable distance and then moved closer gradually so as not to alarm Peter. This is another example of how teaching in small steps is a very successful method.

3. Playing with friends helped to relax Peter and was probably reinforcing to him. When Peter was relaxed, it was more difficult for him to be fearful. The reinforcers of play and friends became associated with the rabbit. This helped to make the rabbit less frightening and more enjoyable.

Peter's fear was easy to identify. But sometimes children show fear reactions to whole situations (a room, an amusement park), and parents may not be able to identify the specific cause. Here, too, parents can reduce fear by exposing children to the feared situation in small steps. The same method can be used to prevent fears from developing. Parents can try to recognize possibly fearful situations. They can then introduce their children to the situations in small, relaxed steps with lots of praise for fearlessness.

COMMON FEARS

Many fears are commonly found among groups of children at various age levels. However, individual children will differ greatly as to what they fear, when they fear it, and how intense the fear is. But there is one general trend: a slow drift from fears of specific events during younger years to more general and imaginary fears in older children.

In Chapter 7, we discussed fears common among children between birth and two years. These fears are of loud noises and things that make noise, falling or loss of support, and pain. Other common fears are of unfamiliar objects, separation from parents, and new situations and people. We now discuss some of these fears in children, and provide examples of how parents can help their children to overcome them.

Fear of Loud Noises

During the first two years of life, children are likely to be most fearful of loud noises. This fear may continue between two and four years, but should gradually decrease.

Toys that make noise may produce fear. Suppose that parents have bought a rubber duck for their three-month-old daughter. When they squeeze the duck, it squeaks. If the toy was squeezed hard near the infant's face, the loud noise might scare her. The baby might tense her body, cry, thrash her arms, and turn away.

It is important to note that the sight of the brightly colored toy did not scare the infant. The loud noise did. By associating the toy duck with the loud noise, a new fear could be learned. The infant may now cry and turn away whenever the toy is brought near to her. Also, if she is exposed to intense or frequent noise, the infant's fear might generalize to other unfamiliar objects associated with the noise.

The way to overcome—or prevent—such a fear is to let the infant experience the noise first at quiet levels. The parents could smile and talk to their daughter in a cheerful and soothing way as they very lightly squeeze the duck to produce a small squeak. By watching the infant's reactions, the parents can easily judge when she is comfortable or interested in the noise. If they increase the level of noise a little bit at a time, the baby may continue to show delighted interest. The child, in this way may show no fear even if the toy is squeezed hard, producing a loud squeak.

Jimmy, at age nine months, learned to fear a vacuum cleaner. To him, the vacuum seemed like a huge, ugly monster as it roared around the room. Jimmy's father accidentally taught him to be terrified of the vacuum cleaner. One day visitors were coming, and Jimmy's father rushed to clean the house. He plugged the vacuum cleaner in and turned it on just five feet from where Jimmy was playing on the floor. Jimmy jumped in fear at the roaring noise, and screamed and cried. The next ten minutes were spent comforting the frightened boy. Before, Jimmy had been only slightly cautious around the noisy vacuum cleaner. Now, he was terrified of it. He would not even go near the machine when it was turned off. He even began to avoid the closet where it was stored.

To eliminate this fear, Jimmy's parents exposed him to the vacuum cleaner in gradual steps while he was kept calm and relaxed. The vacuum cleaner was frequently left out so Jimmy could get used to its quiet presence. From time to time, Jimmy would approach the vacuum cleaner and be praised for his bravery.

Later, when Jimmy was comfortable about touching it, his parents let him become used to the sound of the vacuum cleaner. He was taken across the room from the vacuum and held closely. He parents relaxed him by talking cheerfully and laughing, and then turned on the machine for about one second. This was done several times until Jimmy showed less fear. He was gradually exposed to longer intervals of noise, and was encouraged to move closer and closer to the machine. He began to help to turn it on and off. Then, as his father carried him, Jimmy helped to push the machine and was praised for his efforts. Jimmy's fear of the vacuum cleaner was gone within a few days.

Storms

Many children are frightened by violent storms with loud thunderclaps, high winds, and lightning. How parents handle their child's signs of fearing a storm can greatly influence later reactions. Maria, at two years old, was too young to be told about the real dangers of storms and how to find protection. At her age, her parents' main purpose was to prevent extreme fears of thunder and lightning. When she was six or seven, her parents would teach her about safety during storms.

Maria's father thought about his own behavior during a storm. Was he calm? Did he look nervous or scared? If he was behaving in a fearful way, it was important that he try to control himself in front of Maria. He did not want to serve as a fearful model for Maria to imitate. Instead, he tried to help her to enjoy storms rather than to fear them.

There were faint rumblings in the distance. Another electrical storm was on its way. It was soon dark, and the sky began to flicker with the distant lightning. Maria's father began to speak happily about a storm coming. He described the water it would bring to make the flowers grow. He talked excitedly about how pretty the lightning was, and how loud the thunder would boom. He smiled often as he talked of the fun he and Maria would have that night watching the storm. Minutes later, they sat waiting for the storm, snuggled in a chair a safe distance from a picture window. A nearby plate of peanut-butter crackers and sliced apples made the occasion seem like a picnic.

Excitedly, Maria's father described how the storm was a big cloud high in the sky. He explained that the closer it came, the louder it would rumble and the brighter the lightning would be. He told Maria that the lightning would not last long and that as the storm moved away, the thunder would grow quieter until they could not hear it anymore. During the storm, he hugged Maria and showed delighted excitement at the lightning and loud booms of thunder.

At one point, Maria looked worried and grew quiet. Her father held her closer and assured her that there was nothing to fear. "We're safe at home, and the storm can't hurt us here." When Maria relaxed a little, her father praised her for being interested in the storm. As the storm moved away, they talked about how much fun it would be to watch another storm some day. Maria slept well that night. Perhaps when she grew older, storms would remind her of the warmth and security she felt with her father.

This approach might be varied. Some parents might not want to encourage looking out of the window during their child's first storm. Or they might have their child look only during the less intense stages of the storm. If the storm is especially strong, parents might start some family games in the basement.

In some cases, such as in a tornado area, this approach may need to be carried out in an actual storm shelter. In such situations, parents can admit that big storms are a little scary. But they should reassure the child that the family is protected. Sometimes reading children's books on weather will help children to understand what to expect. This can help them to be more relaxed during storms.

The basic principles of preventing or curing the fear of storms are as follows.

1. The parents model calm and unfrightened behavior.
2. Pleasant activities are arranged during the storm—games, stories, and so on.
3. Thunder and lightning are described as pretty and exciting.
4. The intensity of the storm gradually decreases, thanks to Mother Nature.
5. The parents praise the child for being calm.

Fears of Separation, New People, and New Places

Before the age of seven months, infants may smile happily and coo at almost anyone who comes near. Around seven months, these displays of affection are often shown only to the parents and a few other familiar people. When a new person approaches, children may turn away, hide their faces, or begin to cry. Some may show a fear of new people as early as four-and-a-half months.

Around these ages, fears of separation from parents and of new places usually begin. The fears of new people, separation, and new places are related. Among familiar surroundings and people, infants will probably not be afraid to move away from their parents. In the presence of strange people and places, they may cling to their parents and act fearful. At these times, the parents provide a base of security and comfort in the face of new experiences. Infants will normally show a very special attachment to the mother or father who is the main care giver. If separated from the main care giver around strangers or new places, infants may cry and protest strongly.

These new fears can be upsetting to the unprepared parents. But they are actually a healthy sign of a valuable attachment between parents and infants. Infants, however, must gradually overcome such fears for normal social and emotional development.

Fear of Separation

Infants need love and security for healthy development. But they also need help in becoming adventurous enough to dare leaving the security of their parents' loving arms. This is needed to benefit from an ever-widening range of new and important experiences. An excessive fear of separation can result in limited social, emotional, and even cognitive development. Some parents have too great

a need to be depended upon and loved. Such parents often reinforce the fear of separation. These parents must learn to put their needs aside in favor of their infant's developmental needs.

Parents can best prepare their children to handle separations by teaching them the skills necessary for independent living. They can do this by gradually introducing periods of separation from the parents. They can also reinforce signs of independence, such as a willingness to move away from the parents' sides to meet new people and explore new places.

Figure 24-3. Parents provide a base of security and comfort. When parents move out of sight, young children may show signs of anxiety.

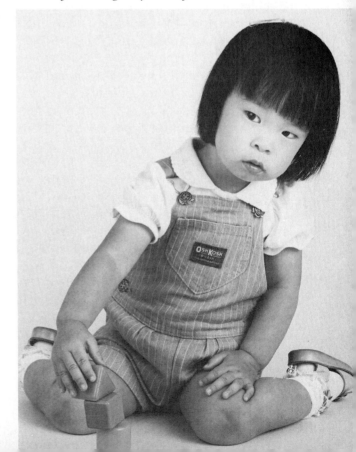

When Richard first learned to crawl at about six months, he soon crawled away from his parents. However, he would not crawl away very far or for very long. Benjamin Spock described the attachment between parent and child as being "elastic" at this point. At first, Richard did not move far out of his mother's sight. In the event of a loud noise or other frightening sight or sound, he would rush back to her immediately. This was an important time for Richard. He had to learn that when he moved away a short distance, his parents would not withdraw their support. He had to know that they would not leave him altogether or withhold their attention when he returned. An infant who feels abandoned is not likely to go exploring very often.

Richard's parents encouraged exploration. They enriched his surroundings with interesting things to investigate. They avoided punishing him for moving away from them, and did not limit his movement about the home without a good reason, such as safety. They childproofed the home so there was no reason why he could not move away whenever he wanted. As Richard moved about, his parents reinforced his actions with smiles and words of encouragement.

Richard's parents taught him to lose his fear of separation in small, easy steps. At first, they praised him and spoke to him frequently as he crawled away to explore. They approached him from time to time to touch him. This sometimes caused Richard to stop what he was doing and follow them. But this was only a temporary effect. His parents' actions had all served as reinforcers for moving away, so Richard would show more of this form of independence later. (Remember that a reinforcer strengthens the *future* frequency of the behavior it follows.)

As Richard seemed to gain more confidence and spent more time away from them, the parents slowly began to increase their distance away from him. They were careful to move farther away in small steps. Richard might have become upset if they moved too far too soon. The parents also continued to praise Richard as he learned to play farther away from them. This was a direct reinforcement of Richard's independence. It also gave him the comfort and security he needed to move off and explore his environment.

Some infants explore happily as long as their parents remain somewhere within sight. When their parents leave the room, they hurry after them or panic and begin to cry. Recall that children at this age do not have object permanence. This means that, to the infant, something which is removed from sight no longer exists in the world. The lack of object permanence in young infants helps to explain their distress at losing sight of their parents.

For infants who are fearful of being left alone, even for a minute, parents can play a form of the game "peek-a-boo." Richard's parents often played this game with him when he was an infant. They stood in the doorway of the room he was in and got his attention. Then they would disappear around the corner of the doorway. A few seconds later, they would reappear with much praise and excitement for Richard's patient waiting. The game was also played while Richard was in his high chair or crib. This prevented Richard from trying to follow his parents.

The amount of time he was made to wait for their return was slowly increased until Richard's parents could leave for several minutes without causing alarm. This game helped Richard to associate the parents' disappearance with a happy situation. It also helped his parents to reinforce Richard's patience and courage.

Richard's parents increased their time away from him very slowly. If they had left him for too long a time and then reentered the room when he was crying fearfully, they would have reinforced his fear of separation. If this had happened, his parents would have shortened their times away the next time they played the game. They would have used smaller steps in the future. But since Richard's parents were patient, they did not have this problem. Richard eventually learned to wait for their return. When they found him happily waiting for them, they were sure to cuddle and praise him.

Eventually, infants will move away from their parents and crawl into another room. This can be encouraged by keeping some toys in other rooms. Now, more than ever, it is important to childproof the home.

Infants should be encouraged to play by themselves. Parents can start by noting how long their infant will normally play alone. If, for example, an infant usually plays alone for four minutes, the parents can watch for longer periods of playing alone to praise. Again, parents should not be surprised if, after the praise, their infant stops playing alone and follows them. The praise still reinforced the playing alone, so this play should increase in the future. As the infant grows more independent and spends more time alone, the parents should continue to visit from time to time.

Fear of New People

It is possible for a child to learn to spend too much time alone. Parents should balance their reinforcement for independent play with praise for approaching and socializing with people. As mentioned earlier, fear of separation is related to fear of new people and new places.

To help Jimmy learn to enjoy the company of other people, his parents held him or let him stay by their sides at first. They gave him the physical security he needed to remain fairly relaxed in the presence of new people. Jimmy's parents tried to keep enough physical distance from new people at first so as not to cause Jimmy fear. As he relaxed with these new people, his parents gradually moved closer. Sometimes they would sit comfortably and wait until Jimmy seemed ready to be moved from their laps to their sides. Sometimes Jimmy would crawl off on his own. To help him forget his fears, his parents often directed Jimmy's attention to toys or other interesting objects.

It is important for infants to learn that new people can be a source of reinforcement—praise, treats, and fun. This usually is learned naturally. Visitors will smile and give attention, other children will offer to play, and relatives and close friends may become involved in care giving. Infants who are raised among many people tend to be less fearful of new people than are infants with more limited social experience.

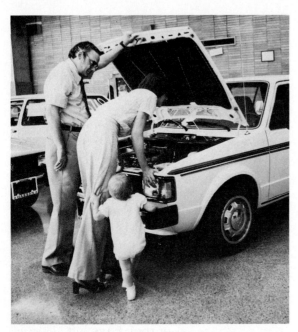

Figure 24-4. When parents often introduce their children to new situations, children are less likely to be fearful.

Fear of New Places

Infants often fear new places. It is a mistake for parents to give in to this fear by not taking them to new places. Parents should also avoid taking their infants home whenever they show any fear. Young children who are often overprotected from the natural stresses of living often have even greater fears at older ages. The same unfortunate effect may be created by similarly giving in to infants' fears of separation or strangers. By using small steps, parents can avoid such unhappy effects.

Maria was taken to a carnival when she was eight months old. She was very frightened by the loud noises, bright lights, and moving crowds. Her parents had planned to push her in a stroller. Instead, they took turns carrying her for the first 15 minutes or so. They walked in the quieter, less crowded sections of the park. They could see her fearful reactions and feel the tenseness in her body.

Maria's parents cuddled her and spoke to her in soothing tones. As she began to relax, they bought a small stuffed animal for her to cuddle, and placed her in the stroller. As they moved, they still talked to Maria and stopped often to touch her. They laughed and pointed out the fun that others were having. They remained in the quieter areas. Later, they moved closer to some of the loud areas. If Maria showed signs of fear, they went no farther until she relaxed. Her parents did not force her to go farther than she was ready to go, and they left the carnival while she was still enjoying herself.

Maria's parents accomplished a lot that day. They took Maria to the carnival, had a wonderful time together, and helped her to overcome some natural fears. When Maria relaxed more, her parents paid less attention to very minor signs of worry. But they continued to reinforce less fearful and more outgoing behavior.

Fear of Babysitters and Day-Care Centers

Parents have often faced the problem of leaving their infants, crying and begging for them to stay, with a babysitter or at a day-care center. (*Day-care centers* are businesses where professionals take care of groups of children for portions of the day.) Such experiences are difficult for both parents and infants. Parents who have strengthened their infants' independent behavior have already done much to reduce the fears associated with these events. But parents must do more to prepare their children to be cared for by babysitters and in day-care centers.

Jimmy's parents invited his first babysitter to come to their home several times to play with him in the parents' presence. This helped both Jimmy and his parents. The parents were reassured that the babysitter knew how to give Jimmy the care and love he needed. Jimmy was reassured because he became familiar with the babysitter. He began to associate the babysitter with reinforcing things such as toys and playing. Thus, the babysitter became an enjoyable person for Jimmy.

After a few visits, the parents sometimes left the room for short periods to let Jimmy become used to being alone with his new friend. His parents were also able to observe the babysitter and Jimmy alone. They were reassured that the two were happy and comfortable together.

Maria's mother returned to work when Maria was two years old. Maria was to spend three mornings a week at a day-care center. Her mother arranged a visit first. This gave Maria a chance to become familiar with the new surroundings, toys, other children, and teachers.

Maria was shy at first, so the teachers introduced her to this new environment slowly and in small steps. They started at an area away from the center of activities. As Maria relaxed, her mother slowly removed her physical support and closeness. The teachers found an interesting toy for Maria to play with alone. Maria was soon playing on the floor near her mother. The teacher stopped by from time to time with smiles, kind words, and other enjoyable activities. Soon, Maria wandered farther away to watch some of the other children. She seemed much more comfortable and relaxed, and began to join in the activities of the other children.

Visits of this sort allow parents to examine the program and teachers in day-care centers or nursery schools. We discuss this matter in greater detail in Chapter 28.

Parents sometimes make errors in dealing with their children's fears of good babysitters and day-care centers. The two most common errors are as follows.

1. Returning to comfort their children's crying or tantrum after they have left. This action increases the likelihood of continued problems by reinforcing extremely dependent behavior. As a result, parents may constantly have to deal with their children's crying or tantrum when they leave.

2. Trying to protect children from the discomfort of separation by never using babysitters or day-care centers. Parents do this sometimes not only to protect their children, but also to protect themselves from separation. As a result, parents and children are likely to miss out on needed social and recreational opportunities. Without some recreation, parents may begin to resent their limited lifestyle. In turn, children may come to notice the resentment.

It is good for both parents and infants to use the services of a good babysitter from time to time. This may begin at about three or four months, depending on the particular infant's health. Younger infants are not likely to show fear, but parents can expect some emotional goodbyes at around six to nine months. This is likely to happen even if the parents have selected the babysitter with great care and the babysitter is known to the child. When leaving, parents may happily kiss their baby goodbye, say that they will be back soon, and walk out of the door. They should keep going even if the baby cries.

Parents sometimes try to calm a child's fear by remaining at a day-care center with the child for a time. Then, once the child becomes involved with an activity, the parents quietly leave without telling the child. When parents leave in this way, the child may become more fearful of separation. This can happen because the child no longer trusts the parents' actions. The child becomes very concerned about suddenly losing the parents with no warning.

In the long run, it is more effective for parents to say goodbye before leaving the day-care center. It is often helpful for parents to leave a personal belonging such as a scarf or hat with the child. Perhaps this helps the child to understand that the parents will return.

SUMMARY

An important ingredient in eliminating or preventing fears is to establish a close and loving relationship between parents and children. Parents are then encouraged to provide reassurance and relaxing activities for their children as they bring them into contact with feared objects or situations through small, easy steps.

QUESTIONS FOR GROWTH

1. Describe several unlearned fear reactions that infants show.

2. Explain three ways in which new fears can be learned.

3. Describe the things that Mary C. Jones did to help Peter lose his fear of a white rabbit.

4. Tell how you would help an infant overcome a fear of some loud noises.

5. Explain how you might help a young child overcome the fear of storms.

6. At approximately what ages can infants be expected to show fear of new people, separation, and new places?

7. Explain what parents might do to help their infant learn to spend shorter, and then longer, periods of time away from their presence.

8. How might you help an infant become more comfortable around strangers?

9. Explain what parents might do to help a child grow more comfortable about being left with a babysitter.

10. Describe some of the things that parents might do to help their child be less fearful of attending a day-care center.

11. Explain the two most common errors that parents make in dealing with their children's fears of babysitters and day-care centers.

CHAPTER

25

Helping Children to Cope With Fears
(Two to Seven Years)

Children are perhaps more fearful between two to seven years than at any other ages. They can see that some situations might be dangerous. But they cannot yet tell the difference between those which are truly dangerous and those which only seem dangerous. Nor have they learned to cope with fears.

In many situations, children's fear is useful and appropriate, as when a five-year-old is fearful of moving cars or of drowning. Such fears help the child to be careful. Other fears, however, are not necessary to the health and well-being of children. They may even harm or limit children's development. Such fears include fear of darkness, thunder, and sleeping alone.

There are many places and activities which present real dangers to the unprepared child.

In these cases, parents must encourage great caution and even a healthy amount of fear. A busy street, a river, and a high ladder are among the things which should come to produce reasonable fear and caution in children in early stages of development. According to Erikson, children between the ages of two and five years tend to believe they can do anything they want. In many cases, children are too young to understand the dangerous consequences for some of their actions. Parents can help by clearly labeling situations which are dangerous. Parents must also enforce their child's avoidance of such situations through effective methods of discipline. Children need to learn the difference between activities which are truly dangerous and those which are not.

COMMON FEARS

Even the most adventurous children will sometimes show a fear of being hurt in fairly harmless activities. Some of the fears common to children between the ages of two and seven years are listed in Table 25.1. This list is by no means complete, because each child can develop fears unique to his or her personal environment.

Although Jimmy had gone down many slides with no problem, he began to show a fear of a new slide in his neighborhood park. This slide was unusually high and spiraling. Jimmy had watched many other children go down the slide, but he mistakenly interpreted their screams of delight as screams of fear. Five-year-old Jimmy was afraid, but he still was interested in the slide. He asked his mother to go down the slide with him.

Jimmy's mother climbed the tall slide and went down, slowing her descent in every

way possible. The height of the slide and the speed of descent were enough to make even the adult a little uncomfortable during the first trip. After a few trial slides, Jimmy's mother took her then-willing son down the slide in her lap. She showed how to slow their descent with her hands, and was careful to show her delight by laughing and cuddling Jimmy on the way down. Jimmy was delighted and said, "Just one more time, Mommy, and I'll be used to it." Eventually, the proud and excited child completed his first of many solo trips down the slide.

Jimmy's mother had avoided ridiculing, scolding, and shaming. Instead, she demonstrated the safe behavior to be imitated, and explained why it was safe. She assisted her child by accompanying him down the slide. Through it all, she praised Jimmy for his courage and safe behavior on the slide. The

Figure 25-1. Children should be helped to overcome their fears of activities that are reasonably safe. (Pocono Mountains Vacation Bureau)

Table 25.1

Common Children's Fears Between Two to Seven Years

Age	Fears
2 to 4 Years	Noises and things that produce noise Unfamiliar objects, situations, or people Animals and insects
4 to 7 Years	Imaginary creatures Darkness Being made fun of Dreams Robbers and "bad" people Threats of harm from accidents

praise was necessary during the early stages of assistance. Later, though, the natural reinforcers involved in a safe, but thrilling, ride were enough. Not only was Jimmy's fear eliminated, but he had also learned a fun new game.

It is important that children be helped to overcome their fears of activities which are reasonably safe. Some parents overprotect their children from all bumps, bruises, and scratches. In so doing, these parents do not teach the difference between real dangers and the minor risks which are a natural part of life. Instead, these parents teach their children to be afraid of many activities which are a part of normal development.

Fear of Animals and Insects

Children can learn to fear animals and insects either through association (having been hurt), imitation, or symbolic representation (imagination). Richard was six and had never been stung by, or taught to fear, bees or other insects. His parents were therefore surprised and concerned when he started to scream, cry, and run away when any insect flew or buzzed near him. They could not understand where Richard had learned this fear.

A few days later, Richard's father watched him playing with a group of slightly older children. The children began screaming and running away from flying insects. They acted almost as though it was a game, with first one child sounding the alarm and then the others joining in. The origin of their fear became clear when Richard's father saw the parents of two of the children react exactly the same way when an insect buzzed by them one day. All of the children had learned the fear of insects through imitation.

There are, of course, certain insects and snakes whose bites are poisonous. Under these circumstances, a healthy fear is wise. Parents should begin early to teach children the differences between these and harmless creatures. In so doing, parents not only expand their children's knowledge, but also teach them to appreciate nature. Parents can read aloud from a good children's book that describes nature and shows pictures of various creatures. Parents can talk about the creatures' habits, and clearly show the differences between harmful and harmless insects and animals.

By educating children about nature, parents can help to remove one major source of fear: *ignorance*, or the lack of knowledge

Figure 25-2. Children who are so fearful that they cannot enjoy safe rides at an amusement park will miss out on some of the normal childhood fun. (Rick Norton/Kings Island)

Figure 25-3. *Most fear is caused by ignorance. It is unlikely that after this safe and fun ride that this child will ever be afraid of horses. (© 1985 Joanne Meldrum)*

about something. In addition, parents will be modeling curiosity about and appreciation of all living things.

When Maria was three, her parents created a small ''pond'' in the backyard so that they could watch the beginnings of life. A small plastic wading pool with some tadpoles and water from a field trip to a pond provided weeks of fascinating nature study. In this ''biological soup'' grew frogs, snails, water insects, and algae. With a microscope, Maria and her parents also looked at the activities of a variety of single-cell organisms which they found in their pond. There is no reason to wait until children reach higher grades in school to learn about these exciting things in nature.

With a little guidance, children can enjoy hours of fascinating and educational play. They can learn to appreciate the beauty and complexity of even the most simple creatures. Children can hold and inspect harmless creatures such as frogs and worms. This kind of teaching is a part of parenting which should not be neglected. Short trips into the garden or to a pond can prevent unnecessary fears and open new sources of fun, beauty, and natural mystery for children. Such experiences lead to a respect and appreciation for our relationship with all living creatures.

Fear of the Dark and Imaginary Creatures

Some children will begin to fear being alone in the dark at about two years. Most, though, grow increasingly fearful between the ages of three and six. Exactly why children develop such a fear is not fully understood. Some people believe it has a genetic origin. They reason that fear of the dark would have held survival value for primitive peoples, preventing them, for example, from blindly falling over cliffs or being attacked by night predators. Yet a more obvious source of fear of the dark is children's imagination based on learned information.

During early childhood, children's powers of observation, understanding, memory, and imagination are increasing dramatically. It is during this period that children are taught in various ways that scary things happen in the dark. They hear stories of monsters which hide in the dark, either from other children or from parents. (Some parents even use the idea of monsters to scare their children into obedience.) Children can also see dangers in darkness as shown in some television programs and movies.

One child, for example, had become a Michael Jackson fan. She had been excited when she was given a poster of the rock star to put on her bedroom wall. Then she saw Jackson's short film, *Thriller*, in which he turns into a frightening monster. After that experience, she was no longer able to sleep with his poster on her wall. She was afraid that his picture would turn into a monster when the room was dark.

To avoid or decrease extreme levels of fear of the dark and imaginary creatures, parents can start early to accustom their children to darkness. They can do this by pairing reinforcing activities with being in the dark and teaching their children to sleep alone in their darkened rooms. Parents must also avoid exposing their children to terrifying television programs, horror stories, and scary fairy tales. The following are some guidelines that parents can follow.

1. Let children become used to sleeping in the dark. Young infants will probably go to sleep in a darkened room. But it is possible that they may sleep more soundly if there is a small, dim light present for several months. A small night light can also make it easier for parents to look in to check on sleeping children. Parents may wish to keep the light off after the first few months. In this way, infants will not become totally dependent upon light for sleep. After sleeping with a light on for years, children may not be able to go to sleep without a light.

However, as with Maria, this problem can result from other sources. Maria became fearful of sleeping alone in the dark shortly after her parents were divorced when she was five. When children experience the loss of a loved one or other painful or sudden changes, they sometimes become generally more fearful. In Maria's case, this was shown by her fear of separation from her mother at night.

For a few nights, Maria's mother let her sleep in bed with her. She then firmly instructed Maria to return to sleeping in her own room. Maria was allowed to keep the light on. But after several weeks, the mother decided to help Maria adjust to sleeping alone in the dark again. Taking away the light suddenly would be an extreme step, neither necessary nor desirable. Instead, Maria's mother let her become used to sleeping in the dark in small steps.

Over a period of days, the mother gradually reduced the amount of light in Maria's room. At one point, Maria asked her mother to increase the amount of light in her room. The mother increased the amount of light a little, and waited for several days before dimming it again. Soon, Maria was able to sleep with just a lamp turned on in the hallway. Her mother was patient but determined, and Maria eventually learned to sleep in a darkened room.

2. Provide enjoyable activities in the dark, and model fearlessness. There are many ways that parents can help children to feel more comfortable in the dark. Some parents of four- to six-year-olds have played hide-and-seek games outdoors at sunset, allowing nature to "dim the lights" slowly. Some have played games with their children in darkened rooms, using flashlights. One useful and enjoyable method is to take relaxed walks in the dark. Even having children help to take out the trash at night can assist them in dealing with fear of the dark.

When Richard was five years old, he and his father sat on the grass one evening before Halloween. The father was trying to explain the meaning of the holiday. As darkness began to fall, Richard's father encouraged him to walk around the house all alone. Richard walked around the house while it was still fairly light. He received much praise for seeing that there was nothing to fear. During the next 30 minutes, Richard walked around the house several more times in the gathering darkness. His father praised him heartily, and they laughed and talked together. They lay on the grass and talked about the moon, the stars, and the planets which were beginning to appear. Later in the evening, they went for a walk in the woods behind their home. Using a flashlight, they looked for animals and talked about the activities of animals that come out in the night.

Some people never completely lose their fear of the dark. But parents can stop such fears from becoming extreme by exposing their children to darkness under relaxed and enjoyable circumstances.

3. Teach children to sleep alone at night. Many parents like to have their young children in bed with them from time to time. It is fun to cuddle, tell stories, and sing and laugh together. Children sometimes climb into their parents' bed in the morning, or sleep there on some special occasions.

Most children visit their parents' bed less often as they grow older. Some, however, develop an extreme dependency and resist sleeping anywhere but with their parents. The causes for this overdependence are often easy to see—and just as easily avoided.

Jimmy was often allowed to sleep with his parents after he had wet his own bed and had been cleaned up. Maria was allowed to sleep with her mother when she had nightmares. Sleeping with the parents was a reinforcer for these behaviors. Jimmy began to wet his bed almost every night, and Maria often complained of nightmares. Sleeping with parents had become a habit for Jimmy and Maria. Their parents each decided that they would teach their children to sleep in their own beds.

Maria's mother comforted her briefly when she had a nightmare. She assured Maria that she was near. She then gave Maria a stuffed animal to cuddle, and tucked her into her own bed. Maria learned to sleep in her own bed, even when she had an occasional nightmare.

Jimmy's parents praised him when he did not wet his bed. They were also careful to not give him many liquids to drink for several hours before bedtime. When Jimmy did wet his bed, his parents quietly and calmly helped him to finish urinating in the bathroom and to change his clothes and bedding. They then put him back to sleep in his own bed. Jimmy learned that he was to remain in his own bed at night. He also began to wet his bed much less frequently.

4. Teach children the truth about imaginary ''dangers.'' Parents should try to protect their children from frightening stories and television programs. But children are still

Figure 25-4. *A friendly stuffed bear to cuddle at night can help ease this child's fear of the dark. (© Ron Meyer/White Eyes Design)*

likely to hear about imaginary monsters from friends, picture books, and television. Therefore, it is important to answer children's questions about such monsters with clear and truthful statements.

Richard's parents told him that people make up such stories to entertain other people, and that they are paid to make up the stories. They explained that the stories are only make believe, and just for fun. Richard's parents said that monsters in movies are just ordinary people in costumes and makeup. They borrowed a book from the library to show Richard pictures of actors in costume and as they appeared in real life. Richard enjoyed hearing the truth about these so-called monsters.

If Richard was fearful of noises or shadows, his parents showed him the source of the noises or shadows in a calm way. They were careful to not reinforce his fearful behavior with special attention, overconcern, or treats. This could have caused Richard to act afraid to get their attention.

It is normal for children to develop certain fears as they live and learn. Yet parents can help to keep such fears to a minimum. Parents should help children to tell the difference between real and imagined dangers such as monsters. In this way, parents can free their children from unnecessary fears to experience a more independent and rewarding childhood.

Fear of Failure—Fear of Success

Children who learn that failure is a very bad thing may come to fear failure so much that they avoid it at all costs. On the other hand, if children are taught that competing and excelling are bad and wrong, they may develop a fear of success. Both of these fears can lead to underachievement.

In an interesting study, J. Atkinson and G. Litwin had college students throw rings at a target to see how well they would score. The students were allowed to choose their own distance from which they would throw. Atkinson and Litwin found that some individuals chose to stand at a middle distance. At this distance, success was possible but not assured. Another group of students more often stood closer to, or farther from, the

target. All students were given a test to see who had low needs or high needs to achieve. Students with high needs to achieve tended to stand at the middle distances. They were not afraid to genuinely test their skills. Students with low needs to achieve stood more often at close or far distances from the target. It is thought that fear of failure influences one's achievement motivation. Children who are too fearful of failure will often *not* try to achieve. If they do try, like the students in the ring toss, some will choose to do things that are so easy that they cannot fail. This, of course, leads to poor achievement. Others will try to do things that are so difficult that no one can expect success. In other words, they do not have to worry about failure, because it is expected. After all, who wouldn't fail when trying to do such a difficult thing?

Matina Horner has suggested that in the past, girls were more often encouraged to take passive roles. Girls were more frequently taught that competition and excelling in areas such as sports, science, business, and other professions was wrong. Hopefully, this is less true today than it once was. Such teaching can lead to a fear of success. It is possible that individuals with such a fear of success would purposely allow others to perform better than they do, in order to avoid disapproval. Recent research indicates that boys can also learn to avoid success for similar reasons.

Fears of both failure and success have to do with fears of looking foolish, being laughed at, or being criticized. Such fears can interfere with children's trying to do things they really want to do. How parents treat their children's successes and failures can influence what they try to achieve in life.

Figure 25-5. *Children's fear of failure, or fear of look-ing silly or clumsy, can prevent them from trying things they really want to do. (Pocono Mountains Vacation Bureau)*

Healthy Attitudes about Failure and Achievement

A cross-country skier was interviewed after he had failed to make a good showing in the 1984 Winter Olympics. The interviewer asked the young man how he felt about his disappointing performance. The skier's an-swer showed his healthy attitude about fail-ure and achievement. He smiled happily as he stated that he had tried as hard as he could, and had given his best effort in the contest. He talked about the thrills and plea-sures he had enjoyed by being a part of the Olympics. He explained that a medal would be "the frosting on the cake," but that the contest was the important thing.

Boys and girls can learn to have a simi-larly positive attitude about both success and failure. To pursue enjoyable but chal-lenging achievements requires that children overcome the fear of failure. The follow-ing are several things to consider when try-ing to help children avoid extreme fear of failure.

1. Avoid punishment and strong disap-proval when children have not done well. Parents often hope that their children will accomplish many things. The parents then show disappointment, frustration, and even anger when their children fail to meet their expectations. Instead, parents should em-phasize enjoyment and socialization while practicing skills. They can use a shaping ap-proach in which reasonable approximations (steps) to success are reinforced. If there is no progress, prompting, fading, backward chaining, schedules of reinforcement, and other methods should be considered. If strong negative attitudes are presented to children when they fail, children will fear failure so much that they may try to avoid accomplishing things.

2. Reinforce good efforts and not just good outcomes (results). It is important that chil-dren feel that parents value trying and doing one's best, no matter what the outcome. It is possible to communicate this appreciation for effort in many ways. Parents can refuse to criticize themselves, others, and their chil-dren for reasonable efforts, even if success is lacking. Parents can talk about how hard a child worked, for example, or how much the child did rather than saying that a good or poor job was done.

3. Model a healthy attitude about fear of failure. Parents should occasionally discuss their own failures openly with their children. Failure can be described in relaxed, cheerful ways. For example, a parent can smile and say, ''Well, it didn't work out the way I wanted it to, but I gave it my best effort!'' Parents should also model a desire to improve for the pure joy of accomplishment. It is important to show self-respect and pride about trying to accomplish things even though one failed to win. The message to present through words and actions is that everyone loses or fails at some things, but that this does not make them failures as people.

SUMMARY

Between the ages of two to seven years, children's fears become more imaginary and social in nature. Parents can help to prevent or reduce their children's fears in small steps. As children become comfortable with each step, another can be added. Parents can also provide factual information about animals, insects, or imagined dangers which may help children to understand them better. Parents are powerful models which children imitate, so it is important that they show their own fearlessness of harmless things. When children show similar fearlessness, parents should remember to praise their actions.

QUESTIONS FOR GROWTH

1. (a) Between what ages are children likely to show the most fears? **(b)** Explain why children are likely to show more fears at this time in their lives.

2. Describe some healthy fears and some unnecessary fears.

3. List some common fears of children between the ages of two to seven years.

4. Review the main ways that Jimmy's mother helped him to lose his fear of going down a slide.

5. Explain how you might help children to be less fearful of insects, frogs, and the like.

6. Provide several suggestions for helping children to be less fearful of the dark and imaginary creatures.

7. Explain what is meant by fear of failure and fear of success.

8. Provide several suggestions for helping children to develop healthy attitudes about failure and success.

CHAPTER

26

Strengthening Independent Thinking

Independent thinking refers to children's growing ability to make important decisions and to solve problems on their own. These are valuable and complex skills.

We all begin life depending upon others to make all of our important decisions and to solve all of our problems. Then, slowly, over years of development, we acquire the ability to do these things by ourselves. This growth in our ability to think independently (without help) earns us greater freedom to be on our own—to live life without direct supervision. Children who can think independently can solve problems, are better able to pursue their own interests, and can better resist blindly following the lead of others.

Independent thinking is not possible without successful cognitive, social, and emotional development, as well as self-care and

self-discipline abilities. Independent thinking is a parenting goal which depends upon a great number of earlier developments.

Parents can strengthen independent thinking by helping children to gain self-confidence and self-esteem. They can also help their children to cope with fears of failure, to make wise decisions, and to solve problems skillfully.

SELF-CONFIDENCE AND SELF-ESTEEM

The development of self-confidence and self-esteem strengthens independent thinking. *Self-confidence* means a belief in one's own abilities to make decisions, solve problems, and cope with life's demands. *Self-esteem* means that a person likes and respects herself or himself. Toddlers who show self-confidence will leave their parents' sides to explore new things or people. In later years, children may seek new experiences with enthusiasm and willingly play a variety of children's games. They will speak up in school, and stand up for their personal rights when they feel mistreated. Children with self-confidence and self-esteem are not afraid of people. They meet people easily, look at them directly in the eye, and are not afraid to talk to others.

Self-confidence and self-esteem go hand in hand. In Chapter 25, for example, we described a ring-toss experiment in which individuals who took chances (self-confidence) also rated high in self-esteem.

Children who are low in self-confidence and self-esteem are likely to have trouble in thinking and behaving independently. They may too often follow the lead of others out

Figure 26-1. Self-confident children meet the world with enthusiasm. (National Easter Seal Society, Inc.)

Figure 26-2. Children who feel loved and respected develop a high self-esteem and a positive self-image.

develop self-confidence and self-esteem. Shaping means to set low-enough requirements at each step of a task so that children can succeed with reasonable effort. As children experience success, they come to see themselves as being competent and good at learning. With a record of success behind them, children are more likely to seek out new opportunites for success.

Success is important. But parents must show their children that they love, value, and accept them whether they are successful or not. When children begin to show self-confidence resulting from both parental support and personal successes, parents should reinforce the signs of self-confidence. Good general goals are to strengthen children's enthusiasm for trying and exploring new things and for working hard at difficult tasks.

of fear of not being liked or accepted. They may avoid social situations because they fear their weaknesses (real or imagined) will be discovered. Such children may withdraw from social, physical, and intellectual activities because they fear rejection and failure.

Self-esteem and self-confidence are clearly important for all areas of a child's development. Children learn to have positive attitudes about themselves based largely upon how they see others reacting to them. If children see that others love, respect, and accept them as worthwhile individuals, they are likely to have the same feelings about themselves. This is only one reason why helping children to feel loved, respected, and wanted is so important.

Parents should learn to shape skillfully to help children learn new things and thus

DEALING WITH FEAR OF FAILURE

The ability to risk failure is an important part of independent thinking and behavior. Every time we try something new and difficult, we risk being seen as inadequate or foolish. Children may stack blocks which keep falling down, or spill a glass of milk while trying to drink it. Whether they improve their skills or give up the activities may have much to do with their parents' reactions. If parents ridicule, scold, or harshly punish children for being clumsy or messy, they may teach that failure leads directly to the loss of the parents' love and respect. This can easily teach children to avoid challenging experiences and hurt their self-confidence and self-esteem.

Parents can teach children to try harder in the face of failure. They can teach that accomplishing the difficult is wonderful, but that trying one's best is also valued and important. When children tie their shoelaces or ride a bike successfully, they should hear, ''Great! Fantastic!'' When children give a good effort but are not quite successful, they should hear, ''Nice try! You'll get it real soon! You try so hard!''

When necessary, parents can physically assist their children to help them succeed. The assistance should be limited enough so that the children can take over and do more and more on their own. If children do not even come close, the task can be made easier by moving in smaller steps. This is important, because almost anyone will eventually give up without occassional successes.

Parents can also help their children to become more persistent. Persistence is necessary for self-esteem and self-confidence because it is a major part of achieving success. If persistence is not present, failure is likely in all but the simplest of tasks. Parents can teach persistence by changing from frequent reinforcers for new skills to infrequent reinforcers. Of course, the change in frequency of reinforcers must occur very gradually. Otherwise, children are likely to become frustrated and quit.

Children tend to imitate their parent's reactions to failure. It is not necessary or even good for parents to hide failures or sadness about failure. Some failures should be discussed openly, but in a positive way. Maria's father talked about the tennis match he had lost to a friend, and how he would have to practice the game more. Maria's father discussed both the good points and the bad points of his playing technique. He praised himself for what he did well, but also discussed working harder to improve. Through this discussion, Maria's father modeled the same perseverance in the face of failure that he hoped to see in Maria. He showed Maria that failure is a natural and sometimes common part of life, and that it is not terrible.

Maria's grandmother also helped her to deal with the fear of failure. She offered Maria much encouragement, and often told her, ''If at first you don't succeed, try, try again!''

Playing games throughout childhood is a good opportunity to teach children to have a healthy attitude about both success and failure. Sometimes we play games for the enjoyment of it. To win can be fun, but losing can be fun, too. Parents can model this attitude about winning and losing in recreational competition.

TEACHING CHILDREN HOW TO MAKE WISE DECISIONS

Making wise decisions on one's own is an important part of independent thinking. Making decisions involves choices. Making independent decisions means choosing wisely from a variety of options with no one present to offer advice. As this ability strengthens, children require less and less direct supervision in everyday life.

People tend to make choices that will increase reinforcement and avoid pain. Babies choose by crawling to one person rather than another, or by pushing one toy away and playing with another. These early choices are the beginnings of independent thinking.

Figure 26-3. Playing games helps children to learn to deal with both success and failure.

Decision making becomes more complex as children mature. The choices available increase in number. It becomes more difficult to figure out which choices will be reinforced by good outcomes. At first, children are likely to make poor choices when they are allowed to make their own decisions. For example, the child who chooses to wear an attractive T-shirt without considering the weather may become cold. The older child who decides to stay up late to watch television may be very tired the next day.

Wise decision making is a learned ability. Parents cannot teach wise decision making through words alone. They must allow their children to gradually make more decisions on their own. Even though mistakes will be made, the experience is necessary for wise decision making in the future.

This is not to say, though, that children should be left totally on their own to make decisions. Especially in the early years, parents should prompt their children and then quickly reinforce the good choices. Decisions sometimes do not show results for hours, days, or even longer. Therefore, young children need some reinforcement and assistance. Whenever possible, children should be allowed to make their own decisions while parents praise those which they know to be good. When needed, children should be guided away from choices which have very painful or dangerous consequences. However, children cannot forever be protected from the consequences of their unwise decisions. These experiences, too, contribute to the learning process.

Figure 26-4. Children can learn to make wise decisions in small steps.

Parents can help their children to identify and consider the advantages and disadvantages of each alternative (choice) before making a decision. To do this requires patience and effort. Impatient parents may express too much criticism and disapproval. Constant criticism or disapproval can lead to loss of self-confidence, and ultimately to failure.

It is good to teach decision making in gradual steps. When Maria was young, her mother laid out her clothes for her. Though Maria was not yet making the clothing choices, her mother praised her for wearing clothes appropriate for various activities and weather conditions. As Maria seemed to understand these factors, her mother began to lay out two sets of clothes for Maria to choose from when she was nearly five. This was no problem for Maria; she nearly always chose the more appropriate set of clothes. Her mother showed excitement and praise. Later, Maria's mother allowed her to choose from a certain area in her drawer or closet. The mother continued to praise wise choices.

If Maria made a bad choice (such as wearing summer clothes to play in the snow), her mother told her to change into proper clothes. When she changed, her mother praised her actions. The extra work involved in changing, along with praise for appropriate choices, encouraged Maria to make better clothing decisions in the future.

As children mature, they become capable of making increasingly difficult choices. The following material describes how parents may guide children to make more and more difficult decisions.

Restricted Choices

In a *restricted choice* situation, children are given very little real choice. A good decision is guaranteed because only a few choices are offered.

For children, restricted choices are a fact of life. Many parents say that they do not restrict their children's freedom, but they really do—and this is often necessary. One parent proudly said that he did not order his child to do things, but preferred to offer her a choice. One choice was, for example, "Brush your teeth alone or I will have to help you." Actually, this parent offered no real choice. No matter what the child "chose,"

her teeth would be brushed. Her father was not wrong in making her brush her teeth or offering her a restricted choice. But he was wrong in believing that he was offering the child a real choice.

It is important that parents recognize what they are doing and why they are doing it when they restrict children's choices. Choices which seem unimportant to adults are often very important to children. Allowing limited freedom of choice in situations where some restrictions are necessary often satisfies children. Children are then less likely to show resistance.

A few examples of restricted choices are listed in Box 26.1. The appropriate behavior

---

BOX 26.1

Examples of Restricted Choices and Appropriate Outcomes

Restricted Choices	**Appropriate Outcomes**
"You can put on your pajamas during these commercials or after the program."	Either way, the child is made to be ready for bed on time. If the pajamas are put on during the commercials, the child is praised for not putting off the task.
"Do you want hot dogs or hamburgers for dinner?"	The child is influenced to choose meat for dinner.
"You may clean your room whenever you like, but it must be done before you go out to play."	The child's room is cleaned early in the day, usually within an hour of awakening.
"If you want to go out to play, you must wear your jacket."	A jacket is worn outside.

described in each case is extremely important. By restricting the options, the parents help the child to make good choices which can then be strengthened with praise and other reinforcers.

Restrictions such as those in Box 26.1 are appropriate for young children who do not yet know how to choose wisely. With prompting and reinforcement, for appropriate decisions, parents help their children to make good independent choices in the future. Remember that any behavior which is consistently reinforced will become reinforcing in itself. Therefore, children will learn a preference for making good decisions.

Simple Unrestricted Choices

Simple unrestricted choices are those in which children make simple but real decisions on their own. Children are allowed to choose from a variety of options, all of which represent acceptable choices.

Parents who try to influence too many of their children's choices often cause great resistance. Children may even come to resist almost all parental advice. Therefore, it is good to let children make as many of their own choices as possible. The following are a few examples of choices which many four- to six-year-olds can make on their own.

• The style or color of a new pair of play shoes or a bicycle.
• How to spend a 50¢ allowance.
• What game to play when the parents offer to play with the child.
• Selecting most of the decorations for the walls of the child's bedroom.

In these situations, any choice can be seen as a sign of a child's individuality which is worthy of genuine appreciation. When children are told that the choice is theirs, it is important that their choice be accepted.

Complex Unrestricted Choices

Complex unrestricted choices are those in which children can make real decisions on their own. However, the choices available are not all good. Children must examine the immediate and long-range consequences of each option before choosing.

Parents should look for decisions that their children can make. They should gradually increase the complexity of choices as children's abilities to reason and understand increase. Wise parents also help children to identify the short-term and long-term advantages and disadvantages of each choice.

When Maria was six, her mother told her that they would do something that Maria wanted that afternoon. Maria said that she wanted to go to the park and also to see a movie. Her mother explained that they would only have time to do one thing. Together, they identified some advantages and disadvantages of the park and the movie. Both activities would be fun. The movie would be funny and they could have some popcorn, but they would have to spend money. The park was free, but it would take 20 minutes to drive there and it looked like it might rain. Maria thought about it for a while and then chose the movie. Her mother felt that the choice was sensible, and praised Maria. If Maria had chosen the park, her mother would have honored that choice. The

Figure 26-5. To strengthen independent thinking, parents can let children contribute to the family's decision-making process as much as possible.

consequences of a long drive and rain would have done the teaching naturally.

STRENGTHENING CREATIVE PROBLEM SOLVING

Making a decision involves choosing from known alternatives. Solving a problem involves finding the best unknown solution available. The problems of childhood may involve how to make a door open, reach a high shelf, or find a lost toy. As life goes on, problems grow in complexity. Children must decide how to arrange toys, how to acquire money, or how to fix a broken toy. For children to gain independence, they must learn how to solve their own problems. Parents must help them learn how to approach problems that they will have in the future, when parents are not available to help.

Creative problem solving means to consider a variety of solutions, some of which may be unusual. Of course, what is creative and new to a four-year-old may be well known to the ten-year-old. The important thing is that children have the self-confidence to try new and unusual ideas to solve their problems.

Creative problem solving requires perseverance. Creative problem solvers will test a possible solution. If it does not work, they will try another and another solution before deciding upon the best one.

At one time, creativity was thought to be inherited. However, recent research shows that creativity is heavily influenced by learning. For example, the Beatles, George Washington Carver, and Thomas Edison all had something in common. They had all learned to persevere in producing new and useful ideas and products even when faced with opposition or criticism.

The following are some guidelines for teaching creative problem solving.

1. Children should be allowed to experiment freely with various objects and tools. Early experience with finger paints, crayons, watercolors, clay, and the like should occur with a minimum of instruction and guidance. Individual creations should be praised and treasured, whatever their appearance.

2. Learning basic skills improves creativity. For creativity to grow, basic tools must be learned. To create from wood, for example, a child will need to learn the uses of various wood-working tools. To paint creatively, a child must learn to use a brush and different kinds of paints. To solve a difficult math problem, a child will need to master the basics of arithmetic. Parents should teach a wide variety of basic skills to help children find the activities which they enjoy the most.

3. Help children learn to brainstorm. To *brainstorm* means to think about and produce as many ideas as possible about how to solve a problem. Brainstorming can be done once a problem to be solved is clearly identified.

In a brainstorming session, no idea should be criticized, no matter how silly or seemingly unworkable it may be. Instead, all ideas should be praised excitedly. Critical thinking should begin only after the brainstorming session is over. At this time, children can be encouraged to think about the advantages and disadvantages of each idea. Ideas that seem good can be kept, and those which seem unworkable can be dropped. This process goes on until one or more solutions to a problem are left. Those solutions can then be tested. Brainstorming can often produce a very creative solution to a problem.

4. Encourage children to act and think independently even if others give criticism or show no interest. Children must learn to value their own judgment enough to act upon it and communicate it often. Parents should treat their children with respect. They should listen to what their children say and observe what they do. Parents should encourage and praise their children's ideas. Encouragement and praise are necessary

because beginning creative behavior is easily weakened if ignored or punished.

Encouragement is the main factor for helping to strengthen creativity. Sometimes, of course, some ideas of children may be unworkable or even ridiculous. One five-year-old thought that she could go bear hunting with a big net. Parents can respectfully suggest that an idea might not work in such cases where experimentation would not be wise. If possible, parents could give assistance in such cases so that children can test their ideas. The six-year-old who thinks he knows how to ride an older child's bike may be allowed to try with some protective assistance. This is better than saying, "No, you're too small." The child who thinks she can save a bird which has been badly hurt can be allowed to try to save it. The real world and its natural consequences can often take the place of unnecessary criticisms.

As children develop and their self-confidence increases, parents may gently begin to disagree with some creative ideas. However, if disagreement is started too early, occurs too often, or is too strong, it may weaken creativity. When parents do disagree, they can try to do so in a light-hearted and cheerful way. They can also explain that people often have different opinions, and that this is not bad but is interesting and fun to talk about.

Examples of Creative Problem Solving

Five-year-old Maria was saddened to find that a squirrel had fallen into her wading pool and drowned. Maria asked her mother how

CASE STUDY

Solving a Problem

Six-year-old Richard had a problem. He wanted to fill a wading pool in the corner of his front yard so he could be near his friends. The garden hose would not reach that far. Richard and his parents had a brainstorming session. There was a lot of laughter and excitement, and Richard thought of the following possibilities.

- Fill the pool using buckets of water.
- Fill the pool with water from the hose, and then move the pool to the preferred spot.
- Get a shovel and dig a hole. Maybe there's water down there!
- Wait until the pool fills up from a rain storm, and then go swimming!
- Buy a longer hose.
- Borrow a longer hose from a neighbor.

After brainstorming, they discussed the advantages and disadvantages of each idea. Richard decided on the last solution, and it was a good one.

During the brainstorming, Richard's parents did not reject any solution right away. They praised any ideas simply because they were new and might be useful. When testing a possible solution, Richard's parents were patient. They let Richard try what he preferred, and went with Richard to borrow a hose from a neighbor.

---

they could save other animals that might fall in. Her mother suggested that they think of all the ideas they could and then try one. Together, they came up with the following ideas.

- Empty the pool when it is not in use.

- Fill the pool with only a few inches of water.
- Make a boat for the animals.
- Put a cover over the pool.

After a fun brainstorming session, Maria and her mother began to examine each idea.

Constantly emptying the pool would be a lot of work and a waste of water. Filling it with only a little water would be no fun for swimming. Making a boat would be fun, but some animals might not be able to climb onto it. Others might be big enough to tip it over and fall back into the water. They finally chose Maria's idea of a pool cover. Her mother bought a heavy piece of plastic, and they laid it over the pool when Maria wasn't using it. Maria was thrilled that her idea had been chosen.

Six-year-old Jimmy wanted to catch one of the animals living in the woods surrounding his home. A neighbor told him that if he put salt on a bird's tail, he could catch it. Jimmy asked his mother if this was true. His mother said that it had not worked for her when she was a little girl, and that she did not think it would work now. But during the next few days, the salt shaker was empty at mealtimes. Jimmy had not taken his mother's word, but had chosen to test the theory out for himself. No one stopped him. However, Jimmy was not rewarded with a catch, and his efforts with the salt gradually decreased.

Soon afterward, Jimmy tried to catch a small animal with a box. His efforts failed because the animal was too fast. At last, Jimmy told his mother that he didn't think he could ever catch anything. His mother suggested that they think of some new ideas for catching small animals without harming them. After brainstorming, they decided to buy a strong basket and place food under it. They placed the basket upside down in the back yard, propped it up with a stick, and tied a long string to the stick. They then waited inside the house so they would not scare the animals. Within 20 minutes, Jimmy had pulled the string and the basket had caught a chipmunk. Jimmy and his mother were excited—and so was the chipmunk. After looking at the chipmunk through the holes in the basket, Jimmy decided to let it go back to the woods.

What was learned? Jimmy had watched his mother model confidence and enthusiasm in trying to solve a problem. When Jimmy imitated these qualities, he was praised and encouraged. The answer had not been given directly, but had been hinted at in small steps. In this way, some of the ideas were Jimmy's.

The project took time and effort, and involved thinking about materials which were not within sight. Jimmy thus learned to look beyond his immediate surroundings when solving problems. Jimmy had persevered and tried a variety of solutions. After much effort, he had solved a problem and achieved success. By letting the chipmunk go free, Jimmy also showed that he had learned about being considerate of the well-being of other living creatures.

Strengthening Other Creative Behavior

There are many other ways to strengthen different kinds of creative behavior in children. Generally, it is important to encourage children and show that their opinions and ideas have value.

Children can learn the meaning of the word *creative* when parents label a behavior as being creative, and by further explaining why it is creative. For example, parents might say, "My, you are so creative! That is a new and pretty way to decorate cookies."

Parents should avoid making their praise too specific. If they say, "I really like the cookie with the red and green hearts," they are likely to see many more such cookies. It is often better to center praise on the fact that something is new and interesting. Also, it is important to avoid limiting creativity by criticizing children's efforts.

The following activities provide enjoyable opportunities to encourage creative behavior.

1. Making things. Parents can provide many creative materials in the home. Such materials are clay, crayons, coloring books, watercolors, paste, chalk, scissors, and colored paper. Parents can spend time with their children while they play with these materials and praise their efforts.

In 1973, Elizabeth Goetz and Donald Baer made an interesting study of preschool children playing with blocks. First, they counted how many different forms the children built out of blocks when not given praise. Then, they offered praise for the first time (and only the first time) a new form was built by each child. When the children were praised for new forms, they created many more new forms than they had when they had not been praised. This study demonstrated the value of praise in encouraging creativity.

Maria's grandfather provided her with a hammer, nails, and some small pieces of wood. He showed Maria how to use the hammer and nails. He then stood by and watched and praised Maria, no matter what she made. The final product was too oddly shaped pieces of wood nailed together. This was a creative beginning for the six-year-old builder.

2. Playing with ideas. Creative people are observant and have a questioning attitude. They often see similarities and differences between things that others do not. Parents should encourage this type of imagination. They can do this by asking their children unusual questions and praising creative answers. In this way, parents can model curiosity and an interest in the unknown. Parents might ask their children, "What do you see in the clouds?" While looking up at the night sky, they might ask, "Do you think there are living things on other planets? What

Figure 26-6. What makes a leaf grow? Why are there veins? Why does the magnifying glass make the leaf look bigger? Parents should encourage children to question—and to think about possible answers.

do you think they look like?'' Parents might ask their children what makes it rain, what makes it get dark at night, or why flowers grow.

The goal in this situation is only to help the child to question, to think about possible answers. Parents should not lecture or insist that children agree with them. Parents can also recognize that humor is a form of creative play with ideas. They can show their own sense of humor, and appreciate their children's attempts to be funny.

3. Making music. Young children enjoy making music with toy drums, guitars, and other instruments. Parents can get involved by singing, clapping hands, and dancing. Later, they might provide their children with music lessons. A good music teacher will not only teach the basics, but will also praise a child's creative efforts. A period of experimental play with music can be used as a reinforcer for learning.

4. Sharing cultural experiences. There are many places to visit which will stimulate a child's imagination and interest in new things. Parents should take their children to museums, art fairs, aquariums, concerts, and magic shows. When visiting these places, they can model curiosity and creative questioning, and reinforce similar behavior in their children.

Encouraging creativity helps children to develop independent thinking. It helps them to have confidence in their abilities, and teaches them a variety of basic skills. Creativity allows children the freedom to make many of their own decisions.

Figure 26-7. Although this 22-month-old's problem (how to stack blocks so they stay up) seems simple, she had to use complex cognitive and physical skills to achieve her goal. Her pleasure in her success is evident.

SUMMARY

Strengthening independent thinking in children is a very important parenting goal. This goal requires progress in many developmental areas. Parents who use basic principles of teaching and learning to strengthen self-confidence, decision making, problem solving, and creativity are also strengthening their children's ability to think independently.

QUESTIONS FOR GROWTH

1. Explain how self-confidence and self-esteem can influence a child's ability to think independently.

2. Tell why dealing with fear of failure is an important part of helping children to think independently.

3. Explain how parents can use restricted choices, simple unrestricted choices, and complex unrestricted choices to help children learn to make wise decisions.

4. What is the difference between "making a choice" and "solving a problem?"

5. Explain the process of brainstorming.

6. Provide an original example of how you might help a child to do creative problem solving using the brainstorming approach.

7. How might you help children to state their ideas and opinions even when they are faced with criticism or disinterest?

8. Describe some of the many things parents and others can do to strengthen creative behavior in children.

CHAPTER

27

Strengthening Values and Moral Behavior

As described in the "child's bill of rights" in Chapter 2, children have a right to learn sound values and moral behavior. Our *values* are the ideas that we have about things that we consider desirable or undesirable, good or bad, right or wrong. *Moral behavior* (morals) refers to one's actions that conform to generally accepted ideas about what is right or wrong.

The development of sound values and moral behavior is important for children, who must learn to work and play with others and live within the rules and laws of society. Children must increase their pleasures in life without making a variety of costly and painful mistakes.

Almost every parent will want to teach certain values. These include honesty, respect for other people's rights, appreciation of beauty, and a love for one's own family.

Other values are very important to some families but not to others. In a democracy such as ours, parents have great freedom of individual choice in such matters. However, equal to such freedom is the responsibility to teach children the values and moral behavior which will help them to develop happily and successfully.

Some people have considered values and moral behavior to be so complex as to be beyond the influence of simple teaching principles. But this is not true. The principles of reinforcement, extinction, shaping, modeling, imitation, and discipline do influence the development of morals and values in children.

Our values and morals have traditionally been defined in terms of our thoughts: how we think about and judge things. For example, we think about and judge the quality of

411

other people (*social values*). We think about and judge beauty (*aesthetic values*) and things which are right and wrong (*moral values*).

But defining values and morals in terms of thoughts and judgments alone is of little help to parents who wish to teach their children to *live out* their values and morals. Parents want their children to *do* desirable forms of social behavior, to *do* moral behavior, and to *do* aesthetic behavior. It is reasonable for parents to begin teaching by "laying the bricks" which will eventually lead to the

Figure 27-1. *Love for nature and respect for other living creatures are important and common values. (USDA Photo by Gordon Baer)*

"structure" called morals and values. This can be done by first teaching appropriate behaviors. The inside thoughts, judgments, and feelings which are known as values and morals are likely to follow later. In other words, one's thoughts are influenced by one's behavior.

Psychologists who study *self-perception* (how one sees or judges oneself) have provided research support for the idea that children's behavior can influence their attitudes. It is thought that children observe their own behavior and then decide, "If that's the way I behave, then that's the way I must feel." Kohlberg's research (described in Chapter 7) indicates that children naturally begin their moral development based upon the consequences they experience for their behavior. This is the first level of moral development.

Sometime between 10 and 13 years, children become concerned with living up to the expectations and rules of others who are close or important to them. This is the second level of moral development. At this time, laws are viewed as right simply because they are laws.

The last level of moral development may be reached in adolescence or adulthood. At this time, judgments about moral behavior are based upon a complex evaluation of the circumstances involved. Moral development, thus, clearly rests heavily upon the progression of cognitive development.

Parents can begin to teach morals and values to young children at the behavioral level first. After all, what good is it if someone feels concern for others, but never helps anyone? What good is it if someone thinks that it is good to be honest, but lies, cheats, and steals? To be of any importance, values and morals must involve behavior.

The development of values and morals is a never-ending process. It is influenced continually by the people that children meet, the things they learn, and their growing ability to think and reason. If parents do not teach their values and moral behavior to their children, the children will learn the values and moral behavior of other people. Friends, teachers, writers, television and movie producers, politicians, and others will try to make them see and do things their way. Parents have a great responsibility to help their children to deal with such sources of influence. Parents must provide a set of basic values and morals to guide their children through life and their relationships with others.

GUIDELINES FOR STRENGTHENING VALUES AND MORALS

Many parents share a concern for values and morals, such as honesty and love for family. However, each parent teaches some values and morals which are unique to the parent's experience and environment. Whatever the values and morals to be taught to children, the following guidelines will be helpful.

1. Parents should not expect too much too soon. Children of three or four years are generally egocentric—concerned mostly with their own wants and ideas. They may have strong ideas about right and wrong behaviors. But these ideas will be closely related to consequences: ''Mommy hugs me when

I share, so sharing is good. She punishes me when I hit my brother, so hitting is bad.'' This level of understanding and teaching is perfectly appropriate for young children and can be very successful.

As children's social experiences increase, they begin to react to the *concepts*, or ideas, alone (''sharing is good''). Children also normally gain in their ability to see things from other people's points of view. They begin to judge an action as right or wrong based more upon the causes or circumstances of someone's behavior (sickness, hunger, and so on).

2. Parents can begin the process of teaching by identifying the various behaviors which are part of values they wish to teach and encourage.

3. Parents can model, prompt, and reinforce these behaviors in as many different situations as they can. Children will not imitate what parents and others only say. They will imitate their parents' behavior. Common sense as well as research strongly show that the ''Don't do as I do, do as I say'' approach should be avoided whenever possible. For example, parents who demand that their children share but who themselves are very selfish will likely not teach the value of sharing. Instead, they are likely to teach selfishness.

4. Parents can take advantage of their children's tendency to imitate others by directing their attention to good models. If possible, they may limit the availability of bad models. Otherwise, bad models may be used as examples of bad behaviors, especially when there is a punishing consequence. For example, a thief goes to jail; a careless driver is in an accident.

5. Parents can explain why certain behaviors should or should not occur. Whenever possible, they should help their children see the influence that their own behavior has on others—making them happy or hurting them. Giving the reasons behind values and morals will help children to behave in appropriate ways.

6. Parents can discipline their children to behave in ways that reflect desired values and morals. Of course, this should be done using the moderate but effective methods of discipline discussed earlier in the text.

Teaching Children to Respect the Rights of Others

Teaching children to respect the rights of others is an important common goal. It forms the basis for futher social and moral development. Maria's mother provided reinforcers for her four-year-old child whenever Maria behaved considerately toward others. The mother was also careful to model her own respect and concern for the rights and feelings of others. Whenever possible, she let Maria see her share with others and help those in need. She often pointed out and discussed her approval of others who treated people or animals with consideration. As they drove in traffic, Maria's mother often praised those drivers who were courteous and followed the law, and she briefly criticized those who were not.

There were many other opportunities to help Maria to respect the rights and feelings of others. During television viewing, when caring for their pet, when playing with friends, or when visiting grandparents,

Maria's mother was sure to identify and label respectful and caring behavior.

Maria's mother knew that it was natural for infants and young children to be self-centered. But she was aware that this egocentrism should lessen as Maria gained more experience with others and was helped to understand their rights and feelings. Maria grew increasingly considerate of others. More rapid progress occurred after she entered school.

Teaching Good Manners

Using good manners is an important way in which people show consideration for others. *Good manners* is a term used to describe some of the ways we show concern and respect for the feelings of others. Good manners are important because children who show them normally enjoy greater social success. This helps their self-confidence and self-esteem.

Maria's mother hoped that Maria would learn to say ''please'' and ''thank you'' to others. When Maria asked for something, her mother waited to hear the ''please,'' along with a polite tone of voice, before giving it to her. If Maria did not say please, her mother told her to repeat the request. When Maria repeated the request politely, she then received what she had asked for. The delay required for Maria to repeat the request was mildly punishing. Therefore, Maria learned that it was easier to say the request politely the first time. Also, getting what she had asked for served as a reinforcer for the polite request. Maria's mother also required Maria to say thank you.

Figure 27-2. Helping children to get along with others will be of benefit to them throughout their lives. (© Ron Meyer/White Eyes Design)

Maria's mother was especially alert for times when Maria said please and thank you on her own. She praised her politeness with enthusiasm.

The mother also helped Maria to acquire and show real concern for the feelings of others. She did this by talking about how polite treatment of others made them feel good, and about how she felt when treated nicely. Occasionally, the mother would ask Maria to think about special ways that she could show appreciation of others. For instance, Maria decided to draw a picture for her grandfather to thank him for his visit.

Teaching Children to Share

Research has shown that simply praising young children for sharing things they greatly value can be a weak approach. Preschool children often do not share things with others very well. In many cases, their toys or treats are just too valuable for them to "trade" for praise. Young children are naturally self-centered. It is hard for them to understand someone else's needs.

It is better to use several approaches to teach sharing. First, children seem to be more generous after they have had successful experiences, and less generous after experiencing failure. This observation suggests yet another reason for parents to teach effectively and to provide children with successful learning experiences.

Second, it is important not to expect sharing at too early an age. Children of two years and younger are not generally able to share. If they play together, it is best that they have their own, similar toys. In this way, they can enjoy being with other children but also enjoy having their own toys. When children show signs that they may be ready to share, it is important that they get back the shared item after a short while. This helps them to see that sharing does not mean a real loss of something.

Third, it is important that parents model sharing themselves. Parents can find hundreds of chances to demonstrate sharing. They may do so as they slice a cake for sharing, read aloud from a good book, or help someone to wash dishes. All of these actions are forms of sharing items or responsibilities. Parents can label what they are doing as sharing, and explain that it is one way to show people that you care about them and their feelings.

Maria's mother often explained that sharing is a way to make others happy. She praised Maria whenever she shared things on her own, and also when she did so at someone else's suggestion. Sometimes the mother would also provide special reinforcers for sharing, such as reading to Maria or playing a game with her.

Teaching Honesty

Researchers have found that honesty is one of the most complex concepts to teach. Honesty is a popular teaching goal for parents, but parents are not always able to be totally honest themselves. For example, parents may be required to compliment a neighbor about the neighbor's new clothes, but later may privately mention that they thought the clothes were awful. The parents, in this case, have decided it is not necessary to honestly tell the neighbor what they really think of the clothes. But how do parents teach children this sort of judgment about when to be honest?

In most cases, honesty is a valuable goal for children. It is a major part of the development of trust, which in turn strengthens the development of human social relationships. Honesty is widely viewed as a learned behavior, and early experiences are very important to its development. However, honest behavior cannot occur without the development of necessary cognitive abilities.

By about three or four years, children have developed the ability to use their imaginations. Normal children sometimes even develop imaginary playmates. This occasional inability to tell the difference between the real and the imagined makes strengthening honesty a goal which requires lots of judgment, understanding, and patience for parents.

Parents begin to work on the goal of teaching honesty in countless ways. Perhaps the earliest step is to reliably provide for an infant's emotional and physical needs. Many professionals believe that this establishes trust in children, thus laying the basis for future honest and trusting social relationships.

Of course, parents themselves are models for honesty. As children mature, they gain the cognitive ability to judge if parents' descriptions match actual events. They can also judge if parents' behavior reflects various common and accepted standards of honesty. If important people in children's lives consistently model honesty, the effects are likely to be beneficial.

Richard's parents wanted to help him to become an honest person. They were aware that their own honesty would serve as a guide for his development. Therefore, they were concerned about their own behavior as well as his. The parents personally demonstrated honesty by being truthful with Richard and each other. They hoped that these efforts would help to strengthen Richard's trust in them. Children who find that their parents are not truthful are likely to think that lying is a quick and easy way to solve problems. It is, therefore, important that children learn that their parents are normally truthful.

Richard's parents also modeled honesty by showing respect for others' property. If they borrowed something, they quickly returned it within Richard's sight. If they found something of value in the street, they turned it over to the police. Once they found and cared for an injured cat. Though they all grew to love the cat, Richard's parents put an ad in the newspaper to find its owners. They explained to Richard that the cat was not theirs, and that its owners were probably worried and sad.

Richard's parents also modeled honesty by sticking to their word. If they promised to fix something for Richard or take him somewhere, they did so whenever possible. They demonstrated that when people give their word, they should try their best to keep it.

Two easily identified parts of what we call honesty are being truthful and respecting the property of others. We discuss these parts in the following material.

Helping Children Learn to Be Truthful

Truthful people describe their own behavior and the behavior of others in accurate ways. Very young children, though, often do not describe events as they really happened. They often make unintentional inaccuracies or slightly exaggerate. Children may also lie purposely when they learn that doing so is a way to avoid harsh punishment or to obtain powerful rewards. These conditions are likely to produce children who lie very frequently.

To teach truthfulness, parents may use shaping. They must fit their requirements for honesty to the child's growing ability to separate fact from fantasy.

Many parents have thought that children would learn to be truthful if they simply punished lying. However, it is much more important to reinforce truthful statements at every opportunity. Jimmy's parents began early to teach him to describe his own behavior accurately. They would ask him simple questions about things they knew he had done, and immediately praised his truthfulness.

Dad: "What happened to the milk?"
Jimmy: "I bumped into it and it fell."
Dad: "Well, accidents happen sometimes. I'm so happy that you told me the truth. I'll help you to clean it up."

The father praised Jimmy's truthfulness and further reinforced honesty by helping to clean up the mess.

Mom: "Jimmy, have you made your bed and put your clothes away yet?"
Jimmy: "It's all done."
Mom: "Good! Let's see how you did. You're right! Just like you said. Your bed is nicely made and the clothes are put away. Thank you for your good work!"

The mother presented her child with an opportunity to be truthful and then praised his accurate description as well as the good job.

Dad: "What happened between you and Sally?"
Jimmy: "She fell down."
Dad: "Jimmy, I saw you push Sally down. If you tell me the truth, I will not punish you as much. Go sit in the other room until I call you."

The father used the timeout method to punish lying. He also promised that telling the truth would help to reduce punishment in the future.

Mom: "Did you put your bike in the garage and shut the door?"
Jimmy (watching television): "Yeah."
Mom (after checking): "You did not tell me the truth about putting your bike away and shutting the door. Please turn off the television and take care of your bike right now."

The television privileges were withdrawn for 30 minutes to punish lying.

In the last two examples, the misbehavior (lying) was labeled and effective discipline was given. If children receive the same punishment whether they lie or tell the truth, they might begin to lie on the chance that they can "get away with it." Parents who severely punish for bad behavior whether or not the child tells the truth probably teach their children to lie skillfully in the future to avoid punishment.

If a child tells the truth about a bad behavior ("I pushed Sally down"), it is wise to praise the honesty and reduce the punishment. If a child lies, parents can explain how lying increases punishment.

Teaching Children to Respect Others' Property

Children should be taught to respect the property of others. This means that children should be taught not to take something that belongs to someone else without permission. They should learn to return borrowed items. They should also learn to try to find the owners of lost-and-found items.

It is too much to expect a young child to quickly understand all of these requirements. Children are naturally attracted to bright and pretty things. They may pick up money or other belongings because they see their parents carry them and they wish to imitate them. Taking things that belong to others is often a problem between four and eight years of age. Children at these ages are not yet mature enough to understand and resist temptations.

But parents should begin teaching children the concepts of ownership early. The approach should be based upon patience and understanding but also firmness and the mild forms of discipline we have discussed.

When Richard was four years old, he walked out of the grocery store carrying a pack of gum which his father had forgotten to pay for. On realizing the mistake, the father explained to Richard that since they had not paid for it, the gum did not belong to them. The father went back to the store with Richard and showed the salesperson the gum. He explained that they had forgotten to pay, and then he paid for the gum. Richard's father explained to him that if they had just taken the gum it would have been stealing, which is a very bad thing to do. He then praised both his child and himself for being honest, and each had a stick of gum.

Six-year-old Maria found a ball in the street in front of a friend's house. When Maria's mother found out where it came from, she asked Maria if she thought it might belong to Maria's playmate. Maria admitted that it might and willingly took the ball to her friend to find out. It did belong to the friend, who happily thanked her. Maria's mother praised her for being honest. She later described Maria's honesty to her grandparents while the child smiled happily and proudly.

In these examples, the parents seized opportunities to prompt or model honest behavior. When the items were properly paid for or returned, the honest behavior was praised. In the second example, Maria was also reinforced by her friend's happiness and her mother's and grandparents' pride. The more often parents prompt and reinforce honesty in its many forms, the more likely it is that future honest behavior will occur.

Children have to be taught the concept of ownership of property. Yet if things are left lying around the home, the idea of ownership will be harder for children to understand. While children are young, it is

Figure 27-3. Parents and grandparents are very influential to children's development. They should be careful to model honest behavior and reinforce honesty in children. (HUD Photo)

probably better if their parents do not leave tempting objects like money lying around.

If parents show too much concern and attention when children do take things, children may learn to take things to obtain attention. The best approach is to prompt honest behavior and then reinforce it heavily. It may also help to include a work allowance system. This gives children an acceptable and honest way to get money. It makes them feel more mature and less like taking money which does not belong to them.

If parents discover that their children have taken some money, the parents should take it back and briefly explain why they are disappointed that the money was taken. Parents might then encourage children to bring any money that they find lying around the house to the parents. When children do so, the parents should hug and praise them for their honesty.

Helping Children to Appreciate Beauty

Parents can demonstrate the many ways in which they appreciate beauty and then encourage their children to develop their own tastes. When listening to music, parents can name their favorite songs and say why they like them. When outside, parents can encourage children to smell the flowers, look at the trees, or watch the beauty of birds in flight. They may make a special trip to enjoy the beauty of a sunset or look for a rainbow after a storm.

Jimmy's parents helped him to plant a garden. They all appreciated and enjoyed the various things that grew in it. They went on field trips together to appreciate and enjoy nature. Jimmy's parents made it a point to talk about the people they knew and the good qualities they saw in them. They also encouraged Jimmy to tell about the people he liked.

Jimmy's parents often discussed people who lived in other cultures, and helped Jimmy to appreciate the beauty of their art, traditions, and way of life. Young children are often fascinated by stories of other ways of life. It is important for children to learn to appreciate the uniqueness and beauty of other peoples. In this way, children can learn that there is no single right way for people to live—there are many right ways to live.

On the other hand, Jimmy's parents did not ignore the ugly side of life. They showed him their disapproval of pollution of the environment and the sights and sounds of violence. They lived their values for Jimmy to see and imitate.

Jimmy's parents watched for times when he showed an appreciation for beauty, and then reinforced these actions whenever possible. They responded with enthusiasm and respect for Jimmy's ways of creating beauty—his songs, pictures, and dances. They warmly praised him for the flowers he admired, the art work he made, and the animals he noted. They also praised him for the good things he noticed and said about people.

Jimmy's parents understood the pleasure that the ability to appreciate beauty could bring into his life. They knew that he could add to his own happiness in the future, simply by noticing the many forms of beauty the world has to offer.

Figure 27-4. Taking trips to zoos is a good way to help children gain an appreciation for beauty and nature.

Strengthening Love of Family

Most people would like the members of their families to show love for one another. The birth of a baby provides an opportunity to enjoy new and rewarding feelings and expressions of love. Richard's parents were sure to take advantage of the principles of modeling and imitation. They often showed their love to each other and Richard through their words and actions. They showed respect for each other's opinions and offered help in times of trouble. Richard's parents praised special abilities and spent time together whenever they could. By letting their love show, they greatly increased the chances that it would be returned.

Teaching the love of family is very important. It is related not only to helping the parents feel loved and appreciated by their children. It is also important in that love of family helps children to feel a sense of belonging. This helps children to feel secure and to develop self-confidence and self-esteem.

Helping Children to Show Affection

Kissing and hugging loved ones comes easily to children who have been encouraged to show these forms of affection. The feelings of love which are represented by these expressions of affection will grow naturally in loving families. Maria's parents started hugging, kissing, and telling her they loved her on her first day of life, and they never stopped. They watched for signs of affection that Maria eventually showed them, and returned such affection immediately. Maria's parents were not smothering in their displays of love. Nor were they too stingy or cautious.

Sometimes Maria was prompted to kiss or hug other loved ones (aunts, uncles, grandparents) during her early childhood. She was praised for her lovingness. While it is valuable for children to show their affection in these ways, it is important that they not be pushed or forced. A shaping approach will allow children to express affection at their own pace and in their own ways.

Maria's parents started assisting her to show affection very early, and Maria did not mind at all. If they had waited until Maria was six or seven years old, it is more likely that Maria may have resisted showing her affection. By teaching Maria early to show her affection, and by speaking warmly and often

Figure 27-5. Everyone needs a sense of belonging. Strengthening the love of family helps children to feel secure and self-confident. (March of Dimes Birth Defects Foundation)

about Maria's relatives, her parents helped her to develop a strong sense of belonging and family love. This was especially valuable for Maria when her parents divorced when she was five. Because she knew that she was strongly loved by all of her family, Maria was able to adapt to the divorce more easily.

SUMMARY

Helping children to develop sound values and morals is one of the major privileges and responsibilities of parenthood. Childhood is relatively short in comparison to an individual's adulthood. Values and morals can change during adult years. However, it is during childhood (and adolescence) that the basis for psychologically healthful values and morals is formed.

QUESTIONS FOR GROWTH

1. Why is it important to teach children morals and values?

2. Explain the three levels of moral development described by Kohlberg.

3. How can parents begin to strengthen values and morals in their young children? Provide several general suggestions.

4. Tell how you might help children to be more truthful and respectful of others' property.

5. Select two examples of moral behavior which you value, and then identify the ways in which you would attempt to strengthen them in a child.

6. Explain how you might help children to appreciate beauty in their lives.

7. Why is helping children to appreciate beauty an important parenting goal?

8. Discuss ways in which you would help a child to feel closer and more loving to other members of his or her family.

CHAPTER

28

Going to School

One of the most important decisions that parents face is whether or not to enter their children in an early childhood program. *Early childhood programs* are group settings which provide opportunities for young children to learn and develop, supervised by adults trained in child development. Good early childhood programs strengthen all areas of a child's growth and development.

Children, of course, benefit from an enriched home environment. But they can also benefit from a well-planned early childhood program. A well-planned program meets the needs of both children and parents. For example, quality day-care programs can provide a safe, enriched, healthy environment for young children while the parents are at work. Or a nursery school program can provide a child with group experiences which the parents cannot provide at home.

Parents and children have many different needs. To meet the needs of these individuals, various kinds of early childhood programs are available in most communities.

Parents must make their choices about early childhood education very carefully. Nursery schools and other child-care settings have a strong influence upon children. By making careful choices, parents can make sure that their children have positive experiences which will help their development while meeting the needs of the family.

Parents' decisions to choose early childhood programs are often based upon the parents' needs. In some families, both parents work, so child care is a necessity. Many parents, though, choose early childhood programs because they can help children to develop socially and expand learning experiences.

When considering an early childhood program, parents must decide upon certain basic factors. These include cost, location, number of hours, and the type of care that best suits the individual child. The parents should visit the different programs available in their area. In this way, they can gather information, check to see if the programs meet state licensing requirements, and, finally, choose the best-quality program for their needs.

KINDS OF EARLY CHILDHOOD PROGRAMS

Several kinds of early childhood programs are available. *Nursery schools* are generally for children between the ages of two to five years. Children usually attend a nursery program two or three times per week, during the morning or afternoon.

Day-care centers commonly provide care for a whole day or less, depending upon the parents' needs. Day-care centers usually have separate programs for infants, toddlers, and three- to five-year-olds. Care may also be extended to elementary school children after their regular school day. The number of privately owned day-care centers is increasing. Some day-care centers are also connected with industries and universities. These associations provide parents with an opportunity to assure good care for their children while they work or further their own education.

Day-care homes involve people's homes which are made available for child care. Normally, the owner of the home is the primary care giver for a small number of children.

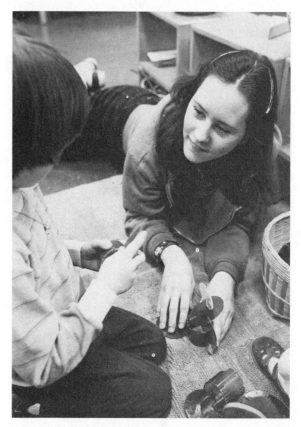

Figure 28-1. Early childhood programs teach a wide variety of necessary skills. (Future Homemakers of America)

In nearly all states, day-care and nursery school programs are required to meet many standards for licensing. The quality of these programs can still vary, however. Many states do not require directors of such programs to have more than a high school education. Further specialized training may not be required. Day-care homes are less likely to be licensed and supervised by states. The quality of these settings can range from very good to very poor.

Parents may also choose to pay someone to come into their home and care for their children. Although this is not an early childhood program, it deserves mention here. The cost of this kind of arrangement can be high. But, more importantly, parents should be certain that such an individual will give their children the quality care they need and deserve. Such individuals are not required by law to have particular qualifications. It is the parents' responsibility to choose in-home care givers carefully. In general, these persons should meet and provide the same good qualities of early childhood personnel and programs.

CHOOSING A GOOD EARLY CHILDHOOD PROGRAM

Some people believe that parents' responsibilities lessen when children enter an early childhood program. In fact, the opposite is true. Parents' responsibilities grow. They

Figure 28-2. *Early childhood programs can provide a middle step between home and kindergarten. (USDA Photo by Jack Schneider)*

must choose programs of good quality. They must also carefully follow their children's program and help to improve their development in the program whenever possible.

It is important to choose an early childhood program carefully. Programs differ greatly in quality. Many states require that they meet licensing requirements. Some states do not. Programs may be forced to meet requirements for safety and cleanliness. But they cannot be forced to provide the high quality of teacher-child interaction essential for learning. This, and more, is what parents must look for in an early childhood program.

It helps for parents to ask friends who have children for their opinions about programs in the area. But it is only by visiting the schools or centers, talking with teachers, and observing them in action that parents can really judge a program.

The Program's Philosophy

Parents must judge the program's *philosophy* of child care and education. That is, the program's ideas about how young children should be helped to develop in the best ways possible. Program directors and teachers have different opinions about the best way to teach young children. Parents should look for a program that has a philosophy about young children that is similar to their own. Several approaches are used, and they are as follows.

• **Loose structure.** Some programs operate under the philosophy that children learn best when left alone, free to explore an environment which is arranged to be stimulating and educational.

• **Medium structure.** These programs are careful to provide a balance between time structured by the teacher and time for the children to follow their own interests.
• **Tight structure.** In these programs, children have very little personal freedom to follow individual interests. Their activities are tightly structured and closely controlled.

All of these approaches have enjoyed success. But it is likely that the medium-structure approach is best. Children need both guidance and control as well as some freedom to do what they want in their own way.

Too little structure can be bad. For instance, children who are often allowed to run wildly around a classroom are likely to learn behaviors that will cause difficulty in kindergarten and at home.

On the other hand, there is too much structure if children are always forced to do things the same way. Children are each unique and enjoy learning in different ways. Some children enjoy learning when a teacher uses flash cards to teach colors. Other children are bored by this method. They would learn more about colors through finger painting or a game of walking around and hunting for various colors in the room. Also, more supervision may be needed for the very young child than for the older child who functions well independently.

In general, early childhood programs need a commitment toward approaches that are individualized for each child's needs. There should also be times for free play and free learning. This medium-structure approach comes closest to what is appropriate for young children.

The Learning Environment

When comparing programs, parents should observe the learning environment. Is the setting bright and cheerfully decorated? Is it big enough to provide areas for group activities as well as areas for children to work alone? Are the children encouraged to participate in these activities? Are there play areas indoors and outdoors which allow for large-muscle activity such as climbing and running?

Parents should notice how many children are in a program. Most states have established ratios of adults to children, depending upon the ages of the children. The younger the children, the higher a ratio of adults to children is needed.

It is important to notice the materials and equipment. Materials and equipment should be plentiful and in good condition. There should also be a wide variety. A program should have many paints, crayons, records, games, building blocks, puzzles, and musical instruments. It should also have plants, fish, and other nature and science materials. Do the children in the program seem to be enjoying and using these materials? If they seem bored, it may be that the teacher has not changed or rotated these materials for a long time.

Parents should note if the furnishings, lockers, clothes hooks, and sinks are suited to young children. Books should be within easy reach. Chairs should be small and easily moved, and doors should be easy to open.

It is essential to check the safety codes that a program is required to meet. Teachers should be able to explain the fire and building requirements which have been fulfilled. Outdoor play facilities are important, and they should be fenced in and supervised. There should be multiple exits from indoors in case of fire. Bathroom facilities should be close by and supervised. Parents should take their time and carefully note whether the setting and its materials are safe for young children. They should also note the cleanliness of the surroundings and ask about the quality of food service.

The Teachers

The teacher's job is a very complex and demanding one. Some even view teaching young children to be an art. The individual human characteristics which teachers bring to their work are very important, even though they are often hard to define. Other good qualities are easier to observe.

Jimmy's parents were looking for an early childhood teacher who had formal training

Figure 28-3. Choosing a good early childhood program is difficult. Parents should be sure that the program and teachers share their philosophy of child care and education. Parents should visit and talk with directors and teachers before choosing a program. (Kinder-Care Learning Centers, Inc.)

in child development, learning, and preschool education. They also wanted a teacher who had several years of successful experience working with young children, and who continued to learn through conferences and workshops. They rightly felt that the teacher should be a warm, open, and cooperative person who was enthusiastic about working with children.

When Jimmy's parents interviewed a teacher, they asked about the teacher's methods, goals, and philosophy. A good teacher should be specific about those skills which he or she considers important, and should state a clear teaching philosophy. Teachers should be detailed about what they are going to teach on a day-to-day basis. If teachers cannot be specific about their daily programs, it is unlikely that they are capable of meeting more general goals such as "teaching children how to learn."

Jimmy's parents observed different teachers in action. They noted whether each teacher used the basic principles of teaching and learning. They made sure that the teachers started by requiring things which the children could do and then slowly increased the requirements in small steps.

Jimmy's parents felt that teachers should treat children as individuals. They wanted them to give extra praise and assistance to those who need it, while allowing the more capable to progress on their own. They looked for teachers who, when praising children, would do so with enthusiasm and describe the specific behaviors which they were trying to strengthen.

Teachers who praise children for "sharing your materials so well today" or who ask children to put their toys away before having a snack are using reinforcers skillfully. This provides for a better learning environment. Some teachers do not provide individual and group reinforcers for appropriate learning activities. Instead, they give their attention to inappropriate behaviors—not sharing, or not putting toys away. Teachers who withhold reinforcers from behaviors which lead to learning, and heavily reinforce behaviors which do not, do not provide the best learning environment.

Jimmy's parents were also aware that a teacher's methods of discipline are extremely important. They watched out for the teacher who scolded and showed frequent disapproval. They felt that positive reinforcement in a warm, accepting environment was important for Jimmy. Teachers who set firm, but reasonable, limits were valued by Jimmy's parents.

Jimmy's parents also asked the teachers whether they encouraged parent-teacher meetings and classroom visits. They told teachers that they wanted to be kept informed of progress through written progress evaluations and frequent meetings with the teachers. Jimmy's parents also stated that they wanted to be able to visit the classroom often.

Were Jimmy's parents asking too much from a teacher? Absolutely not. The positive effects of excellent teaching during a child's first years in school are priceless. It is the parents' responsibilities to provide these advantages for their children.

INFLUENCING CHILDREN'S ATTITUDES ABOUT AN EARLY CHILDHOOD PROGRAM

Richard seemed a little worried about starting nursery school. To relieve his worry, his parents began to teach him good attitudes about nursery school well before his starting date. They associated stories about nursery school with events that Richard already found reinforcing. From time to time, they talked with him about the positive things about school, starting as soon as he was old enough to understand. When reading to Richard, his parents sometimes said that he would someday hear many new stories from his nursery school teacher. When preparing a snack, they sometimes mentioned that his teacher would also make snacks. When praising Richard, his parents told him how his teacher would also be interested in what he did.

Richard's parents were creating new reinforcers for their child. Such reinforcers included the idea of going to school, the activities, the teacher, and the friends he would make. They were careful not to overdo it, though. They made such references only occasionally over a period of several months.

Sometimes Richard would ask questions about nursery school. His parents answered them in positive terms. Richard soon began to make his own positive statements about going to school. (''When I get big enough to go to nursery school...'' ''When I get my own teacher...'') Richard's parents praised such statements and sometimes encouraged more discussion. For example, Richard said, ''I get to finger paint in nursery school.''

His parents replied, ''Isn't that exciting! I'll bet your teacher will give you your own apron so you can paint all you want!''

Richard's parents also allowed him to watch children's television programs about nursery school. The programs showed children in nursery school settings, teachers in action, or groups of children in enjoyable learning situations. Such programs are probably more valuable than parents realize for preparing children for school.

Children may be somewhat fearful of going to school someday, and will express their fears by making negative statements. Parents may find themselves trying to soothe the fears with glowing accounts of how great school is. This is appropriate—occasionally. But too much attention following children's negative statements about school might strengthen negative statements about school. Therefore, it is better for parents to pay only a little attention to such statements. The parents can continue to present school in a positive light at other times.

Most early childhood programs hold open houses, in which children and parents can walk around and become familiar with the school and teachers. This can help to relieve children's natural fear about the unknown. Even after such preparation, though, many children will still show signs of fear when they are finally left at the school alone. Richard's parents thought that he might have this fear, so they warned his new teacher in advance. The experienced nursery school teacher knew how to help children with separation anxiety.

On Richard's first day of nursery school, his parents took him to school and spent some time looking around the school with Richard. When Richard became busily involved with a puzzle, his parents explained that they had to leave but would be back. Richard's parents then cheerfully hugged and kissed him goodbye, and left. Richard's new teacher stayed with him, talking and laughing with him and waving goodbye to his parents. She assured Richard that his parents would be back in a few hours. After several days, Richard went to nursery school happily and with no fear.

FOLLOWING CHILDREN'S PROGRESS IN EARLY CHILDHOOD PROGRAMS

Despite their natural curiosity, Richard's parents avoided asking him too many detailed questions about nursery school. They restricted themselves to occasional casual questions: "What did you do in nursery school today?" "Who are your friends at nursery school?" They then responded to any reasonable answer with warm but quiet enthusiasm. If Richard wanted to talk more, they listened with interest. If he did not want to talk more, that was fine with his parents, too. They also listened with enthusiasm when Richard brought up the subject of school on his own.

Through this approach, Richard's parents were making observations about how he was progressing in nursery school. They also paid attention to his behavior when leaving for school and talking about it. They noticed that Richard was happy when leaving for nursery school. His statements about school were

positive as well. In these ways, his parents were able to tell that Richard liked the care and activities provided by the nursery school. This was a measure not only of Richard's progress, but also of the school's quality.

More detailed information was also available through parent-teacher *conferences*, or meetings, and by visits to the classroom. Conferences should occur near the beginning, middle, and end of the school year. Between these times, parents can gain a feeling for how things are going by an occasional question to the teacher when picking a child up at school. If the parents think there may be some school-related problems, parents should ask for a conference right away. At the conference, they should discuss the exact problems, when they occur, and how often they occur. Parents should ask how difficult the teacher feels the problems are.

It is best to talk in terms of observable actions: "She hits two or three times a day" rather than "She's aggressive." Such specific language tells parents and teachers exactly what the problems are. It also helps to suggest new behaviors to be taught, such as cooperation, sharing, or talking to other children.

Conferences are an important way to follow children's progress in early childhood programs. Often, it is good to schedule a visit to observe before the conference. This may help parents to see exactly how a child behaves. Such observations will give parents something concrete to discuss, and a better basis for communication with the teacher.

Parents would benefit from observing children using the methods described in Chapter 15. The parents should watch and remember the things which are important to them. It is helpful if they take notes. Such notes are valuable even when a child is experiencing no problems, because they are a measure of progress.

When Richard's parents visited the nursery school to observe him, they took notes in the form of a sequence analysis. The events that occurred just before the behavior, then Richard's behavior, and then the consequences were written down, as shown in Box 28.1. These notes contained several valuable pieces of information.

• The teacher seemed to be doing a good job. Within less than an hour, she praised Richard four times for good behavior. She prompted him once to follow instructions, and then praised him for doing so.
• When a fight threatened, the teacher wisely waited to see if the children would work out the difficulties on their own. They did. Richard stood up for his rights to the instrument he wanted. The other child also learned something about "property rights" in a nursery school.
• Richard seemed to be doing well in nursery school. His behavior was appropriate during the story time. He even dared to answer a question in front of the group. He concentrated on his painting and block building during free time. In fact, he enjoyed himself so much that he did not hear, or he ignored, the teacher's instruction to the group. But when he was told personally to clean up, Richard did so immediately. (Any child might become absorbed by an activity and miss a teacher's instruction. But Richard's parents checked with the teacher

to see if this occurred frequently and how the teacher handled the situation.) The conflict with another child was of appropriate length and intensity for children in nursery school. Richard also dealt with the problem appropriately. His willingness to stand up for himself when in the right is a quality he will need throughout life.

Dealing with Problems

Written observations are very important if a child has a problem in an early childhood program. Both the parents and the teacher must know how often a problem occurs and the conditions which produce it. They must also be aware of what reinforcers are present or absent for the behavior. Sometimes parents might observe that the teacher is actually strengthening a problem with consistent attention for misbehavior and little attention for appropriate behavior. A written record might help to convince the teacher to try another approach.

Once a problem is identified, it should be observed closely by the parents and the teacher. By noting how often the behavior occurs, they can find how serious it is and choose methods likely to improve it. For example, the teacher who finds that a child hits other children from five to ten times daily might use the time-out method. This will help to reduce hitting to once or twice a day and eventually to eliminate it.

Parents and teachers must cooperate with one another. They should identify and discuss which behaviors to reinforce both at home and in school. Frequent telephone calls

BOX 28.1

A Sequence Analysis of Richard's Behavior in Nursery School

What Happened Before the Behavior	Richard's Behavior	Consequences
Children seated in a circle around teacher. Story time (9:00)	Richard listens quietly.	Teacher looks directly at Richard.
Teacher asks where the bear gets honey.	Richard raises his hand.	Teacher calls on him.
Teacher calls on Richard.	Richard says, ''In a bee's nest up in the tree.''	Teacher praises good answer.
Free time (9:10). Richard paints enthusiastically with watercolors. (9:17)	Richard is hard at work.	Teacher stops by and encourages him.
Teacher stops by and encourages him.	Richard still paints.	Teacher praises Richard and pats him on the shoulder.
Teacher instructs children to clean up. (9:45)	Richard still paints.	Teacher tells Richard personally to clean up. (9:47)
Teacher tells Richard personally to clean up.	Richard cleans up immediately.	Teacher thanks him for following instructions.
Children are asked to choose a musical instrument from the box. (10:00)	Richard runs to the box and grabs a small cymbal.	Another child tries to pull the instrument away.
Another child tries to pull the instrument away.	Richard pushes the child and yells, ''I had it first!''	The other child stops pulling and chooses something else. Teacher observed the interaction but said nothing.

may be necessary to follow progress at home and in school. Or, the teacher's wink or nod of the head may communicate all the parents need to know when they pick up the child from the program. This might tell the parents to be prepared to reinforce the child's improving behavior at home.

What if a teacher refuses to cooperate in ways essential to solve the problem? In this case, it is certainly reasonable to take the child out of that early childhood program and look for a better one. Such a change can be made without telling the child the reasons. It is best to act quickly rather than waiting out the time until the child enters kindergarten. By then, the problem may have grown worse. If the problem continues to be serious, it may be important for the parents to ask a child psychologist for advice.

Whatever the setting, parents must choose day-care services with care. There is no substitute for quality child care. Parents should look carefully at many different centers, homes, and individual care givers. They should speak with many other parents about the level and quality of care provided at different centers, homes, or by individuals. It is wise to choose a day-care service which most closely resembles the parents' philosophy about child rearing.

Many professionals have found that a child's first five years of learning and experiences are the most important for further development. These years are also the time of parents' maximum influence. However, involvement in a quality day-care setting or nursery school can provide new and valuable experiences. They can also help parents to prepare their children for school situations before starting kindergarten.

READINESS FOR SCHOOL

As described throughout this book, development is a continuous and gradual process. It occurs in a predictable, orderly manner. Yet each child has his or her own rate of development.

It is helpful to think of children as different trains going along a track. They all follow the same, predictable path, but they go at different speeds, slowing down and racing ahead at different points. Some of them even stop for a while at different points before speeding ahead again. It is thus important that parents consider an individual child's readiness for the formal school experience.

A level of *maturation* refers to the readiness of a child to take the next step forward before learning can be most effective. Maturation can be enhanced and encouraged, but it cannot be forced if a particular child is not ready. It is important that parents consider all areas of development (physical, emotional, and social) when judging a child's readiness.

Maria's parents were quite sure that she was ready for kindergarten. They felt even more sure when they talked with her nursery school teacher. The teacher agreed that Maria had demonstrated skills and abilities that showed she was ready for kindergarten.

Richard's parents, though, made a different decision. Richard was quite advanced intellectually. But he too often showed signs of immature social and emotional development. His small motor skills were slower to develop. Richard's parents thought that he might experience frustration with some of the tasks that would be expected of him in kindergarten. After talking with Richard's nursery school teacher, his parents decided to wait a year to enter him in kindergarten. This did not mean that Richard had failed, but simply that he was at a different point in his development. He needed more time to benefit from an early childhood program before entering kindergarten.

It is important that parents gather as much information as possible by talking honestly with the teachers or other care givers who know their child. In this way, parents will be better able to make their decision in their child's best interests.

Skills Needed for Kindergarten and Later Schooling

In kindergarten, children face a new teacher, longer hours, and new classmates. More is expected from them in following instructions, self-control, the amount they must learn, and so on.

A casual observer might think that kindergarten does not involve much. But kindergarten makes demands upon all areas of

Figure 28-4. Most children enjoy learning and the activities in kindergarten, even though this new situation places more demands on them. (Kinder-Care Learning Centers, Inc.)

children's development. Children find themselves among a group of 20 or so strangers, and are required to become a successful member of the group. They will be asked to respond appropriately to a variety of a teacher's instructions. They will be expected to learn to share, cooperate, and take turns with classmates. They must learn to deal with children who may disagree with them. They must eventually control their emotions as appropriate for a variety of frustrating or even frightening situations.

Children need to learn and accept that they cannot always be the center of attention. They must face the fact that they cannot always be the best at everything—the smartest, fastest, or strongest. Children in kindergarten are expected to join in group projects, to sing and dance freely, and to speak up and express ideas to the group. They will gradually learn to influence others in skillful and appropriate ways. They must also adapt to certain structures. Sometimes it will be appropriate to sit quietly or move slowly, and other times it will be okay to play loudly and joyfully.

Being a successful member of a group requires adapting to the group in certain ways. However, group membership also requires children to show some independence. Children should learn not to follow the lead of others who misbehave. They need to learn to care for their own belongings, to clean up their own messes, and to dress themselves. Hopefully, children will develop a good understanding of their own rights and the rights of others. Sometimes they must stand up for their own rights, and sometimes they must protect those of their classmates.

CASE STUDY

The First Day of Kindergarten

The father recalled Jimmy's first day of kindergarten.

As my son and I drove away from home, the emotions of the moment were powerful and mixed. While there was pride, joy, and excitement, there was also a lump in my throat as I thought about how quickly Jimmy was growing up.

I waited as Jimmy stood in a line of many children in front of the brick school. He was unusually quiet and, except when he turned to the car and waved, he didn't smile. After the children had entered the school, I experienced nagging doubts: ''I hope Jimmy will like his teacher. I hope the teacher's good. I hope Jimmy will learn well and be happy. I hope … I hope all goes well for our little boy!'' When I returned home, my wife expressed the same feelings.

Jimmy's parents had done their best to prepare him for kindergarten. They were sure he was ready. Why, then, the concern? Perhaps it was because they loved him and cared about him, and because they knew that kindergarten, while similar to preschool, involved many new demands.

Clearly, kindergarten is a demanding experience for children. Fortunately, though, most children look forward to kindergarten with great excitement. Going to school is a big event in the life of a child.

During the summer, many school systems provide counseling and books for parents whose children will enter kindergarten in the fall. These efforts are good and useful. But parents should not try to prepare their children for kindergarten in only two months. It is wise for parents to ask for these aids a year or two in advance. This early planning will allow parents the time to develop slowly and effectively those skills known to be important for success in kindergarten.

First grade is a rewarding experience for children. However, first grade is quite different from kindergarten. There will be much to learn in order to help children's success in the years to come. In first grade, the room size is usually smaller, so the area to move about in is more limited. Each child is normally assigned a desk and must spend longer times in one place. The time is more structured to teach subjects such as reading, writing, and arithmetic. Children's work is scored by teachers, and competition becomes greater between children.

Following Children's Progress at School

As in an early childhood program, children's progress in later schooling should be followed closely by parents. Parents can do this by listening to what children say and observing their behavior. If children mention the same problem several times, it is wise to call the teacher to gain a better understanding of the situation. If children's behavior at home changes in alarming ways (crying, stomach aches, bedwetting), this may be a sign of trouble at school.

Children bring home important information in the form of art work and projects from kindergarten. In later schooling, information is also available in the form of workbooks completed at school and graded by the teacher. Jimmy's parents were careful to show interest and congratulate him on his good work. They happily told each other about Jimmy's achievements in front of him. They taped his work on the refrigerator or pinned it up on a bulletin board.

Jimmy's parents noted any problems in private, not in front of him. They discussed such problems as uncompleted work. They helped him with these problems during homework and tutoring sessions. Jimmy's parents were careful not to use negative labels or statements ("You are so sloppy"). Children tend to believe such labels if they hear them often.

Progress Reports

Progress reports differ from school to school, but they are an important measure of children's growth and development. In kindergarten, progress reports often take the form of a checklist divided into different categories. The categories may be social and emotional skills (shares, gets along with others, etc.), physical development, independence (works alone, finishes work, etc.), and intellectual achievements (prints name, knows alphabet, etc.). A kindergarten progress report often will include general comments on the individual's progress.

In the first grade, progress reports often still include social skills. But they begin to emphasize independence, study habits, and progress in math, reading, and writing. Many schools are replacing letter grades with a more detailed report. Such a report categorizes learning areas. But the skills involved in each category are described carefully and marked with a comment rather than a grade. The comment may be, for example, "outstanding," "satisfactory," or "needs improvement." In the areas of reading and math, skill levels may be represented in even greater detail. For example, one level in math may read as follows.

Level 1

Compares objects in terms of height and
    length.
Writes numbers 0 through 5.
Identifies sums of numbers 2 through 5.
Identifies subtracted differences of numbers
    2 through 5.

This method of dividing children's learning into small steps and recording progress through each step provides important information. This is better than the more general progress reports. With the more detailed report, parents can identify exactly what the school is trying to teach and how their child is progressing. They can also identify any particular weaknesses to help the child overcome.

Parents should sit with their children to review progress reports. It is important to sit in a relaxed way and strongly emphasize and praise any strengths or improvements. Nearly all children will show some areas of concern on reports. When discussing these, it is wise that parents not deal with all of them at the same time.

Maria had three areas which needed improvement. Her mother mixed the discussion of these among Maria's many achievements, which were praised enthusiastically. When she discussed a weakness, she was serious and showed her concern. She clearly identified ways in which she hoped Maria would try harder. Yet she spent more time on Maria's areas of strength.

Maria's mother did not show anger or extreme disappointment about the areas which needed improvement. She knew that showing anger might make Maria feel negative about school. Maria also might begin to avoid discussions with her mother about personal problems. By using a concerned approach, Maria's mother was able to relax Maria and give her confidence for future improvement.

Parent-Teacher Conferences

Poor performance in any area should prompt parents to call the teacher and arrange a conference. Conferences are also valuable when there are no performance problems. Parent-teacher conferences are an important way for parents to gain information about their child's school performance and activities.

Conferences are normally scheduled by the school. They first occur after children have attended school for a month or more. Teachers need about a month to get to know the children.

If the school does not schedule a conference during the first part of the school year, parents should request such a meeting. If possible, both parents should go to the conference.

Some parents find it difficult to talk with teachers. They may be overly agreeable and afraid to speak up about their concerns. Others can be too aggressive and demanding. Such difficulties are sometimes due to the teacher's manner. Most often, though, they are due to the parents' previous experiences with teachers. (Teachers have had a great deal of power over us all in our school years, and this may well influence how we react to teachers.) But parents should remember that they and the teacher have at least one thing in common—a concern for the child's happiness and success. This common concern should help parents and teachers to work together.

Parents should be organized and ready to contribute to the conference. In advance, they should be aware of what kind of information they want to know. This kind of preparation will help both the parents and the teachers during the conference, as teachers cannot be aware of all of the parents' concerns. The following is an example of an effective meeting between Jimmy's parents and his teacher.

Parents: "How is Jimmy at following instructions?"

Teacher: "I think he is doing reasonably well. He's shown good improvement during the last two months."

Parents: "It's probably too much to expect a five-year-old to follow all of a teacher's instructions. But are there any kinds of instructions that Jimmy has special difficulties with?"

Teacher: "You're right. Most of the children need an occasional second request. If I were to pick an area that Jimmy can improve in, it would be following instructions when he is playing alone."

Parents: "Can you give us an example of this kind of situation?"

Teacher: "If Jimmy is playing with a small group and the group moves to follow an instruction, he will also. But if he is playing alone with a toy, he sometimes needs a reminder."

Parents: "About how often a day does this happen?"

Teacher: "It really doesn't happen all that often. Some days it happens once or twice. Many days, not at all. Jimmy is really doing just fine in kindergarten, and there is no cause for concern. He and I have worked on following instructions and he's doing much better now. However, if you want to help him at home, be sure he follows your instructions with reasonable speed, and praise him warmly when he does."

This conversation was very informative. In response to the parents' general question, the teacher reassured them that Jimmy was doing reasonably well. This helped to relax the parents, who were happy to hear that there were no major problems. The parents showed their understanding that five-year-olds are not always perfect in following instructions, and then began to question more closely. The more specific the questions, the more the parents learned of the difficulty. The teacher reassured them, but also asked for specific help from the parents at home. The parents and teacher were working as a team.

The following are other useful questions that parents should ask during a parent-teacher conference.

- Is the child learning well?
- Does the child appear to see himself or herself in a positive way?
- How does the child usually respond to the teacher? Is the child polite? Cooperative? Rude? Uncooperative? Cheerful?
- Does the child work well alone and with others? Does he or she complete tasks?
- Does the child pay attention during stories or demonstrations? Does the child ask questions, volunteer answers? Is the child curious?
- Does the child speak well and have a good vocabulary?
- In general, is the child's conduct appropriate to various activities?
- What can we do at home to help?

If answers to these and other general questions suggest any problems, parents should ask specific questions. They should ask how often the behaviors occur, under what conditions, and what can be done to bring about improvement. This approach allows parents to learn exact information about a child's

Department of Information, NWT, Canada

Kinder-Care Learning Centers, Inc.

Figure 28-5. *A good teacher knows the children well, and can help parents identify special skills and interests as well as behavioral problems.*

performance. It also provides an opportunity for parents to help with any problems before they become serious.

SUMMARY

School experiences represent a new phase of learning and development for children. Children normally enter enriched environments where specially trained care givers help to facilitate growth and development in many important ways.

Parents still have the main responsibility for helping to prepare their children for school. They must choose quality schools, follow their children's progress, and cooperate with teachers to solve any problems.

QUESTIONS FOR GROWTH

1. Describe some of the main points to consider and compare when parents search for an early childhood program.

2. In what ways can a good early childhood program help to prepare children for kindergarten?

3. Explain the importance of an early childhood program's philosophy of child care and education.

4. Describe some of the main things to look for in an early childhood program's learning environment.

5. What are some important things to consider when choosing an early childhood program teacher?

6. Tell some of the ways in which parents might positively influence their children's attitudes about an early childhood program.

7. Explain what parents can do to follow their children's progress in an early childhood program.

8. What would you recommend that parents do if they discover that their child is having problems in an early childhood program?

9. (a) What are some things that parents should consider when determining their child's readiness for school? **(b)** Explain why Richard's parents decided to wait another year before starting him in kindergarten.

10. Describe some of the skills that children will need to begin kindergarten.

11. Explain how parents can follow their children's progress once they have entered kindergarten and later schooling.

12. (a) Explain the importance and objectives of parent-teacher conferences. **(b)** How should parents prepare themselves for such a conference, and what kind of an attitude should they show during the meeting?

GLOSSARY

Abstract problems—Problems which involve ideas rather than concrete items.

Accommodation—Creating a new way of thinking when old ways of thinking do not work.

Active labor—The birth process or period of contractions preceding the delivery of a child.

Active labor pains—Involuntary contractions of uterine muscles which help to move the fetus into the birth canal.

Adolescent—A person growing up from childhood to adulthood, especially from the ages of about 12 to about 20.

Afterbirth—The placenta and other membranes which leave the mother's body after the birth of a child.

Alternatives—Available choices.

Amniocentesis—A medical test which may determine the presence or absence of fetal abnormalities during pregnancy.

Amniotic fluid—The watery substance that surrounds and protects the developing child in the uterus.

Amniotic sac—A sack which holds the amniotic fluid and the fetus.

Androgeny—The ability to creatively combine characteristics of traditional male and female roles.

APGAR—A medical testing system used to evaluate a neonate's health.

Approximation—Each teaching step in the shaping method which moves closer and closer to the desired behavior.

Assimilation—Using old ways of thinking to understand something new.

Association—Previously neutral stimuli can gain new abilities to change behaviors and emotions when they are paired (associated) with other stimuli already capable of producing a response.

Authoritarian parents—Parents who often use harsh punishment and who seldom explain rules or praise their children for good behavior.

Authoritative parents—Parents who often praise their children in warm and loving ways but who also set appropriate rules and use mild discipline when it is necessary.

Autonomy—Independence.

Babbling—Repeating consonants followed by vowel sounds.

Baby talk—Language adapted to make it more understandable to a young child.

Backward chaining—An operant-learning method used to teach sequences of behavior; the last step in the chain is taught first.

Behave—Act in a certain way.

Behavior—A certain action.

Behavioral goal—A teaching goal which is described in terms of specific behaviors to be learned.

Behavioral objective—A behavior to be learned, the circumstances under which it should occur, and how to tell when it has been learned.

Bond—An emotional tie between people.

Bonding—The early formation of a relationship between infant and care giver.

Bonus response cost—A mild punishment method in which extra tokens are given which may be lost, during a time period, for specific misbehavior.

Brainstorm—To think about and produce as many ideas about how to solve a problem as possible.

Cephalo-caudal—The head-to-tail progression of physical growth.

Cervix—The opening in the uterus which leads to the vagina.

Chain of behaviors—A skill which is made up of a sequence of several or more behaviors, such as getting dressed.

Characteristics—Special qualities or features.

Child abuse—Mistreatment of children; may be sexual, physical, or emotional in nature.

Child neglect—Mistreatment of children as a result of not providing the essentials for healthy physical or mental development.

Chromosomes—Tiny strands of DNA protein matter which carry the genes.

Classify—To group or categorize things.

Cognitive development—How the ability to think and know about things grows in human beings.

Complex unrestrictive choices—The choices available to children are not all good; children must consider the immediate and long-range consequences before choosing between them.

Conception—The moment at which sperm and ovum unite and pregnancy results.

Concrete illustration—To show what will happen if a certain behavior occurs.

Concrete operational period—Piaget's third period of cognitive development, during which children learn the principle of conservation and begin to think logically.

Condition—To create a new learning through association or providing consequences.

Consequence—The outcome or result that follows a behavior.

Conservation—The ability to understand that liquids or solids can change in shape but remain the same in volume or mass.

Continuous reinforcement—Reinforcement happens each time following the behavior.

Cooing—An infant's open vowel sounds.

Cooperative play—Children play together and each contributes to achieve some result.

Coordination—Skillful movement.

Cope—To appropriately deal with or handle a situation of potential stress.

Correction—A mild punishment method in which children are required to correct an inappropriate behavior.

Counseling—The exchange of ideas and advice.

Crawl—To move about on hands and knees.

Creative problem solving—To consider a variety of solutions, some of which may be unusual.

Creep—To inch forward while lying on the stomach.

Cross-sectional studies—A research method in which different groups of individuals of different ages are measured or studied at the same time.

Cue—A signal or reminder.

Day-care center—An early childhood program which commonly provides care for a whole day or less; with separate programs for infants, toddlers, and three- to five-year-olds.

Day-care home—A private home that provides care for a small number of children.

Decision making—The action taken in choosing among known alternatives.

Deferred imitation—Children watch someone do something and then remember the actions and imitate them sometime later.

Dependent variable—In an experiment, the specific behavior under study.

Deprivation—A situation in which someone's reinforcers are withheld.

Deprivation trap—A situation in which parents deprive their infant until he or she protests. Then the parents give reinforcers for fussiness and crying.

Despair—A feeling of unhappiness and disgust with one's efforts.

Differential reinforcement—A method of learning in which reinforcement is provided for desirable behaviors but is withheld from less desirable behaviors.

Discipline—To help children to learn, accept, and believe in beneficial rules for self-conduct.

Discriminate—To tell the differences between people, places, and things.

Displace aggression—To take out anger on someone who is not the cause of the anger.

Disruptive children—Children whose extreme misbehavior is upsetting to those nearby.

Divorce—The legal ending of a marriage.

Duration—The amount of time a behavior is done.

Early childhood program—A group setting which provides opportunites for young children to learn and develop, supervised by adults trained in child development.

Egocentrism—Self-centeredness; concerned mostly with oneself or seeing things only from one's own point of view.

Emotional development—The development of feelings and emotional behaviors and how children come to manage them.

Environment—All of the surrounding non-genetic things, conditions, and influences which affect children's development.

Expansion—Retaining the meaning of a child's statement but saying it back in a more grammatical way.

Experiment—A research method which is used to identify cause-and-effect relationships.

Expressive language—The ability to speak.

Extension—Using a child's statement by relating it to a similar but different idea, then restating the new idea in a grammatically correct form.

Extinction—An operant-learning method in which reinforcers are withheld following operant behavior, with the result that the behavior decreases in future frequency.

Eye-hand coordination—The ability to look at an object and then accurately reach out and touch it.

Fading—Removing prompts or assistance.

Fallopian tube—The structures which connect the ovaries to the uterus in the female reproductive system.

Fertile—Capable of producing offspring.

Fetal alcohol syndrome—A condition that can cause serious physical and mental harm to an unborn baby, caused by maternal alcohol consumption during pregnancy.

Fetus—The developing unborn infant, from eight weeks after conception until birth.

Frequency count—A count of how often a behavior occurs.

General goal—A general statement or idea about something one wishes to accomplish.

Generalize—Skills or emotions spread to other similar situations.

Generativity—The ability to extend one's interests and concerns beyond oneself to others.

Genes—Inherited special biochemical messages which strongly influence a person's mental and physical characteristics.

Genetic counseling—A medical estimate of the likelihood of genetic problems in a couple's future children.

Genetic inheritance—The characteristics that a child receives from the genes of both parents; heredity.

Genetics—The study of how genes function to influence development.

Growth spurt—A period of unusually fast physical development.

Guilt—A feeling of having done something wrong.

Habituation—The process of getting used to things.

Handicap—A physical, mental, or emotional disadvantage.

Heredity—Genetic inheritance.

Holophrase—A child's single word which may mean many different things.

Ignorance—The lack of knowledge about something.

Imitate—To match someone's behavior.

Incidental learning—When learning a skill (coordination, etc.), other less obvious abilities and skills are learned at the same time.

Independent thinking—The ability to make important decisions and to solve problems on one's own.

Independent variable—In an experiment, a specific treatment that will be applied to identify its effect on a behavior (dependent variable).

Industry—Steady effort and busy application.

Inferiority—A feeling of being worth less than other people.

Initiative—Actively planning and trying to accomplish things.

Integrity—A feeling that results when individuals are satisfied with their efforts and would change little.

Interact—To communicate both ways, from person to person.

Interfering variable—In an experiment, a factor other than the independent variable that can influence the dependent variable.

Intermittent reinforcement—Reinforcement which is given only after more than one behavior or action.

Interview—A research method in which someone asks questions and records the answers.

Intimate—A close relationship in which feelings and thoughts are shared.

Isolation—A sense of apartness from others.

Kindergarten—A program for five-year-old children that usually begins their formal education.

Label—Name, identify.

Language—Any form of communication.

Language period—After the prespeech period, the period in which children can say meaningful words.

Law of effect—A principle of operant learning that states that many behaviors are influenced by their consequences.

Laws of developmental direction—The progression of physical development; the cephalo-caudal principle, and proximal distal development.

Learned reflex—A reflex which is acquired through experience.

Longitudinal studies—A research method in which the same group is studied over a long period of time.

Manipulate—Handle and move or change.

Manners—Some of the ways that people show their concern and respect for the feelings of others.

Maturation—Physical growth and development.

Maturity—The achievement of full development.

Measurement—Using numbers to describe behaviors that have been observed.

Meiosis—A process by which sex cells divide.

Menstruation—In the female's monthly fertility cycle, the bleeding which occurs as the uterus sheds its lining.

Miscarriage—Spontaneous abortion.

Mobility—Ability to move.

Model—To show or give examples of behavior.

Moral behavior—Actions that conform to generally accepted ideas about what is right and wrong.

Moral code—A set of rules that people follow in controlling their behavior.

Moral values—What we think is right and wrong.

Negative reinforcement—The subtraction of something unpleasant following a behavior, which increases the future frequency of the behavior.

Negative reinforcer—The unpleasant stimulus which is subtracted following a behavior, which increases the future frequency of the behavior.

Neonate—A newborn infant.

Neutral stimulus—A stimulus which produces no measurable response.

Nonconsequence—The withholding of reinforcers following operant behavior (more technically: extinction).

Nonselective social smiling—A time period when infants will smile at nearly everyone.

Nonverbal communication—Feelings which are not expressed in words but through gestures, tone of voice, and facial expressions.

Nursery school—An early childhood program for two- to five-year-olds, usually for two or three afternoons or mornings a week.

Object permanence—The ability to represent an object in one's thinking when the object is out of sight.

Observational learning—Learning which occurs by watching people's behavior and other events.

Obstetrician—A physician who specializes in caring for pregnant women and delivering babies.

Offspring—A person's children.

Onlooker—A form of play in which a child watches others play.

Operant behavior—Behavior which is influenced by its consequences.

Operant learning—Learning which results from operating on or manipulating the environment and experiencing the consequences.

Oppositional behavior—Refusing to follow nearly all reasonable requests or instructions.

Oppositional children—Children who refuse to follow nearly all reasonable requests or instructions.

Oral language—Spoken language.

Osmosis—In pregnancy, the process by which the chemicals necessary to maintain life are exchanged between the mother and developing child.

Ovary—A storage structure for ova (the female sex cells).

Overcorrection—A mild punishment method in which a child is required to do work following an inappropriate behavior.

Ovum—The female sex cell (plural **ova**).

Parallel play—Playing close to others and using similar materials but not cooperating on a common goal.

Parenting—Assuming the responsibility for rearing a child.

Pediatrician—A physician who treats infants and young children.

Period of the embryo—The fertilized human ovum from about two weeks to eight weeks after conception.

Period of the fetus—The period of development which extends from about eight weeks after conception until birth.

Period of the zygote—A fertilized human ovum from conception to about two weeks.

Permissive parents—Parents who do not set rules or discipline their children, and who do not encourage independence.

Persistence—The quality of continuing to try to achieve something rather than giving up.

Physician—A medical doctor.

Placenta—A special layer which forms in the uterus to protect and nourish the developing infant.

Positive practice overcorrection—A mild punishment method in which after inappropriate behavior, a child is required to practice a substitute proper action several times.

Positive reinforcement—The addition of a stimulus following a behavior, which increases the future frequency of the behavior.

Positive reinforcer—That stimulus which is added and which strengthens the behavior it follows.

Power struggle—A conflict in which someone has to lose and someone has to win.

Premack principle—A principle which states that if people are allowed to do an activity which they prefer immediately after they do an activity which they do not prefer, the nonpreferred behavior will be positively reinforced.

Premature infant—A premie, an infant born at less than 37 weeks of development with a body weight of less than 5½ pounds.

Premoral level—The first level of moral development.

Prenatal—Before birth.

Prenatal development—The growth of the new life in the mother's body from conception until birth.

Preoperational period—Piaget's second period of cognitive development, during which language, imaginative play, and delayed imitation appear.

Prespeech period—The time preceding the language period, when the child is unable to say words.

Principled level—The third level of moral development.

Prompting—Helping a child to do the desired behaviors.

Proportion—Relationship in size.

Psychologist—A person who studies human behavior, learning, feelings, and other mental processes.

Puberty—The physical beginning of manhood or womanhood that results in being able to produce offspring.

Punisher—The stimulus which is added or subtracted following a behavior, and as a result the behavior happens less often in the future.

Punishment—A procedure in which something unpleasant is presented or positive reinforcers are removed following a behavior, and that behavior happens less often in the future.

Pyramid of needs—Maslow's theory that human beings have basic needs which must be met before the highest forms of human growth can occur.

Rational approach—Obtaining the available information about a question or problem and reaching a conclusion through logical thinking.

Rearrangement—Childproofing a child's environment by removing fragile or unsafe objects or changing schedules to suit the child's needs.

Reasoning—A mild discipline method in which the parent explains why the child should or should not behave in some way.

Receptive language—The ability to understand other people when they speak.

Reflex—A biological reaction to a specific stimulus; a stimulus-response connection.

Reflexive smiling phase—A period in which an infant's smile is more of an automatic reaction to something than a social response.

Representation—A memory of an experience.

Reprimand—A mild punishment method; a brief scolding showing clear disapproval.

Respondent behaviors—The behaviors observed in reflexes.

Respondent extinction—A learned stimulus is no longer associated with an unlearned stimulus. This causes the learned stimulus to lose its power to cause a response.

Respondent learning—A form of learning which occurs when a neutral stimulus is associated with an unlearned stimulus. The previously neutral stimulus gains new powers to cause a response.

Respondent stimulus generalization—Responses occur to stimuli which are similar to, but different from, a learned stimulus.

Response—An action or reaction caused by a stimulus.

Response cost—A mild punishment method in which a certain amount of reinforcers are lost following a behavior, and the behavior decreases in future frequency.

Restitution overcorrection—A mild form of punishment involving work. A child is made to intensively correct the mess or trouble caused by his or her actions.

Restricted choices—Children are given very little real choice; a good decision is guaranteed because only a few acceptable choices are offered.

Retardation—A condition in which a child's development is much slower than others of the same age.

Risk—Possible danger.

Role conformity—The second level of moral development.

Sacrifice—To give up something in order to achieve something else.

Satiation—Letting a child get tired of some behavior.

Schedule of reinforcement—A way to teach persistence in operant learning; how much one must do, or how long something must be done, before reinforcement is given or achieved.

Selective social smiling—A period in which infants smile at parents and other familiar faces, but do not smile when unfamiliar people approach.

Self-absorption—The opposite of generativity; concerned only with satisfying one's own needs and wants.

Self-actualizing—The top of Maslow's pyramid of needs; the achievement of developing and using all of one's unique talents and capabilities.

Self-centered—Egocentric; concerned only with one's own needs and views.

Self-confident—Feeling that one is capable of succeeding in most situations; showing that one is able to try to do new or difficult things.

Self-control—The act of purposely motivating oneself to do or not do some action.

Self-perception—How one sees or judges oneself.

Self-punishment—Using mild punishment methods to control one's own behavior.

Sensorimotor period—Piaget's first period of cognitive development, during which infants and toddlers learn through their senses, repeated bodily movements, and manipulation of objects.

Sensory—Receiving stimulation or learning through the five senses.

Sequence analysis—An observation which shows how certain consequences are affecting a child's behavior; what happens before, during, and right after the behavior.

Sex cell—A cell whose function is to produce new life.

Sex-role differences—Behavioral differences between males and females caused by social expectations and teaching.

Shaping—An operant-learning method in which small improvements are taught in a series of steps toward a desired behavior or new skill.

Siblings—Brothers and sisters.

Simple unrestricted choices—Children make simple but real decisions on their own. They are allowed to choose from a variety of options, all of which represent acceptable choices.

Small-for-date infant—An infant born after 38 weeks who weighs less than 5½ pounds.

Social development—A child's growing ability to form and maintain relationships with others.

Social reciprocity—People treat others as they themselves wish to be treated.

Social values—How we think about and judge the quality of other people.

Solitary play—Playing alone.

Spanking—A potentially dangerous punishment method which involves slapping with an open hand to eliminate misbehavior.

Sperm—Spermatozoa; the male sex cells.

Spontaneous abortion—An unplanned, naturally occurring death of a fetus.

Stereotype—Traditional role.

Stillbirth—An infant is born dead.

Stimulus—Something that may cause an action or response (plural **stimuli**).

Stranger anxiety—A fear of unfamiliar people.

Stress—Pressures or tension.

Survey—A research method in which someone asks questions and records the answers; questions can be in verbal or written form.

Symbol—Something that represents something else.

Symbolic consequence—A description of what will happen (the consequence) if a certain behavior occurs.

Symbolic play—Dramatic, imaginary play that reenacts life's situations.

Theory—A possible explanation for some event.

Threshold—The amount of size or strength that a stimulus must have in order to produce its particular response.

Timed running description—The observer writes down everything he or she sees or hears that relates to the child being observed.

Timeout—A mild punishment method in which the child is removed from opportunities to receive reinforcement for a period of time.

Toilet training—Teaching children to want to use the bathroom, to recognize their urges to go to the bathroom, and to master the self-help skills necessary in using a toilet.

Token—Something, such as money, stars, or points, which may be earned and exchanged for other reinforcers.

Trust vs. Mistrust—Erikson's first stage of psychosocial development in which consistent and loving care of an infant leads to feelings of trust. The absence of consistent and loving care can lead to mistrust.

Umbilical cord—The lifeline that supplies the developing baby with nutrients from its mother.

Unlearned negative reinforcer—Stimulus which, if removed following a behavior, will strengthen the future frequency of that behavior; the power of this stimulus is genetically based and does not depend upon learning.

Unlearned positive reinforcer—Stimulus which, if presented following a behavior, will strengthen the future frequency of that behavior; the power of this stimulus is genetically based and does not depend upon learning.

Unlearned reflex—A reflex which is present at birth.

Unlearned response—An ability, action, or reflex which occurs without learning.

Uterus—The female reproductive organ in which a fetus will grow during pregnancy.

Vagina—The passage leading from the female's external genital organs to the uterus; the birth canal.

Values—The ideas we have about things; what we consider to be important, desirable, bad or good, right or wrong.

Vicarious learning—Learning by observing another person's behavior and the consequences.

Wean—To part or detach from something, as a mother's milk or continuous reinforcement.

Work allowance—A token system for chores.

Zygote—The fertilized ovum, from conception to about 10 to 14 days.

INDEX